Karl Barth

Karl Barth

Theologian in the Tempest of Time

Karel Blei

TRANSLATED BY
Allan J. Janssen

EDITED BY
Matthew J. van Maastricht

CASCADE *Books* · Eugene, Oregon

KARL BARTH
Theologian in the Tempest of Time

Copyright © 2021 KokBoekencentrum Uitgevers. All rights reserved. Except for brief quotations in critical publications or reviews, no part of this book may be reproduced in any manner without prior written permission from the publisher. Write: Permissions, Wipf and Stock Publishers, 199 W. 8th Ave., Suite 3, Eugene, OR 97401.

Cascade Books
An Imprint of Wipf and Stock Publishers
199 W. 8th Ave., Suite 3
Eugene, OR 97401

www.wipfandstock.com

PAPERBACK ISBN: 978-1-7252-6959-0
HARDCOVER ISBN: 978-1-7252-6960-6
EBOOK ISBN: 978-1-7252-6961-3

Cataloguing-in-Publication data:

Names: Blei, Karel, author. | Janssen, Allan J., translator. | van Maastricht, Matthew J., editor.

Title: Karl Barth : theologian in the tempest of time / by Karel Blei ; translated by Allan J. Janssen ; edited by Matthew J. van Maastricht.

Description: Eugene, OR: Cascade Books, 2021. | Includes bibliographical references and index.

Identifiers: ISBN 978-1-7252-6959-0 (paperback). | ISBN 978-1-7252-6960-6 (hardcover). | ISBN 978-1-7252-6961-3 (ebook).

Subjects: LCSH: Barth, Karl, 1886–1968. | Theology—20th century.

Classification: BX4827 .B3 B546 2021 (print). | BX4827 (ebook).

11/12/21

Scripture quotations are taken from the New Revised Standard Version Bible, copyright © 1989 National Council of the Churches of Christ in the United States of America. Used by permission. All rights reserved worldwide.

Contents

Foreword by Matthew J. van Maastricht | xv
Note on the Translation | xix
Abbreviations | xx

1. Introduction | 1
    1.1 Then It Happened   1
    1.2 The Barmen Declaration   2
    1.3 The Theology of Karl Barth   3
    1.4 Relevance   4
    1.5 The Aim of This Book   5

2. Early years | 6
    2.1 Youth and Education   6
    2.2 Ministry: Geneva, Safenwil   7
    2.3 The Outbreak of the First World War   9
    2.4 Meeting with Blumhardt   10
    2.5 Reading the Bible Anew: *The Epistle to the Romans*   11
    2.6 The Christian's Place in Society   13
    2.7 Towards the Second Edition of the *Epistle to the Romans*   14
    2.8 The Accidental Bell-ringer   15

3. Dialectical Theology | 17
    3.1 From Pulpit to Lectern   17
    3.2 Göttingen   18

3.3 Honorary Doctorate   19
3.4 The Task of Theology   20
3.5 The Impossibility of Theology   20
3.6 Clashes, Reservations   22
3.7 Associates   23

4. Towards His Own Dogmatics | 25
4.1 Theology as Footnote   25
4.2 Problems in Göttingen   26
4.3 A Path through the Jungle   26
4.4 Acquaintance with Reformed Orthodoxy   27
4.5 The Church Fathers and Scholasticism   28
4.6 Münster   30
4.7 Accountability to the Nineteenth Century   31
4.8 "Church and Culture." The Speech at Amsterdam   32
4.9 Dutch Reactions   33
4.10 Dogmatics in Service of Preaching   34
4.11 A Dogmatics in Draft   35
4.12 Charlotte von Kirschbaum   37

5. The 1930s: On a Definite Theological Course | 39
5.1 Anselm as Crown's Witness and Ally   39
5.2 Anselm's Proof for the Existence of God   41
5.3 On Anselm's Theological Program   41
5.4 Anselm: No Apologete but Witness   42
5.5 Theology of the Name   44
5.6 New Beginning: The *Church Dogmatics*   45
5.7 Self-correction   46

6. The German Church Conflict | 49
6.1 Hitler Comes to Power   49
6.2 "The Need of the Evangelical Church"   50
6.3 Dogmatics over and against the Self-Consciousness of the Church   52
6.4 In Continuing Discussion with Schleiermacher   54

6.5 The Church Following Hitler   57
6.6 "Theological Existence Today!"   59
6.7 The "German Christians" and the Vulnerability of the Church   61
6.8 Tensions among Comrades   63

7. Barmen 1934 and Consequences | 66

7.1. The Onset of Ecclesiastical Protest   66
7.2 The Barmen-Gemarke Declaration   67
7.3 The Barmen Theses   68
7.4 Barmen and the Jews   69
7.5 Barmen and National Socialism   71
7.6 Leaving Bonn   72
7.7 Utrecht Lectures on the Apostles' Creed   74
7.8 The Situation of the Church in Germany compared with That in the Netherlands   76
7.9 Back to Switzerland   78

8. A More Radical Rejection of National Socialism | 79

8.1 Parting Words to Germany: "Gospel and Law"   79
8.2 Further with the *Dogmatics*: On God's Revelation   81
8.3 Sympathy for Germany   83
8.4 Appeal for Political Resistance: Letter to Former Students   85

9. On the Eve of the Second World War | 87

9.1 Solidarity with Czechoslovakia: Letter to Josef Hromádka   87
9.2 On the Scots Confession: Armed Resistance May Be Necessary   89
9.3 On the Relation of Church and State   91
9.4 Criticism Focused: The Jewish Question as a Question of Faith   94
9.5 In the Netherlands. Christian Faith and Threatened Humanity   96
9.6 The Problem of Infant Baptism   97
9.7 Speaking of "God" in a Catastrophic Time   99

CONTENTS

10. A Voice from Switzerland in the War Years | 101

    10.1 Advice on Personal Authority   101

    10.2 The First Months of the War: Letter to France   102

    10.3 It is about Life, Including for the German People   103

    10.4 Following the French Defeat: The Facts and the Word   104

    10.5 Letter to Great Britain   105

    10.6 Faith in Christ as the Deepest Reason to Struggle   106

    10.7 Christmas Greeting to Germany   107

    10.8 Radio Message to Norway   108

    10.9 Questions from the Netherlands   108

    10.10 The "Illegal" as the Genuinely Legal   109

    10.11 The Neutrality of Switzerland: A Matter of Principle   110

    10.12 A New Part of the *Dogmatics*: On God as an Electing God   113

    10.13 Israel and the Church: Distinct but Together   114

    10.14 "Then I Shall Know Fully . . ."   116

11. 1944–1945. "How Can the Germans Be Cured?" | 117

    11.1 A Period of Silence on the War   117

    11.2 "The Teaching of the Church Regarding Baptism"   118

    11.3 The War Changes. What the Church Is in a Position to Do Now   120

    11.4 Striking a New Key. "The Germans and Ourselves"   122

    11.5 "How Can the Germans Be Cured?"   124

    11.6 Direct Contact with Germany Renewed   126

    11.7 First Post-war Visit to Germany: New Beginning of the German Church   128

    11.8 Necessary Steps to a New Way of Being Church   130

    11.9 The Stuttgart Confession of Guilt, a Compromise Text   132

    11.10 Again in Germany: "A Word to the Germans"   133

    11.11 Further with the *Dogmatics*. The Doctrine of Creation   134

12. Guest Professor in Post-war Germany | 137

    12.1 Summer, 1946: Guest Professor at Bonn   137

    12.2 "Dogmatics in Outline"   138

12.3 "Christian Community and Civil Community"   141

12.4 Frustrations with the German Church   144

12.5 A Contribution to the Ecumenical Reflection
on the Church   145

12.6 Summer, 1947. Again in Bonn   147

12.7 The Christian Doctrine according to
the Heidelberg Catechism   149

12.8 Again with the Apostles' Creed   151

12.9 On the Sacraments   153

12.10 "Protestant Theology in the Nineteenth Century"   154

13. Further with the Dogmatics. On the Human | 156

13.1 A Critical Look at the German Church   156

13.2 The Darmstadt Declaration   157

13.3 Reactions   158

13.4 Dogmatic Reflection on the Human Existence: Jesus as
the True Human   159

13.5 Human Nature: In Relation to God and the Fellow Human   160

13.6 The Human as Soul and Body   162

13.7 The Human, Living in Time   163

14. Between East and West | 168

14.1 Continuing to Live and Work in Basel   168

14.2 Visit to Hungary, March–April, 1948   168

14.3 The Church and the Changing Structures in the State   170

14.4 Concrete Questions   172

14.5 Reportage to the Swiss Home Front   174

14.6 The Critical Reaction of Emil Brunner   175

14.7 Again: Theological Existence Today   177

14.8 Amsterdam, Summer 1948: Founding Assembly
of the World Council of Churches   178

14.9 The Church between East and West   181

14.10 "Now No Choice of Parties!"   182

CONTENTS

15. Does Life Stand under God's Leading? The Doctrine of Providence | 185

    15.1 *Church Dogmatics* continued   185

    15.2 The "Christological Thread" of Belief in Providence   186

    15.3 The King of Israel is the King of the World   188

    15.4 The Jews as Sign   189

    15.5 Reactions. Questions   192

    15.6 The Reality of Evil   194

16. Swimming against the Tide | 197

    16.1 The 1950s: Discussion of German Rearmament   197

    16.2 Rumor in Swiss Media   199

    16.3 The Accusation of Politician Markus Feldmann   200

    16.4 Again on "Christian Community and Civil Community"   203

    16.5 A Short Retrospect: Democracy or Theocracy?   204

    16.6 Distance from Pre-Communist Standpoints. Letter to Albert Bereczky   205

    16.7 "Political Decision in the Unity of Faith"   207

17. Ethical Reflection: The Command of God the Creator | 210

    17.1 Ethics as Part of Dogmatics   210

    17.2 The Human as Creature under God's Command   212

    17.3 Called to Freedom Before God: Sabbath   213

    17.4 Called to Freedom in Co-humanity: Man and Woman   215

    17.5 Called to Freedom to Live   217

    17.6 Called to the Protection of Life: Limit Cases   219

    17.7 War: Not Normal, but Sometimes Necessary   221

    17.8 Called to Active Life: The Meaning of Work   223

    17.9 The Social Question   224

    17.10 Affinity with Socialism   226

    17.11 Called to Freedom within Limits   227

18. The Heart of the *Dogmatics*: The Doctrine of Reconciliation | 230

    18.1 Still not Retired   230

    18.2 Reconciliation as a Dogmatic Theme? Rudolf Bultmann   231

18.3 Critical Questions to Bultmann   233

18.4 The Doctrine of Reconciliation: Incomplete
      Last Great Undertaking   234

18.5 Reconciliation as Fulfillment of the Covenant   235

18.6 Jesus Christ, the Mediator   236

18.7 Christ's Humiliation and Exaltation   238

18.8 A Different Doctrine of Reconciliation than
      that of Anselm   239

18.9 The Way of God's Son into the Depths, "Into the Far Country":
      Jesus, the Jew   240

18.10 The Way of Obedience. The Unity of God   242

18.11 Reconciliation: God as the Triune God in Action   243

18.12 The Judge Judged in Our Place   244

18.13 The Judgment of the Father: The Resurrection of Christ   245

19. The Doctrine of Reconciliation from Another Perspective | 247

19.1 Continuing Concentration on Reconciliation   247

19.2 The Human is also the Subject of Reconciliation   247

19.3 Jesus Christ: The Exalted Human   249

19.4 Again, the Meaning of Easter   250

19.5 A Paragraph on the Life of Jesus   251

19.6 Dogmatics as Re-narration of the Gospel Story:
      Jesus, the Royal Human   252

19.7 Jesus' Royal Speech   253

19.8 Jesus' Royal Action   254

19.9 The Cross as Coronation   255

19.10 Jesus' Human Nature and Ours   256

19.11 Sin as Pride and as Sloth   256

19.12 Reconciliation Focused: Justification, Sanctification   258

20. Other Activities. Current Discussions | 260

20.1 Lecture on "Freedom," September 1953   260

20.2 "In Theology, Begin at the Beginning, with God"   261

20.3 Wiesbaden, November 1954: Speech in Memory of Victims of War   263

20.4 Involvement in Ecumenical Work: "Continental" vis-à-vis "Anglo-Saxon" Theology   266

20.5 The Discussion of Christian Hope   268

20.6 The Commission Report on Christian Hope   269

20.7 Missing: Hope for Israel   271

20.8 Critical Voices: Dietrich Bonhoeffer on Barth's "Revelation Positivism"   272

20.9 The Dutch Neo-Calvinists: The New Barth-interpretation of G. C. Berkouwer   274

21. New Accent on the Humanity of God | 277

21.1 The Doctrine of Reconciliation: Still Incomplete   277

21.2 Seventieth Birthday: The Festschrift *Answer*   278

21.3 "The Humanity of God"   279

21.4 Protestant Theology in the Nineteenth Century: A Revaluation   281

21.5 Rising Tensions between East and West: The Hungarian Crisis of 1956   283

21.6 Letter to a Preacher in the German Democratic Republic (DDR)   285

21.7 The Letter as Theology-in-Action   287

22. The Doctrine of Reconciliation as a Theology of Hope | 289

22.1 The Doctrine of Reconciliation Thus Far   289

22.5 Reconciliation as a Communicative Event   290

22.3 Jesus Christ, the Living, the Resurrected   291

22.4 Jesus and the Old Testament   293

22.5 Note: Judaism Unfruitful?   294

22.6 The Light and Other Lights   294

22.7 True Words from the Profane World, Recognized in Faith   295

22.8 Reconciliation as Victory   296

22.9 The Battle Is not Illusory   297

- 22.10 Reconciliation Intends to Be Acknowledged and Accepted   298
- 22.11 Reconciliation: Already and Not Yet. The Doctrine of Reconciliation, a Theology of Hope   299
- 22.12 Sin as Lie   300
- 22.13 Reconciliation Focused: Call, Mission   302
- 22.14 Again, the Jews   304

23. Towards an Ethics of Reconciliation | 307

- 23.1 Again on the Path of Ethics   307
- 23.2 Lectures on "The Christian Life"   309
- 23.3 "Zeal for the Honor of God"   310
- 23.4 "The Battle for Human Justice"   311
- 23.5 Seventy-fifth Birthday: "The Idol Falters"   313
- 23.6 Work on the *Church Dogmatics* Broken Off   314
- 23.7 Swan Song: Retirement as Professor   315

24. Retired, in a Changing Theological Landscape | 318

- 24.1 Trip to America   318
- 24.2 Panel Discussion on the Relation between Jews and Christians   320
- 24.3 The Conclusion of the American Trip   321
- 24.4 Discussion of Being Church in a Totalitarian State   322
- 24.5 "The Time for Big Lectures Is Past"   323
- 24.6 Confrontation with "God Is Dead" Theology   324
- 24.7 Searching a "Top-class" Contradiction   327
- 24.8 Organized Opposition: "No Other Gospel"   328
- 24.9 Difficult Years. Eightieth Birthday   330

25. In Discussion with Rome | 332

- 25.1 Visit to the Vatican   332
- 25.2 From Early On: Objections to Roman Catholicism   333
- 25.3 Rome and the Ecumenè: Discussion with Jean Daniélou   334
- 25.4 Ecumenical Approach? Hans Urs von Balthasar   336

25.5 Hans Küng, an Ecumenical Mayfly?   337
25.6 Encounters in Rome   338
25.7 Critical Questions   339
25.8 God's Mills Grind Slowly   340

26. A Late Dogmatic Fragment on Baptism | 342
    26.1 Plea for the De-Sacramentalization of the Church   342
    26.2 Sacraments: Indispensable Means of Grace? Early Views   343
    26.3 "Jesus Christ, the One and Only Sacrament"   345
    26.4 Baptism: Not a Sacrament but a Human Answer   346
    26.5 Late Dogmatic Fragment on Baptism   348
    26.6 "Spirit Baptism" and "Water Baptism"   349
    26.7 Basis, Goal, and Meaning of Baptism   350
    26.8 No Place for Child Baptism   352
    26.9 Questions with This New Conception of Baptism   354

27. The Close of a Life | 356
    27.1 The *Church Dogmatics* as an Unfinished Symphony   356
    27.2 Nonetheless, Back to Academic Work   357
    27.3 Again: Schleiermacher . . . and Bultmann   358
    27.4 A Dream of the Future   360
    27.5 "What Jesus Christ Means to Me"   361
    27.6 "My Theology Always Had a Strong Political Component"   362
    27.7 Orthodox or Liberal?   363
    27.8 Life's End   364

Appendices | 367
Bibliography | 381
Name Index | 387

Foreword

HENDRIKUS BERKHOF, IN HIS essay in the volume, *How Karl Barth Changed My Mind*, recounted his own experience of being underwhelmed at first with *Der Römerbrief* but saw Barth in a new light when he studied volume I/1 of the *Church Dogmatics*. Berkhof notes that he saw something that he had missed in his previous encounter with Barth, and he refers to this as "beginning again with Barth." Berkhof writes,

> I never encouraged my students to read Barth during their first academic years. That was easy advice because most of them disliked Barth . . . From their fourth year on, however, many stopped [their other] reading when they discovered Barth. They needed the boat of experience, but now they could start on new ground . . .
>
> We can hardly begin with Barth, but eventually we have to make our second start in him . . .[1]

This experience of needing to begin again with Barth is not unique to Berkhof. Many need to begin in the same places that Barth began, standing before a congregation every week needing to say something about God, but also wondering how, exactly, a human can speak the Word of God. Indeed, Barth's work was, itself, beginning again in light of his experiences and his education. It is this proclamation-oriented experience which launched Barth's theological path, and the church remained in his sight throughout his life, and in which he always encouraged his students to begin at the beginning. And this ecclesiastical orientation of Barth is one thing that one will (re)discover in this volume by Karel Blei.

---

1. Hendrikus Berkhof, "Beginning Again with Barth" in *How Karl Barth Changed My Mind*, edited by Donald K. McKim (Grand Rapids: Eerdmans, 1986; reprint, Eugene, OR: Wipf & Stock, 1998), 26.

I first met Karel Blei in 2016 in a classroom at the Protestantse Theologische Universiteit in Amsterdam. I knew of Karel only through two of his previous books, both of which were translated by Allan Janssen, *The Netherlands Reformed Church, 1571–2005* and *Oepke Noordmans: Theologian of the Holy Spirit*. I was in Amsterdam participating in the long-running International Summer School of Theology through New Brunswick Theological Seminary. This day, Blei was speaking to us about Dutch theology, its history and milestones. Blei is a scholar who is smart and insightful, engaging and interesting. Even in hearing him cover familiar ground, I always learned something new, a new insight, a new way to hear or think about the topic at hand. No doubt this will come through in this volume. Even those who are acquainted with Barth, his work and his context, will certainly find value within these pages.

Blei is probably unknown to most in the American scene, and perhaps a little introduction may be helpful. Blei is well known in the theological world in the Netherlands. A minister in the (then) Netherlands Reformed (Hervormde) Church (now a part of the Protestant Church in the Netherlands), he served in the local church at the beginning of his career, during which time he earned his doctorate from the University of Leiden under Hendrikus Berkhof. For ten years from 1987–1997, Blei served as the general secretary of the Netherlands Reformed Church. His doctoral dissertation was a study of newer Roman Catholic ecclesiology, which led to him being heavily involved in the ecumenical movement, including serving as a member of the World Council of Churches Central Committee, and also as president of the theological department of the World Alliance of Reformed Churches. He has published writings in biblical theology, ecclesiology, the sacraments (especially baptism), church-state relationships, and church history.

Blei is a theologian in his own right, and his broad and significant experience with the Netherlands Reformed Church, the World Council of Churches, and the World Alliance of Reformed Churches (and others), and his broad experience in ecumenism and European context give him a unique perspective in this contextual reflection on Barth.

Allan Janssen, the translator of this volume, tragically passed from the church militant to the church triumphant, from COVID-19 complications, before this went to the publisher. This was the last thing on which he was working. Janssen was a minister in the Reformed Church in America and as pastor served three churches in the northeastern United States. He had long been influenced by Dutch theologians (and I am indebted to him on this front, among many others), especially A. A. van Ruler. It was on Van Ruler's doctrine of ecclesiastical office that Allan wrote his doctoral dissertation at the Vrije Universiteit, Amsterdam. For many years, he served on the faculty at the New Brunswick Theological Seminary in New Brunswick, New Jersey, where he taught, among other things, the Reformed confessions and Reformed church polity, fields in which he is widely published. Janssen was also a General Synod Professor of Theology of the Reformed Church in America. A translator of Dutch and frequent traveller to the Netherlands, Janssen is probably more well known outside of the United States than inside of it. He was a true transatlantic theologian. More personally, he was my mentor and friend.

While this is sadly the final collaboration between these two theologians and ecclesiastics, it is an excellent one. In addition to telling the story of Barth, this volume aids us in contextualizing or recontextualizing Barth's theology.

All theology is contextual. That is, all theological work is always influenced by its context. This is not to say that theological work is bound to its context as though it cannot transcend the context. Nor does the reality of theology being contextual mean that it can only speak to the immediate context. Rather, in order to more fully understand a theological work, we must understand the context from which it arose. Over time, the contextual impact is lost and enters into the realm of history and we have an increasing tendency to lift theological work out of its context and drop it into our own.

Context is particularly important for understanding theologians who worked in times of great theological and social upheaval. We might also think of the theologians of the sixteenth century Reformation. The Protestant Reformation of the sixteenth century was like a wildfire that burned over Europe, and the theologians working in that context were not somehow isolated from the contextual realities, but were embroiled with them. There is enduring value to their work, that is to be sure. But we cannot just take their theological statements from the sixteenth century and place them in today's world without doing our work of contextual understanding and interpretation.

Similarly with Barth. The break from the classic German liberal Protestant tradition, as well as the first World War and its aftermath, the Jewish question, the rise of National Socialism and the second World War, the partition of Germany, and others are all in the background of Barth's theology. Blei also shows us, here, that Barth's consistent eye was always on the church, even in his criticism of it. As we move farther from the tempest in which Barth lived and worked, the potential of separating Barth from his context becomes easier and more likely. This, however, is important to avoid. This contextual maelstrom is not incidental to Barth's work, but is deeply embedded in his work, and is important for a fuller understanding.

Blei has given us, and Janssen has made available to English-speaking audiences, a book which covers the story of Barth's life, the context of his work, the path of his development. This book provides an engaging narrative and theological depth, and it covers a significant amount of Barth's voluminous published corpus. The present volume is accessible enough for non-specialists, but students and pastors will find this particularly useful. In these pages, people who are familiar with Barth will find the pieces put together and will find new insights into his work; people who are new to Barth will find an excellent introduction to Barth, his work, and the contexts from which his work arose.

Finally, this book is unique, particularly in the United States, in that it comes from the Netherlands. This explains the frequent connection to the Netherlands throughout the book. However, do not think that the references to the Netherlands are unimportant for an American audience. Indeed, as Qoheleth proclaims, "What has been is what will be, and what has been done is what will be done; there is nothing new under the sun" (Eccl. 1:9). The references to Blei's country are rooted in a context, but their value extends beyond that. Perhaps, if they pay attention, American audiences may also hear echoes of this contextual maelstrom where they are, even today.

This volume offers great aid in helping us to revisit the context in which Barth was working, and helps us encounter his work in a renewed and refreshed light. To return to the anecdote from Berkhof at the beginning, this volume is not only a good way to begin with Barth, it is also a very good way to begin again with him.

Matthew J. van Maastricht

The Altamont Reformed Church
Altamont, New York

The Reformed Church Center
New Brunswick Theological Seminary
New Brunswick, New Jersey

September 2020

Note on the Translation

THE ORIGINAL DUTCH VERSION of this book did not include footnotes and literary references in the text, but did include the works consulted in an Appendix. However, for the English translation, we have added footnotes for direct quotations, and a new comprehensive bibliography is presented in this translation. As much as possible, we have referenced English translations of texts. When this is so, the quotations themselves are not translated from Dutch, but rather, are taken from the particular English translations cited. It is the hope that this will make the volume more useful to English-speaking audiences and enhance its cohesion with Barth's English-language corpus. When the reference is given in German, the translation is the author's. Particularly where previous English translations of Barth's works are used, the reader will note the masculine language. This is retained within quotations for no other reason than quotation accuracy and ease of reading. More than anything else, this serves as a remnant of the era from which they originated.

Abbreviations

BB Barth, Karl and Rudolf Bultman, *Karl Barth–Rudolf Bultmann Letters, 1922–1966*

BT *Barth–Thurneysen Briefwechsel 1921–1930*

BV *Barth–Visser't Hooft Briefwechsel 1916–1966*

CD Barth, *Church Dogmatics*

OB Barth, *Offene Briefe 1945–1968*

RT *Revolutionary Theology in the Making*

1

Introduction

1.1 Then It Happened

SOMETIMES THE VOICE OF the church speaks from an unexpected quarter. Articulated not by church leaders (pope, bishops, synods) but by ordinary church members. Not by virtue of official mandate but from a particular initiative, under the press of need. People appear in the time of crisis who advance something that clarifies the situation and points a way forward. That which is so convincing, so in sync with the biblical message that others hear and recognize what must be said today in the name of the church. Or put more strongly, the authentic voice of the church itself is recognized in these words. Recognition will become widespread at a later time.

Something like that occurred in Germany in 1934. Adolf Hitler had very recently come to power to massive acclamation. From the outset he left no doubt as to what he intended—the aim of his *Kampf*. For him and his compatriots in the National-Socialist movement, it was about the purity and the possibilities of the German race embodied in the German people. That must be strengthened and maintained. To that end, every element alien to this race must be eliminated, including, specifically, the Jews. As representatives of a different race, they should have no home in Hitler's Germany.

Among his efforts, Hitler intended to involve the churches, beginning with the Protestants. He succeeded. A unified structure was instituted. The German Evangelical Church (an umbrella organization of a number of regional churches) came under the control of the state. A "bishop," a henchman of Hitler, became the central leader. A new ecclesiastical rule was instituted on the order of the new powers, one that determined that Jews (Jewish Christians) could no longer be church members in a real sense. Enthusiasm for the "new Germany" also reigned among German Protestants. A group who called themselves "German Christians" (and of whom representatives had in the meantime taken all the leading positions via ecclesiastical elections) declared the complete agreement between Christian faith and National Socialism. Had the difference between races not been given in God's creation? In the rise of Hitler, one saw a great event, a new opportunity given by God, for the German people and for the church.

Still, this did not happen without resistance. A church conflict broke out in Germany. A small minority protested. They organized themselves within the German Evangelical Church as a particular, alternative church body: the "Confessing Church." In May 1934, this "Confessing Church" held a first synod, in Barmen. There a declaration was accepted in which the view of the "German Christians"—and hence implicitly National Socialism—was rejected. The declaration consisted of six theses, each beginning with a positive confession and continuing with the rejection of what was called a "false teaching."

The main author of the declaration was the Swiss theologian Karl Barth, active in Germany beginning in 1921.

1.2 The Barmen Declaration

The first thesis puts it strikingly:

> Jesus Christ, as he is testified to us in the Holy Scripture, is the one Word of God, whom we are to hear, whom we are to trust and obey in life and in death. We repudiate the false teaching that the church can and must recognize yet other happenings and powers, images and truths as divine revelation alongside this one Word of God, as a source of her preaching.[1]

It is not said in so many words that the events of 1934 with the rise of Hitler as the new leader (*Führer*) are what is meant concretely by the last part. But at the time it would have been clear to everyone.

Consequences are drawn in the theses that follow. They speak of obedience to Christ as valid for all of life, the organization of the church, the relation of church and state, and the freedom of the church in the fulfillment of her task. No area falls outside obedience to Christ, including politics and society. The organization of the church, or the formation of its leadership, cannot and may not be left to a particular politics or worldviews that may dominate at a given moment. The state, an instrument given by God in the aid of justice and peace, exceeds its authority if it would regulate all of life and society and thus, as it were, itself becomes "church." The church retains

---

1. "The Barmen Declaration," 520.

its peculiar task over and against the state reminding rulers (and the ruled!) of God's kingdom and command; it may not allow itself to be co-opted by political powers as an "organ of the state."

However generally formulated, the conditions of the time stand in the background of these theses. It was the pretension of the National Socialist state to regulate all of life and society, including one's philosophy of life. State policy had as its goal, the co-optation of the church. And there was a readiness within the church itself to allow that to happen. A church that allows itself to be co-opted apparently gets wonderful opportunities and an influential position in the society. But it has become speechless as far as its real task is concerned. In 1934 that was the case.

We already saw that the synod of Barmen represented only a small minority of the German Evangelical Church and of the German people as a whole. Afterwards, the German resistance to Hitler found in it its source of inspiration, but that resistance was never very successful. Only later, was the Barmen Declaration recognized by many as a clarifying and guiding word, as an authentic witness of the Church of Christ and thus also as important in new situations.

1.3 The Theology of Karl Barth

As said before, the main author of the draft Barmen text was Karl Barth.

The first thesis, especially, is a concise summary of his theology. It also shows how much that theology, as *real* theology, was committed to the trend of the time. Theology, as Barth had stated it before and as he would continue saying, totally lives on God's Word, God revealing himself in Jesus Christ. One should refrain from looking for bridges through which people could come from themselves in the direction of God. One should stop looking for clues in humans themselves to understand who "God" is. The idea that bridges or clues would exist is an illusion. God is different; not just greater or more powerful or wiser than we are, but completely different. In theology, as in faith, we simply have to bow before the Word, which authoritatively comes to us; before Jesus Christ in Whom God has already mercifully come to us.

Barth's concentration on Jesus Christ as "the one Word of God," where over and against or where alongside nothing other can count as God's revelation, sounds strong, cold. Can human religious effort and feelings be simply, radically cut off? Is this not in essence a seriously narrow outlook? Does that not enclose Christians as if they alone are right, in the midst of a world that is completely mistaken religiously? So, it was questioned, and still is.

Certainly, in a time like our own where alongside Christianity (other) world religions emphatically manifest themselves and all sorts of private forms of religiosity bloom lushly, a theology like Barth's appears to have little more to say. It certainly hardly appears to be appropriate in the interreligious discussion as that is the order of the day.

Despite these and other reservations, old and new, it is good to note that Barth's radical concentration on Jesus Christ as "the one Word of God," was not an arm-chair theology in the Germany of 1934; not the thinking of a scholar isolated in his ivory tower. His thought was directly related to what was going on in society and in the church. It warned of threatening dangers, and it pointed a way out of the confusion.

In some situations, matters cannot be left open. Decisions and choices must then be made. That was the situation in Germany, 1934. Barth did not shrink from speaking decisively. Not everyone praised him, even then. Later, few would find that to be unnecessary, and there were even voices that argued that it should have been still more radical.

1.4 Relevance

The question, however, is whether decisiveness in theology and in the church is not *always* necessary, in other contexts as well and precisely in times of meeting with those who think and believe differently. Does not the Christian faith in its particularity threaten to be overwhelmed in an (inter)religious vagueness? That question makes clear that Barth's theology cannot be written off for good.

A number of churches have referred to the Barmen Declaration in their church order. That is the case with the Protestant Church in the Netherlands. Article 1-5 of its church order reads: "The church acknowledges the significance of the theological Declaration of Barmen for confessing today." It is true: this is very carefully formulated. It is not said in what significance this declaration consists. Still it says a great deal that the declaration is referred to here. "Barmen" obtains as a model for how confession can (could) occur in the modern era (in the twentieth century). Does that not say something about the significance that Karl Barth's theology itself still has today?

This theologian and this theology still deserve consideration. No other theologian has so dominated (Protestant) theology of the twentieth century. This is certainly the case in the Netherlands. His influence on ecclesiastical life in that country has been immense. He inspired the ecclesiastical resistance to Hitler, not only in Germany but also in the Netherlands (and elsewhere). Moreover, the renewal that took place in the Netherlands Reformed Church in and after the Second World War—in the context in which it transcended the conflict between the "orthodox" and the "liberals"—cannot be properly understood apart from the influence of Barth's theology. He also offered his own contribution to the reflection on the relation of church and state, of Christian faith and politics.

Certainly, there was criticism alongside acclaim, as we have already heard. Barth's *magnum opus*—his thirteen-volume expansive, albeit uncompleted, *Church Dogmatics*—was characterized as "an awesome building—without doors." But the criticism also showed the extent to which many were affected by Barth's theology.

His work was not only an ("accidentally" well aimed) reaction to incidental political conditions in a concrete situation (the 1930s). It had and has a broader importance. It is still studied. The contemporary theological discussion can only be followed when one sees it against the background of Barth's theology.

1.5 The Aim of This Book

Karl Barth died on December 10, 1968, and 2018 was the fiftieth anniversary of his death. This book appeared in the context of this remembrance. We follow the course of Barth's life. How did he become the Barth of "Barmen?" And how did his life develop following that crucial period? We observe how his theological insights developed; how he shined a new light on traditional ideas of the Christian faith from his concentration on Jesus Christ. Specifically, all parts of his *Church Dogmatics* pass in review. We will inquire in what period and in what contextual climate each part originated and how the thought represented therein is related to what was going on at the time. We will note how Barth remained faithful to himself and how he also corrected himself in particular instances. A change in accent took place in the last years of his life, but there was a sharpening of his vision as well. He theologized within the ambit of the church, in service of the church, but that also meant that he did not spare his criticism of the church in all its practices. This criticism still echoes today.

Very basic footnotes and literary references are taken up in the text. At the end of the book, in appendices, the reader will find information on Barth's works as well as a comprehensive bibliography of the works quoted and consulted.

2

Early Years

2.1 Youth and Education

KARL BARTH WAS BORN on May 10, 1886, in Basel, Switzerland. His father, Johann Friedrich (Fritz) Barth was a preacher, like his grandfather. When Karl was born, he had just begun his new task as teacher at an institution of theological education ("preacher's school") in Basel. A few years later the family would move to Bern where Karl's father would become a professor of church history and New Testament. His mother, Anna Sartorius, was also from a minister's family. Thus, the family tradition was thoroughly ecclesiastical. Karl grew up in this atmosphere as the oldest of four children. It more or less speaks for itself that he would study theology following his education at gymnasium.

He began his studies in Bern in 1904. There he followed lectures from his own father among others. After having passed his first ("propaedeutic") exam, he continued his studies in the fall of 1906 at various universities in Germany (Berlin, Tübingen, Marburg) interspersed with semesters at Bern. Traditional doctrine did not attract him. Instead, in Berlin he was attracted by the well-known church historian (and liberal theologian) Adolf von Harnack; and later, in Marburg, by Wilhelm Herrmann, professor of dogmatics and ethics. The latter became his true teacher.

For Herrmann, student and follower of Schleiermacher, religion was by definition a question of individual experience. Dogma, the doctrine of faith, is necessary for the church, which, after all must be able to maintain itself within modern culture and must not allow itself to be ruled by fanaticism. But, said Herrmann, dogma cannot be laid on people as a law of faith. Believing is being-on-the-way, in experience and action. The human is on the way to the kingdom of goodness and truth. One lives in the tension between the "is" and the "ought." One is saved from this tension where one experiences God's revelation (which is historically unprovable) inwardly. The fact of the "wondrous man" Jesus of Nazareth belongs to this revelation. Jesus is not historically provable; nor is he to be explained away. The point is: living for yourself the "inner life of Jesus." Thus, the foundation of the moral good originates in the human and therewith the kingdom of God. Herrmann emphasized that this can happen to every human because it is not totally alien to any human.

Barth eagerly became acquainted with these modern insights. Through Martin Rade, one of his Marburg professors, he was editorially connected with *Die Christliche Welt*, a Lutheran periodical aimed at "educated congregants." Barth became an assistant editor. He read and evaluated incoming manuscripts. Now and again he wrote a short review himself. He met Eduard Thurneysen, a fellow student, later a colleague and kindred spirit. It began a life-long friendship.

At the end of his student years, 1909, he summarized his own experiences and convictions in an article. How is it, he asked, that so few theological students become active as preachers? Modern theology, with its emphasis on individual experience and with its historical-critical research of the Bible, is so distant from ecclesiastical practice. Must you now toss that overboard to be able to work sensibly in the church? No, Barth found. The theologian may not be unfaithful to himself. So long as he does not consider science itself the gospel to be proclaimed!

2.2 Ministry: Geneva, Safenwil

Church work in Switzerland for Barth began in Geneva. There, in the fall of 1909, as a 23-year-old, he became an assistant minister in the German congregation. That year, the 400th anniversary of the birth of Calvin was being commemorated. That received a great deal of thought in the "Calvin city" of Geneva. It stimulated Barth to do further study of Calvin alongside the work of Schleiermacher. It did not give him different insights. He deemed modern and Reformation theology to be very compatible. At the time, he also planned to pursue a doctorate at Marburg. But that would not happen.

In Geneva he met a talented violinist, Nelly Hoffman, who had come with her mother intending to study languages and music. She was seven years younger than Barth and belonged to his first catechism class. They were engaged in 1911. The engagement meant that Nelly would abandon her intended music studies (so it went at the time!). They married in 1913. Five children would be born of the marriage: Franziska (1914), Markus (1915), Christoph (1917), Matthias (1921, who would die in a Swiss mountain accident in 1941), and Hans Jakob (1925). Barth's three oldest sons would, like their father, choose to study theology, although for his third son those plans would be cruelly ended by his sudden death.

At the time of his marriage, Barth was already a preacher in Safenwil, a village in the canton Aargau. He was called there in 1911 and installed in office by his father (who shortly thereafter died, only 55 years old, unexpectedly as a result of an acute illness). Safenwil was populated by farmers and workers. Village society at the time was developing considerably as a result of growing industrialization. Here, more than in Geneva, he was involved with the problems of which he had written at the end of his student years: the discrepancy between scholarly theology and ecclesiastical practice. He spent a great deal of time on sermon preparation. His sermons did not come easily. Later, speaking in 1922 for a gathering of preachers, Barth told how he, as preacher, had to deal with "the problem of preaching." The problem is not solved by the possession of theological baggage! Having to preach means finding a way "between the problematic of human life on the one side, and the content of the Bible on the other." Making a real connection between those two, human life and the Bible, is that really possible? The question arises: who is able to preach? Can a human really speak God's Word?

In 1913, his friend Thurneysen came to work as preacher in neighboring Leutwil. Barth had regular and intensive contact with him. The two friends understood and supported each other.

In Safenwil, Barth came up against the social question. Many members of his congregation worked for local companies for extremely low wages. They were subject to the arbitrary will of business leaders. Unions were not yet in existence. However, there was a workers' organization. Barth saw it as his task to help. He sought contact with the local workers' organization and appeared at its meetings as speaker on subjects like "Human rights and the citizen's duty," and "Profit, work, life." It motivated him to deepen himself in questions around employment legislation, insurance, worker's organizations, and economics.

He came into contact—primarily through Thurneysen—with the contemporary Swiss religious-social movement. It viewed socialism as unconscious Christianity. It explained the atheism of many socialists as a justified reaction to conservative Christianity. That had appeal to Barth. Later he would concretize his sympathy for socialism—albeit for a short time—in his choice of political party.

He did not hide that fact while in Safenwil. So, he held a lecture on "Jesus Christ and the Movement for Social Justice," in which he typified Jesus as a partisan for the poor. The press reported this lecture. It led to sharp reactions, from industrialists among others. Tensions also emerged in Barth's own congregation: a prominent member of the church council, from a family of a director of a factory, immediately resigned from his church responsibilities.

Barth also involved himself practically in the realization of better working conditions for the employees in Safenwil. When fifty-five workers of the local sewing machine factory had organized themselves and were promptly threatened with being collectively fired, Barth visited the director who was involved at his villa in an attempt to reverse that dismissal. He was courteously welcomed but achieved nothing. Meanwhile he became known as the "red pastor."

Still, he had his critical questions for socialism. He would not simply identify Christianity with socialism. At the least, according to him, a distinction must be made between factual, party socialism and genuine socialism. "Genuine socialism" is what Jesus practiced—and what socialists also essentially aim for (albeit unconsciously). The way "beyond themselves" must be pointed out to socialists. In the socialist conflict it would have to be not about self-interest but about a "better justice." And socialists would have to be unambiguously against a war conducted out of nationalist motives. That however did not mean that naïve pacifism was an option for Barth.

2.3 The Outbreak of the First World War

On August 1, 1914, the First World War broke out. There was great enthusiasm in the Germany of that time for the German cause. Protestantism stood at the forefront. Had the Reformation not been a German affair? With the development of the unified state of Germany in the nineteenth century under the imperial house of the Hohenzollerns, it was the Protestants who had felt themselves closely connected. For the German Protestant churches, the war was a national *and* Christian affair at the same time. The Protestant churches saw it as their special task to equip the German people spiritually in and for this conflict. One had certainly not desired war. But the war—as was it experienced—was forced on Germany. Now it would and must then also be waged. With all power, with God's help!

A manifesto was published on the very day the war broke out, August 1, signed by ninety-three prominent intellectuals. That manifesto offered unreserved support for the war politics of the emperor, Wilhelm II. To his dismay, Barth saw the names of almost all his German teachers among the ninety-three signatories. He asked himself: is that where all the esteemed theology of our time leads? The entire theological world in which he was educated was compromised for him at one stroke. A theology that had given itself to sanction a war politics must certainly be somehow foundationally amiss.

Barth did not refrain from voicing his disagreement in a letter to one of his teachers. His puzzlement concerning the question of what to do in his church work, specifically in preaching, with the theological insights he had received from university, had now only deepened. He had the feeling, as preacher and theologian, that he had to begin completely anew.

How much Barth clashed with the ruling German theology (by which he had himself been influenced) appeared at a particular moment in 1915. In April of that year he witnessed the marriage feast of his youngest brother, Peter, in Marburg. In his friendship with the Barth family, Thurneysen also attended. Among the guests, they met the prominent German theologian (and politician) Friedrich Naumann, uncle of the bride. They found themselves together in a small circle that had withdrawn from the feast for a moment. They had a short conversation on the war situation. Naumann said, "All religion is now right for us, whether it is the Salvation Army or Islam, if it only helps us to hold out through the war."[1] Barth reacted immediately with a strong protest. Using "religion," Christianity, to achieve one of our goals? That is the most serious abuse of God's name!

This was possibly the occasion for Barth to see clearly for the first time what the point would be in all his further theological work. A battle must be waged against a Christianity (and a society) that only called on God for the accomplishment and the affirmation of human plans. The "fear of the Lord," the "awe before the Lord," should, in the words of Proverbs 9:10, not be a florid coping-stone, but rather a beginning, a starting point of all human wisdom, including all theology!

2.4 Meeting with Blumhardt

On the return trip from the wedding, Barth and Thurneysen traveled via Bad Boll. There they visited Christoph Blumhardt. Thurneysen had known him since 1904 and introduced Barth to him. Barth had come under the impression of Blumhardt's peculiar sort of preaching and attitude of faith, an attitude of tense waiting for the coming of God's Kingdom, preaching about God as the radical renewer of the world. Already in 1899, Blumhardt had drawn the consequences of the political choice for social democracy from the insights of his faith. He was even a member of parliament in Wittenberg for a few years as a socialist. That had brought him into conflict with the leadership of the church. He did not become a "professional politician."

---

1. Barth, "Past and Future," 39.

What moved him went beyond the framework of political action. But in his view it also transcended the interests of the official church. In his mind, the gospel points firstly to those who—in the church and in society—stand at the margins. He desired to be in solidarity with just such persons. Barth recognized in Blumhardt's attitude something of that "genuine" socialism that he himself envisioned.

Having returned home, he also read about the work of Blumhardt's father, Johann Christoph, the founder of the work in Bad Boll. It had been Blumhardt senior who in his pastoral work, his engagement with the sick among others, had learned to understand the gospel as the message of Jesus' victory over the powers of death and darkness. The younger Blumhardt continued building on his father's work. Both Blumhardts advocated an understanding of the gospel that simply did not fit with the theological climate that ruled in Germany at the time. But Barth recognized, precisely here, something of that new understanding that he, too—since the outbreak of the First World War more than ever—was searching for.

2.5 Reading the Bible Anew: *The Epistle to the Romans*

To satisfy his own need, and stimulated by his meeting with Blumhardt, Barth began to read the Bible anew. Not in the way that he had been taught at university, but differently, more directly, more openly. He had learned to approach the Bible with the help of a number of scholarly presuppositions, according to the historical-critical method, and study it as a collection of writings from a particular time and culture, and comparable to other writings and documents of the time, a study method that also had as its starting point the fact that the biblical text itself is substantially only relevant insofar as it is connected to what the human also finds, believes, and feels of oneself. As they take the Bible in hand, humans already know something of God; and in reading, of course, they discover that confirmed.

One thing, in the judgment of the theological elite of those days, was not possible: that the Bible itself proclaims something new, something for which the reader or listener is not prepared. In their new reading of the Bible, Barth and Thurneysen attempted to reckon with just that as with an unheard-of possibility. Barth's sermons displayed a different content, surprising, sometimes scandalous. That was not what the congregation was either used to or wanted to hear. His church services did not thereby become more popular. Barth himself suffered from that, but he could do no other. He began, in particular, to read Paul's epistle to the Romans and to write about it. What he found there sounded strange to him but also sounded liberating. The God whom the epistle to the Romans is about was not the one of whom the theology of the time used to speak. *This* God is not self-evident, is not to be verified. He is other: holy, just. It was for that message that Barth became ever more open.

Together with Thurneysen, he published a collection of sermons in 1917: *Suchet Gott, so werdet ihr leben* [Seek God and Live]. It was the first result of a shared theological quest. According to its introduction, the book was aimed at people who "with us are troubled by God's great hiddenness in the contemporary world and church and rejoice with us in his still greater readiness to become one who breaks all ties."

In 1919, *The Epistle to the Romans* appeared, the product of Barth's study of Paul's epistle to the Romans. It was a commentary, but not in the style of the usual scholarly commentaries. A reviewer called this book a relevant, albeit at the same time unmodern, paraphrase. Barth himself set forth his intentions in the preface:

> Paul, as a child of his age, addressed his contemporaries. It is, however, far more important than that, as Prophet and Apostle of the Kingdom of God, he veritably speaks to all men of every age . . . The historical-critical method of Biblical investigation has its rightful place: it is concerned with the preparation of the intelligence—and this can never be superfluous . . . Nevertheless, my whole energy of interpreting has been expended in an endeavor to see through and beyond history into the spirit of the Bible . . . What was once of grave importance, is so still . . . our problems are the problems of Paul; and if we must be enlightened by the brightness of his answers, those answers must be ours . . . It is certain that in the past men who hungered and thirsted after righteousness naturally recognized that they were bound to labor with Paul. They could not remain unmoved spectators in his presence. . . The mighty voice of Paul was new to me: and if to me, no doubt to many others also.[2]

It cost Barth considerable effort to find a publisher for his book. When that finally succeeded, the (limited) edition quickly sold out. A reprint appeared to be desired. But instead of that, Barth set himself to completely re-write his book. The same thing would have to be said in yet a different way. The second, revised printing of *The Epistle to the Romans* would appear in 1921 and elicit reflection far and wide.

---

2. Barth, *The Epistle to the Romans*, 1–2.

2.6 The Christian's Place in Society

But Barth had already become well known in broader circles by his appearance at a gathering of German religious socialists at Tambach (Thüringen) in 1919. The gathering was arranged by people who sought a new course for the church in post-war Germany. They did not form a defined group but were in contact with the Swiss religious-social movement and desired to make that better known in Germany. They originally attempted to involve leading representatives of Swiss religious socialism at the deliberations at Tambach. When that did not succeed, Barth was invited as the speaker. He, too, counted as a representative of Swiss religious socialism.

The theme of his presentation was "The Christian's Place in Society." However, those who had expected that Barth would offer a good word for socialism left cheated. We Christians cannot boast the establishment of the Kingdom of God, for example in our social democracy, he claimed. Some such thing is in fact an attempt to clericalize society. But we thereby do no justice to society as it is. God's Kingdom does not begin with our protest movements as little as it does with our conservatism, not even as we propose that protest or that conservatism as ecclesiastical or Christian. It is a revolution that precedes all revolutions as well as all established situations. It is the radically new. And as little as we desire the clericalization of society, so little may we desire the secularization of Christ. The latter occurs where Christ is annexed to our own human struggles, whether it is about social democracy or liberalism or nationalism. But then Christ is betrayed anew. The renewal of society must come from God himself. And will also come from God himself.

God stands radically opposite the human. He is "other." But that other exists precisely in that he comes to have mercy on the world. The same God who warned Moses at the burning bush to keep his distance (pay attention! This is holy ground!), also declared there that he had heard the cry of the people and had "come down" to save (Exodus 3). To be able to know that, to believe in it, presses us not to lose hope. For God's sake there is a revolution on the way, a revolution of life against the powers of death! Thus, we finally can do no other than understand all the contemporary movements of concerns and protest (however ambivalent they may be). Certainly, protest movements are to be criticized. In his radicality, one often goes too far. But we can, knowing what God is actively doing in our world, again find something of that in these protest movements. So, we can better understand them than they do themselves.

But we must not only pay attention to protest movements and revolutions. The God of the Kingdom is also the Creator. The world too, as it *is*, already belongs to him. Comprehending that gives us the possibility to recognize a deep reasonability and sense in this world. Hence it is that the Kingdom of God can be represented in images derived from worldly conditions. Hence it is that Paul can say that the "invisible being of God" is "perceivable for reason" in his works (Romans 1:19–20). Proverbs and Ecclesiastes include expressions of life's wisdom and sound reason. Whoever believes in God has the occasion to assent to life.

That does not mean that we must idealize the existing world. That would be a denial of the brokenness of life. We know God as Creator *because* we know him first and primarily as Savior, liberator. God's kingdom is not only the "kingdom of nature," but also and primarily the "kingdom of grace." Indeed, it is not for nothing that there are protest movements. God's kingdom itself turns against the society to confront it. Jesus certainly used worldly images in his parables, but he did so to point to a completely different matter. We must, also as social democrats, reorient ourselves to God. However, a new day *has* dawned. "The Kingdom of God is at hand."

But the Kingdom does not lie in the extension of our protest nor of our revolution. Nor can social democracy organize it. We can only look outward, hunker down. It is God's own business. God is also the One who consummates. We are, beyond creation and salvation, directed to the consummation, the "kingdom of glory." Just that offers us the possibility of a positive affirmation of life and a critical attitude without having to stick to the one or the other.

What is the conclusion to the entire argument? Barth summarizes: "We can indeed do only one thing. But it is just that one thing which *we* do not do. What can the Christian in society do but follow attentively what is done by *God?*"[3]

"2.7 Towards the Second Edition of *The Epistle to the Romans*

In fact, this address signaled Barth's departure from religious socialism. It included core ideas that Barth would elaborate in his later work. It provoked many reactions among his listeners and among the broader public. What for one signaled a regrettable lack of concreteness was precisely for another an inspiring guide into the heart of the matter. This appearance at Tambach offered Barth many new contacts in Germany with those, who, like him, were searching for a truly new beginning for theology, church, and society.

In their turn, these contacts stimulated him to a renewed study of Paul's letter to the Romans. He gave particular thought to becoming

---

3. Barth, "The Christian in Society," 327.

acquainted with the work of thinkers and writers who had taken uncharted paths in the nineteenth century like the Danish theologian-philosopher Søren Kierkegaard, who had turned with great fierceness against the "self-evident Christianity" of his day. Or the Russian writer, F. M. Dostoyevsky, who in his novels shed extraordinary light on the depth of human existence. Or the German religio-critical philosophers Ludwig Feuerbach and Friedrich Nietzsche, who were talked about with horror in official nineteenth-century theology, but who for Barth had a great deal to say, and with whom he recognized what hovered before his very own eyes.

Therefore, Barth saw all the more reason to completely rewrite his *Epistle to the Romans*. Barth wrote later, in the preface of this new edition, that in it "may be claimed that no stone remains in its old place."[4] In fact, it became a new book. Now only, now completely, he emphasized that God is "wholly other"[5] and that knowing God brings the human "to the limits of humanity." God's Yes to us is, he claimed "hidden dialectically in the form of a No."[6] And being Christian does not mean to glory in possession of the truth but "an honest, a fierce, seeking, asking, and knocking."[7]

In the original *Epistle to the Romans* Barth had understood God's revelation primarily as a (renewing) factor *in* history. He had turned against individualism and pietistic inwardness, conversely to advocate for the objective, universal character of God's revelation. In connection with salvation he then still gladly spoke in terms of process, progress, from the past via the present to the future. The new edition moved within a completely different language world. Here often fall terms like moment, decision, judgment, crisis. God's revelation is no longer understood as a renewing presence *in*, but as a critical stance *over and against* history. So, Barth would now do justice to Paul's witness by placing what was peculiar, unique, at the forefront, more than he had before. According to him now, revelation is that God gives new names, new qualities (creating "New-Predication") to what exists. This vision had already announced itself in his presentation in Tambach.

2.8 The Accidental Bell-ringer

This second edition appeared in 1922. But Barth had already received—and accepted—an appointment as professor for Reformed theology at the university in Göttingen. His new theological involvement, already set out in the

---

4. Barth, *The Epistle to the Romans*, 2.
5. Barth "Biblical Questions, Insights, and Vistas," 74.
6. Busch, *Karl Barth*, 114.
7. Barth "Biblical Questions, Insights, and Vistas," 87.

first edition of the *Epistle to the Romans,* had found an echo. Not so much among the theological elite. They reacted with rejection. But elsewhere his message was understood. Certainly in the Germany of the time, a land in crisis so shortly after the misery of the First World War.

So Barth's university theological career had begun. With his *Epistle to the Romans* he had accomplished more than he had thought possible. Later, looking back on these developments he compared himself with someone who climbs high into a church tower, and suddenly, unexpectedly, instead of a support receives a rope in his hands that appears to be a rope for the clock. To his dismay, he hears how above him the great clock tolls and that not only for him. That was not his intention. But what can the tower-climber do now other than continue climbing as carefully as possible?

That was the task that Barth saw set before him.

3

Dialectical Theology

3.1 From Pulpit to Lectern

IN 1921, BARTH BECAME professor in Göttingen, Germany (Lower Saxony). He went there, to the Lutheran theological faculty, to occupy a newly established chair of Reformed theology.

The chair had not originated as a matter of course. At the time Lutherans and Reformed (Calvinists) were on different pages. From the earliest years, the Reformed have been in a minority in German territory. Their center lays in northwest Germany. They have their own regional church (*Landeskirche*) in that area, around Emden and Leer. There are a few other Reformed centers elsewhere in Germany (e.g., Erlangen, North Bayern). But the great majority of German Protestants are Lutheran. At that time, in Göttingen, only ten of about one hundred students were Reformed.

But the minister of the Reformed congregation in Göttingen had worked hard for the establishment of a chair of Reformed theology within the Lutheran faculty. He had found fellow supporters among various local Reformed groups. Financial help was offered by an American kindred spirit (Presbyterian). For a dozen years, he had to undergo difficult negotiations with the German (Prussian) minister of religion before confirmation of the establishment of the chair of Reformed theology was received.

For Barth, the appointment came as a bolt from the blue. He asked himself whether he was fit for this professorship. Now, for the first time, he found himself addressed as a "Reformed" theologian. Whatever that meant, he first had to make it his own. He was appointed on the basis of the first edition of his *Epistle to the Romans*. In any case, in his opinion it could not be said that the book had a particularly Calvinist character. That one had seen it as an occasion to propose the appointment of him as a "Reformed" professor would be, he supposed, because of the passion by which he had engaged already in the first edition, in the witness of Holy Scripture.

There had been intensive discussions in the board of the faculty of Göttingen theological professors prior to Barth's appointment. The board had had no objections to the appointment, provided that Barth's courses be limited to the "introduction to the Reformed confession, Reformed doctrine and Reformed church life."[1] Barth accepted these conditions. He desired to truly theologize in the footsteps of the Reformed tradition. But he did not understand that in a narrow confessional sense. To his mind, "Reformed" and "ecumenical" did not exclude each other. In that sense he had also negotiated with the ministry over his appointment. Thereby his request, to not restrict him confessionally in his educational activities, was granted. This was done quietly, not through a formal decision. That would make for problems during his stay in Göttingen.

3.2 Göttingen

However, he took his Reformed courses seriously. He had to study a great deal in the Reformed tradition. He had to catch up, for example, by getting to know the Reformed confessional writings in preparation for his courses. He thereby directly addressed these confessional writings. He began immediately with the discussion of the *Heidelberg Catechism,* thereby indicating the necessity to pay attention to the sixteenth century, the era in which it was written, in order to interpret it well. Afterwards, he lectured on the theology of Zwingli and Calvin. In just these years, he said later, he gained a real understanding for himself of the significance of the Reformers.

From the outset, alongside this reflection on the Reformed tradition, stood his reflection on the interpretation of the Bible. Just so, he continued in the path of his *Epistle to the Romans.* And that also fit, in his mind, his Reformed curriculum. Thus, he held a course on the letters to the Ephesians and the Philippians, and the first letter to the Corinthians. From the latter came *The Resurrection of the Dead*, an interpretation of the "resurrection chapter," 1 Corinthians 15. Barth viewed that chapter as the center of that letter. Just as with the interpretation of the letter to the Romans, his exegesis here differed from that given by New Testament scholars of the time. For him it was not about an historical-critical textual inquiry but about a theological exegesis, of listening to what the text itself has to say.

Barth was an honorary professor in Göttingen. That means that his courses were not required for students. Still, ever more auditors attended,

---

1. Quoted in Busch, *Karl Barth*, 128–29.

including those outside the circle of Reformed students. He enjoyed his contact with these young men and was inspired by their questions and their own contributions. As a professor in his first years, he saw himself as a student among the students. He had an open manner with them, challenging, not without self-mockery, critical of everything that presented itself as authority.

3.3 Honorary Doctorate

Barth had begun in Göttingen without himself having earned a doctorate. But already in February 1922, the University of Münster conferred on him an honorary doctorate in theology. Over the course of years, he would receive many more: from the University of Glasgow (1930), Utrecht (1936), St. Andrews (1937), Oxford (1938), Budapest (1954), Edinburgh (1956). Geneva (1959), Strasburg (1959), Chicago (1962), and Paris (1963). But the first, from Münster, had and retained a special meaning for him. For him, it was like an after-the-fact legitimization of his professorship begun just a year before. It would retain its value even when later, in 1938, the honorary doctorate was withdrawn on the order of the National Socialist state. It would, in fact, be conferred on him again directly after the fall of Hitler in 1945.

What motivated this honorary doctorate? The University of Münster remarked that the honorary doctorate was conferred on Barth "by virtue of his many contributions to the review of the religious and theological inquiry."[2] Barth's work was strikingly typified by this motive. This existed in conceiving theology—in the literal sense of the word—as really speaking about God. Thereby Barth had turned around the contemporary notion of theology 180 degrees.

Theology is (and was) often experienced as scientific reflection on religion, on human piety, thus as a human science. To turn one's attention to the fact that theology is about God, God's self, was (and is) not usual. That was precisely the anvil on which Barth had hammered already in his *Epistle to the Romans*, as well as in various lectures and readings he held in a number of places. In his opinion, that meant that theology must be about completely different questions than theologians had normally had on their agenda. He articulated that strikingly in a lecture he held in October, 1922.

The core question is specifically: can we humans really talk about God? Are we in the condition to speak the Word of God? To ask the question, said Barth, is its answer: no, of course. That exceeds our capacity. Precisely that is

---

2. Barth to Thurneysen, January 31, 1922, in *RT*, 60–61.

the emergency in which theology finds itself. Because theology also cannot walk away from that task.

3.4 The Task of Theology

What else would theology have as its task? Talking about life-questions? On what can and cannot be? On matters of religions or piety? People do not need us for such things. They have the answer for themselves. After all, it is part of their own life. Certainly, if we can help them go further in such an area, that is to be done. But that is not what theology is about. It is not what people really expect of us. They do not call for a "solution, but for salvation." There is a need that runs deeper than everyday needs. That has to do with the question of the origin, the meaning, the real goal of life. Thus, in essence, the question of God. People have placed us in pulpits and lecterns to talk about that.

Hence theology is also experienced in the university. Apparently, one deems that to be important among the sciences. Science is also not certain of its matter, where it is about the foundation, its ultimate presuppositions. But to be valued for its place in the university, theology must desire to be genuine theology. This is something other than religious science. A separate faculty for religious science is meaningless. After all, the phenomenon "religion" is already studied. Historians, psychologists, philosophers, are intensely busy with it. But a separate faculty of theology does make sense. For in such a faculty there is no hesitance (highly "unscientific"!) of placing God on the foreground. And that can critically engage religion, piety, Christianity. Those are human possibilities. But God stands directly against the human as the impossible against the possible; The impossible that itself—O wonder!—becomes possible, in a new event, from this God.

3.5 The Impossibility of Theology

But how must, how can theology now put that into words? It has been attempted in various ways, along diverse paths. Barth distinguishes three. The first is the dogmatic way. Here appeal is made to the Bible and dogma. It is from that, then, that well-known, orthodox thinking about Christ, salvation, "last things" develops. In any case, that is better than to remain with the human spiritual life or human piety. The orthodox realize that in the Bible and dogma it is about what is objective outside and over and against our own state of being. Still, God's self is not spoken of where dogmatic statements are offered. For God is the One who reveals himself, who comes, who becomes human. So that the human is not dogmatically gob-smacked, but knows oneself acknowledged and cheered up.

The idea of the insufficiency of the dogmatic path has motivated people to set out on a different path: the critical way, the mystic way. Here persons are not called to simply "believe" this or that; here it is much more that they die as humans, give up what is peculiar to them, their "I," become completely receptive to God. The idea, here, is good that God is more than an objective dogma, that God does not leave humans cold. But here too the real God is not spoken of. Here the human is spoken of purely negatively. So, the human is, in fact, yet again, busy completely with himself. While the genuine negative, that what the gospel is about, is still only the counter-side of the positivity of God. He is the God who enters our emptiness with his fullness. That is not talked about in mysticism.

While the dogmatic and critical, mystical path finally lead to a dead end, there is yet a third way: the dialectical. That is the way of Paul and the Reformers. Here the "yes" of the dogmatician and the critical "no" of the mystic are taken up and mutually connected with each other, in the notion that the meaning of the "yes" becomes clear precisely through the "no," and the other way around. Knowing, for example, that God's glory in creation can only be spoken of by whoever considers that precisely in creation God is hidden. Or that the glory of the human can be spoken of where it is also understood that the human (as we know him) is a fallen human. Think of Luther's statement that the human justified by God is "justified and sinner at the same time." Every "yes," every positive statement, immediately receives a "no," a counter-statement with it, and can thus only be ventured together, to pinpoint that neither the one nor the other is in itself God's truth, but that both are only witnesses of that truth; after all God's truth transcends all our yes and no. Still, this dialectical talk cannot of itself bring about that God's truth becomes apparent. The dialectical path also breaks off, comes to a dead end, where that happens. The dialectical, too, cannot speak about God. God becomes apparent in his own time and way. And that can happen equally via the words of the dogmatician and the mystic.

Theology is thus, Barth claims, an impossible possibility. As theologians we are called to talk about God, but as humans we cannot do that. Every theology, every theologian, however (rightly!) fastidious, also must fail. It is well for us to be conscious of that. Then we can stand open before the possibility that it pleases God thereby to use our theological words to speak his Word. So viewed, the emergency of theology is also its promise.

3.6 Clashes, Reservations

Barth had indeed executed a drastic review of theological inquiry with these ideas. This position simply did not apply in the world of those who had become official, authoritative theologians. Barth primarily clashed with his earlier Berlin teacher, Harnack, leader of liberal theology. Harnack saw in Barth's trajectory a great disregard of "scientific theology." Can one really persist in the fact that theology has as its task speaking "of God"? Can one simply claim that the "Word of God" is "the" task of theology? And that thus the task of theology is really nothing other than the task of preaching? That, then, comes down to the fact that the theological chair has been transformed into a pulpit. If that becomes the new trend, then the door is opened to an unbridled subjective arbitrariness. Then theology gets revival preachers as the authority.

A sharp exchange of letters began between Barth and Harnack. Barth rejected the reproach that he would despise scientific theology. His objection to this theology concerned, he said, not its "scientific nature" as such, but the fact that it had—just in its scientific nature—departed from its real theme. The two opponents did not agree. Even after this discussion, Harnack could not see it otherwise than that Barth's effort would demolish what church and theology were about, rather than edifying it.

Did Barth have associates? One could imagine that there would certainly be some on the right wing, in the circles of orthodox theologians. Barth's emphasis on the authority of the Word of God, vis-à-vis the criticism of the liberal, "scientific" theologian, must have sounded like music to their ears. But we recall that in his lecture cited above Barth had also qualified the dogmatic, orthodox path as insufficient and leading to a dead end. Barth found the orthodox too certain of themselves, too convinced of their own rightness. So it is evident that there were also considerable reservations from that side against Barth's efforts.

That was also clearly the case with the Lutherans. At the time there was a true "Luther-Renaissance" underway. Following the disaster of 1918, Germany found itself in a crisis. At the time, many turned away from the (until then) dominant civil liberalism. They sought refuge in a new conservatism with a strong dependence on the intuitive and the irrational. With that, a new reflection on Luther originated, primarily of Luther's inner life, how he had known doubt and finally experienced that God was graceful to him, that he was "justified by faith alone." One recognized in that something typically German, something peculiarly national. Was not Luther German par excellence? And was the Reformation thus not the origin of the German character, *the* German contribution to the history of the European Christian people?

As a Reformed theologian, Barth was certainly not blind to Luther's significance. Indeed, we saw that he viewed Luther as one of those who had followed the dialectical path in theology. But precisely for that reason, he could not find within himself the inclination to a confessional absolutizing of Lutheranism. He had little to do with the motto "back to Luther." And he certainly felt nothing for the propagated glorification of German nationality via Luther. For him, it was about bringing up what Luther (like Calvin) had discovered and newly articulated in and with an eye on his own time. Whereby he could also point to limitations of Luther and Lutheranism, reasons why his Lutheran colleagues in the faculty at Göttingen, friendly as they were, stood by him in a skeptical and mistrustful way.

3.7 Associates

Still, Barth did not travel his path as a perfect loner. A small circle of kindred spirits took shape around him. First among them was Eduard Thurneysen, already a friend of Barth's from their student years in Marburg and his closest colleague in the years of Barth's ministry in Safenwil. Thurneysen was a partner in Barth's theological change of course in the years of the First World War. He was directly related to the production of Barth's *Epistle to the Romans*. Barth and Thurneysen kept close contact through a long, intensive change of letters.

Another associate was Friedrich Gogarten, minister of the German Stelzendorf (Thüringen). In 1919, he had been present at the gathering at Tambach and was deeply touched by Barth's speech on "The Christian's Place in Society." Like Barth, he was a sharp critic of the modern, liberal culture and theology. He published a number of times on that, among others an article under the title "Zwischen den Zeiten" [Between the Times]. This "between the times" typified his own position as not belonging to the "course of time," "the world," of modernism, but standing without, in openness before God.

Zwischen den Zeiten also became the name of a new journal, co-founded by Barth, Thurneysen, and Gogarten in 1922. This journal served as a mouthpiece for the new dialectical theology. The editor-in-chief was the German Lutheran and publisher Georg Merz. In the first number what the three founders had in mind was set out: "a theology of the Word of God as it has pressed itself upon us as young preachers from the Bible and as we find it exemplarily practiced by the Reformers."[3] The periodical appeared bimonthly.

One of the closest associates in this periodical was the Swiss Emil Brunner. Already in 1919, he had publicized a wide-ranging and approving discussion of Barth's *Epistle to the Romans*. Just like Barth, he had felt himself connected with the Swiss religious-socialists but had distanced himself from them in the war years. He very critically turned against the experiential theology of Schleiermacher. In 1924, he became professor of systematic theology at the University of Zürich.

Still one other name must be given, that of the German New Testament scholar, Rudolf Bultmann, since 1921 professor at Marburg. Barth had also gotten to know him when both were contemporaries as students. Bultmann had critically written on the first edition of Barth's *Epistle to the Romans*, but expressed himself positively on the second edition. Bultmann also worked repeatedly as a writer in issues of *Zwischen den Zeiten*.

Barth knew himself indeed at one with Thurneysen. But the cooperation with Gogarten, Brunner, and Bultmann was tense from the outset. They developed gradually into genuine differences of opinion. In 1933, *Zwischen den Zeiten* would cease to appear. Barth would see himself forced to go his own theological way in sharp delimitation. But even so many would recognize themselves addressed by what he had to say. Barth was and remained a leader and figurehead of the new theological school that one had called "dialectical theology."

3. Barth, "Abschied," 63.

4

Towards His Own Dogmatics

4.1 Theology as Footnote

IN THE PREVIOUS CHAPTER we saw how Barth described the dialectical character of all true theology. Theology is called to speak of God, to speak the Word of God. It is impossible to do so, for theologians as well as for everyone else. Still, they may not and cannot walk away from the task. Just so theology is an impossible possibility. It can only be practiced when people have no illusions of the eventual success of the theological task. Only then can one be open to the reality that God can use the theologian's word and speak his own Word through it.

Is this the starting point of a substantial theology as a project alongside (and over and against) others? Is not every effort to do something like a "theological project" thereby undermined from the outset? Was it not a misunderstanding that Barth was increasingly seen as leader and figurehead of a new theological school?

The designation "dialectical theology" did not come from Barth himself. For that matter, he did not reject it either as an indication of what he had in mind. To be sure, he emphasized that he had no intention of propagating his "own theology." Rather he saw his own contribution as nothing more than the placement of a (correcting) footnote ("marginal note," "gloss") *alongside* what already exists in theology. Barth said, "every one . . . may well *remain* in his own school and with his own masters."[1] Provided that their representatives would not overlook the footnote.

Thus, Barth put it in an address, held at a gathering of preachers in July, 1922. It sounds somewhat unbelievable from the mouth of the author of the *Epistle to the Romans*. But Barth himself referred here, by way of an illustration,

---

1. Barth, "The Need and Promise of Christian Preaching," 98.

to his *Epistle to the Romans* commentary. That too was, he claimed, in essence nothing more than an (extensive) form of this "footnote."

4.2 Problems in Göttingen

So, Barth did not have his own theological project in mind, one that would concur with other theological projects. Still, he was now professor of Reformed theology. He had accepted the appointment with the understanding that one who says A (*Epistle to the Romans*) must say B (theology). The placement of his "footnote" could not leave what is in fact practiced as substantial theology undisturbed. The "footnote" would itself have to be theologically considered. "*Speaking the word of God*"[2]—what does that mean concretely?

In the first instance, Barth did not yet come to this question. We saw that, in conformity to his curriculum, he had dedicated himself to begin with a discussion of documents (confessional writings) from the Reformed tradition. Next, he gave consideration to the interpretation of portions of the Bible in line with his studies of the letter to the Romans. But in 1924, Barth began with lectures in dogmatics. He felt compelled to provide a further, systematic account of his own theological path.

That did not proceed without problems with the Göttingen (Lutheran) faculty. It had objections when Barth wanted to announce his treatment of the theme "introduction in dogmatics." It deemed this general theme to conflict with his specific, Reformed curriculum. Barth would at least have to mention that his lectures would be about *Reformed* dogmatics. Barth protested. As if "Reformed" would be something strange, sectarian, only intended for eccentrics! He referred to the arrangement when he took office, that he would not be limited confessionally in his educational activities. But the arrangement was not in writing. The faculty persisted in its objection. Ultimately, it came to a compromise. Barth need not use the word "Reformed" in his announcement; in its place he would use as the theme the title of Calvin's magnum opus, "Instruction in the Christian Religion."

4.3 A Path through the Jungle

The preparation for these lectures cost Barth a great deal of thought. It would have to be about a dogmatics in service of preaching. He was very conscious of the fact that he himself would have to forge a path through

---

2. Barth, "The Need and Promise of Christian Preaching," 124.

the jungle. Looking back eleven years later, he described how it was for him that Spring of 1924:

> I sat in my study at Göttingen, faced with the task of giving lectures on dogmatics for the first time. No one can ever have been more plagued than I then was with the problem, could I do it? and how? My Biblical and historical studies to date had more and more expelled me from the goodly society of contemporary, and, as I began to realize ever more clearly, of almost the whole of the more recent theology; and I saw myself, as it were, alone in the open without a teacher. That H. Scripture must be the controlling element in an evangelical dogmatics I also realized to the full. I was equally quite clear that the right thing was, in particular, to link up again with the Reformed, as more than one designed to do at that time. But how to do it, without a guide?[3]

Bowing before the authority of Scripture sounds nice in principle. But it easily becomes biblicism. And that is precisely where he did not want to go. Yes, biblicism turns against modern rationalism. But is it itself not also rationalist? Does it itself not appear too much like what it fights against? How can its method of battle then be effective?

And what does it mean to take the Reformers as the starting point? That is a motto that has been used all too easily in the last two centuries, left and right. What has it offered? On the one hand, modernism, scholarship without piety. On the other hand, piety, piety without scholarship. In fact, from either side little of the Reformer's preaching remains. Thus it must be different. But how?

4.4 Acquaintance with Reformed Orthodoxy

In that situation, Barth got hold of an old book, Heinrich Heppe, *Die Dogmatik der evangelisch-reformierten Kirche*, 1861. This book (it would be republished in 1935) offered a systematic summary of the ideas of the leading orthodox-reformed theologians from the sixteenth, seventeenth, and eighteenth centuries. It clearly gave too much of the appearance of a uniform, generally valid Reformed system of thought. Still it was very well suited for becoming acquainted with the main lines of post-Reformation, orthodox Reformed thought.

The dominant theology had long since written off this Reformed orthodoxy as "no longer contemporary." But in reading this book, Barth was

---

3. Barth, "Foreword," in Heppe, *Reformed Dogmatics*, v.

wonderfully fascinated. Here, he came across thought that wanted to take both the Reformers and Scripture seriously—thought that at the same time wished to continue the work of the church fathers from the first centuries as well as the scholasticism of the Middle Ages.

> I found myself visibly in the circle of the Church, and moreover . . . in the region of Church science, respectable of its kind. I had come to be amazed at the long, peaceful breathing, the sterling quality, the relevant strictness, the superior style . . . with which this "orthodoxy" had wrought . . . I saw that it can be worth while to reflect upon the tiniest point with the greatest force of Christian presupposition, and, for the sake of . . . "life," to be quite serious about the question of truth all along the line.[4]

So, Reformed theologians have worked in the past in a strongly ecclesiastical and scholarly manner. Would Reformed theology be able to return to the same attitude of churchliness and scholarship? That was what Barth had in mind.

Naturally he did not intend a noncritical acquisition of seventeenth- and eighteenth-century orthodoxy. He noted that the same derailment that he had found in neo-Protestant, modern theology had announced itself in this old Reformed orthodoxy as well. One could see the tendency to place not God's self but the human and their religious experience at the center of thought already there in the beginning. The orthodox reasoned very schematically. They also trusted their "enlightened reason." Thus, they thought they could get a grip on revelation, as though revelation would be a reasonable principle that we humans would be able to manage.

From that perspective, Barth wrote, the old Reformed theologians are not to be followed. It must be different, better. On the other hand, those who would return too directly to the Reformers too easily end up either in rationalism or pietism. In both cases one loses sight of the fact that the Reformers were teachers of the *church* and that theology is to be a matter of ecclesiastical *scholarship*. "That precisely may be learned, nay must be, from the early Orthodox."[5]

4.5 The Church Fathers and Scholasticism

Barth not only deepened his knowledge of Reformed orthodoxy, but he also read the writings of the church fathers from the first centuries. There he found

---

4. Barth, "Foreword," v–vi.
5. Barth, "Foreword," vii.

the roots of the reflection of faith from which Christian dogma, specifically the dogma of the Divine Trinity, had originated. He was also confronted, there, with a passionate battle for Christian truth, the likes of which he no longer came across in the prominent Protestant theologians of his own day. These were used to relegate the church fathers as writers who, through their Greek-philosophical way of thinking, would have deformed the "simple" gospel. Barth, however, came more and more to the conviction that one did not thus do justice to the church fathers, that on the contrary there is every reason to continue to work with their articulation of Christian truth.

So too with the scholasticism of the Middle Ages. That appeared unfruitful in the eyes of modern, practically interested Protestants. But Barth deemed that judgment to be too hasty. He—just he, the man of the new path!—began to realize that church history did not begin with the Reformation of 1517. Things had happened in previous centuries that had produced thought that must be taken seriously. It must be possible to cite such eminent Medieval thinkers as Anselm and Thomas without thereby immediately showing signs of revulsion.

Thus, Barth prepared for his own, first classes in dogmatics. He began them in the summer of 1924. In four successive semesters he would treat the entire content of dogmatics, from introductory questions (the "prolegomena," on which dogmatics is based), via the doctrine of God and the doctrine of reconciliation, to eschatology (the doctrine of the last things). By the way, he would not get to this last part in Göttingen. In 1925, he would continue his activities in a new post as professor in Münster.

In these classes, he also stated his conviction that dogmatics must serve preaching. The claim with which he opened was:

> The problem of dogmatics is scientific reflection on the Word of God which is spoken by God in revelation, which is recorded in the holy scripture of the prophets and apostles, and which now both is and should be proclaimed and heard in Christian preaching.[6]

From this point, under this sign, Barth set himself to a new consideration of the old doctrines: the Trinity, God's "attributes," election (preceding creation), creation, covenant (preceding the fall), the person and work of Christ, etc. To his surprise, he wrote later, he had to agree with Reformed orthodoxy on nearly every point. He heard himself saying things that he could never have dreamt earlier, to be able to take them into account.

---

6. Barth, *The Göttingen Dogmatics*, 3.

4.6 Münster

As we said, Barth's work in Göttingen came to an end in 1925. He never felt particularly at home in Göttingen. The tensions with the theological faculty there that had led to the confrontation in 1924 over the scheme for Barth's lectures in dogmatics had always been latently present. As an honorary professor he did not have the same formal rights as his Lutheran colleagues, and moreover he received a lower salary.

For a long time, he looked for a possible escape "from this mousetrap."[7] In June 1925, a chance presented itself for a return to ministry in Switzerland via a call to Zürich (the congregation of the Neumünster). His friend, Thurneysen, had mediated and encouraged him to seriously consider this call. Barth did so but had difficulty with it. Is the pulpit not "the actual arena of the kingdom of God?"[8] But on the other hand, may he curtail the work of theological reflection just begun in Germany?

However, before he had to decide on this point, a new possibility presented itself. In that same summer, Barth received an appointment to Münster (Westphalia). This time it was not an honorary but an ordinary professorship with dogmatics and New Testament exegesis as its curriculum. In any case, a quick decision was required. That happened; Barth accepted the appointment. A more Reformed climate ruled among the Protestants in Münster; he would be able to work more freely there. An additional advantage was that as ordinary professor he would be able to retain his Swiss nationality. And (as he wrote Thurneysen) he had the additional sense that "this will not be our last stop."[9]

How would things now go in Göttingen? Would Thurneysen be able to become his successor? Then things could be worked out in the same spirit there as well! Once Barth had accepted his appointment to Münster, he approached his friend about it from his side. With enthusiasm, he told him that students and authorities, including from the Reformed side, already had let it be known that they would be very much taken with Thurneysen's eventual arrival. But Thurneysen (at that moment, since 1926, minister in Bruggen, Switzerland), called it off. He deemed teaching dogmatics not to be his business. Moreover, he wrote Barth, the acceptance of a curriculum in Göttingen "not because somehow my scholarly work opens the way . . . but because *you* are transferring from Göttingen to Münster," would be an all too accidental, arbitrary course of events. And

---

7. Barth to Thurneysen, March 4, 1924, in *RT*, 175.
8. Barth to Thurneysen, June 23, 1925, in *RT*, 231.
9. Barth to Thurneysen, July 22, 1925, in *RT*, 235.

above all, what would be the sense of "the opening of a branch in your neighborhood? The students who are interested should hear *you* on Calvin and Dogmatics and New Testament."[10] "I see in the fact that I am called only a recognition of *your* work and achievement."[11] It is good in any case that that continues in Münster.

4.7 Accountability to the Nineteenth Century

Barth indeed felt more at home among his colleagues in the Protestant faculty at Münster than at Göttingen. Moreover, there were enriching contacts with the professors of the (larger, older) Roman Catholic theological faculty, also established at the University of Münster. Barth could thereby make further acquaintance with the Catholic world of thought, a world of thought that evoked his criticism but at the same time alerted him that the substance of the Christian faith had remained better retained there than it was in modern Protestantism. The relation to Catholicism would continue to engage him in his further work.

In Münster, Barth began with classes on the history of Protestant theology of the nineteenth century. He was educated in and with that theology (stamped by Schleiermacher). He had himself turned away from it during and after the First World War. At the same time, he was of the opinion that this nineteenth-century theology must not be spoken of only negatively. After all, it also had developed with the intention of articulating the gospel. At the least, it must be about evaluating it fairly, according to its intention. However that may be, Barth had the growing need to be expressly responsible in his own new theological course vis-à-vis this modern Protestantism. He did so through discussions with individual theologians (and philosophers) representing this world of thought. He would continue to do so in later years.

In the collection of lectures, *Die Theologie und die Kirche*, which Barth published in 1928, a few sections of lectures Barth held in the summer of 1926 are to be found, specifically lectures dedicated to Schleiermacher and Feuerbach. Later, Barth's activities in this area would result in his great book *Die protestantische Theologie im 19. Jahrhundert, Ihre Vorgeschichte und ihre Geschichte*, published in 1947. Barth would remain in conversation particularly with Schleiermacher for the rest of his life.

---

10. Thurneysen to Barth, July 29, 1925, in *RT*, 238.
11. Thurneysen to Barth, July 30, 1925, in *RT*, 239.

4.8 "Church and Culture." The Speech at Amsterdam

In 1926, he traveled to the Netherlands along with his wife and a number of students. This first visit to the Netherlands was a positive experience for him. Here, he wrote later to Thurneysen, he smelled something of the "sea air that pleases me so much in Bremen and Danzig and that can be so healthy in the German hinterland (to say nothing of Basel!)." The Calvinism that he met there also pleased him. To his perception, it was more engaged with moral questions than with "the problem of the assurance of salvation." It did not take much pleasure in "liturgical play"; it was "a bit dry and heavy-handed," but still "in movement." Barth recognized something of "the Syndics and the Nightwatch of Rembrandt, before which we sat for a long time in wonderment." He met a number of kindred spirits, including Th. L. Haitjema, J. Eijkman, D. Tromp, and O. Noordmans. The last of those especially made an impression on Barth. He judged him as someone who "surpassed the others in independence and caliber."[12]

At the close of his visit, Barth spoke in Amsterdam at a European congress for internal mission on the theme "The church and culture"; in different words, the same theme as that on which he had spoken seven years previously in Tambach (see 2.6). Like there, he considered that from the three viewpoints of creation, reconciliation (salvation), and consummation. First, creation. God's Word, as Word of reconciliation, says that the human, even as sinner, has not ceased to be a creature (human) of God. In Christ, it is confirmed that the world, the human, is God's own. So it still obtains that grace does not remove nature but perfects it. The work of culture, oriented as it is on humanity, can thus refer to that to which the human, as creature of God, is destined. It is not only that it can do that; viewed from Christ it in fact does so. Culture, then, is the promise given to the human of what he will become. Culture does not of itself effect the inbreaking of the Kingdom of God, but it can certainly be a sign of it (or display signs) that the Kingdom has actively approached (in God's way). The church, of course, is attentive to that. The culture is also its business.

Then the viewpoint of reconciliation. We are justified in Christ and called to sanctification, to new obedience to the will, the law, of God. Just as the human as creature stands under the promise of humanity, so he stands as reconciled, justified under the command of humanity. So viewed, culture is thus a form of the law, as appeal to human existence. If the culture is for the human as creature the promise of what he will become, for the reconciled,

---

12. Barth to Thurneysen, June 4, 1926, in *BT*, 417.

justified human it is the command whereby he is called. And under this viewpoint, the church can only but affirm the culture.

Finally, the viewpoint of the consummation. We are reconciled, but not yet fully saved. Certainly, "the old is past, the new has come," we are "a new creation" (2 Corinthians 5:17). But that obtains in Christ, for faith. It is not yet a visible, palpable reality. The consummation means that this restriction to faith, this "not yet," will be removed. Then, the foreordination of the human, humanity, will be realized. Then the genuine, true culture will be reality as a gift of God. What at present is called "culture," so viewed, is only the limit beyond which God's self will make all things new. From this point it is clear that the connection of church with culture can only be of a critical nature. Before we know it, culture as such is the building of the tower of Babel which intends to storm heaven. The church cannot meddle with that. "The hope of the church rests *on* God and *for* men; it does not rest *on* men, not even on religious men—and not even on the belief that men *with the help of God* will finally build that tower."[13] This eschatological reserve, oriented to God's coming judgment, does not mean a disdain of culture but just the highest esteem for that to which all culture (in art and science, economics and politics, technology and education) points. True, it can appear disturbing. Perhaps it makes the church unpopular in society. But only by asserting this reserve, if necessary, against societal protests, can it really be in service to society.

It is just this last point of view, so Barth concluded his argument, that matters today. To think that it is God's self who, in Christ, will make all things new and that thus we will not and cannot do so (in our cultural work), we had also, and just, in the church (in modern cultural Protestantism) forgotten that. Just where that is again considered, the notion also appears that the culture is promise (for the human as creature) and law (for the human as reconciled, justified).

4.9 Dutch Reactions

That is the way that the Netherlands became acquainted with Barth in 1926, and Barth with the Netherlands. Of course, one had previously heard of Barth in that country. His *Epistle to the Romans* and other works had attracted attention. But thus far not in broad circles. That changed in 1926. That was also the year in which the first Dutch publications of (Reformed) kindred spirits appeared on Barth's theology: a book from the confessional leader Haitjema (*Karl Barth*) and a collection of contributions from the

13. Barth, "Church and Culture," 349.

Ethical party in the Netherlands Reformed Church (including Noordmans, under the title *Nieuwe Theologie*). The personal meetings and Barth's speech in Amsterdam stirred interest in broad circles.

There was also criticism of course. Barth's accent on the eschatological reserve of everything, even at the Christian, cultural engagement, had touched a sensitive nerve. There was a deep commitment to a "Christian culture" especially in circles of the Reformed Churches of the Netherlands. Here one could not easily tolerate Barth's drastic relativization of this effort. One could not share the notion that it is just in this relativization that it gets its due. This was viewed as decidedly too little. Is not the Christian unambiguously called to social labor? That must be stimulated, not slowed! In later years, it would also be an often heard reproach directed at Barth, that he misunderstood the human vocation in history.

4.10 Dogmatics in Service of Preaching

In Münster, as well, Barth's primary attention was on dogmatics. Here he picked up the dogmatic thread that he had to let lie in Göttingen. There he had not yet come to a treatment of eschatology. That was still on the agenda. Barth kept himself from every inclination of a curious speculation of the "last things." He claimed that eschatology is not about *what* the future is, but about Who is future. It is not about "the last things" in themselves, but that God's Word as such is "the last," that which comes and what we do not have within our power. That too must be considered. To realize that, that is eschatology.

In the following three semesters, from 1926 to 1928, Barth again offered an entirely new cycle of lectures on dogmatics. Just as he already had done in Göttingen, he carefully wrote out these lectures beforehand. And this time he also conceived the plan to prepare them for publication. Yet again, just as with the writing of his *Epistle to the Romans*, he felt like a pioneer. As he would write later, "I could not and cannot find a place in the line in which Protestant dogmatics, of whichever sort, where I . . . would be able to connect." The thinkers with whom he felt at home (among others he named the two Blumhardts, Kierkegaard, Hermann Friedrich Kohlbrügge) had not "walked in the path of the newer theology."[14] Just like them, Barth felt like a loner. Thus, he could not do other than present his own dogmatics as a proposal, a proposal that he knew was pressed upon him, if only because of his curriculum. And aside from that, he felt urged thus to render account of the course that he had struck with his *Epistle to the Romans*.

14. Barth, *Die christliche Dogmatik im Entwurf,* 4–5.

Dogmatics is in the service of preaching, thus in the service of the church. Barth remained firm in that starting point. As he formulated it this time, dogmatics strives to understand the proper content of Christian talk about God and the human. Such Christian talk (preaching) itself, with its pretension of truth, is already risky. Thus, the practice of dogmatics is so as well. For here the aim is to hold that pretension of truth to the light. What about the content of what you think you have to say? What is really the content? One cannot just speak at random. Truth stands over and against falsehood. It matters that one speaks the truth!

4.11 A Dogmatics in Draft

In 1927, the first part of Barth's dogmatics appeared, in essence the content of what he had treated the first semester, held in the winter of 1926/27: the "prolegomena," the introduction to the dogmatics. Just as in Göttingen, Barth also had begun with that in Münster. The intention was that the substance from the later semesters would also be published in the following parts. The whole would have as its title: "Die christliche Dogmatik im Entwurf" [Christian Dogmatics in Draft]. That title was also already given to the first part.

Why a separate discussion of "prolegomena" to dogmatics? How can the search for the substance of Christian thought be introduced? Can one not come straight to the point, just like that? The newer Protestant theology generally presupposed: no. Whoever wants to speak the truth of God's Word would in any case have to search for steps to be able to make this Word plausible to humans. For "prolegomena," preliminary considerations. One called on the science of religion, for example, for help in taking such a step. Would a reference to the general phenomenon of religion not be able to contribute an openness for the Christian faith? For is Christian faith not a specific phenomenon in the general field of religion? Others, rather, sought the approach via the philosophy of religion. Would whoever thinks about the Word of God not be able to start from the reasonability of belief in God? Still others argued primarily psychologically. Would not the dogmatics be able to connect with human psychological need to (believe in) God?

Besides, it is not only newer Protestantism that is interested in such steps. Already earlier, in Reformed (and Lutheran) orthodoxy, one had begun with an introductory chapter in dogmatics. That treated "the authority of Holy Scripture." If that is certain, the doctrinal truth of the Christian faith can be firmly constructed on that basis, so it was reasoned. And an extra introduction was soon added to that treatment, on "the concept of religion."

The thought behind that was that the substance of the Christian faith can be expanded upon only for those who possess that insight.

But Barth claimed that this entire search for steps into the dogmatics is a sign of weakness. The theologian is apparently not sure of his business. That makes for a bad proof. After all, every science works with hypotheses, axioms, in the confidence that its correctness will appear in the progress of the work! Why would it be different in theology, in dogmatics?

Still, Barth believed he could not avoid the generally existing custom of beginning with a prolegomena, not to let himself be drawn along by the spirit of the time but just to be able to show in this prior talk "about" the matter that the matter stands by itself. Whoever would argue that dogmatics, as reflection on the substance of the Christian faith, is sensible and possible, must naturally refer to the *norm* of the truth of this faith. But then it comes down to making clear that talk of the norm is also a matter of faith. The norm becomes clear where it is actively applied—in dogmatic practice itself. Thus, the introduction to the dogmatics is already, in itself, a form of dogmatics.

Barth made that concrete by giving his own prolegomena the form of an elaborated "doctrine of the Word of God." He found the reality of the Word in the preaching of the church that in its turn is based on the witness of the prophets and apostles, and behind that, on revelation. In the chapter on God's revelation the dogma of God's tri-unity already emerges, with separate paragraphs on the "incarnation of the Word" (the birth of Christ) and the "outpouring of the Holy Spirit." Other separate chapters are dedicated to "The Holy Scripture" (how Scripture and tradition, Scripture and the church are related to each other) and to the question of how the preaching of God's Word and the human word correspond.

In his preface to this lecture-in-book-form, Barth again explored the question that had been put to him by many friends (and that also came up at the beginning of this chapter): how could he, champion of "dialectical theology," of "theology as footnote," become a dogmatician? Has he, himself, not now succumbed to the "danger of orthodoxy"? Has it not now been that with him the "Springtime of Reformation theology" (O jubilant sound!) was followed all too quickly by "a questionable scholastic Autumn?" Has Barth become his own epigone? Has the earlier "prophet" become an ordinary theologian?

Nonsense, he said. It was never my ambition to be a prophet. I have never intended anything other than to practice theology, and that with both feet on the ground. And I now have dogmatics as the curriculum. Labels like "orthodoxy" and "scholastic" are too easily affixed. Besides, we need not be anxious about it. Let us be about what there is for us to do. Or would it be like before, that somewhere a "great clock" will toll? That was and is not my intention. And that is not what matters.

4.12 Charlotte von Kirschbaum

The plan to publish the entire dogmatic course from the years 1926 to 1928 did not come to fruition. New parts of the *Christliche Dogmatik* would not appear; the published "first part" would remain as one volume. Just as with the *Epistle to the Romans*, he would, on further consideration, conclude that in his dogmatic work the same thing must be said differently. It would lead to a completely new beginning. In 1932—we will come back to this—the first part of what from now on would be called "Church Dogmatics" would appear. True, it would have the same point of departure. Barth would remain active with it the rest of his life.

Barth would be assisted by Charlotte von Kirschbaum in that further work. She had already helped Barth in preparing the above named *Christliche Dogmatik* for publication. As a nurse, she had also followed classes for secretarial work. She was also theologically grounded. Barth had met her, thirteen years younger than himself, already in 1924 and made further acquaintance in 1925. From that point, at the age of twenty-seven, she became his closest fellow worker, indispensable for the progress of Barth's work.

The collaboration included much more than secretarial support. She made Barth's way of thinking more and more her own. Barth's business became her business, her life's work. She not only took care of all Barth's arrangements as well as his correspondence but developed into his conversation partner. A more or less fixed pattern developed in their mutual way of working. In the preparation of his lectures and classes, Barth first made brief notes. She worked them out into the text that Barth would subsequently put into final form. This is how all Barth's further work originated. That could not have happened without Charlotte van Kirschbaum. Her part has always been only dimly known. Given the conditions, that could not be otherwise. But that must not have been easy for her.

There was a great deal to do on the relation between Barth and Charlotte von Kirschbaum ("Lollo"), primarily in Barth's family, but not only there. The relationship became more than a working one; it became a relationship in life. So much so that she became part of Barth's family in 1929. That was coupled with unavoidable personal tensions. Barth's wife, Nelly, could manage this triangular relationship only with difficulty. There was talk that the marriage would break up. But a divorce would have conflicted with the social status that was important for Nelly. Thus, things did not come to that. Nelly accepted, with difficulty, Charlotte's presence in her home and the life of her husband. Just as Charlotte accepted that she would not become the only wife in Barth's life.

Barth himself would always be open about his particular relationship with Charlotte, including with those who addressed him critically about it. He would make no secret of the fact that he could not do without her. He would dedicate the last part of his *Church Dogmatics* to be published, the "fragment" on baptism (1967), to his wife "with great gratitude," but in the preface to the same part he would at the same time expressly note the "great part" that Charlotte had had in his work. At that moment she had definitively been set "out of action" through illness.[15] The consequence was that Barth would no longer continue with the *Church Dogmatics*. Charlotte died in 1975, seven years after Barth's death. At his wish, she was placed in the Barth family grave. Nelly was also buried there a year later.

---

15. Barth, *CD*, IV/4, viii.

5

The 1930s: On a Definite Theological Course

5.1 Anselm as Crown's Witness and Ally

IN 1930, BARTH WAS appointed professor of systematic theology at Bonn. Here he met congenial colleagues. A period of growth began in the Protestant theological faculty with Barth's arrival. Bonn was now considered the center of Protestant theology. There was a large number of students. Barth attracted many students, including those from outside Germany, even from beyond Europe. Students flocked to his lectures. To keep the number of participants within limits he offered two parallel courses. He also instituted a sort of entrance exam for candidates.

One would have expected that Barth would have immediately picked up the thread of his own dogmatic research and teaching in Bonn that he had begun in Göttingen and continued in Münster. But instead he began with the study and discussion of the work of Anselm of Canterbury, theologian of the eleventh century and one of the first representatives of medieval scholasticism.

The central theme of scholasticism was the relation between faith and reason. According to Anselm there is no contradiction between the two. Whoever believes seeks, automatically, to understand. "Faith" is by definition "a search for reasoned insight" (*fides quaerens intellectum*, as Anselm put it). And the search cannot be for naught. Faith is to be made reasonably accessible.

Anselm had applied this axiom to belief in God. Belief accepts that God exists. But Anselm had developed reasoning according to which the existence of God could also be proven. He had also made the belief that Jesus Christ, the incarnate son of God, had borne the punishment for human sin through his crucifixion a subject of reasoned reflection. That the incarnation and crucifixion of the Son of God were necessary for the reconciliation between God and the human, can, so he claimed, be understood by a reasonably thinking human, even apart from the fact that the Bible (and behind that God's revelation) says it.

Little value had remained of such reasoning and medieval scholasticism in the circles of the leading modern Protestantism since the nineteenth century. Such reasoning was considered unfruitful speculation. But Barth was more and more convinced that the great thinkers of the past cannot simply be written off.

He had also been busy with Anselm earlier. In particular, he had been affected by the way in which Anselm saw insight, reasonable thought, related to faith. Anselm wrote concisely on this in the first chapter of his *Pros-logian*, a text that closes with the words "I believe in order to understand" (*credo ut intelligam*). Belief is prior for Anselm. It is the starting point of his thinking. Barth recognized in that his own theological method. He had already written on this foundational notion in his *Christliche Dogmatik* of 1927. There he had quoted Anselm as the crown's witness for his own claim that the Word of God—and that Word alone as a reality resting in itself—is "the meaning and the possibility of dogmatics." With that claim, Barth had turned against the modern Protestant conception as if dogmatics, theology, was about investigating the human spirit in its own "God consciousness," as though God would be the "God of our consciousness" or "of our believing idea"! In Anselm, Barth had found an ally in his rejection of this modern position.

First, he reflected further on Anselm's theology. On further review, he was dissatisfied with his own *Christliche Dogmatik*. It was intended as a first part, but he didn't get to working on a further part. Barth had concluded that it would have to be completely different in the dogmatics. In his search for the right course he again looked all the more for support from Anselm.

The result of his study of Anselm was his book *Fides quaerens intellectum. Anselms Beweis der Existenz Gottes* (Anselm's Proof for the Existence of God). Barth dedicated it to the theological faculty of the University of Glasgow in gratitude for the honorary doctorate conferred by this faculty the previous year (his second, following the one from Münster in 1922, see 3.3). It is the least well-known of all Barth's publications. But he later stated that he had written this book out of the greatest love and that it contained the documentation of the change of course that he took at the time, a change of course that set him on the path that he would strike in his later theological work. Thus, we expend further thought to this book.

5.2 Anselm's Proof for the Existence of God

First something on Anselm's own argument. He begins his argument for the existence of God with a definition of what must be understood by "God." He states this in the form of prayer: "We believe that thou art: Something beyond which nothing greater can be conceived." Strictly taken, this definition as such is not only the starting point but, at the same time, the concluding point of the argumentation. Or better: it *is* itself the entire argument. For, so he reasons, the thought and expression of this definition means already in itself that you must accept the existence of the God so defined. After all, something that exists in reality is greater than something that only exists in the human spirit. Whoever only thinks of a God as "that above which nothing greater can be conceived," without reckoning with the existence of this God, contradicts himself. After all, he must then see, however unwillingly, that there is still something conceivable "beyond which nothing greater can be conceived."[1] He appears to have misled himself.

Anselm claimed in a following chapter that that "beyond which nothing greater can be conceived" cannot even be *considered* as non-existent. For again, something of which non-existence is inconceivable is of course greater than something of which, albeit exists, its non-existence is still conceivable (imaginable).

At this point Anselm accomplished the identification of his thinking with his faith. This essence "above which nothing greater can be conceived," that thus exists not only in reality but that cannot even be conceived as non-existent, is nothing other than God's self. Again, Anselm expressed himself in prayer: "That Thou art, Lord our God. So truly art Thou thus . . . Thou alone (possess) being in the most real sense."

5.3 On Anselm's Theological Program

In his book, Barth first devoted a reflection on Anselm's theological program as such. He emphasized that Anselm, in his search for understanding, did not "intellectually storm heaven" (he was no rationalist; after all, his thought began with belief!) and even less did he sacrifice reason (*sacrificium intellectus;* after all, precisely as a believer he aimed at thought and understanding!). For Anselm it is belief itself that yearns for thought and understanding (although it is not dependent on it for certainty). That makes theology both necessary and possible. Whereby it is to be thought (so

---

1. Barth, *Anselm,* 74.

Anselm had elaborated elsewhere) that faith lives from the preached and heard Word of God that comes from without.

This attitude brings with it a very particular view of "the way of theology." Barth notes that for Anselm, theology is nothing other than thinking-after what is pre-said in the faith (the credo). The issue is: that the truth given in the faith is understood as truth, that its essential meaning, foundation and coherence is recognized (if only so to a certain extent). So the human bows with one's *ratio*, one's capacity to think reasonably, before the authority of the truth. But that does not mean irrationality. Indeed, it affirms the *ratio*, reasonability, that is peculiar to the truth (revelation) itself.

What is the goal of theology? In any case Anselm does not theologize (argue, reason) with the intention of bringing unbelievers to belief. He apparently presupposes humans who, like him, stand in faith as conversation partners, but who do not (yet) see the inner coherence of what is held before them to be believed (as revealed). He makes no special apologetic (defense of faith). His "argument" consists simply of his struggle to elaborate the faith such that it becomes understandable for everyone in its transparent reasonability.

Is that naïve? Barth thinks not. Instead he sees Anselm here as taking the "*via regia* of divine simplicity."[2] Maybe, Anselm presupposed, the unbelief of the unbeliever need never be taken so seriously. Perhaps he did not believe his unbelief, rather (in opposition to everything) his belief! This assuredly not from a supposition concerning the presence of piety or religiosity with every human. More, he presupposed, Anselm will have let himself be led by the notion that the reasonability of that faith has itself the capacity to educate and convince humans. After all, Anselm had experienced that capacity personally! It was from experience that he could not address unbelievers other than as though they were already believers. Thus, it is understandable that he could not continue to admit to the chasm between believers and unbelievers but bridged the chasm as conqueror. With, as his only weapon, that he put himself on the same wavelength as unbelievers and conversely accepted them as being on the same wavelength as himself.

5.4 Anselm: No Apologete but Witness

It is this theological program that Anselm also applied in his proof for God. Barth noted that already with Anselm's definition of "God": "Something beyond which nothing greater can be conceived." He pointed out the negative in this definition. Nothing is said of God's essence, nothing of

2. Barth, *Anselm*, 70.

"what" God is. Only the "who" of God is spoken of. God is thereby indicated as someone is indicated with his name. In fact, said Barth, with this definition Anselm refers to God's name. Anselm expresses that in faith: "We believe that Thou art . . ." Anselm had not invented that himself. The Name is nowhere derived; nor can it be derived from anywhere. It has apparently imposed, revealed itself to him.

Thus, the proof of God is about the question whether this God only exists by means of human thought or also as Reality outside and over and against the human spirit. That question is, said Barth, already answered for Anselm as believer. And at the same time, it is called to mind. *Credo ut intelligam*, "I believe in order to understand."

In this way, Barth saw that Anselm speaks not only as a philosopher but as a believer. He saw that interpretation confirmed in the way in which Anselm sees himself positioned over and against the "fool," just like the Psalmist. "The *fool* says in his heart: there is no God" (Psalm 14:1). Whoever speaks like that is not lacking in intelligence or erudition, but in faith. And that cannot be the final, definitive word. Of course, the believing human thinks differently than the "fool." But at the same time, one implicitly considers that one, from oneself, is in the same state as the "fool." After all, whoever believes does so thanks solely to God's grace—and that grace could also overcome the fool. The fool "of today might be the believer of tomorrow."[3]

Anselm, it is true, did not say that in so many words. But in any case, said Barth, he goes to work particularly unphilosophically in his argument. For the fact that in his answer to the objection of the "fool" ("there is no God") he takes his point of departure in God's revealed name means that he does nothing other in this entire answer than call this "fool" to faith. His argumentation is proclamation. Anselm's main issue is that the "fool" hears God's name ("something above which nothing greater can be conceived"). If that happens then it cannot be other than that he understands what he hears. Then this God is, in any case, present in his understanding, his thought. And if he then continues thinking he must conclude that this God cannot be only present in his thought. After all, what exists in reality, not only in the human spirit but also outside it, is greater that what exists exclusively, as concept, in the human spirit. That also goes for the created world. A God "above which nothing greater can be conceived" that still would exist only in human thought is an inner contradiction. Such a God would be a pseudo-god. Barth agreed with Anselm:

> In so far as it has been shown that God exists in the knowledge of the hearer when the Name of God is preached, understood and

3. Barth, *Anselm*, 106.

heard. But he cannot exist merely in the knowledge of the hearer because a God who exists merely thus stands in impossible contradiction to his own Name as it is revealed and believed.[4]

5.5 Theology of the Name

Barth gave particular thought to the way in which Anselm focused his argument: in the claim that on that, "above which nothing greater can be conceived," and thus this must really exist, it also must be said that it cannot even be *conceived* as non-existent. Here, Barth said, Anselm is articulating God's existence as an existence of an entirely peculiar nature. It says something of God that can be said of nothing and no one else. What cannot even be *conceived* as non-existent does not exist in the way that other things and essences exist; it exists "as the reality of existence itself, as the criterion of all existence."[5]

Anselm also derives God's *unique* way of existing from the Name that God bears. The Name is a given. It is not thought up by theology. The theologian has only the task (and possibility) of understanding the underivable, peculiar reasonability and necessity of this Name and what is given with it (God's existence).

The prayerful conclusion to Anselm's argument is also to be noted: "That Thou art, Lord, our God. So truly art Thou thus, Lord, my God . . . Thou alone (possess) being in the most truthful sense." Barth pointed out that here God is first spoken of as "our," thereafter as "my" God. That "our," he said, is from Anselm himself as a member of the church; God is the Lord of the (praying, believing) church. In the "my" he speaks—in *this* context—as the theologian seeking understanding. Again, Barth noted with agreement the lack of any philosophical doubt, along with any inclination to apologetics (defense of the faith). Theology is nothing other than affirmation, acceptance, of the decision taken because of its "object" (the Lord), acknowledgment of the self-communication of the Lord.

Anselm sees the human standing over and against God as creature over and against their Creator. That, too, is belief on the basis of God's revelation. The creature would not be able to think something greater than the Creator. If it nonetheless intended to do so, that would be "most absurd." Besides, for the creature it not only obtains that God, the Creator "also" exists, but primarily that *He* really (*verissime*, "in the truest sense")

---

4. Barth, *Anselm*, 128.
5. Barth, *Anselm*, 142.

exists. Barth commented: this unique existence of God makes it possible that general objective reality exists (and that the existence of God can also be conceived in general terms).

5.6 New Beginning: The *Church Dogmatics*

Thus far, Barth's interpretation of Anselm in outline. Has Barth done justice to the Medieval thinker? Expert critics (church historians) have not spared him. It was supposed that Barth had committed eisegesis. He would have read Anselm with problems in his mind that were not those of Anselm himself, at least not in the modern way.

Barth did not deny that particular subjective character of the work that resulted by virtue of his own questions. He even deemed that to be self-evident. "Who can read with eyes different than his own?" he wrote in the preface to his book. Still he stood his ground having advanced nothing other than what he had read in Anselm himself. It was this further acquaintance with Anselm that pointed him in the direction of his further theological work.

In the summer of 1931, Barth began his lectures in dogmatics. Again, as in Münster (and also in Göttingen) on the "prolegomena," the introductory matter: the "doctrine of the Word of God." That God expresses himself in his Word, reveals himself, is the norm for all dogmatics. It is just that that is to be considered. The result of the lectures held through the Spring of 1932 appeared later that year in book form. It was a republication of his Christliche Dogmatik, at least of its first part. But then in foundationally reworked form.

The title already was new: no longer "Christliche," but "Kirchliche [Church] Dogmatik." Barth had learned from Anselm to clearly see that the theologian, the dogmatician, is first of all a member of the church. With the new title he intended to show in a more disciplined way than previously that dogmatics is in service of the church and can only be practiced within the ambit of the church (namely of what "church" is in essence: the communion that lives by faith).

The arrangement, the division of the matter, remained the same. But it was treated much more expansively. Less than half of what had been discussed in the previous publication could be contained in one hefty volume. Hence the numbering: I/1. A separate volume would be needed for the remainder.

In his preface, Barth himself explained how the more expansive volume had come about. He had seen himself required to elaborate more broadly and to ground the matter more deeply. Specifically, he had had to expend more thought in indicating how his dogmatic ideas rest on exegetical, biblical-theological presuppositions and how they relate to what earlier thinkers in church history have said. One could, if necessary, skip these exegetical and church historical excurses (often very expansive, and printed as separate paragraphs in small letters) in following Barth's own argument. But Barth would not encourage it. After all, the excurses refer to the "voices which were in my own ears as I prepared my own text, which guided, taught, or stimulated me, and by which I wish to be measured by my readers."[6] What must be said today in dogmatics becomes clearly heard, said Barth, in the other voices from Scripture and tradition.

5.7 Self-correction

Compared with the *Christliche Dogmatik,* the approach was substantially new. True, it certainly was not a completely new approach. In the earlier dogmatics, from 1927, he had already maintained that dogmatics must not begin with something like the human religious idea but must find its starting point and substance in the preaching of the church, that it is thus in essence reflection on the Word of God. He had come to terms with the notion that a human intersecting point for that Word must first be sought out, to imagine possibilities of being able to make this Word plausible for humans. Prolegomena, introductory considerations would, to his understanding, have to be about that and how dogmatics also—or better, precisely—is possible under the abandonment of such plausibility considerations. They must point to the Word of God as the norm for the preaching of the church. To do so is already a matter of faith. So that the introduction to dogmatics is already itself dogmatics. Barth now defended this position anew but (stimulated by his study of Anselm) still more sharply and consistently.

At the same time, he maintained that he had been too unclear in his earlier dogmatic project. There he had posited that the Word of God takes on three forms: concretely in the preaching of the church, behind that in the witness of the prophets and apostles (set down in the Bible as guide), and again behind that in God's revelation itself (thus in that of which the Bible and proclamation witness). Just as now in 1932. But in addition, connected paragraphs on what the Word of God is in "essence," and on its knowability. This too was already there in the 1927 dogmatics. But then it was presented as considerations in which, differently than previously, the relation of humans (as proclaimers, hearers, believers) with the Word

6. Barth, *CD,* I/1, xii.

is discussed. This theme meant, so Barth opined in 1927, a "change of the manner of consideration,"[7] no longer "phenomenological" (on the Word as objective phenomenon), but "existential," thus reckoning that the Word touches human existence.

At the time, he inferred further delimitations of the Word of God from this analysis of the human as preacher, hearer, and believer. Barth had considered that humans are preachers: the Word is really word, spoken from person to person, not aimed at emotions but insight; word indeed that in essence is spoken by God himself and that the human never as something, even the preacher, has at his disposal. He saw disclosed in the fact that humans are hearers that they stand at a distance from God, estranged from God; that thus human existence is a question and that the Word is an answer to it, or: revelation that happens ever and anew. That humans accept the Word in faith caused him to underline that the Word of God is really addressed such that the believing human must be deemed as already taken up in the concept of the Word. Whoever speaks of the Word of God thereby speaks, per definition, immediately of the believing human. And humans can only be met humanly, thus: to be capable of being addressed, the Word must enter in a human, earthly and sinful way of being and take on a form ("flesh") in Christ, then also in the human witness of prophets and apostles in preaching and sacrament (that again does not mean that the forms themselves would be the Word of God apart from their service of God.)

It is precisely here that Barth came to criticize himself. Not so much about the *content* of all the considerations about the Word of God (the content is maintained in his new dogmatics), but in the way in which he had presented them at the time, as derived from an analysis of the human situation. That was, he now saw, not only unnecessary, but above all misleading. As though the human self-understanding would have to become a point of contact to be able to come to a correct concept of the Word of God! As though theology could be founded on human considerations! As though theology would have to be based on a particular kind of philosophy (existentialism)! He now avoided a way of speaking that has the Word of God as an "answer" to the question of human existence. Just like the formula as if the believing human would already be 'included' in the concept of the Word. With that, the graceful nature of this Word addressed to the human would be deformed to something automatic and self-evident.

Barth had not intended that already in 1927. This is a misunderstanding. But as far as he then had given himself occasion, he now had expressly

---

7. See Barth, *Christliche Dogmatik im Entwurf*, 69–71.

corrected that. Here he saw the danger that he deemed present not only in modern Protestantism but above all also in Roman Catholicism, the notion that there would be an *analogia entis* (analogy of being) between God and the human. Together, God and the human would share the same being. So, the truth and reality of God could be approached already from natural, earthly existence. And so, grace becomes something self-evident. God's actions in their uniqueness disappear from view. Barth deemed this notion absolutely unacceptable. He even writes in his preface that he viewed that as "the invention of Antichrist."[8] If an "analogy" between God and the human can already be spoken of, then only by faith (*analogia fidei*). After all, Barth also had learned from Anselm that one has to begin with faith.

Barth would never leave the theological path that he struck in 1932 with the publication of *Church Dogmatics* I/1. It would now result in further construction. Barth would work on that the rest of his life. The *Church Dogmatics* would, remaining however incomplete, grow to a body of thirteen volumes, altogether over 9,000 pages.

---

8. Barth, *CD*, I/1, xiii.

6

The German Church Conflict

6.1 Hitler Comes to Power

FOR BARTH, THE YEARS in Bonn were not only years of new theological focus. He was more and more involved in societal and ecclesiastical developments. This involvement was closely connected with his dogmatic reflections.

He had become a German citizen, alongside his Swiss citizenship, already at the beginning of 1926. This was connected to the fact that he had entered the service of the state as professor at Münster (and remained so as professor in Bonn). In May 1931, he also became a member of the SPD [Social Democratic Party]. His opting for socialism was in line with his earlier course in the Swiss Safenwil; it was not motivated so much principally as practically (see 2.2 and 2.6). He felt pressured to do so by the course of events.

The world-wide economic crisis that broke out in 1929 had consequences primarily in Germany. There was unemployment, inflation, poverty. From the left the Communists advocated action with their work for revolution and the "power of the proletariat." National Socialism emerged from the right. It called for strong leadership. Adolf Hitler stood as a candidate to fill that role. He promised restoration of employment and prosperity in a Germany that would again be great and strong. National Socialist propaganda culminated in the glorification of the German ("Aryan") race. It would have to be purified of alien stains, concretely of Jews. Hitler's party, the NSDAP, gained a great following. This all meant a serious threat to the democratic system of the Weimar Republic (which functioned since the Peace of Versailles in 1919). Barth's renewed choice of social democracy was a protest against that threat.

The election of 1932 resulted in a stalemate. Extremists from left and right, Communists on one side, National Socialists on the other side, achieved great gains. The parliament (*Reichstag*) was hamstrung. In that situation, beginning in 1931, the President of Germany, Paul von Hindenburg, appointed Hitler as chancellor (premier). He hoped that Hitler's action would help to rein in the Communists. Hitler's first act following his acceptance of power on January 30, 1933, was to call a new election. That was held in March. Intimidation and violence delivered the National Socialists an overwhelming majority.

The newly elected *Reichstag* "temporarily" ceded the legislative power of the parliament to the government. This was represented as a measure "for the lifting of the emergency of the people and the empire." In fact, the chancellor thereby received dictatorial authority. All other political parties were banned. The National Socialists self-titled their assumption of power as a "revolution." In his declaration of governance, Hitler maintained that this was "extremely disciplined and bloodless." The first anti-Jewish measure directly followed his acceptance of power.

6.2 "The Need of the Evangelical Church"

Already at the end of the 1920s. Barth had viewed with horror how much giving up on the institutions of the Weimar Republic had become popular in Germany. Circles within the German Evangelical Church, an umbrella group of (partly Lutheran, partly Reformed, partly Lutheran-Reformed, "united") regional churches (*Landeskirchen*) also shared this attitude. There was a great deal of sympathy in the church for National Socialism as it beat on the anvil of "German nationalism." The church saw itself as the highest religious authority in a renewed Germany. It detected opportunities in the new trend. The leadership of the church made this known in official publications. It would be good times for the church, so it was said.

Barth expressed his displeasure in a short but sharp article in 1930. He spoke of "a scandal screaming to heaven" and an "extremely dangerous attack" on the "substance," the essence of the German Evangelical Church. With this wager on the "religious thought rooted in the German religious soul" and on its own existing interests, the essential church had, in his opinion, ceased to exist. Where church leaders advertise for their own business they betray God's business. The title of this article, "*Quousque tandem . . . ?*" "How long . . . ?" was a reference to a warning address of the Roman senator

Cicero from the first century BC. "How long does it continue?" That was now also Barth's question.[1]

One year later, in January 1931, Barth elaborated his vision of the church situation more broadly. He held an address to a packed university hall in Berlin on "The Need of the Evangelical Church." There is a need, he said, that lies within the evangelical church itself. There is also a need that the evangelical church has brought upon itself in which it denies its essence. That is now acute.

The first need identified, coheres with the church itself that it, as the church of the crucified Christ, is the "church under the cross." It cannot presume to present the world with either power or pretense. It does not exist to advance human interests nor to sustain its own influence. It is not itself the Kingdom of God. It is not the continuation or embodiment of the revelation and reconciliation in Christ. It cannot make Christ active nor propagate nor spread salvation. God himself will do that. It can only serve that end. It lacks the saving word, the divine authority. It is impoverished.

That is not serious. It belongs to its essence. But just when, like the evangelical church at this time, it flees from that, it comes upon another, serious need. In the post-war misery, the German people appealed for a new order, a strong authority, for the dedication of the individual to the "great Whole." One speaks readily, deeply, of unavoidable societal developments. Church spokespersons readily take up this jargon. But that it is about a particular visibility of the church, a visibility that recalls the cross of Christ, of that there was silence.

The evangelical church must display character and vigor, its leaders say. It must manifest itself publicly. It must pursue a place for itself to live (*Lebensraum*). But one doesn't bother oneself about "what" the church really is. Yes, one says "the church has the gospel," as if the church had the gospel at its disposal. As if the gospel must not be received in faith, over and again. The church presents itself as self-assured. It is thereby, unconsciously, in serious trouble. Moreover, it proclaims law (a particular kind of law) rather than gospel. It appeals to religious renewal, moral purity, communal meaning, the support of the community of the people instead of speaking of God's mercy to humans in guilt and need. Of course, the law too must be preached. But that can be the case only where God's grace is taken seriously.

It was Barth's primary reproach that Christianity and the nature of the people, gospel and German were paired directly with each other in official statements of the evangelical church. He claimed that just so, the church does no service to the fatherland. "What the German people need today is the

---

1. Barth, "*Quousque tandem?*," 28–29.

existence of an *evangelical* and precisely *not* a *German*-evangelical church."² A church on this nationalistic track is on the way to its own demise.

Among the audience in the Berlin hall was Otto Dibelius, head of the evangelical church in Prussia. Eight days later he held an address in the same hall in which he dispatched Barth's criticism as theoretical; and "as a practical man," Dibelius defended the concrete, existing church. Barth's remark on the pairing of "German" and "evangelical" was dismissed as coming from a foreigner. Someone of Swiss birth "cannot really sympathize with what lives in German hearts." Barth reacted bitterly that this only strengthened his criticism. "I hope for another, new day for the German evangelical church."³

6.3 Dogmatics over and against the Self-Consciousness of the Church

The discussions identified above took place at the same time that Barth was very busy with his study of Anselm and the new version of his dogmatics that it inspired (as described in the previous chapter). That he also was very much involved with the church in this work (his real task as professor) appears already from the fore-mentioned fact that from that point on, he published his dogmatics under the new title, *Church Dogmatics*. This was not to present his work as a sort of ecclesiastical "court theology," not to the adulation of the official church and its doctrine. No, it was precisely to address the church on what it, by virtue of its essence, must be and do—and what at the same time it threatens to fail to do.

The political and ecclesiastical relevance can be heard in the preface of the first part (*CD* I/1), 1932. He laments "the constantly increasing confusion, tedium and irrelevance of modern Protestantism, which . . . has lost an entire third dimension . . . we may describe as mystery," with the consequence that one seeks it in a number of "meaningless surrogates," such as the "German church" (German-national churchliness), and that many preachers or believers "hope to discover deep religious significance in the intoxication of Nordic blood and their political *Führer*."⁴ For sure, a lot of things have to be clarified in politics. And the church can and must have its say on that. But to be able to do so, theology itself must come to clarity. "One" expects much of the church in society these days. But, said Barth, we must not take that too seriously. We must keep to our own, real, task. Just then it can happen that "one" again, takes us into account. The church's

2. Barth, "Die Not der evangelischen Kirche," 57.
3. Barth, "Die Not der evangelischen Kirche," 62.
4. Barth, *CD*, I/1, xiv.

best contribution to the solution of the contemporary German problems consists "in a better church dogmatics."[5]

Thus, Barth developed his views on what dogmatics really is as well as its necessity. It is critical inquiry of the preaching of the church. Is it in fact a configuration of the Word of God (as it would have to be)? That is not self-evident. Critical inquiry is not a superfluous luxury or an academic game; it is, rather, the church's act of obedience to its Lord. It is measured against nothing other than the Word of God itself as that is concretized in the witness of the prophets and apostles, in the Holy Scripture of the Old and New Testaments, standing authoritatively over and against the church and applied ever again as such. Besides which, by the way, God's Word, God's revelation, is yet again to be distinguished from Scripture. It is that—better, the One—to whom the Scripture (just as preaching, when it is good) points, Jesus Christ, in the Person of the incarnate Word of God.

That the church, preaching, dogmatics exist presupposes that there are people who can know the Word of God. Just as in the earlier version of his dogmatics, Barth now argued that the "can" is not a human capacity, present beforehand, by nature. The modern Protestant conception is that this is indeed the case and thus that the human can know God from his or her own self. Barth deemed that as disregarding the totally other-nature of God and his Word vis-à-vis the human. Where the Word is received by humans, it is thanks exclusively to the Word that creates of itself the capacity of the hearer to receive the Word. Thus, it becomes possible for humans to "experience" the Word of God.

But even so, everything is not yet clear. Does this now mean that the human receives one's own new capacity where this "experience" occurs? Is human-existence thus elevated to a higher plane in this event? Then from that moment the experience of the Word would yet become something of the human—the Christian, the believer, the pious human—themselves. The human would then have become an active fellow player in the participation of the reality of the Word. And to know this reality, one could thus take as a starting-point the experience, not of every human, but certainly of this particular, graced human. Then dogmatics can (must) find its criterion for its inquiry in the content of preaching in the particular experience of the pious human. It would in fact become a doctrine of faith. Then the church would have reason (in gratitude) for self-consciousness, for an attitude of self-assurance.

Barth himself discussed this conception already in the earlier version of his dogmatics. Meanwhile it manifested itself more emphatically. The

5. Barth, *CD*, I/1, xvi.

self-consciousness of the church, so Barth now maintained, is borne out by many "positive," enlightened preachers of the German Evangelical Church. It is also dominantly present in the newly emerged pietistic community movement. It was articulated by church leaders like Dibelius. It was expressed with ever more pomposity. Barth had already turned against it in his speech on the "Need of the Evangelical Church." Here, in his re-written dogmatics, he did so anew and foundationally. He elucidated what was theologically behind it, the claim that the human who experiences God's Word thereby and therein becomes, oneself, a "particular human."

Barth said that here the "pious human," and thus also the church, is placing oneself (itself) in the middle, instead of the Word of God. While the one who is really touched by the Word just so is aware that he cannot boast on the basis of his own experience, that "experience of the Word" is nothing other than respectful acknowledgment of the authority of that Word, an acknowledgment that more overcomes him than that it would be his own act. See as an illustration the apparent paradoxical appeal of the father of the sick child with Jesus, "I believe, help thou my unbelief." (Mark 9:24). Knowledge of the Word is possible; otherwise there could be no church. But the church "has" that knowledge only and insofar as it is given it, ever and anew, and in the hope that it will happen.

Barth made no mention of the German situation in this connection, but it certainly played a part in his considerations. The German Evangelical Church consciously placed itself in the midst of society. It participated, albeit unconsciously, in German nationalism. Barth's dogmatics is not exclusively a continual participation in the German church struggle, but it is also certainly this.

6.4 In Continuing Discussion with Schleiermacher

With these views of the Word of God and of how the human can know or even experience it, Barth must have continually thought of the nineteenth-century Schleiermacher. After all, in his theology, Schleiermacher had concentrated on the human pious consciousness, on feeling and experience. It is not surprising that Barth cites him several times in this connection. In general, Barth was always conscious of the particular character of his own way of thinking compared with the course of the liberal Protestant theology of the nineteenth century (which he detected as still active). Schleiermacher was its prominent representative. A simple rejection of this theology was certainly not Barth's intention. So far as it set out to keep in mind that the Word of God is about to meet the human, including the modern human,

Barth found that it deserves to be honored as legitimate. But then it comes down to putting the matter precisely and not allowing misunderstandings to be undisputed. We see him busy with that in the preceding cited passages of the first part of his new dogmatics.

Besides, we see Barth busy with that in lectures dedicated at this time to nineteenth-century Protestant theology as such. We heard (see 4.7) that he had begun to treat this theme in courses in Münster. Now, in Bonn, he picked up that work again. In 1932 and 1933 he treated a series of leading (eighteenth and) nineteenth-century philosophers and theologians for his students. The underlying thought was that one cannot be a theologian today without an open eye for the work of yesterday's predecessors. His book on this subject *Die protestantische Theologie im 19. Jahrhundert: Ihre Vorgeschicht and Geschichte* [*Protestant Theology in the Nineteenth Century*] would appear in 1947 (prepared for the press by his son Christoph). That book in essence included nothing other than the lectures from 1932 and 1933.

Of course, Schleiermacher received special consideration in connection with these lectures. It is documented in the book. The positive way that Barth treated him is surprising. As a Christian theologian, Schleiermacher wanted to construct a bridge between the gospel and culture. He saw himself set before the task of apologetics, to present the Christian faith such that it is recognizable for the modern human as an indispensable element for the completion of culture, namely of the mature human being. A feeling of absolute dependence belongs to that human-being, said Schleiermacher; cultured humans can understand that. Theology and preaching would have to intersect with that feeling of dependence. So Schleiermacher developed his theology as a theology of feeling, a theology of piety that is recognizable in his origin from the Evangelical Brotherhood (established by Ludwig, Count of Zinzendorf in Herrnhut) and his relationship with nineteenth-century romanticism.

Barth carefully analyzed all that. He noted that Schleiermacher always saw the Christian pious self-consciousness as related to God, as the Other. That he started from this Christian self-consciousness and thence from that question to human action in view of God is not to be seen as blameworthy in itself. One can even find it an understandable approach given the fact that the modern human is concentrated on oneself in one's thinking; however, it is also dangerous. In any case, starting from the human who stands before God's face, one can certainly develop a good theology, namely as a theology of the Holy Spirit. And so Schleiermacher himself must have intended it. He would also certainly consider the reality of God, of the Word of God, of Christ in his own theology.

Except that this was apparently difficult for him just because he also would, in his talk about Christ, approach the modern human, concentrated on himself and so on his own consciousness. Thus, he came to present Christ as a factor in the development of the human in the direction of an ever less sensate, ever more spiritual existence—thus also in the direction of an ever stronger God-consciousness. That God-consciousness is, so he claimed, a perfect reality in Christ's self. And from that point it influences humanity in general. So Christ's spirit also reaches the Christian in the Christian community. His God-consciousness then appears to be more and more that of Christ's. And thus the human is ultimately saved by Christ. As a Christian, he comes to stand on a higher plane and reaches his ultimate destiny. Thereby then the creation of the human is also completed and crowned. Barth remarked that here Christ is distinguished from the Christian, but that distinction is only relative and provisional—quantitative, not qualitative. What is already, though imperfectly and still growing, seen present in the Christian is considered more perfectly present in Christ. Schleiermacher intended that they will ultimately coincide; thus there then can no longer be talk of the particularity of Christ.

So with Schleiermacher, everything turns around human feeling. The human knows oneself related to God in one's piety. But looked at that way, God does not stand over and against the human. He is there only as experienced by the human in their feeling. That means that when the human talks about "God," one always talks about oneself. That the human experiences "God" is in fact nothing other than that one experiences oneself as "absolutely dependent."

Barth's conclusion was that with all good intentions, Schleiermacher's theology is still not a genuine theology of the Holy Spirit. The Word of God is not acknowledged as its own, independent factor over and against faith. The consequence of Schleiermacher's apologetic work is that it is not the Spirit but the human religious consciousness that has become the real theme of theology. And among nineteenth-century Protestant theologians, Schleiermacher was not just anybody; he is, Barth said, rightly called the "Church-father of the Nineteenth Century."[6] He stands first and foremost as a model for the theological approach that places the human—one's consciousness, one's struggle—at the center. This means mediation between the gospel and culture. However well-intended, the gospel is thereby short-changed. Here, too, Barth omitted a direct reference to the current situation of his day. But there is no doubt that a direct connection existed between this theological perspective and his own in the current

---

6. Barth, *Protestant Theology in the Nineteenth Century*, 411.

situation of the church. It was a theological approach like Schleiermacher's, this form of culture theology, that in Barth's judgment had caused the derailment of the German Evangelical Church.

6.5 The Church Following Hitler

Barth was quickly pressured in the German church conflict to choose an explicit position. Directly following Hitler's acceptance of power on January 30, 1933, it was already apparent how many in the German Evangelical Church were inclined to get carried away by the general enthusiasm over the new National-Socialist state.

A movement in the church calling itself "German Christians" stepped forward. They experienced Hitler's inauguration as a sort of new Pentecost. The passion for National Socialism and for the equation of the church with the new state was not simply a political conviction for them but a matter of faith. The German people are active in National Socialism, they claimed, reflecting on the deepest sources of their life and thereby also rediscovering the way to the church. The German churches must respond. They must help the German people to see and fulfill their own vocation just as the new policy does the same. The church must consist of true Germans, that is to say of Christians of the Aryan race. The "German Christians" did not hesitate to propagate their convictions via intimidation, with violence, via mass political meetings and marches.

On the analogy of the centralization of the power of the state, they would also centralize power in the church. The German Evangelical Church must be more than a federated connection of regional churches. It would really have to become one church led by an administration headed by one man. In an official declaration at the end of March, Hitler assured the churches that their rights would be respected under the new policy. That gave many extra assurances. The "German Christians" received massive support among church members.

The leadership of the church intended to keep the matter in hand, but it was not insensitive to the efforts of the "German Christians." A troika received the task to determine the new course for the church. They made a direct appeal that left no doubt about their own sympathies:

> A mighty National Movement has captured and exalted our German Nation. An all-embracing reorganisation of the State is taking place within the awakened German people. We give our hearty assent to this turning-point of history. God has given us this: to Him be the glory.

> Bound unitedly in God's Word, we recognise the great events of
> our day a new commission of our Lord to His Churches.[7]

Indeed, it was a concrete attempt to rebuild the federal connection of churches as one new national church (*Reichkirche*). This restructuring was deemed necessary because of the "historical reversal" of "our beloved German fatherland." There would have to be a national "bishop" (*Reichsbischof*) at its head, just as a regional "bishop" must be the head of each regional church (*Landesbischof*). Hitler was informed of these plans. He signaled his agreement and designated an army chaplain from among the "German Christians" as fully empowered, who participated in the discussions on the restructuring of the church (later the new position of *Reichsbischof* would fall to him by virtue of his appointment by the national synod). The new organizational form of the church was declared legally binding by the state.

The state also determined that to fill the new church structure, church elections would take place in July 1933. This resulted in victory for the "German Christians," massively supported by National Socialist propaganda. All the leading positions in the various regional churches (*Landeskirchen*) were occupied by persons from their circle. At the beginning of September, the synod of the largest regional church, the one in the Prussian areas (among others, Berlin and environs, Westphalia, Rhineland), established a new law concerning the rights of preachers and church functionaries. An "Aryan paragraph" contained the determination that "non-Aryan" (read, Jewish) or those married to "non-Aryans" (Jews) may no longer be active in the ministry of the church.

Was there no resistance to this in the church? There was at least one group—the "Young Reformation Movement"—that raised objections to the efforts of the "German Christians." They at least rejected the plans to exclude "non-Aryans" from the church. These "young reformers" were supporters of the introduction of a national "office of bishop." They hoped that a powerful central authority would counter "arbitrary proclamation." Thereby, however, they advocated the retention of the independence and freedom of the church over and against the state. They saw just that independence threatened in the efforts of the "German Christians," though they sought no confrontation. They aimed for peace and cooperation within the church. But they were drowned out by the "German Christians." Their candidates in the church election of that summer had no chance against those of the "German Christians." In reaction to the outcome of the election, an "emergency coalition" of ministers, the *Pfarrernotbund* [Pastors' Emergency League] was formed. And "confessional groups" sprang up in a number of places,

---

7. Barth, *Theological Existence To-Day*, 23.

groups of church members who were troubled by the course of events. But for the time being little resulted.

Barth noted to his dismay a sympathy among his friends, or at least understanding, for the new course. Georg Merz, the Lutheran theologian with whom Barth, already since 1921, had worked together on the publication of the journal *Zwischen den Zeiten,* (see 3.7), wrote him a letter in April intended as wise advice:

> I understand that you now only continue your work in Germany with discomfort. Whoever is liberal and thinks democratically will have a good deal of resignation necessary . . . Your sons, too, will only have a good time in German schools as they can find themselves within the fortunes of the German people. Or is that now possible for you? for them? . . . I am of the opinion that one can exist in the coming years only then in Germany if one does not set himself against these things.[8]

6.6 "Theological Existence Today!"

Barth reacted furiously. A church that, as now in Germany, wants to have the totalitarian state as a systematic presupposition for its own existence, he wrote, has already at root betrayed its Christian character. Christ and Caesar cannot be so combined! Whoever claims that that must still be the case because it is the "German fate," "because the holy stream of history leads to this moment," says the impossible.[9] One may not set oneself against "these things"? But I cannot declare solidarity with "the things" that happen today, like what is now happening to the German Jews.

In a later letter, from the end of April, he turned directly against the "careful" position of those like his old friend Merz. Certainly, they advocate for the freedom of the church. But by not resisting the appeal of the troika (cited above), as Barth had, they have themselves in fact already betrayed the church, and have also expressed a "thankful yes" to Hitler. Thus, this "yes" to Hitler has been made the foundation of the church. All else that is brought forward—however "biblical" and "confessional"—is unworthy of the faith from the outset. The church has become a wagon hitched to a particular political party. How fatal that is will appear "as the hypnosis, in which now nearly all of Germany finds itself, will no longer work one day."[10]

---

8. Stoevesandt, introduction to Barth's *Theologische Existenz heute!,* 12.
9. Stoevesandt, introduction to Barth's *Theologische Existenz heute!,* 13.
10. Stoevesandt, introduction to Barth's *Theologische Existenz heute!,* 14–16.

Would a new structure for the church have to be immediately proposed? Must, can, the unity of the church come about as the byproduct of the intoxication of a political unity? Must we allow ourselves to be told by Hermann Goering what "authority" is, to infer from that what "authority" a church must have? "No, I say, not so."

What Barth already maintained in these and other letters in the Spring of 1933 he elaborated at the end of June in a brochure entitled *Theologische Existenz heute!* [*Theological Existence Today!*]. It is for theologians and the church, so Barth claimed, really to remain with theology and not to do (church) politics. It is not on the current situation (*zur Lage*), but on the matter itself (*zur Sache*) that must be spoken. As theologians, we are bound to the Word of God. That is our "theological existence," and we must maintain that. Just that is of church-political, and who knows also of political, significance. The temptation exists that "under the stormy assault of 'principalities, powers, and rulers of this world's darkness,' we seek for God elsewhere than in His Word, and seek His Word somewhere else than in Jesus Christ, and seek Jesus Christ elsewhere than in the Holy Scriptures of the Old and New Testaments."[11] Giving in to this temptation means the betrayal of our theological vocation.

Barth again denounced the immediate call for reformation, restructuring of the church. Does this call emerge from obedience to the Word of God? It is surprising how positively church proclamations evaluate the recent political upheaval and the new National Socialist state. One hastens to state that the church is prepared to cooperate in the construction of the new state. In just that framework then the church's own declarations, programs follow. Has the church not become unfaithful to itself?

Barth referred again to the (above cited) appeal of the ecclesiastical troika. One claimed to be "bound to the Word of God." But in saying that, one has understood the "'new commission of the Lord to the church . . . in the great events of our days.'"[12] As if the task from the Lord to his church could be heard in something other than Holy Scripture! Contrary to the "events of our day," God's Word would have to be listened to as a correction.

In particular, Barth directed his arrows at the figure of the bishop advocated by the supporters of church restructure. For them, he said, it was apparently about more than a nice title for those who already practice leadership and oversight in the church. One desires a real bishop, à la the Roman Catholic Church, someone with spiritual power, standing above the congregations and other office-bearers. How so? This is pure imitation of the state. The state

---

11. Barth, *Theological Existence To-Day*, 15.
12. Barth, *Theological Existence To-Day*, 27.

has a Führer, and the church must now also have one. Can, may that be so in the evangelical church? A reversal is necessary here.

Barth referred in this way to a double series of theses on "the shape of the church" formulated and publicized recently (May 20 and June 4, 1933) by a number of German Reformed theologians, including himself. The first (the "Dusseldorf Theses") was a theological declaration on what the church is in essence; the second (the "Elberfeld Theses") derived from that a number of demands concerning the organization of the church. The idea of an authoritative bishop was rejected on theological grounds in both documents. Up to this point, said Barth, there has been no reaction by others, including Lutherans. Theological reflection remains absent. The institution of this new "office of bishop" is common recklessness. After all, the German Evangelical Church—as part of the one, holy catholic church—already *has* its *Führer* in Christ himself!

6.7 The "German Christians" and the Vulnerability of the Church

In this connection, Barth sharply rejected the ideas of the "German Christians" as the real driving force behind the effort to restructure the church. The German Evangelical Church, he said, is certainly a church *for* but not *of* the German people. It serves only the Word of God. It believes that the state is instituted by God as a representative and a sustainer of the public order, but it does not believe in a particular type of state, and that includes the National Socialist state, as commanded by God. It proclaims the gospel *in* contemporary Germany but not *under its supervision* nor *in its spirit*. And it is not blood or race, but the Holy Spirit and baptism that determines who belongs to the church. If the German Evangelical Church excludes Jewish Christians or treats them as lower-class Christians, it is no longer a Christian church.

Moreover, more than worrying about the movement of the "German Christians," Barth said, one needs to worry about the "stunning vulnerability" in all parts of the evangelical church. One simply goes along, he maintained, either out of conviction or caution, out of ecclesial political considerations or with the intention of "adjusting" from "inside out." Some rejoiced that at least there is "life in the church brewery." Others would primarily be relieved of anxiety. But the question whether what the "German Christians" advocated is Christian *truth* was asked by no one.

More than the effort of the "German Christians," he also said, it was the internal "opposition" of the "young reformers" that worried him. The opposition is not powerful, not principled, not sufficiently theological. One advocates for the freedom of the church, but out of considerations of church politics and with church political means. While the "German Christians" would abandon the church to the desires of the "people," the "young reformers" are people of compromise. They would combine "Creation *and* Redemption, Nature *and* Grace, Nationalism *and* Gospel."[13] That is dangerous. They do not consider that the true freedom of the church and its proclamation consists in the fact that the Word of God rules in proclamation (and theology). That is anything but self-evident in the church; it was not that anyway.

Barth deemed the danger of "we as church" losing the Word of God as a much more serious danger than the "German Christians." No actions or demonstrations, manifestos, or protests defend against that danger. The only thing necessary is conversion. Something like a resistance center against dangers threatening from without can originate only where the Word of God is again what matters for us. We will not save the church by sharing in a general lament. Besides, such lament is superfluous. Let the church *be* the church! as the congregations gather—are gathered—around the Word. Then the church *is* already saved.

So at the end of his brochure, Barth returned to his starting point. He claimed that only the church that really *is* church can be there for people, and thereby also for the German people. We German theologians are entrusted to serve the Word of God among this people. Hence, not to go along with this people. Where we continue with our real task, our "theological existence," we can truly be there for the people, even when this service is not accepted with gratitude. To the German people have today, in 1933,

> been appointed to it something quite extraordinary in its prospects—that the people should be united and free on one way which its leaders have made plain to its understanding, and which the people have elected to travel with those leaders. But the nation will need the admonition and the comfort of the Word of God, even when it shall have reached its goal, all the more to-day when it is standing at the beginning of the road.[14]

Besides, it appears, so Barth concluded, to be a difficult way. The German people have already had to give up much: democratic freedom, independent courts, freedom of academic research. "All that was called Liberty, Justice, Spirit only a year ago and for a hundred years farther back, where has it all

---

13. Barth, *Theological Existence To-Day*, 70.
14. Barth, *Theological Existence To-Day*, 83.

gone?"[15] Now, true, those are temporal, earthly goods. In the past, many peoples have had to go without these goods under totalitarian policies.

> "But the word of our God abideth forever" . . . Because of this, theology and the church cannot enter upon a winter sleep within the "Total State"; no moratorium and no "assimilation" can befall them. They are the natural frontiers of everything, even of the "Totalitarian State."[16]

Thus, it is there for "the salvation of the people, *that* salvation that neither the state nor the church can bring about; the salvation, the proclamation of which the church, however, is called."

6.8 Tensions among Comrades

The brochure *Theologische Existenz heute!* was in bookstores on July 1, 1933, six days after the completion of the manuscript. Copies sold quickly. The piece attracted a lot of attention. Many responded by letter. Critical reviews appeared in a number of periodicals. In their turn, opponents published brochures. From this point on, Barth was a genuine public figure in Germany.

Now tensions came to the breaking point in circles around *Zwischen den Zeiten*. The publication of this journal had begun in 1922. It was meant to be the mouthpiece for "dialectical theology" (see 3.7). Many of Barth's texts, essays, lectures, and articles were published in it. *Thelogische Existenz heute!* was published as an supplement to this journal. But the cooperation among the principals faltered. Differences of opinion had already appeared earlier.

It was above all the train of thought of his fellow-initiator, Gogarten (in the meantime professor at Breslau) who raised critical questions with Barth. Gogarten had always given a great deal of thought to the secular (worldly, profane) background of the gospel. He argued ever more clearly that modern secularization is no threat to Christian faith but is precisely a consequence of the gospel. But then it appeared as though worldly reality interested him more than the gospel itself. He claimed that theology cannot be developed apart from human view. He had discussed Barth's first dogmatics, from 1927, critically (in *Zwischen den Zeiten*). In his opinion, Barth had spoken of "God" and "man" too abstractly, as though they were two isolated subjects. God and the human belong together. That had appeared in Christ par excellence. Since Christ, God cannot be spoken of apart from the

---

15. Barth, *Theological Existence To-Day*, 83.
16. Barth, *Theological Existence To-Day*, 84.

human, said Gogarten. It was precisely this that he saw almost completely lacking in Barth's dogmatic views.

Barth engaged this criticism in his re-written dogmatic part, from 1932. It touched a sensitive point. He had given the impression in particular passages in his first dogmatic project that he too had derived the correct understanding of the Word of God from human self-understanding and thus based theology on a view of humanity. But he had come to correct himself on just that point (see 5.7). Now he squarely claimed that theology cannot be delivered up to philosophy. What (who) God is cannot be inferred from what (who) the human is. It cannot even begin with the human being as creaturely-being who would already (prior to the "real" revelation in Christ) have been given a revelation of God. That was what Gogarten had in mind. He thought theologically from the *human, bound by one's creaturely-being with God*. Here Barth had asked Gogarten, what makes this different from pure natural theology à la Roman Catholicism? An answer to the question had failed to appear.

More and more, Gogarten began from the created reality in his theology. He had recently written, again in *Zwischen den Zeiten*, on "creation and the nature of the people." Along the same line he was now apparently sympathetic to the new trend among the people and in church for what was peculiarly German. He was a co-signatory of manifestos from the young reformers movement. He even signed a declaration from the German Christians in which it was claimed that the "law of God" is identical with the "German order." In August 1933, he joined the movement of the "German Christians," although he would withdraw a few months later. Barth's opposition to all that grew. Was *Zwischen den Zeiten* not established to help to be done with the old, liberal theology that saw God and the human, the divine and human, blend into each other and to bring a theology of the Word of God in opposition? Barth saw in Gogarten's theological thought the old theology raising its head again.

He saw comparable tendencies in another important co-worker in the journal, Emil Brunner. True, this theologian would not meddle with the starting-point that the human fully relies on the Word of God that comes to him, but he also gave consideration to the question how this Word can come to, come within, the human. He considered reflection on that question "the other task of theology." He developed the notion that a natural "intersecting point," a natural susceptibility for the Word, must be presupposed as present with the human. So in his own way, Brunner again came to place "nature" and "grace," "reason" and "revelation" alongside each other. Barth again noted disloyalty to what *Zwischen den Zeiten* had been about from the outset. We heard him already in his new dogmatics claim that the Word itself creates the capacity for the hearer to receive the Word; there can be no talk of a natural human capacity given the "strangeness" of the Word. That was already a polemic against Brunner.

It also bothered Barth that the editor, Georg Merz, appeared to have no difficulty with articles at cross-purposes placed alongside each other in the same journal.

This all brought him to end his own participation in the journal. He communicated that at an editorial meeting on September 30. In a short, sharp word of resignation, published shortly thereafter in what appeared to be one of the last issues, he elaborated his reasons for stepping down. Thurneysen declared his solidarity with Barth. At the end of 1933, the publication of *Zwischen den Zeiten* was discontinued.

A year later, Barth would continue his polemic with Brunner more intensely. In October 1934, he would publish a brochure titled "No!" Brunner had attempted to clarify his own intentions vis-à-vis Barth. In his opinion, there was not much difference between what he had in mind and Barth's position. But Barth would make clear in this "answer to Emil Brunner" that he thought differently. In his opinion, an unbridgeable difference of opinion had grown between him and Brunner.

Barth and Thurneysen continued their own way. To fill the empty space that was created by the cessation of *Zwischen den Zeiten*, they decided to initiate immediately a new publication, a series of brochures titled after Barth's June piece, *Theologische Existenz heute!* Barth's own essay with that title was the first in the series.

The series also received attention in the Netherlands. Different parts appeared in Dutch translations. So immediately Barth's *Theologische Existenz heute!* under the title: *Bezinning* [Reflection].

7

Barmen 1934 and Consequences

7.1 The Onset of Ecclesiastical Protest

THE "GERMAN CHRISTIANS" HAD achieved victory in the church elections, but radicals in their midst were not satisfied. On November 13, 1933, they organized a mass meeting in the Berlin stadium in commemoration of the 450th anniversary of Luther's birth (November 11). Luther was celebrated as the man of the German people. The renewal of the church in the National Socialist spirit would, it was said, be the culmination of the Reformation. There was a plea for a consistent implementation of the Aryan paragraph to include church membership. A separate church body must be established for Jewish Christians. The Old Testament must be "purified" of "Jewish elements." "True Christianity" must focus on the "hero Jesus." A resolution to this intent found general agreement among the 20,000 attendees.

But beyond that there was protest. Many found that matters had gone too far. The Pastors' Emergency League under the leadership of the Berlin pastor, Martin Niemöller, considered action. Barth participated in the deliberations. The "confessional groups" originating in various places organized as a national body. A national administration was formed from the local administrations, a *Reichsbruderrat*. They presented themselves as a "church" called the "Confessing Church." As such, they did not intend to take a position outside or in opposition to the German Evangelical Church. They wanted to support the church, to keep it on the right track. They saw themselves as the legitimate continuation of the church.

Barth was happy to be involved. He found it important to contribute to it so that the ecclesiastical opposition would not run aground in emotions and confusion. His radical rejection of the ideas of the "German Christians" was not generally shared in the "confessing" circles, however. He did what he could in preaching and in lectures to make clear to congregations what was at issue. He did so primarily in the Rhineland and in areas where the Reformed tradition had for many years a great deal of influence proportionaly.

A special gathering ("free synod") was held on January 4, 1934, in this region, in Barmen-Gemarke, with representatives from 167 congregations of the Reformed tradition from throughout Germany. Barth had summarized his ideas in a proposed declaration. It was accepted without change by the representatives of the meeting. The following day, also in Barmen-Gemarke, the yearly meeting of the *Reformierter Bund* (Reformed League, an organizational coalition of all the Reformed in Germany) took place. This group also stood behind the declaration. Moreover, they stated that a "German Christian" could not be a member of this League.

7.2 The Barmen-Gemarke Declaration

The Declaration of Barmen-Gemarke includes a series of theses grouped under five main points. The "German Christians" are not specifically named, but their ideas are firmly rejected. For example: besides being led by the Word of God spoken by Christ and heard in the Holy Scripture, the church can be led by God's revelation in nature and history; in the Bible, only the New Testament matters; a new action of God could be detected in current events; the church would have to serve people and state by adjusting its message and form to human desires and aims; the church would need a central office of leader (the office of *Führer*); to be a member of the church and to serve the church one must belong to a particular race; and the state would be all-determinative and the church must allow itself to be "coordinated" with the state.

Meanwhile, this declaration also claimed that the "German Christians" are not the real problem. What happened in the church in 1933 has become much more apparent, so says the first thesis, an error that had afflicted the evangelical church for centuries, that is the opinion that "alongside God's revelation, a justified human self-sufficiency may also be decisive for the message and form of the church."[1] The Reformation confession was already directed against this error. Nothing less than the validity of that confession is at stake.

It is the relevance of that confession that is presented point for point in opposition to the ideas identified above. The church indeed exists exclusively by the Word of God that it hears together in the Old and New Testaments. Contemporary events stand under God's patience and command

---

1. The full text of the Barmen-Gemarke Declaration can be found in Barth, *Gottes Wille und unsere Wünsche*, 9–15.

but are limited in their right by God's kingdom that comes. The church serves people and state by its obedience to God's Word alone. It stands under God's promise and command, with congregations that must themselves provide for church services (hence a special "office of a *Führer*" is misplaced). The unity of the church is not based on race but on Christ. The church, just as the state, has its own particular office, one that it cannot allow itself to be removed by the state.

On the evening following the synod session of January 4, Barth spoke in a local church before a crowd of a thousand on "God's will and our desires" (he would do the same the two following evenings in Bochum and Lübeck, there too before large crowds). He again set out just why it was stated the way it was in the declaration just accepted. It is often said that we also hear "God's Word" by listening to our own voice. "In this sense one speaks today of God's revelation in the voice of the blood and of history, and thus of a realization of God's will in Germany's awaking to its national nature and political will." This concept is usually based in reference to the creation of the world and of the human. The goodness of creation would not have been ruined by sin such "that God's Word and God's will could not be heard as well in the ordinariness of our created existence."[2] And then it is added that we would not be able to hear God's word in Christ if we did not, in one way or another, bring it along ourselves, via a variety of "intersecting points."

This is thus the central question: Is there a "natural revelation" by virtue of which God's will corresponds with our desires? Barth said that the focus of this question was not on the agenda in the time of Luther and Calvin. We do not get an unambiguous answer to the question from them. But this is the question today. And the answer, so said Barth with great certainty, cannot be other than negative. For God is God and the human is human, bound with God by virtue of God's will, not by virtue of our desires.

7.3 The Barmen Theses

In the growing pressure from the regime on the church, the opposition gradually took greater shape. In order to confirm the newly existing "Confessing Church," it was decided to hold a "confessing synod" of Reformed and Lutherans from all of Germany on May 29–31, 1934. Barmen again was the meeting place. A small theological commission of three, including Barth, would prepare a new theological declaration for this broad synod. In fact, Barth became the main author. The proposed text would later be called the "Barmen Theses." Following an explanation of the text by the co-author, the

---

2. Barth, *Theologische Fragen und Antworten*, 152.

Lutheran Hans Asmussen, it was discussed by the synod in detail. That in turn led to an amended text but not to an essential change. The 139 synod members, representatives from eighteen regional churches, did not form a homogeneous community. Still, the amended declaration, consisting of six theses, the "Barmen Theses," was accepted unanimously on May 31.

We already spoke of the *Barmen Theses* in the first, introductory chapter. The text includes, shorter and yet with more of the tone of a confession, the same foundational ideas as the Declaration of Barmen-Gemarke cited above. That one was accepted by a Reformed synod. Still the earlier declaration had also aimed for an agreement by the Reformed and the Lutherans together. They would have to agree, against the acutely emerging error, to the one confession of the One Lord, rather than working for separate Reformed or Lutheran interests. In this later synod meeting, of May 1934, Lutherans and Reformed have now indeed spoken with one voice.

The *Barmen Theses* were the witness of a minority. It did not find general agreement—certainly not among the Lutherans. Shortly after the synod, a group of theologians, very closely aligned with what is peculiarly Lutheran, expressly indicated their resistance. They specifically objected to what one called the "predominance of the influence of the theology of Karl Barth."[3] Still the appearance of these Theses was important. For the first time, a gathering of the evangelical church had expressed itself critically on the problem of natural theology.

7.4 Barmen and the Jews

The *Barmen Theses* have become well-known as a courageous witness of resistance. Are they overvalued as such? They objected to a particular theology, to the course of the church. But was that also an objection to the political tendencies in the society? Or were they—to put it precisely—only of intra-ecclesiastical importance?

It is said that they are less concrete than the earlier Declaration of Barmen-Gemarke. And indeed, foci appear in the earlier text that are lacking in the Theses. There are theses in Barmen-Gemarke that oppose the (ruling) notion that would abolish the Old Testament; that oppose the notion that would open church functions or church membership only for persons of "a particular race." The lack of such foci in the *Barmen Theses* is to be seen in connection with the fact that the latter theses were drawn up for a joint Lutheran–Reformed synod. Lutherans were less inclined than the Reformed to stand critically against the state. Was that why Barth

---

3. Busch, *Karl Barth*, 246.

perhaps used a less explicit wording in the construction of the Theses? He wanted support for his ecclesiastical opposition to be as broad as possible. Has he thus expressed himself in these theses more carefully? In any case, as stated, the foundational thoughts are the same. Besides, Barmen-Gemarke was also opposed to ideas *regnant in the church* and held back from directly criticizing the Hitler state.

In any case, it is striking that the *Barmen Theses* are silent concerning the Jews. Discrimination against the Jews had already begun at that time. And an Aryan paragraph was already in place in the state; Jews were no longer eligible for service to the state. Did Barmen not have to declare solidarity with the Jews? At the end of his life, Barth himself declared that such a declaration of solidarity would not have been acceptable for the synod of the Confessing Church in 1934, but that he did not consider that an acceptable excuse for himself. He should, he said looking back, at least have proposed a sentence to this effect in the proposed text.

Why had he not done so in 1934? Was he anxious that an express advocacy for the Jews would put him in a tight corner with his central point, his opposition to "natural theology"? Anyway, how he thought about the treatment of the German Jews is clear; that belonged to the "things" of which he had absolutely no peace (see 6.5). Also in a sermon, delivered on December 10, 1933, in a university church service in Bonn, he had shown that to be so. There, speaking from the text for that Sunday (Romans 15:5–13), he had pointed to Jesus' Jewishness. "The blood of *this people* was, in his arteries, the blood of the Son of God. He took on the nature of *this* people," not because of this people, its blood or its race in itself, but "because God chose to make a covenant with *this* people." "The Jew is . . . among all the other peoples the living proof that God is free to choose whomever he will." Thus "it could be" that whoever "defends himself all too passionately from the Jews" thereby "defends himself against the God of free grace." During this sermon a number of listeners had left the church in protest. In their opinion an apparently pro-Jewish statement was too clearly articulated.[4]

In the *Barmen Theses*, as in the earlier Declaration of Barmen-Gemarke, an *implicit* criticism of discrimination against the Jews in Hitler's Germany is certainly articulated. After all, that criticism is included in the rejection of the racist ideas of the "German Christians."

---

4. Barth, *Die Kirche Jesu Christi*, 14–15.

7.5 Barmen and National Socialism

The *Barmen Theses* did not in fact oppose the National Socialist state in so many words, nor did it oppose National Socialism. In form and content, the text is a confession of faith in which what must be seen as erroneous teaching *in the church* is repeatedly stated. Theology stands over and against theology.

In this connection we must again return to his brochure discussed above, *Theologische Existenz heute!* (6.5 and 6.6). There is a passage in it that presupposes Hitler's leadership as a fact. Barth argued there that genuine leadership is something that happens, manifests itself, even without the institution of a formal, special leadership position. To illustrate, Barth referred to the political course of events. As a kind of experiment, he identified with the National Socialists. They could say that Hitler is the *Führer* not because he has his position as chancellor (leader of government); no, he is chancellor because he already was, indubitably, actively, *Führer*. Barth had not intended this—he said later in a clarifying explanation—as Hitler propaganda, but exclusively as a formal point of comparison for the church. Genuine leadership is also necessary in the church. And there too it obtains that genuine leadership happens, manifests itself; a new, central position of bishop need not first be instituted for that to happen. Still, the reference to Hitler as a model for genuine leadership continues to surprise. The fact that Barth saw himself pressured to a later clarifying explanation is telling.

Also surprising are the above cited closing passages of *Theologische Existenz heute!* We heard Barth speak there of "extraordinary prospects" that were offered to the German people by the new regime; prospects of unity and freedom. He characterized the way thereto as "difficult," without rejecting it by definition. "Liberty, Justice, Spirit" (or, democratic freedom, independent justice, academic freedom) had long been highly honored in Germany and had fallen away with the coming of the new regime, he said. He immediately appeared to relativize the seriousness of that loss. These lost matters, he claimed, were after all "temporal, material, earthly goods." They were matters that "many" people in the past living under totalitarian rule "had to do without."[5]

It is also striking that directly after its appearance, Barth had also sent copies of *Theologische Existenz heute!* to the Prussian minister for religious affairs and even to Hitler personally. He explained in the accompanying letter, "This is a word to the German Evangelical pastors. I am recommending that they should reflect on their special position and their particular work in

---

5. Barth, *Theological Existence To-Day*, 83.

light of the most recent events in church politics."⁶ Was that to allay Hitler? A commentator remarked that had Hitler really read *Theologische Existenz heute!* he would then have had no reason to take offense.

Some commentators characterize Barth's position as well as the *Barmen Theses* as "apolitical." It is said, in a manner of speaking, that Hitler himself could have accepted these theses. But that is a misunderstanding of the critical content of the theses. They kept the possibility of criticism of the state firmly in view. They spoke not only of the church but also of the state, of what in the name of God does and does not belong to the task of the state. Like the church, the state is also reminded of its limits. It is completely unimaginable that Hitler could have accepted anything that clearly relativized the authority of the state (represented by him).

The notion "that the state can and should ... become the single and total order of human life, and also thereby fulfill the commission of the church" is not acceptable; hence, the concept of the totalitarian state belongs to the rejected errors of the fifth Barmen Thesis.⁷ The National Socialist Germany became and was indeed such a totalitarian state. That is not said in so many words, it is true. It uses general terms for "the state," that "could become" totalitarian. That corresponds with the character of the *Barmen Theses* as a confession of faith. It speaks principally. But it does so with an eye on contemporary events. For so far as Barth had expressed himself neutrally as to the totalitarian state in his *Theologische Existenz heute!* he had in any case abandoned that neutrality in Barmen. In the fifth Thesis cited, an appeal was made to the state to be conscious of its limits and to act accordingly. It would quickly appear that the Hitler state was not open to such an appeal.

7.6 Leaving Bonn

A second "confessing synod" was called at the end of October, 1934 in Berlin-Dahlem. Relations within the Evangelical Church had grown more tense. The new, central church leadership, inspired by Hitler, had promulgated further church regulations in order to the strengthen its authority. The state supported that move; some protesting pastors were placed under house arrest. It was necessary to resist such intimidating actions. That happened. The membership of the *Reichsbruderrat* grew. Barth also joined.

But now disagreement arose in this *Reichsbruderrat*. Some members advocated a more careful, less confrontational course. That would also improve the relation to the state, they thought. It would avoid a split in the one "people's

---

6. Quoted in Busch, *Karl Barth*, 227.
7. "The Barmen Declaration," 521.

church." And one could better respond to the lived experience among the people. More members signed on to this course. There was no formal meddling with the decisions of Barmen—the *Barmen Theses*. But they were in fact reversed by the decisions of Berlin-Dahlem. Barth could not agree. In his opinion, this development meant the end of the "Confessing Church." At the end of November, he, together with a few others (including Martin Niemöller) resigned his membership in the *Reichbruderrat*.

At that time, he also collided directly with state authorities. On August 19, 1934, Hitler had, following the death of von Hindenburg, assumed the presidency. As chancellor and president at the same time, he now held all the power (see 6.1). By virtue of a decision issued on August 20, all the officers of the state had to swear loyalty to the *Führer* as the new head of state. This was also required of state professors. November 7 was designated as the date for this ceremony. Barth was not exempted from this duty. He was Swiss, but at the same time had been a German citizen since 1925. As professor at Bonn, he was also in service to the state. He was called up. But he let it be known that he was willing to take the oath with a reservation. The reservation was that his loyalty to the *Führer* would only obtain "*so far as I can do so responsibly as an evangelical Christian.*"[8] That could appear to be an unimportant addition, but it was not. It raised the specter that the *Führer* with his regulations could oppose the command of God. It held open the possibility that an appeal to the Word of God would limit the validity of the *Führer's* authority. That suggestion was already unacceptable for the authorities. They detected an incorrect, critical attitude toward the National Socialist state.

On November 26, Barth was summarily suspended. The following day his students stood in front of a closed lecture hall. They protested, as did Barth himself, without result. On December 7, just before Barth's official dismissal was a fact, the students were informed that the continuation of the lectures in dogmatics had been taken care of. A theologian from among the "German Christians" was appointed as Barth's successor. On December 14, the provisional "leadership" of the Confessing Church published a declaration that included that every oath, solely by its character as an appeal to God, already *by definition* excluded disobedience to God's command. Referring to that, Barth let it be known that he deemed that a separate, extra reservation in taking the oath was no longer necessary. But that did not make things any better for him. On December 20, he was formally dismissed. It meant an abrupt halt to his professorship in Bonn

---

8. Barth to Bultmann, November 27, 1934, in *BB*, 78.

and in Germany. Again, protests followed, from Barth and his comrades. Their protests also were not allowed to succeed.

On February 10, 1935, Barth took leave of his students. That could not take place (any longer) in the lecture hall of the university. The meeting took place in Bad Godesberg, at a Bible study meeting. In his departing words, he spoke of how good the years in Bonn had been and that he would gladly have continued working. He encouraged his students "very simply" to invest themselves in the reading of God's Word. Look first at what is there. That is more important than developing a particular theology. "Exegesis, exegesis, and again exegesis. That is what is necessary for us. If I have become a dogmatician, that is because I had long ago invested in being an exegete . . . Keep to the Word."[9]

7.7 Utrecht Lectures on the Apostles' Creed

Barth was not yet completely silenced in Germany. He appeared now and again in church services. He appeared as a speaker at conferences. He held Bible lectures and was involved in church consultations. But on March 1, 1935, he was forbidden to speak at all.

At that time, Barth had received an invitation to give a series of guest lectures in the Netherlands, at the University of Utrecht. The ban on speaking did not apply there of course. He spoke on "the chief problems in dogmatics."[10] He did so by offering an elucidation of the Apostles' Creed. Beginning on February 8, he traveled weekly to Utrecht on Fridays. He gave two lectures over eight visits. The text of the lectures was published with the title *Credo*. Here, in brief, he offered his theological vision *in toto*, as, in the meantime, he had begun to work it out in his *Church Dogmatics*.

He opened by setting forth the meaning of "dogmatics" and of what it consists. Dogmatics and faith, so he held before his Utrecht audience, correspond closely. Faith is nothing other than the acknowledgment of God's reality that is concerned with the human; it is a human decision that, however, wholly and completely lives from its Object, God's self. The same applies to dogmatics. That too is an act of faith, of acknowledgment of the reality of God's concern for the human; namely, the act of faith that would understand and explain itself; that aims at unpacking and considering God's reality and truth and pointing out its mutual coherence (*credo ut intelligam*, "I believe in order to understand"). Faith is an act of confession, thus primarily an act of the church. So too dogmatics is in service to the church, so

---

9. In *Antwort*, 875–76.
10. Barth, *Credo*, 1.

that it can understand its confession ever anew and also, where necessary, can come to a new confession.

All the central themes of dogmatics appeared in the following lectures in connection with the Creed. The doctrine of God, Christology, the meaning of Christ's passion, death and resurrection, belief in the Holy Spirit, the meaning of the church, the future expectation, it was all discussed. In a short, nearly staccato manner, but so that one could overlook the whole.

"I believe in God," so the confession of faith begins; Barth immediately found in it the occasion to set out the heart of his theological thought. Here it is, he said, not about a concept of God that we already knew before we came to Christian faith. In that belief we learn that we do not know from ourselves what we say when we say "God." All our eventual representations of God must recede before the revelation that comes to us. Where that happens, there Christian faith is confessed and thereby acknowledges that God, this God, remains incomprehensible to us. That we find God is not the result of our seeking. God has already found us, and we have thereby looked for this God. The word "God" in the confession of faith is not used in a general sense. It refers to God in his revelation, as Father, Son, and Holy Spirit (as it is later set out in the confession of faith).

Barth did not intend to involve his Dutch audience in the battle that he had to engage in at "home," in Germany. A phrase comes through only here and there. So, for example, in the lecture dedicated to the passage on belief in "Jesus Christ, his (God's) only-begotten Son," Barth explained that the words "God's only-begotten Son" mean that the human Jesus is one with God. Thus, God has himself in Jesus, gracefully, reconcilingly, begun anew with us humans (and we must not intend to infer this divine initiative from a preceding analysis of human guilt and need!). This, this divine initiative, is what the church later would secure against qualifications and misunderstandings when (in the Nicaean Creed) it called Jesus "the only-begotten Son of God," also "God of God, light of light, true God of true God." Strange mythology? Unsustainable philosophy? No, simply the unfolding of what is presupposed in the biblical witness. Whoever would meddle with this relapses into pagan religiosity. That is what has happened in modern Protestantism, Barth said. In that connection he spoke of "the great theological-ecclesiastical catastrophe" in "contemporary German Protestantism," the consequence, he said, of the circulation there—already "for more than two hundred years"—of a number of weakening interpretations of this "only-begotten Son." The real, sharp meaning of this phrase was no longer kept in mind.[11]

11. Barth, *Credo*, 49.

One could find another phrase concerning current affairs in Germany in the lecture on the passage "I believe in the holy catholic church." The church, Barth said, must be distinguished from other communities such as that of people, state, race, or culture. Of course, they also exist. They have their right. Church members too must "give to Caesar what is Caesar's" (Matthew 22:21). They, too, are called to obedience to those who are set over them (Romans 13:1–2). But the church has its own goal and struggle in the midst of other communities. That is not prescribed for it by others, by other powers. It is everywhere and always the same. That is why it is called "catholic." "No tie to a people, a state, a culture must ever cause the church to forget this *catholica*."[12] However it is organized, as a people's church or state church or free church is of subsidiary importance. The first question is whether or not it is faithful to its real essence and task, thus, whether it is "catholic." These reflections were particularly telling for those for whom the German situation was known.

There was great interest in Barth's appearance in Utrecht in the theological circles of the Netherlands. As a result of this great interest, the lectures were also opened to pastors, and people were directed to the Building of Arts and Sciences. It was primarily K. H. Miskotte, at the time pastor at Haarlem, who set himself to making Barth's theology better known in the Netherlands. In the space of a few weeks, he prepared a Dutch translation of Barth's lectures with the addition of many explanatory notes (the text of which was nearly as expansive as that of the lectures themselves). In May, the book, titled *De apostolische geloofsbelijdenis*, was in Dutch bookstores. This was even earlier than the German edition that Barth himself later (also quickly, in 1935) helped to see the light.

7.8 The Situation in Germany Compared with That in the Netherlands

Following the completion of his series of lectures, Barth returned to Utrecht once more to respond to questions that were submitted in writing. The stenographic report of the response was added to the German edition. It is primarily Barth's introductory, personal words that offer a fascinating picture of his view of the Netherlands and of the situation of the Dutch church and of the Dutch view—as he had experienced it—of him and his theology. In particular, he also spoke of his own conditions in Germany:

---

12. Barth, *Credo*, 139.

All your questions betray to some extent that you are still able to pursue theology in comfort, with a certain calmness and detachment in regard to its problems, such as we once knew in Germany but to-day know no longer. Here the delectable possibility is still yours of actually standing *over* and *against* theological matters, of observing them, of having them approach in themselves. And now this Professor has blown in from Germany and with regard to many matters has said something very definite in a somewhat binding fashion, and you from your situation—that became very clear in your letters—are making a more or less cautious *defensive* movement. You would prefer that all questions, or as many as possible should be left open . . . And further, you can still afford to cultivate certain favourite lines of thought; you wish to have certain *specialties* substantiated, others rejected. A profusion of parties was evidently waiting to hear what I had to say to their special interests. From this point of view disappointment could not be avoided . . .

I come from a Church and I come from a faculty whose life outwardly and inwardly is different from the life of your Church here—and of your faculty. Be clear about what has been happening during these last months in Germany and Bonn . . . Where such things are possible a very different wind is blowing. And it is not as if these things began in Germany only some months ago; actually they have been going on for years, and in their presuppositions properly speaking ever since the end of the [First World] War . . . All this has in Germany been a challenge to the Church and to theology, has been and is a challenge to each individual theologian to make a stand, to decide, to confess . . . [Y]ou must reflect that such is the situation from which I am speaking. This situation, this direct call from the exigency of life, from the affliction the Church in Germany is at this moment suffering, has naturally its good *and* its dangerous sides. But there is no denying that the situation of an *ecclesia militans* can show a closer kinship to the great times of the Church's past, to the times in which Church dogma arose. Quite a different inner attitude is involuntarily adopted to this dogma than will be adopted in a quiet ecclesiastical situation in which it is merely honoured and probably also criticised as legacy of a past that no longer exists.[13]

---

13. Barth, *Credo*, 173–75.

7.9 Back to Switzerland

Returning to Germany, Barth waited uncertainly for a few months. But a new possibility opened for him at the end of June. He was appointed professor with a special chair at the University of Basel. So he returned to Switzerland, the city of his birth. There he would continue to live and work for the rest of his life.

8

A More Radical Rejection of National Socialism

8.1 Parting Words to Germany: "Gospel and Law"

FOLLOWING HIS DEPARTURE TO Switzerland in June 1935, Barth once returned to Germany on a visit. On October 7 of that year, he was again in Barmen. The organizers had invited him as speaker on the subject "Gospel and Law." Because Barth had been banned in the meantime from speaking, his appearance as a speaker could not take place. Police authorities made sure that this ban would not be taken lightly. But Barth brought along the text of his lecture. It would be read by the local preacher in his presence, in a crowded church. Thus, Barth spoke indirectly.

"Gospel and Law," apparently only a simple theoretical theme that, in fact, was completely practical. The law is God's will for human living. The question is always, how do we know that? Can it be inferred from the course of events? Does it coincide with natural law? Or with the nature of the people? So the "German Christians" said. Yet again, Barth opposed their ideas, although this time the "German Christians" are not specifically named. And it is immediately clear that Barth's fight has a further aim, pushes deeper. The fundamental fault that Barth identifies and of which the ideas of the "German Christians" are, in his opinion, but exponents, is the notion that God's law, God's will, could be known apart from God's revelation in Christ.

Barth would know nothing of that. Whoever engages the law this way is, before he knows it, actively calling on natural law or the nature of the people to help in the interpretation of the law. Or one appears to have relapsed to paganism with its appeal to natural facts and to instructions to be deduced from the stars.

In this connection, Barth also opposed the claim (primarily by Lutherans) that the law must precede the gospel in consideration of the faith. Must the human first learn to know their sin from the law to then be able to hear the gospel as the message of the forgiveness of sins? Barth claimed that whoever first says law, and then gospel, is, in fact, speaking not about the law *of God*, and consequently not about the real gospel. That all too quickly makes the law a means to self-justification, and wherever this self-justification fails, to an accusatory and judging instance, and then not much more of the gospel remains than Jesus as one who "inspires" and who makes all things good. It must not be so. The law comes to light in its intention precisely when we hear it from and in the context of the gospel. Hence, we must first say "gospel" and then "law," "gospel and law," not vice versa.

For, so he claimed, talk about God can only begin from God's Word. And that is first and centrally *gospel*, a message of grace. The Word has become flesh. Christ has become human, has taken the place of us humans, has in our place, before us, said yes to God, and also to God's judgment of our disobedience. Thus, he has fulfilled the law. The gospel says that. And as that is proclaimed to us it is also—in second place—*law*. "From what God does *for* us, we infer what he wants *with us* and *from* us."[1] "[T]he Law is nothing else than the necessary *form of the gospel*."[2] Said differently, the law is the way the gospel addresses human life, takes it on. In the law we are called to love God and thereby to follow Jesus Christ. That is the substance of the First Commandment. All other commands are nothing other than extensions thereof. They are a call to faith in Jesus Christ.

Thus, Barth's argument in outline. He had expressed this earlier. In March 1933, in Denmark, he had delivered a lecture on "The First Commandment as Theological Axiom." He had interpreted this commandment, to have "no other gods alongside me" ("before my face"), as guide for theology, namely as an indicator that it has to concentrate completely on the God of revelation and thus should not allow itself to be led by reason or experience, by contemporary events, by the nature of the people, the morality of people or the state. Barth had thereby said that this same axiom is to be heard in the gospel, (for example in John 1:14, "The Word became flesh), but that a particular word from the Bible just speaks at a particular moment." There Barth had thus already placed the word of the gospel and command (gospel and law) alongside each other, as essentially witnessing the same thing. In the lecture of October 7, 1935, he provided broad support to this claim.

Following the close of the gathering in Barmen, he departed quickly. Accompanied by the police, he was brought that same evening by special

---

1. Barth, "Gospel and Law," 78.
2. Barth, "Gospel and Law," 80.

train to the Swiss border. He would not walk on German soil for ten years. The address, "Gospel and Law" was more or less his parting word to Germany for this period, a word that would echo for a long time in German discussions. Later, Barth himself would take this argument seriously by including ethics in the context of his dogmatics.

8.2 Further with the *Dogmatics*. On God's Revelation

Barth picked up the work on his dogmatics in Basel that he had to set aside in Bonn. For several hours during the week he gave lectures; he also held seminars on various topics. Besides the Swiss (among whom were two of his sons Markus and later Christoph), there were among the participants students from elsewhere, for example, from Scotland and France. They also came from Germany as long as the borders were still open. That came to an end, of course, when the Second World War broke out. Earlier, at the beginning of 1939, it had been officially determined that the time students spent with Barth would not count as theological study in Germany. That would mean the (provisional) end of the presence of German students in Basel.

On May 10, 1936, Barth celebrated his fiftieth birthday. On that occasion, a thick festschrift with contributions from students, friends, and kindred spirits appeared. Most authors came from Germany and Switzerland, but they also came from England and Scotland, Denmark, France, Japan, and the Netherlands. The list of contributors gives evidence of Barth's influence, even beyond German-speaking lands. The book appeared from the publisher that had also prepared the publication of most of Barth's writing, Chr. Kaiser Verlag in Munich. But the German censor had been watching with Argus eyes. The book would have originally been called "Freedom of Those in Bondage," but the title was politically suspect and thus had to be abandoned; it was replaced by the more neutral *Thelogische Aufsätze*, "Theological Essays." Moreover, on the order of the German authorities, a contribution by Asmussen on Barth's significance for the Confessing Church had to be omitted; it remained in the table of contents but the relevant pages were omitted from the book (Asmussen's contribution would be published separately later, including in a Dutch translation). Not much later, the publication of Barth's writings would be banned in Germany. From then on they would appear in Switzerland.

Barth's primary concern went into—and from then on would go into—continuing to work on his *Church Dogmatics*. In 1932, the first part was published, officially still only its first half (*CD* I/1; see 5.6 and 6.3). That included introductory considerations of what dogmatics in essence must be. It discussed the Word of God as the measure of all dogmatic reflection. That Word was therewith further defined in three ways: it is "revealed," it is "written" (contained in Holy Scripture), it is "proclaimed" (by the church). These three must be considered further.

With that a beginning was also made in *CD* I/1 in a first series of paragraphs on "God's revelation." What does the statement "God reveals himself" mean? Barth analyzed it: a God exists who reveals himself (the Subject of the action) and the event of revelation exists (the action itself). The result is a form of being-revealed. There are thus three aspects to consider. First there is the form. That is to be distinguished but not to be separated from the God who reveals himself. God himself is present in it. He becomes his own "double." He distinguishes himself from himself and is God *in yet another manner*. But—that is the second aspect—it is to be considered that is not about the form as such. Rather, it is about *God*, the One who in his essence, in himself, is *unknowable to humans*. It finally obtains—that is the third aspect—that God's revelation *falls to the human*. In that it reaches its goal. It is thus essential that it plays itself out as a unique event *in* history. We find these three aspects testified to in the Bible. They caused the church to speak in its dogma of God as Triune: Father, Son, and Holy Spirit. That dogma, so often dismissed as incomprehensible and speculative, is in fact rooted in what the Bible testifies: that God reveals himself.

Barth had elaborated this in *CD* I/1. In that first part, he had, differently than was usually the case, fully discussed the doctrine of God's trinitarian nature. But these considerations would still have to be filled out. Still further to be discussed were the "incarnation of the Word" ("the incarnation of Christ") and the "outpouring of the Holy Spirit." And to that the two other matters that determine the Word of God; that it is "written," and that it is "proclaimed" would have to be discussed. Thus, there would have to be paragraphs on "Holy Scripture" (and the nature of its authority) and "the proclamation of the church" (the question of how far the human word can really obtain as the "Word of God"). Barth's earlier dogmatic project, the *Christliche Dogmatik* from 1927, had already displayed something similar (see 4.11). But Barth deemed that here also a new consideration and formulation was necessary.

That would require a few years. The manuscript would be ready in the summer of 1937, so that it could appear at that time as *CD* I/2, the second, concluding half of the introductory considerations. That book, a large volume of 1,011 pages, included the product of Barth's dogmatic lectures from the preceding years.

In Basel, Barth met his old friend Eduard Thurneysen. He had been the pastor at the Münster, the principal church in the city, since 1927, and moreover a docent in practical theology from 1930; in 1941, that position as docent would become a part-time professorship. Barth regularly attended Thurneysen's church and preached there repeatedly. Earlier, he had published a collection of sermons with Thurneysen (see 2.5). In 1935, a new collection of sermons from the pair appeared. In it, sermons from 1924–1934 were bound together with the title *Die grosse Barmherzigkeit* [The Great Mercy].

In the preface the authors set out what, in their opinion, preaching must be: not the treatment of one theme or another, but the interpretation of the Bible. "Preaching is reading out loud what is written, and a reading out loud that is oriented to the contemporary person, but then so that this person, in turn, becomes a student of Holy Scripture. That is . . . the old, clear method of the forefathers, that is presented to us anew by the theological work of these years."[3] For Barth, dogmatics and preaching indeed stood side by side.

8.3 Sympathy for Germany

Barth continued to have intense sympathy for developments in Germany. He maintained contact with theologians and church leaders, friends and acquaintances, by post. He intensely followed reports that reached him. He still understood himself to be connected with the Confession Church, in the existence of which he had been so involved in 1933 and 1934. He also reported what happened in Germany in Switzerland where he could, convinced as he was of the importance of information about it in broad circles internationally. He held lectures on it and published articles in newspapers and magazines. Among other things, between 1935 and 1939 he wrote expansive reports in the annual Zwingli calendar, specifically offering a portrayal of what was occurring in the German church and in politics along with his perspective on those events.

He was very concerned. There was the Confessing Church, that part of the German Evangelical Church that did not want simply to be carried away by the intoxication of National Socialism. But even that, so he writes in 1935 (for the Zwingli calendar of 1936) is not a success story. There is indeed a thin thread of evangelical clarity and bravery to be detected. But at the same it is drowned by avalanches of political caution and hairsplitting. The "old bond of gospel to human reason, of church to the state" can also be perceived here.

---

3. Barth and Thurneysen, *Die grosse Barmherzigkeit*, 3–4.

Barth's reports show how he had become radicalized in his rejection of National Socialism. It was no longer about the retention of the particularity of the church or the defense of the freedom of the gospel. He understood more clearly that the National Socialist state itself must be resisted and that that resistance was also part of the vocation of the church. He was concerned that the church, including even the Confessing Church, repeatedly apparently, did not hear that vocation. It has not yet understood, he wrote already in 1935, how dangerous its enemy is. "She has fought hard to a certain extent for the freedom and purity of her proclamation, but she has, for instance, remained silent on the action against the Jews, on the amazing treatment of political opponents, on the suppression of the freedom of the press."[4]

Later, yearly reports sound somewhat more positive concerning the Confessing Church. New men had taken over its leadership in 1936. They showed more spine vis-à-vis the German authorities. The state continued in its efforts to take control of internal church affairs. Within the German Evangelical Church, one tried half-heartedly to remain free, but the new leadership of the Confessing Church actively resisted. Barth, writing in 1937 (for the *Zwingli-Kalender* of 1938), noted with thanks that the Confessing Church had protested directly to Hitler, now not only against the assault on the freedom of the church, but also against "the general injury to law and humanity, which in the Third Reich had become systematic." With this protest, the Confessing Church had spoken in the name of the whole Evangelical Church (although it could have been more powerful, and although other sectors of the church remained silent; the leaders of some—mostly Lutheran—regional churches even found it necessary to expressly distance themselves from this). Whether the protest would result in anything was a question. But that it was lodged—and that it had also been publicized internationally—was already a signal. "[W]e shall no longer in future be able to accuse the Confessing Church of being silent in this matter."[5]

In his two final yearly reports, from 1938 and 1939, Barth described how the pressure under which the Confessing Church had to live had been increased. The state had set up everything to execute a real "coordination"—that is its shutting down—of the church. Nazi-thinking persons were placed in leadership everywhere. Whoever would not walk on the leash of the Nazis found work made nearly impossible. It was not rare for the latter to be treated heavy handedly, via arrest, as happened to the Berlin pastor Martin Niemöller, arrested in 1937, then held without formal process in a

---

4. Barth, *The German Church Conflict*, 60.
5. Barth, *The German Church Conflict*, 83.

concentration camp (where he would remain until the end of the Second World War), isolated from the outside world, given over to the personal whim of Hitler himself. Niemöller's fate (who shortly before had been with Barth in Switzerland on a visit) affected Barth deeply. In his yearly reports he emphatically asked that he be remembered. Humanly speaking, Niemöller was in a hopeless situation, but

> We know that . . . he is richly comforted by the Word of God, despite the human hopelessness of his situation. But no-one (especially any naïve travellers in Germany) should forget for one moment that he is there and what his situation is: in our very midst a man who is plainly and simply suffering brutal injustice for the sake of our evangelical faith.[6]

Not everyone was so steadfast. Barth noted in 1939 that many pastors in the Confessing Church still appeared to be unable to cope with the pressure.

> Much curious talk was spread abroad of a "Christian suffering" which one must accept by becoming even more passive towards the attacking state than some members of the Confessing Church had unfortunately always been, and by breaking off one's struggle for justice and order in the Church and devoting oneself to parish work, still possible, even if in ruins.[7]

One must also have nothing more of serious theology, Barth wrote. One now prefers to keep things, remarkably neutral, "simple." Pay attention, that is a simplicity "which in fact has the not at all simple but very clever power of calling black white, and white just as easily as black."[8]

8.4 Appeal for Political Resistance: A Letter to Former Students

The resistance to the National Socialist state would have to become *political* resistance. Barth wrote a letter to that effect, which he sent to his former students on his fifty-first birthday, May 10, 1937. He knew himself connected primarily with them, his earlier students from Göttingen, Münster, and Bonn, now all working, most as pastors. He was conscious how difficult and responsible their positions were, and he described that himself. Opposition

---

6. Barth, *The German Church Conflict*, 90–91.
7. Barth, *The German Church Conflict*, 100.
8. Barth *The German Church Conflict*, 101.

to the gospel today, he wrote, comes not from "the sinner" in general, or from this or that anti-Christian segment. It is the contemporary German state itself that, ideological as it is, has emerged as the opponent of the gospel. The contemporary German state has abused the authority given by God to it by ascribing to itself divine power. In those conditions, Christian existence includes a political choice by definition. That must also become evident in Christian proclamation, with the consequence that the pastor brings hatred and persecution on himself from the side of the authorities.

Listen closely. It may not be about the choice of a political position *in itself*. Barth also knew that. It must be clear that the church intends nothing other in its choice of a political position than being obedient to the gospel. The church may not identify with a particular purely political opposition movement. In that sense it is not allowed to "do politics." Anger is not good, but recklessness even less so. You may not withdraw to the "sacral" (as the "peculiar domain" of the church), but even less may you engage in the ventures of the secular, the worldly. We may not be blind to political reality, but that is something different than wanting to lead the way.

9

On the Eve of the Second World War

9.1 Solidarity with Czechoslovakia: Letter to Josef Hromádka

How Barth had begun to see the political question "as such and in its totality" as a question of faith appears in the letter that he wrote on September 19, 1938, to the Czech theologian and professor, Josef Hromádka, in response to his condolence on the occasion of the recent death of Barth's mother. Conversely, Barth signaled his sympathy for Hromádka and the Czechs as they faced the current threat.

That summer, Hitler had claimed Sudetenland, just across the German border (arguing that he thereby "liberated" the Germans living there under Czech "oppression"). German troops had mustered at the Czech border. England and France were in negotiations with Germany hoping to rein in Hitler's aggression and to avoid a new war. It was at that time that Barth wrote his letter. He was concerned with the possibility that the western powers, hoping for peace, would grant Hitler's territorial demand. Was Czechoslovakia being sacrificed for the sake of the "general interest"?

Barth saw that the freedom of all of Europe stood in the balance along with that of the Czech people. He encouraged the Czechs, should they be left in the lurch by England and France, to persevere and, if necessary, to defend themselves with arms. This was also an encouragement from the perspective of faith. He wrote, "Every Czech soldier who fights and suffers will also do it for us—and I say that today without reservation, also for the Church of Jesus Christ." For "in the atmosphere of Hitler and Mussolini that Church can simply fall prey to either ridiculousness or extermination." We would naturally avoid violence and keep the peace, but, Barth wrote, it is now the time to give second place the aversion to violence and the desire for peace "for the sake of the faith," and to give first place to the aversion to injustice and the desire for freedom. "And I cannot repress the expectation that if Prague remains steadfast, London and Paris might also become steadfast." Now: all hands on deck! And do not trust in people, politicians, cannons, airplanes, but in the living God, the Father of Jesus Christ. That is trust that really matters. That is decisive against the stronger German battalions, "that alone is finally important and defensible."[1]

On September 30, somber suspicions were confirmed. The British and French leaders agreed to Hitler's demands concerning Czechoslovakia (and were celebrated upon their return as "peacemakers"). In the meantime, Barth's letter to Hromàdka was cited, in whole or part, in many newspapers internationally. Protests rained down. The German papers (under state control, of course) let loose with headlines like, "Theology Professor as Warmonger." But Barth also received criticism and even indignant reactions from friendly sides.

Others expressed their concern in letters and asked questions. Some asked, should not the church have to keep its distance from armed violence and encouraging its use? Barth answered a representative of the Dutch union "Church and Peace": unconditional pacifism is theologically impossible for the church. God's command is not to be identified with a principle, with an "ism"—with pacifism no less than with militarism. The church must, for the sake of the gospel, intercede and work so that the state can be a genuine, true state; that means that it protects the peace, but a genuine peace is in service to justice and peace. A "peace" based on oppression is only the appearance of peace. In such a "peace," the gospel becomes an object of oppression and ridicule. Violence is sometimes necessary to keep genuine peace. Dictatorship is systematic injustice, planned servitude. Thus, there is, also for the sake of the gospel, much to do to keep the dictator out where possible and to take up the cause of saving democracy.

But had Barth not gone too far in his identification of the interest of the (Czechoslovakian) state and the interest of the church? That "every Czech soldier who fights and suffers" for his fatherland thereby also would do that "for the church of Jesus Christ"—can that really be said like that? The question came from a Dutch pastor. Barth answered: for me it is not about identifying the interest of the state with the interest of the church. Still, with the threat of the political order and of freedom it is indeed the case that the church is, indirectly, threatened. It is not an indifferent matter for the church whether it lives in a democratic system rather than under a dictatorship. Barth clarified what he had written to Hromádka on the dilemma that the church "in the atmosphere of Hitler and Mussolini" can

---

1. Barth, "Brief an Prof. Hromádka in Prag, 1938," 58–59.

either make itself ridiculous or meet its demise.[2] The church is called to the proclamation of the total claim of the Word of God. For just that proclamation, there is no place under a dictatorial rule. If the church allows that claim to disappear, it becomes ridiculous, meaningless. If it still retains the Word uprightly, then it is threatened with its own elimination. The church must be spared this abhorrent dilemma where possible. Thus, where the state (as in Czechoslovakia) stands against chaos and tyranny, the church must be in solidarity with the state.

9.2 On the Scots Confession: Armed Resistance May be Necessary

The letter to Hromádka caused a breakdown of trust in the relation between Barth and the Confessing Church in Germany. The leaders of that church recalled that previously Barth, at the time of Barmen, had sharply opposed the entanglement of the gospel and politics by the "German Christians." Now, they claimed that Barth himself was also guilty of the same entanglement. He had abandoned the way that he had previously followed as a teacher of the church. He had lost sight of the fact that the freedom of the church of Jesus Christ rests solely in the heavenly Father.

A forceful criticism, but it came from a misunderstanding. Was Barth in fact unfaithful to himself? No, he now drew the consequences of what he had said earlier. In his earlier essay critical of the church, he had never intended to view the church as a reality unto itself apart from the world. His critique, originally directed at the (German) church (where it was inclined to be carried away in the stream of National Socialism) had now moved to what it had implicitly been from the outset: a critique of the (German, National Socialist) state. Here too the Word of God was the sole criterion for him.

It is that Word that obtains not only for the church (in its proclamation) but also for the state (in the fulfillment of its vocation: the maintenance of justice and peace). Christ is not only Lord of the church but also Lord of the world, of the society. The latter, of course, in a hidden way. It can only be about a provisional, outward sanctification of life in the society, in politics. Outward justice and outward peace that the state can effect (including by violence) are still not identical with the peace and justice of God's Kingdom as it is proclaimed and confessed in the church. But they are signs of the kingdom. In their way, they serve the welfare of humans. So then, if it is good, God is also served in politics, by the state, in a proper way (Romans 13:1–7). And where

2. Barth, "Brief an Prof. Hromadka in Prag, 1938," 67.

that happens, Christians not only have a duty to respect the state. They are also called to cooperate in the work of the state.

But does the concrete state act in agreement with its vocation? Church and state stand together before the same critical question: do they do what they must do? Are they what they must be? Is what is called church really "church"? And here too, is the state really the state as it, for God's sake, must be? Just like the church, the state can degenerate, go off the rails. The authority of the state can become tyrannical.

Barth had elaborated on that in a lecture a half a year earlier, in March 1938, in Aberdeen, Scotland, one of a series in which all the articles of the Scots Confession of 1560 were successively considered. The lecture treated the article on civil authority. It contains what Barth underscored: authority is a "servant of God," and so too in politics, in the policies of the state, when things are done rightly, God (the Father of Jesus Christ) is served. And there the possibility that those who bear authority do not do that to which they are called is also spoken of, albeit implicitly.

Barth had pointed out that the Scots Confession also talks about the relation between church and state. He underscored that as well. Whether political power is used well appears from how the state stands over and against the church. The state cannot be concerned with the reformation and renewal of the church. But the state can certainly be expected to guarantee the church the freedom to proclaim its own message. What if that freedom is now limited "out of the interest of the state"? Then what if the state absolutizes its own goals? Then it behaves as "church." That is the degenerate state, not as what is intended in Romans 13 (servant of God) but as typified in Revelation 13 (the beast from the sea).

Where the state fulfills its vocation, we owe the state obedience and cooperation, Barth said. But *not* where the state *forsakes* its vocation. *Resistance* against the state may even be necessary. That is not, in fact, stated in the confession's article on civil authority. But it is alluded to in an earlier article, on the question, what are "good works." The question is answered by referring to the Ten Commandments. There it is stated that to "resist tyranny" is part of the fulfillment of the command, "thou shalt not kill." In his discussion of the article on authority, Barth picked that up and worked it out. There are conditions conceivable, he claimed, in which *active*, thereby including violent, resistance against the power of the state is allowed, and even is demanded, for God's sake.

Suppose we were dealing with "a Government of liars, murderers and incendiaries, with a Government which wished to usurp the place of God, to fetter the conscience, to suppress the church."³ Then the "prayer for the authority" (1 Timothy 2:1–4) can only be the prayer for the end of the existing regime. And hence praying also means acting to that end, if need be with violence.

Does that last bit not go too far for Christians? Barth had already put the question to himself that would later be laid before him by the representative of the Dutch "Church and Peace." He had already answered it here. We live in a world not yet saved. In it we cannot do without violence. Whoever would be obedient to God in this world is thus, however directly or indirectly, also involved in the practice of violence (or at least in preparation). Not just in resistance against unjust authority, but also already with the required support and cooperation in the work of the just authority. Of course, violence is always the last resort, to be used where nothing else can do. But Christians cannot withdraw in advance from ever being involved in the use of violence.

Barth had not specifically mentioned German National Socialism in this perspective. But of course he had that regime concretely in mind with his reference to the "possibility" of a confrontation with "a Government of liars and those who don't keep their word, of murderers and arsonists." It would appear just how concrete a half a year later in the above cited letter to Hromádka.

9.3 On the Relation of Church and State

That the letter was not an unreasoned outburst, not the expression of a theologian who had violated his role, also appears from the lecture Barth had held in June 1938 in Switzerland for various gatherings of preachers. Barth gave it the title "Justification and Justice" (later to be published in English as "Church and State"). He set out his views on the "political service of God" in a still broader framework, now with a special appeal to the New Testament. He claimed that a correspondence indeed existed between "justification" (God's justifying actions in Christ) and "justice" (what is intended in society, in politics). That had incorrectly been omitted in Reformed confessional writings. Human justice (and its maintenance, the practice of political power) does not exist on its own (eventually to be inferred from a general divine "providence"). It is based on justification (what God has done in Christ).

Thus, Barth had again put the relation between gospel and law on the agenda (as earlier in October 1935). God's Word takes hold of human life. Hence, it is law that is also to obtain in politics and society. But it is first of

3. Barth, *The Knowledge of God and the Service of God*, 230.

all gospel, the message of God's justifying grace in Christ. The law, including where it engages human society in the state, cannot be heard apart from the gospel. The authority of Christ also obtains in politics and over the state.

Barth had emphatically pointed to the positive significance of the state for the church in a more extensive elaboration of what he had already put forward in his lecture in Scotland. The starting point for his views here was the scene from the gospels of Jesus before Pilate. Pilate represented the (Roman) state. The state was unmasked in the Passion Narrative as demonic. Still, it first confirmed that the state has power, power that (in Jesus' words) is "given from above" (John 19:11). Pilate abused it; he did not let Jesus go free, although he established Jesus' innocence. At the same time, the gospel testifies that Pilate cooperated with what must happen in God's way for the justification of the sinful human; the innocent is condemned in the stead of the guilty. Here the demonic state acts despite what he must, for God's sake, do.

Further, speaking on Romans 13:1-7, Barth pointed out that the word used there for "authority" refers elsewhere in the New Testament to the angelic powers. They are (according to representations of the time) created heavenly powers that manage the world and maintain its order. Apparently, Barth said, the state is also considered such an "angelic power." These angelic powers can degenerate, become demonic. Yet, according to the New Testament, they remain destined to serve Christ. They will be subject to him forever (1 Peter 3:22). And now already, they belong to Christ. They are "created in him" (Colossians 1:16) and thus owe their existence to Christ. This also obtains, then, for the state, as political "angelic power."[4] It can become demonic (and yet serve God's righteousness as was the case with Pilate). But it can also be a good state, maintaining justice. The state, too, belongs to Christ's sphere.

Barth found that the state is called to guarantee the church freedom to proclaim the gospel expressed in a particular way in 1 Timothy 2:1-7. That passage encourages prayer for "all people" and then, in particular for "kings and for all in authority." And this in order that "we can live a quiet and peaceable life" what is thus viewed as the business and concern of the same people in authority who must be prayed for. But for Christians, quiet and tranquility is not a goal in itself. It is "good and acceptable in the sight of God" who "will have everyone be saved." It is apparently for that reason, in this context, that the "restful and undisturbed" life of the church (guaranteed by the state) is deemed important.[5] Hence, it can proclaim its message of the

---

4. Barth, "Church and State," 114.
5. Barth, "Church and State," 128.

God who desires to save all. Barth also pointed out that, in Romans 13:1–7, the state is identified as "servant (deacon) of God," and its administrators as "liturgists of God." Apparently, the state is considered (in a certain sense) a constituent part of the sacral order of the church.[6]

Barth also went into the significance that the church has for the state. The central point is intercession on behalf of the state (1 Timothy 2:1) in contradistinction from the worship of the state. After all, intercession for the state is by definition a reminder of its limits. In Romans 13:1, respect for ruling authorities is encouraged. Here too a misunderstanding threatens: as though the concept would mean that the church would simply have to welcome all plans and measures of the state positively. The state can become unjust and repress the proclamation of the church (the preaching of justification). Respect for the state then will appear as critique of the (this concrete) state, and this to the benefit of the (true, just) state. Nowhere in the world is there a stronger notion than in the church of the importance, even the necessity, of the state. The church sees the authority of the state as included in the authority of its Lord Jesus Christ and always expects from it the best, that it maintain justice and protect the freedom of proclamation. Where the state does not fulfill that expectation, the church defends the (just) state *against* the (concrete) state.

In any case, Christians are bound to be prepared to fulfill their duties toward the state. That includes the payment of taxes (Romans 13:6–7). There Barth, referring to the Reformers, added: including the fulfillment of military service. The state may and must defend itself against threats, even with violence. If Christians were to reject this principle, they would then reject the state as such; that they cannot do.

The threat can come from another state, one that has become an unjust state instead of a just state, a qualification that, so Barth had said, was applicable to "more than one other state."[7] Hitler and Mussolini still remained unnamed here. Their names would be mentioned a few months later, in the letter to Hromádka. Defense and protection of the borders is indeed necessary against that threat. And it is incomprehensible why the church would not decisively support the defensive struggle of its own government.

Barth had continued the lines of Romans 13 to make yet another point. The New Testament knows nothing of a democratic state (as we mean it). But the appeal for intercession on behalf of the state certainly points in that direction. After all, in interceding, Christians are actively involved in what the authority does. Praying for one's own state, namely praying that it

---

6. Barth, "Church and State," 135.
7. Barth, "Church and State," 143.

continues to exist as a just state, respectively that it may become a just state anew, cannot happen without being prepared to cooperate actively to that effect. Here too Barth had, as in the Scottish lecture, alluded to the possibility that, for the sake of the just state, one would have to resist tyranny and to revolt against the concrete authority of the state.

9.4 Criticism Focused: The Jewish Question as a Question of Faith

With this broad theological argument on "justification and justice," Barth had laid the foundation on which he aligned himself politically in these months and throughout the Second World War, as sharply as in the letter to Hromádka cited above. It appeared separately as a brochure, but not in the series started by Barth himself in 1933, *Theologische Existenz heute!* (see 6.7). He was no longer allowed to publish in Germany. Besides, the series had abruptly ended. In its stead Barth started a new series in Switzerland, *Theologische Studien*. "Justification and Justice" appeared as its first number.

On December 5, 1938, Barth again discussed very concretely the current situation (as he had done in the letter to Hromádka). He held a lecture in Wipkingen, a suburb of Zürich. He was invited by the Swiss Protestant "Hilfswerk für die Bekennende Kirche" (Aid Agency for the Confessing Church, recently established, with Barth's cooperation). This organization, established to show solidarity with the (preachers of) the Confessing church in Germany, had quickly taken on the cause of the reception of Jews and Jewish Christians fleeing from Germany. Barth spoke on "The Church and the Political Question of Our Day." A few hundred ministers and theologians were present; German refugees were also there. As an introduction, the chairman read the long list of German preachers who were known to be imprisoned or persecuted.

Barth spoke comprehensively of the character of National Socialism. That is, he said, a political experiment, aiming at the principle breakdown of the just state. And it has, with its religious pretensions, all the characteristics of an (anti-Christian) "counter-state." Hence it is impossible for the church to accept the lordship of National Socialism. In fact, it can only pray that accounts be settled. The anti-Christian character of National Socialism appears already from its efforts to deprive the church of its freedom and take it under its control. But it appears primarily from its anti-Semitism. This, especially, also touches the church. He implicitly referred to the "Kristallnacht," of November 9/10, of just a few weeks previously, the night in which under the passive presence of the police the windows in all Jewish shops were shattered and synagogues everywhere went up in flames. In Germany, he said, the "physical extermination" of the people of

Israel had in fact begun. And the church is thereby attacked at its root. No Christian can be indifferent. For

> Objectively, what are we then, without Israel? He who rejects and persecutes the Jews rejects and persecutes Him who died for the sins of the Jew—and then, and only then *thereby* for our sins as well. He who is a radical enemy of the Jews, were he in every other regard an angel of light, shows himself, as such, to be a radical enemy of Jesus Christ. Anti-Semitism is a sin against the Holy Ghost. For anti-Semitism means rejection of the *grace* of God.[8]

That this antisemitism is now the life world of National Socialism, makes it clear par excellence that the church can only say "no" here.

With this express rejection of antisemitism and persecution of the Jews, Barth focused his critique on National Socialism all the more.

His lecture provoked immediate, intense discussion already at the gathering. Many reacted anxiously and fearfully. Could this be said so crassly? Had Barth not gone too far with his appeal to pray against Hitler? Was a more careful approach not better? Would voices like these from Switzerland not provoke the German powers? Could that not unloose a greater threat to Switzerland itself? Barth's position could certainly not count on general agreement in Switzerland. He was conscious of that. After all, directly after he left Germany, he had begun to provide information on the German situation.

In his last calendar report, written in 1939 for the Zwingli-calendar (see. 8.3), Barth again went into the Jewish persecution in Germany with reference to the "Kristallnacht." That requires, he said, a reaction from the church. Alas, to a large extent, such a reaction had not come. True, here and there, by individual Christians, in local congregations throughout Germany, more for the persecuted Jews had been done than could be made known publicly and to other lands. But official church authorities in Germany kept aloof. In particular areas, church authorities even allowed anti-Jewish state policies and the ban on baptizing Jews to obtain in the church. And the situation was not much better even among the best in the Confessing Church. They still closed their eyes to "the truth that the Jewish question, and thus the political question as such and as a whole, has become today a question of faith."[9]

The ecclesiastical inclination to passivity and aloofness in view of politics emerged, so Barth supposed, in adherence to the Lutheran "doctrine of two kingdoms": "Luther's very dubious teaching on Matt. 28:18,

---

8. Barth, *The Church and the Political Problem of Our Day*, 51
9. Barth, *The German Church Conflict*, 103.

concerning the separation between the kingdom of Christ and all 'worldly spheres.'" How can one desire to maintain that separation in light of Christ's word, "All power is given to me in heaven and on earth" (Matthew 28:18)? Still, the shadow of this doctrine lies "over the ecclesiastical thinking and action of more or less every course taken by the German Church. Will the Gospel in Germany (and elsewhere too) ever be really free from the Babylonian captivity of this teaching?"[10]

In this way, Barth made it clear to all sides where he stood. His continued outspoken criticism of the Hitler regime had, of course, won him an extremely bad reputation with the German Nazi authorities. He was already forbidden to speak in Germany and furthermore, to publish. Moreover, in the course of 1938, the honorary doctorate conferred on him in 1922 by the University of Münster was officially withdrawn (see 3.3).

9.5 In the Netherlands. Christian Faith and Threatened Humanity

In the Spring of 1939, Barth again visited a number of Western European countries: France, Denmark, and (in March of that year between these two visits) the Netherlands. His visit, on the invitation of the VSTF (Union of Students of the Theological Faculties in the Netherlands), was the third, following his visits in 1926 and 1935. On a long tour of the theological faculties of Utrecht, Leiden, Kampen, Groningen, and Amsterdam he spoke on "the Sovereignty of the Word of God and the Decision of Faith." That God's Word is sovereign, takes all our life in tow, does not make faith superfluous, he argued. It evokes it and asks for concreteness in a decision of faith here and now. It is not only something of the heart, of personal morality nor is it intra-ecclesial. It also touches the life without, in the world. In closing, Barth also alluded to the current situation:

> We stand today in horror before the phenomenon of a Europe, a so-called Christian Europe, which is threatened with the loss of its humanity. The problem lies not with those forces which would take its humanity away and would lead it into chaos. The problem lies in the fact that Europe itself has chosen not to decide, that it does not dare to choose and thereby has chosen evil, which means it has chosen inhumanity. But honest choice ... for humanity exists only as the decision of faith, and the decision of faith, in turn, exists only under the sovereignty of God's Word

---

10. Barth, *The German Church Conflict*, 103.

... Is it that the Christian Church itself knows too little of the sovereignty of God's Word?[11]

Here, for the first time, Barth put the theme of threatened humanity on the agenda. Already earlier, faced with the rise of National Socialism, there was talk about that in the Netherlands, for example by the historian Jan Huizinga (one of the professors in Leiden among Barth's audience). But that it is a matter of Christian faith to advocate for humanity, that was not said before. Barth would go into it further in his later work.

But here he avoided references that were all too direct. That had to do with the circumstances. His visit took place in a nervous and tense atmosphere. Dutch authorities had asked Barth for his text ahead of time. They were concerned about provocative statements and did not want the neutrality of the nation put at risk.

Still, Barth was not intimidated. He refused to allow his text to be precensored: "If those countries which are still free resort to such methods for fear of Germany, then we shall soon have a Hitlerite Europe, and I would not want to give even the slightest support to that."[12] It had been demanded of Barth that he refrain from political expressions. That was not possible for Barth. "Wherever there is theological talk, it is always implicitly or explicitly political talk also."[13] To be sure, he promised to respond to concrete questions on the political situation only in closed sessions.

During his entire visit to the Netherlands he was observed by the police on the order of (as Barth wrote later) the "Christian minister-president" Hendrikus Colijn. To ease pressure from the government, the student committee had previously abandoned the idea of arranging Barth's appearance during public meetings. It had been decided to hold closed meetings, with the sale of entrance tickets. That had, in the meantime, strongly fueled interest.

In preparation for the meeting in the hall of the University of Amsterdam, the police even wanted to see the questions to be put to Barth ahead of time. Certain questions were deemed too risky. At the last moment it led to the banning of the entire meeting in the hall. It took place at a another venue: in a café.

9.6 The Problem of Infant Baptism

One matter drew particular attention in this visit. In the discussion following his appearance in Utrecht, a question was put to him concerning

---

11. Barth, "The Sovereignty of God's Word," 32–33
12. Quoted in Busch, *Karl Barth*, 292.
13. Quoted in Busch, *Karl Barth*, 292

infant baptism. In his answer, Barth opposed its legitimacy. Baptism must not, he said, precede the faith of the baptized, but must follow confession; its administration presupposes that faith is already present. The baptism of infants takes place in a climate in which Christianity, church membership, is self-evident and in which church and the population nearly coincide. That situation is undesirable and must be ended.

Giving this answer, Barth undoubtedly had the situation of the *volks*-church in Germany and Switzerland in mind, specifically the way in which the "German Christians" had reshaped the church into an institution of the state, as in National Socialism (see 6.4). More and more he saw the practice of infant baptism as a pattern that formed an easy connection for a similar disastrous development. Thus, he had come to the critical question of whether Luther and Calvin had not retained too much of a medieval perspective in their defense of infant baptism. If asked, Barth firmly denied that his critical view of infant baptism had emerged purely from current ecclesiastical developments. His critique was really the result of theological considerations.

He wrote that later in a letter to Miskotte, who had witnessed this discussion in Utrecht and had voiced his dismay of Barth's critical evaluation of infant baptism in an earlier letter, immediately after the meeting, Miskotte had already been a friend and kindred spirit of Barth for years (see 7.7), but he could not follow him in this. Besides, he had heard Barth speak like this already two years previously in a personal meeting in a small circle in Basel and been dismayed at that time. But that Barth had now offered his critical view of infant baptism publicly, Miskotte wrote, was "like a bomb fallen on our church and exploded."[14] Miskotte's reaction reveals something of the commotion that originated in broad circles in the theological and ecclesiastical world of the Netherlands over Barth's statements. The *volks*-church tradition was still valued in the Netherlands of the time as a beloved asset. Not that Miskotte himself still shared that tradition, but he feared subjectivism in Barth's vision, and thus a misunderstanding of the ecclesiastical objectivity of salvation, a misunderstanding that the grace of Christ engages us already before we open ourselves to it—a notion that in contemporary theology had found too little approval. He deemed Barth's critique of infant baptism an alien element in his theology, all the more to be regretted because it had only played into the hand of resistance to Barth (always present among church people).

Barth answered in the returning post. He urged to reconsider calmly what he had advanced and summarized his view in a series of pointed questions. Is there really a reception of the sacrament apart from the faith of the

---

14. Miskotte to Barth, March 22, 1939, in Miskotte, *Karl Barth*, Verzameld Werk, 2:449.

one who receives? Infant baptism indeed illustrates that God's grace precedes everything, but is that a proper justification of infant baptism? God can also use a human misuse like infant baptism for his purpose, but is that an argument to retain the misuse? Questions that he had himself answered negatively—that is clear.

Later, Barth would engage the theme of baptism, and thus also of infant baptism, much more expressly. And Miskotte would come to a more positive understanding of it.

9.7 Speaking of "God" in a Catastrophic Time

It is unimaginable that Barth saw an opportunity in this tumultuous time to work further on his dogmatics. That was and remained his main task, his real work. Still, in the summer of 1939, just before the outbreak of the Second World War, he could finish the manuscript of a new part of the *Church Dogmatics*, II/1. The two previous parts, I/1 and I/2, had treated the "doctrine of the Word of God." There the Word was spoken of as that which comes to us in revelation as testified in Holy Scripture and proclaimed by and in the church. These "introductory perspectives" were in themselves already fully substantial in nature. But the substance would now have to be further elaborated thematically.

So, Barth placed the "doctrine of God" on the agenda in this new part. How "God" could be talked about, in reflection and preaching, had been a pressing question for Barth from the outset. In reading Paul's letter to the Romans, he was more and more convinced that God is other, not self-evident, not to be reasoned from ourselves. He had written about this in his *Epistle to the Romans*. He had also, in his own dogmatic work, resisted the way in which the "other"-being of God was not respected in much of traditional and modern dogmatics. In his *CD* II/1, he advanced that resistance in his own, positive, consideration of who and how God is.

Traditional dogmatics was inclined to speak of God's "attributes." But that word already evokes misunderstanding. As if God would be an object of human inquiry, like so many other "matters." Barth avoided the term. Instead, he spoke of "perfections,"[15] a term that can be used only in connection with God. Thus, Barth immediately emphasized the unique nature of this God, whose "essence" can only be inferred from revelation. The richness of God's essence is reflected in the plurality of his "perfections." At the same time, it obtains that in each "perfection" we have to do with the total, the one God. The one who makes himself known as the one who *loves* and who, as such, is *free*, is himself. God is the one who *loves in freedom*.

---

15. Barth, *CD*, II/1, 322.

Each "perfection" of God, as we find it testified in the Bible, is, so Barth claimed, an expression either primarily of God's love, or of his free-being. That God's love emerges from his "grace," his "mercy," his "patience." But that it is *he* who loves in *his* way, in freedom, emerges in such "perfections" as God's "holiness." "righteousness," "wisdom." These do not offer "additional information" about God, but help to see that other, of whom it is first spoken, in the correct light. The one cannot be heard without the other. One can also, conversely, begin in his reflection from God's freedom, and then for example, prioritize his "omnipotence" or his "omnipresence." That happens in a lot of talk about God. There it has become the occasion for all sorts of speculation, about the God who "can do everything." Barth argued to the contrary that God's "omnipotence" is seen in the proper light as we see it as the counter-side of God's faithfulness. And God's "omnipresence" (that is, his all-embracing lordship) can be properly understood only when we see it against the background of God's "oneness," "unity." The God who is free and sovereign is none other than the God who loves. He brings his freedom to expression precisely in love. Again, the one cannot be heard without the other.

I just mentioned Barth's continued work on his dogmatics as his main task, his real work. But that was not in the sense that it was separate from his involvement in the events of his day, and even less in the sense that it offered only a foundation for his political position. No, he understood his dogmatic reflection itself as politically important. What he wrote on God's omnipotence could not be read without thinking of the brutal power of the Third Reich, of which the power of God is the precise counter-image. Where he wrote where and how God is one, that is unique, that implied the rejection of the pseudo-religion of National Socialism. "It was on the truth of the sentence that God is One that the 'Third Reich' of Adolf Hilter made shipwreck," he wrote.[16]

The book in which he wrote this, *CD* II/1, appeared in 1940. The Second World War was in full course. That Hitler's kingdom would become a "disgrace," did not appear to be the case, in the least at the time. Hitler's troops had gained one lightning victory after another. In the midst of the need of the time Barth's voice was an appeal to reconsideration, in theology, in the church and in society. The following chapter will consider such matters.

---

16. Barth, *CD,* II/1, 444.

10

A Voice from Switzerland in the War Years

10.1 Advice on Personal Authority

BARTH WORKED HARD ON his dogmatics in the war years. At the outbreak of the war in the fall of 1939, he began to consider a new part of Christian belief in God, the doctrine of election. God is an "electing" God; that must be considered more fully. It became the main theme of the next part of the *Church Dogmatics*, II/2.

In the meantime, he was fully involved in the events of the war. He was convinced that it was precisely for the sake of the free proclamation of the gospel and the practice of theology that both spiritual and (now also active) military resistance against Hitler and National Socialism was required. Barth could not undertake foreign travel in these years. But he maintained contact with churches and church leaders elsewhere by letter. Those outside Switzerland repeatedly reached out to him seeking counsel and encouragement.

So, he weighed in over and again on his own authority. He found that unpleasant. He would have preferred official church leaders to have weighed in. He had specifically pressed the secretariat of the (pre-formed) World Council of Churches in Geneva. But it was said that such an action was impossible. It was claimed that the council did not have an ecclesiastical mandate. The World Council existed only in provisional form. It had not yet been officially established. The outbreak of the war had blocked further work. Barth certainly understood the reticence of the institutions of the church. Still it was difficult for him to come to terms with it. Does one not run from responsibility?

In any case, he would not walk away. In some extended letters he answered principle and practical questions that were submitted to him for response. A number of times he held short radio addresses broadcast outside the country via the BBC microphone. He also lectured in many places in Switzerland on current events and the stance that he thought Christians churches should take toward those events. He published texts of these letters, lectures and addresses himself in a collection on June 1945, under the title, *Eine Schweizer Stimme* [A Voice from Switzerland]. He thereby discharged his responsibility for his own activities during the war years.

10.2 The First Months of the War. Letter to France

He wrote to his friends and kindred spirits in France in December 1939 that England and France had done well in declaring war on Germany. He opposed voices he heard from Christian circles that war is wrong by definition and that Christians must by definition distance themselves from armed violence. Such general statements overlook reality. This war is not like the one of 1914–1918 or most other wars of the previous century. Now it is about calling a halt to tyranny and injustice as propagated and practiced by the National Socialist German regime. Hitler has already spread terror and anxiety in Germany and now threatens all of Europe. A remnant of order and justice always exists by virtue of God's goodness in the midst of all sin and shame, in the life of the peoples, but "where Hitler rules it is done with the remnant."[1] It would not have been responsible before God and humanity, if one would not have engaged in this war, as an attempt to make an end of Hitler's efforts.

The church as such certainly does not wage war, of course. Its task is the proclamation of the gospel. This is something different than viewing England and France's business with Germany directly as God's business. Thus, it does not appeal for a crusade against Hitler. "He who has died on the cross has also died for Hitler."[2] The church knows that we humans cannot ourselves provide justification of existence. We receive that from God; no war needs to be waged for that. But, so Barth put it to his French readers, the church also knows that there is a correspondence between justification given by God and the justice worked by humans, now, already on earth (Barth had already argued this in his *Church and State*, on 'Justification and Justice'; see 9.3). Therefore, the church today cannot remain neutral in view of attempts like this war of establishing and maintaining a bit of justice, no matter how fragile, against an injustice that screams to heaven. After all, it

---

1. Barth, "Ein Brief nach Frankreich," 110.
2. Barth, "Ein Brief nach Frankreich," p.111.

has to witness that that is precisely the task of the authorities as servant of God: to advocate for justice:

> It would be regrettable if the Christian churches, after they have spoken so often thoughtlessly in a nationalistic and militaristic manner in earlier wars, would thoughtlessly wish to remain silent, pacifist and neutral in this war. Today they must pray in all penitence and sobriety for a just peace, and in the same penitence and sobriety testify to everyone that it is necessary and worth while to fight and to suffer for this just peace ... The churches also owe it to the Christians in Germany, and to the entire German people, to hold out to them: Your business is not good! You are on the wrong path! Separate from this Hitler![3]

10.3 It is about Life, Including for the German People

Just as the church can say that openly it can, Barth argued, also say that this war can only be waged for the sake of life, including the life of the German people. It is ultimately about healing, helping. That Germany will suffer following defeat is, humanly speaking, hardly to be avoided. Then the disaster which Germany has brought upon itself will come to light. Then, the German people should not be left in the lurch!

The German people is not worse than other peoples. Every people has its own heritage mixed with Christianity. It is typical for German paganism that that is tinged with Lutheranism. Luther claimed law and gospel, worldly and spiritual orders, as two kingdoms alongside each other, as though the world could go its own way apart from the gospel. Just so, German natural paganism is ideologically confirmed and strengthened. "Hitlerism is the contemporary evil dream of the German pagan, Christianized as Lutheran."[4] Consider that in Hitler one has to do with a sick man. He will have to be treated as a patient. And the German people must then be helped in waking from the evil dream of Hitlerism. For that it must get a new, fair chance. It did not get that chance following the First World War, from 1919. The hard measures to which Germany was then subjected have engendered a spirit of resentment in the German people, as fertile ground on which Hitlerism could take root. Such a thing must not happen again.

Anyway, so Barth concluded, "man proposes, God disposes." Will Germany really lose the war? It is a colossal opponent. Perhaps that the fight

3. Barth, "Ein Brief nach Frankreich," p.111–12.
4. Barth, "Ein Brief nach Frankreich," p.113.

against this enemy will appear to be for naught and that then all European peoples will be as the German people is now. Then only our defenseless confession in Jesus Christ will remain. It can be that God will make it so clear to us how much our advocacy for humanity and justice and freedom to proclaim the gospel have come up short. If we are to be sustained, that is only thanks to God's grace. But if not, are we then also prepared to understand that as God's grace? Only then may we defend ourselves today with good conscience and therewith pray for his assistance.

10.4 Following the French Defeat: The Facts and the Word

Did Barth recant his own audacity in this latter consideration? Is this a defeatist voice? In October 1940 he sent another letter to France, again as before, on request. Much had happened in the ten months since the previous letter. The French army was defeated by the Germans within the space of a few weeks. Much of France was occupied by Germany; a new French "government," established at Vichy, had entered an armistice with Germany. How would the church have to position itself in the new situation?

No wonder that many whom Barth had addressed in France first recalled the close of Barth's first letter, as though there he had already presupposed the French defeat. But in his new letter, Barth assured them that that had not been his intention. Do not forget the rest of my letter, he appealed to his readers. That Hitler had been so successful in France and elsewhere does not mean that the fight against him must be discontinued. It remains as necessary and justified as it had been. "A sea of reality . . . does not mean a drop of truth for us Christians."[5] The language of brute facts must be distinguished from God's Word. At least turn your whole heart to the French who have been turned aside and are determined to continue with waging the war for France.

That there is in France much talk about "humility" and "penance" in Christian circles sounds beautiful, but it looks too much like apathy. Genuine humility and penance mean the acknowledgment and acceptance of God's judgment, but not that one may walk away from one's responsibility and may renounce obedience to God's command. Genuine penance does not remain stuck in a passive regret for committed faults but leads to a new engagement in the good fight. It is good to give a great deal of thought to the crucified Christ; but it is not to be forgotten that this crucified Christ is proclaimed as the Resurrected, "as the King whose kingdom has no borders and whose servants know no fear because He has overcome the world." However, with

---

5. Barth, "Eine Frage und eine Bittean die Protestanten von Frankreich," 150.

the armistice of the Vichy-government with Hitler, there can be no talk of such an armistice in what concerns the French church.

10.5 Letter to Great Britain

In April 1941 Barth sent a long letter to the Christians in Great Britain, also on request. Following the defeat of the French in June 1940, that nation stood completely alone in the war against Hitler's Germany. Barth assured his readers: your (British) business is also mine, is that of all Christendom. He again opposed "the well-known arguments of Christian pacifism."[6] The war that must now be waged is not simply a necessary evil, it is a just war, not only permitted but commanded by God. It is about the defense of justice; German military might can be countered by no other means than military. Christians cannot but affirm that; to do so is a matter of Christian obedience.

Here again Barth refers to the witness of the New Testament on the role of the state. It is instituted by God, not as a sort of prefiguration or beginning of the Kingdom of God, but to check the chaos that is the consequence of sin. It is precisely the state that has the vocation of defending justice against injustice, if necessary with the sword (Romans 13:4). That in itself is an indication that the life of all people, Christian or not, is objectively included in Christ's rule; that it rests in God's patience. The state that meets this vocation is a right, good state. When the British government declared war against Hitler's Germany in September 1939, it had indeed acted, by Christian measures, as the government of a just state. Christians who read the Bible as well as the newspaper know that they cannot remain neutrally outside this war.

Here, Barth referred to the message of Easter. This world is the place where Jesus Christ was raised from the dead. God has exalted the name of Jesus Christ above all names and thereby the world is definitively imprinted. Hence, it is not a dark space in which Fate or Accident reign, in which various powers could indulge themselves without limit. Such powers assuredly exist—Paul talks about them in his letters—but he also talks about how Jesus Christ has now already disarmed them (Colossians 2:15), to definitively subject them under his feet in his return (1 Corinthians 15:25). Christians, who know Jesus' resurrection, thus need not respect nor be anxious of these powers. They are called in Jesus' name to meet these powers courageously and with determination. Hitler is such an anti-power. Here it must become apparent whether we really believe in Jesus' resurrection.

6. Barth, *Letter to Great Britain from Switzerland*, 4.

10.6 Faith in Christ as the Deepest Reason to Struggle

So, Barth knew himself to be closely connected with the British and their struggle. Still, he was not completely at ease with the British attitude to the war. Was one receptive in Great Britain to the fact that the resistance to Hitler is commanded ultimately from the resurrection of Christ? It appears to me, he wrote to his readers, that in British statements on what is at issue in this war usually matters like "Western civilization," "freedom," and the "infinite value of the human person" are mentioned. Important matters, undoubtedly. But those who appeal only to such human ideals are not sufficiently strong to resist Hitler. One remains caught in arguments derived from natural law. And one can come dangerously close to Hitler's National Socialism with an appeal to natural law. It is those who resist Hitler in the name of Jesus Christ who really have hold. That is the experience in the German church struggle of the 1930s. That central reality is articulated in the Barmen Theses of 1934. Thus far, there has been little interest in that document in England and Scotland. Has that changed?

That is not theological hair-splitting. A great deal depends on it. Whoever appeals only to ideals derived from natural law easily continues to drift in a "spiritual" atmosphere. Hard politics all too easily remains out of view. Precisely those who base their attitude on Jesus Christ cannot leave that out of view; they are also sober. This war is not in itself, directly, "the" war of God against his enemies, let alone a crusade. It has become simply "a large-scale police measure which has become absolutely necessary."[7] Those who are of the opinion that they must base themselves on natural laws set their aims all too high. Moreover, the sobriety of faith also knows that everything depends on God and is wary of human optimism. That does not mean pessimism, but rather seeing things as they are, while those who play around with beautiful ideals all too easily operate with misplaced self-confidence. Misplaced, because the devil always appears somewhat more cunning, quicker, and stronger that we think.

But perhaps, Barth wrote, my unease is unjustified and in the matter of the deepest motives for resistance to Hitler we are much closer than it appears. In any case, we are very edified by what we have heard since August 1940 of the steadfastness and mutual assistance among the population of London and other British cities that have endured the heavy German air raids. That attitude is an example for us to follow.

---

7. Barth, *Letter to Great Britain from Switzerland*, 21.

10.7 Christmas Greetings to Germany

In the course of 1941, Barth received a number of visits from Germany. Among them was Dietrich Bonhoeffer, whom he had known previously as a comrade in the German church struggle. At the outset of the war Bonhoeffer had worked with the *Abwehr*, the domestic security service of the German authorities. That was, in fact, a cover for his involvement in illegal activities. Bonhoeffer belonged to a group of comrades who secretly conspired to overthrow the Hitler regime. From his official position as a traveling diplomat for the security service he could pass on information on the situation in Germany to allied and ecumenical ecclesiastical contacts. Barth was one of those whom he visited—and did so repeatedly. So, Barth was well informed of the situation in Germany.

In December 1941 Barth received the opportunity to offer a short Christmas greeting to German Christians via BBC-radio in London. He grasped the chance with both hands. In it he referred to "the distress it costs you to confess the gospel." He also did not fail to speak of the fate of the Jews: "the fearful events that your and our sisters and brothers from Israel have to go through in Germany." "You must know that you are being prayed for. Pray for us as well!" And most importantly: God himself thinks of us all "in that he became and is our brother, to take away all our sin and hurt and death itself and be our Savior the true Lord and Victor over all the kingdoms and powers of this dark earth."[8]

Without using Hitler's name, he spoke of the promise and vocation of Christians with an eye on current events:

> This is the great promise given to us Christians, but that obtains for the entire world: there are no human lies, presumptions, and disorder that do not have their limit in truth, righteousness, and peace. This is our great freedom: that we in the world—including the world of political events—need not be anxious because He has overcome it. But that also reminds us that we cannot limit our Christian responsibility to the quiet inner chamber and to our private life or to the life of the church; rather more we may observe that joyfully and everywhere.[9]

---

8. Barth, "Weihnachtsbotschaft an die Christen in Deutschland," 240–241.
9. Barth, "Weihnachtsbotschaft an die Christen in Deutschland," 241.

10.8 Radio Message to Norway

In April 1942 Barth again was given the occasion by the BBC for a short radio address, this time to Christians in Norway. That nation had been occupied by Hitler since April 1940. Hitler's Norwegian henchmen were now in power. From that point, the Church of Norway also was under pressure to adjust its policy and public stance to the ideology of Nazism. It had, he knew, thus far resisted that pressure under the leadership of Bishop Berggrav. The pressure had increased. But, said Barth, now that your faith is tested, it can alone become purer and stronger:

> You may discover how clear and powerful it then becomes when from a matter of tradition and custom, as in the age of the forefathers, it becomes a matter of obedience and adventure. It is a privilege to be able to offer great and decisive assistance in the reestablishment of freedom and justice in your fatherland.[10]

Alongside his assurance that he would continue to remember the Norwegian Christians in prayer, he also spoke of the opponents: "We think with care of those who persecute you: they are to be pitied; you are not."[11]

For Barth, the courageous resistance of the Norse church, including its official leaders, was all the more heartening because it was a Lutheran church. On the (according to him) fatal role of the Lutheran tradition in Germany (which he deemed as sharing responsibility for the passive attitude of the German churches toward National Socialism) we have already heard his condemnation. But he could see in Norway that Lutheranism does not by definition mean passivity.

10.9 Questions from the Netherlands

A number of practical questions were put to Barth from the Netherlands on the attitude one is to take toward the occupier from the perspective of faith. The questions were formulated by the "Lunteren Circle," a group of young Reformed ministers who embodied the unofficial ecclesiastical resistance (as the "louse in the fur" of the official church leadership). Hebe Kohlbrugge was the contact person. She succeeded in avoiding the border patrol, proposed the questions to Barth in Basel and brought Barth's response (on microfilm hidden in her mouth) back to the Netherlands. There the letter was translated in August 1942 and illegally distributed.

---

10. Barth, "An die Christen in Norwegen," 242.
11. Barth, "An die Christen in Norwegen," 243.

The questions reflected the discussions that had taken place in Protestant Netherlands from the outset of the occupation. One of the questions concerned the intercession for the queen during church services. In May 1940 Queen Wilhelmina had left the country for England. Prayers "for the queen" during church services could easily be considered by the occupier as a provocation. The prayer was not formally forbidden but preachers who had done so in their Sunday service were repeatedly interrogated or arrested. Was it then not sensible to omit this prayer and so to avoid giving offense? But on the other hand, did the omission of this special prayer in fact not mean an acknowledgment of the legitimacy of the occupation? Would not just this intercession have to express that one continued to acknowledge the queen as the legitimate head of state? The Reformed synod had affirmed the latter meaning. A formal prayer with intercession for the queen was made available to preachers for use in church services. But many preachers chose caution and set the synodical guide aside. What was wisdom in this case?

Other questions concerned whether it was morally (from the Christian viewpoint) legitimate to cooperate with the activities that aimed at intersecting with the policies of the occupier. May the church diaconate give social support to the Dutch who refuse work in Germany? May one as a Christian be involved in illegal activities? How must the biblical command "thou shalt not bear false witness" (Exodus 20:16) be understood in this connection (when it comes to police interrogation)? The inclination to obedience to authority and to biblical faithfulness resided deep within Dutch Protestants.

10.10 The "Illegal" as the Genuinely Legal

Barth offered his unambiguous opinion. To the question whether intercession for the queen could be omitted he answered briefly: unconditionally no! For you it is about the confession of the just state instituted by God vis-à-vis National Socialism as a robber's band. Today, that is the heart of what must be confessed. Prayer for the queen is now for you the article on which the church stands or falls.

To the question whether the diaconate may support Dutch who refuse to work in Germany, Barth was equally brief: unconditionally yes! Even if the Dutch concerned are not church members and particular regulations would forbid it. After all, that they refuse service and so have problems is because they would not cooperate in a business that no Christian would make his own. Whoever supports them acts in the spirit of Christ.

Barth deemed cooperation in illegal activities not only legitimate for Christians but commanded. For you today "illegal" is genuinely legal, he wrote. "German National Socialism that has overcome you is not an authority instituted by God; it deserves only apparent and temporal obedience, in truth, however, resistance." Naturally, the church cannot as such identify with particular "illegal" organizations; after all, the area of its work is proclamation, not the public order. But it also cannot intend to distance itself from such organizations. It must consider "that it finds itself with each word of genuine proclamation factually in the arena of that so-called 'illegality.'"[12]

Concerning the command to bear "no false witness" Barth wrote that the Truth is God himself in the revelation of his will. To serve the truth is thus confessing God's revealed will in word and deed as that now happens in the Netherlands in the participation in the struggle to reestablish justice. It is about whether what (in a particular situation) is a part of this struggle. Whether it agrees with certain "objective" facts is thus a matter of the second order. It can appear that one utters a truth (namely serves the Truth) that seen objectively is "false," and that then what is seen as objectively "true" word would mean to lie. Not the end, but certainly obedience to the will of God sanctifies each means. Consider that God's command is always *concrete*. Its aim is *concrete* obedience.

In this connection—also in answer to a question—Barth encouraged his readers in the Netherlands not to walk anxiously on the leash of official church leadership. Church leaders must always pay attention to regulations and finances, to the unity and preservation of the church, to relations between church and state. Thus, it is good when there are free progressive groups alongside the leadership of the church who freely bring to light that which is under discussion. So long as such groups keep the unity and preservation of the church in mind that presents no danger of schism.

The "Lunteren Circle," that had put the questions, was such a group. In writing this last bit, Barth must also have considered his own position as a critical loner alongside and in opposition to official church institutions.

10.11 The Neutrality of Switzerland: A Matter of Principle

Barth's anti-Hitler position became an ever-greater thorn in the eye of the authorities of his fatherland. They were extremely concerned that Barth's letters, mentioned above, could harm Switzerland's neutrality. Barth's Easter letter to Great Britain of April 1941, which had become quickly known

---

12. Barth, "An meine Freunde in den Niederlanden," 247.

in broader circles, was in July declared forbidden reading matter by the Swiss censor. Barth's statements were, it was judged, so critical toward Germany that "the proper relation of Switzerland to Germany" could be disturbed. Barth's radio address to German Christians of December 1941 also gave Swiss authorities the occasion to distance themselves expressly from it. Moreover, the address was not well received by the curatorium of the University of Basel. The same goes for the message to Norway of April 1942. In August 1942 Barth received an official reprimand from the curatorium for this double radio appearance.

This corrective and censorial attitude of the Swiss authorities was absolutely unacceptable to Barth. Not that he was an opponent of Swiss neutrality. In his letter to France of December 1939, he even defended it principally. This war is rooted in the international decisions of 1919 (the peace of Versailles), very humiliating for Germany, he wrote. Differently than France and Great Britain, Switzerland was not involved in that peace, and even less in later developments in Europe. Switzerland would appear arbitrary and in conflict with its own earlier declarations if it were to get involved militarily in this war. Allow Switzerland's neutrality to continue as long as it is possible.

But then it is important that Switzerland remain what it has always been, not a power state, but a community of free peoples and free persons bound by justice; a state ordered so that the church is allowed space for the proclamation of the gospel. As such, this neutral Switzerland is a reminder how human life and society can be lived in order and at the same time be an invitation for all to imitate. Barth spoke of that in a speech held in July 1941 in various Swiss locations on the occasion of the celebration of the 650th birthday of Switzerland as an independent state ("confederacy"). The speech, held before large audiences, had as its title, "In the Name of God Almighty," a reference to the opening words of the Swiss constitution. This constitutional reference to "God," as the cross (not a swastika!) in the Swiss flag, does not make Switzerland a church. But it certainly shows that this confederacy exists on the foundation and in the sphere of influence of the church. As a state, Switzerland is not "Christian," but is confronted with, and thereby claimed by, the gospel of Jesus Christ. That had influenced the nature of the Swiss society. It is about justice, not power.

The character of a community bound by justice may not be lost. That, said Barth, is not self-evident. Switzerland can only exist as a neutral nation in the midst of powers that hold each other in balance. Germany, along with Italy, however, is out to distort and destroy this balance of power. Hence, England, in its war against Germany, fights for a cause that is also Switzerland's. In that perspective, Switzerland cannot remain neutral. Are the Swiss aware of that? They live under great pressure. In fact, Switzerland is no more than an island in the great sea of German/Italian power. What now? Give in to the pressure, maintaining as many conditions for life as possible, but having lost freedom, and in fact functioning as a cog in the German war machine? Or: resist the pressure? That can mean that a military attack will ensue, against which we must defend ourselves and, in the worst case, suffer defeat. But we have then retained our spiritual freedom. It is only with the last choice that there is still a future for Switzerland.

Barth was not at ease in view of his fatherland. At the conclusion of his speech he cracked a few hard nuts. In Switzerland it must be about justice, he said. That is implied in the reference to "the name of God Almighty" in the constitution. How does that then fit with care for the economically weak? And why then is freedom of the press and of speech reined in by censorship in Switzerland? Censorship exists in the cause of defense of the nation. But now it is used to defuse statements that could be "painful to surrounding powers." As if such statements may and could remain in abeyance! Still more: why are immigrants who have fled German oppression treated in Switzerland as undesirable aliens, while henchmen of the German political system are more than welcome? And why does Switzerland continue to do business with Germany and Italy and even offer arms to these nations? Even Swiss Christians may not run away from questions like these. Indeed, exactly they themselves may be expected to have a sense of what is valuable in the order of the Swiss state and society, of the significance of the words "in the name of God Almighty" of the constitution and of what is evil in the spirit that currently is in pursuit of supreme power in Germany.

It is primarily this last part that engendered review and evoked criticism. Swiss authorities intervened and within a few weeks also banned publication. But by that time 16,000 copies had been distributed. Barth's speech had reached an extensive readership.

His plea to stand in the breech against the German/Italian threat for the maintenance of Swiss neutrality and independence not only addressed others. How much he himself took this seriously could be seen when he volunteered for military service in April 1940, now almost 54 years old. Helmeted, in uniform, armed, he thus served from time to time for a few weeks and stood guard at the border near Basel. Military service too can be service to God. Barth had written that earlier. Here he put it into practice. It also means that now and again he would have to appear at speeches and lectures in military uniform.

10.12 A New Part of the *Dogmatics*: On God as an Electing God

As already said, the lectures continued, and hence also the work on the *Church Dogmatics*. The manuscript of *CD* II/2, the second, concluding volume of the doctrine of God could be completed in the winter of 1941/42. The book appeared in the spring of 1942. As we already saw, an important portion was dedicated to the doctrine of election. It was specifically the Reformed tradition, going back to Calvin, that sees it as an important issue that people have to thank their salvation to God who in his grace has chosen for them. Barth shared that conviction. Except that he had objections to the way in which this insight has been worked out in the Reformed tradition.

That God has chosen humans to salvation logically implies that he has rejected other humans, so it was traditionally said. Genuine election must be "double election": some are elect and others not. And the question why the one is elect and the other not is not to be answered. It is God's free, sovereign will. Thus, one intended to honor God's supremacy and holiness. But is one not left uncertain on whether he belongs with the elect or the rejected? And where does this image of God come from? How is it clear here that we know God only from his revelation, that is, in Christ? How is logic related to faith?

In the classic Calvinist notion, Christ is spoken of when it is about election to salvation. He has given himself for humans and whoever believes in him will live. So one sees election to eternity realized in time. Christ is the "means" of salvation. The eternal divine decision (to elect some and "thus" to reject others) has already been taken, outside Christ.

For Barth it was clear: this is operating with a self-constructed, philosophical concept of God. This thus leads to dead ends. Whoever reckons that God cannot be known, or even thought, outside his revelation, his Word, thus outside Christ, also cannot see God's electing actions, his eternal decision to election, apart from Christ. He must also confess: Christ is not only the means but also the ground of election. God has chosen us "in Christ," "before the foundation of the world." (Ephesians 1:3).

Barth saw in this "in Christ" a double dimension. On the one hand it refers in his understanding to Christ as the one in Whom God himself has come to us; so understood he is himself *the electing God*. On the other hand, Christ is a human among humans. The gospel calls him *the elected human* par excellence, the man of God's good favor (Matthew 3:17) and that as representative of all who belong to him. In that sense too we are "in Him," for with Him, elect. Election, said Barth, is the decision of God in which he has destined himself in Christ to be God for the human, and at the same time thereby has determined the human to be human of and for God.

Does not rejection also exist? Yes, but, seen biblically, only as the back side of election, as a shadow is the back side of the light. The "yes" of God's grace, addressed to the human is no easy indulgence. It is *at the same time and as such* a "no" addressed to the same human in his unbelief. God's gracious turn toward the human is *at the same time and as such* a radical condemnation of the human as one is. But this "yes" and this "no," this turn toward, and this condemnation do not imply an even balance of the two. Such a construction of a balance would be the result of logical reasoning, but the gospel speaks differently. It proclaims that it is about the "yes," the turning toward. That is what is decisive, what is real. That is where God is with the human on the way.

10.13 Israel and the Church: Distinct but Together

All this looks highly theoretical with no connection with the perilous war conditions of those years. But the appearance does not exist any more for those who see how Barth went on to speak about the relation of Israel and the church, Jews and Christians. That theme was not considered in the classic Reformed doctrine of election. There it was exclusively about the (elect or rejected) individual human. Barth, however, noted that in the Bible election is seen not primarily as related to the individual human as such, but to a community of persons. It is about an elect people, Israel, and an elect community, the church, consisting of Jews and pagans.

Those are, said Barth, the two configurations of the one community. They exist up to the present. The distinction between Israel and the church is still there. But they are both the object of God's election. That is what binds them together and relates them to each other.

Here the relevance of the dogmatic views strikes anyone who realizes the time in which this was written. National Socialism would make a pact with the churches, "neutralize" them. At the same time, it was the driving force for an anti-Jewish policy. The churches would have to be "purified" of their Jewish elements as well as of their connection with the Jewish people. Persecution of the Jews was in full swing. In January 1942, shortly before the appearance of *CD* II/2, the meeting of Nazi leaders at the conference center in Wannsee near Berlin decided to completely eliminate the Jews in Europe. We saw above, that for Barth this anti-Jewish policy had more and more become the real offensive, demonic, element of National Socialism. It had made it crystal clear to him that there existed an irreconcilable contradiction between National Socialism and Christian faith. Christians and Jews, church and Israel, may not and cannot be played off against each other.

Barth worked out his view of the relation between Israel and the church from an interpretation of Romans 9–11. In those chapters of the Epistle to the Romans Paul considers at length the fact that the Jewish people as a whole, apart from individuals, has not acknowledged Jesus as Messiah, and not accepted the gospel. It looks to be justified by its own good works and is not open to the fact that the human can by justified before God only by faith. For Paul, himself a Jew captured by Jesus, that is a pressing problem. After all, Israel is the people that has first been allowed to receive God's promises, the people also from whom Christ has come. One would say that Israel would have to have been the first to accept the gospel of Jesus Christ. It was the closest. Has God's Word now lost its validity for Israel? God had chosen Israel, prior to all other peoples; does this election no longer obtain? Paul wrestles with the question and comes to answer "no." The Israel that is still disobedient to the gospel has not fallen from God's election. The rejection by the Jewish people has been instrumental in a particular way in that the gospel has reached the pagans, the peoples of the world. Israel has stumbled but for just that reason salvation could come to the pagans. If that is so, the rejection of the gospel cannot be ultimate for Israel. Then it may be assumed that ultimately "all Israel" (11:26) also will be saved.

Barth attempted to honor Paul's elaborations in his dogmatic reflection. It brought him to accentuate the distinction between Israel and the church and at the same the connection of the two and that in three ways, corresponding to chapters 9, 10, and 11 of the Epistle to the Romans. First, the gospel is the message of God's judgment and of his mercy, it is "no" and "yes," we heard him say already. The one is the back side of the other, cannot really be heard if the other is not heard at the same time. Barth claimed that Israel is the configuration of the community that brings God's *judgment* to expression; the church is the configuration that shows God's *mercy*. Barth set a second description alongside the first: the community is called to hear God's promise and to believe it; Israel is the community that *hears*, the church is the community that *believes*. Finally, Barth's third description: in his graceful election, God effects the human's death, to raise him to new life; Israel represented the community that *dies*, the church the community that is *resurrected*.

It is not accidental that at the same time as his lectures on the doctrine of election, Barth held a series of lectures on the Letter to the Romans at the people's high school at Basel (held in the winter of 1940/41; they would be published in book form, later, in 1956, as *Kurze Erklärung des Römerbriefes*

(*A Short Commentary on Romans*). Chapters 9–11 were, of course, considered in that connection. He had published on the Epistle to the Romans twenty years previously (see 2.5 and 2.7). But the relation between Israel and the church was not a topic in the earlier book. Then, in 1922, he had related what Paul said in Romans 9–11 about "Israel" immediately to the church, its need, its guilt, its hope. At the time, he did not have the existence of the Jewish people as a reality distinct from the church in mind. In 1940/41 he clearly did. Now chapters 9–11 of Romans were summarily discussed under the title "the gospel among the Jews." And moreover, Barth made it clear that the relation between Jews and Christians is the central theme not only of these chapters but of the entire Letter to the Romans. After all, the question of the right interpretation of the Old Testament is also at issue. Paul sought to answer just that question by pointing out that Abraham is already justified by faith, not by works (4:1–15), and that by faith the law is not set aside but is in fact confirmed (3:31). The events of the 1930s and 1940s have decisively contributed to Barth's reading of the letter to the Romans with new eyes.

His argument of Israel as manifestation of the community that is dying, going under (contrary to the church as manifestation of the living, coming community) can sound ominous to superficial readers. But whoever reproaches Barth here as approving or justifying the Nazi effort to eliminate the Jews does not understand his intention. Whoever hears and reads it rightly sees that Barth's distinction between Israel and the church does not minimize his fundamental insight, derived from Paul's Letter to the Romans: that they are both objects of God's election.

10.14 "Then Shall I Know Fully..."

Barth and his wife suffered a personal loss in the summer of 1941. In June of that year their son Matthias perished in the Swiss mountains. He was just twenty years old and had just begun his theological studies. Barth himself presided at the burial. He preached on 1 Corinthians 13:12, "Now we see in a mirror darkly, but then face to face. Now I know in part, but then I will know fully even as I am known."

11

1944–1945: "How Can the Germans be cured?"

11.1 A Period of Silence on the War

AFTER NOVEMBER 1942, BARTH did not appear in print or in open letters on current events for some time. In the collection *Eine Schweizer Stimme* [A Swiss Voice], in which Barth's documents on the struggle against a National Socialist Germany in the years 1938–1945 are collected in chronological order (see 10.1), the text that follows immediately is from 1944, about one and a half a year later.

He later accounted for this period of silence. It was the time in which the course of the war changed. In North Africa, German troops were forced to retreat following the defeat at El Alamein; Tripoli fell on January 22, 1943. The German advance ran aground on the Eastern front as well; on January 31, 1943, the German troops had to end the siege of Stalingrad, following which the Red Army took the initiative. On July 10, 1943 the attack on Italy began with the invasion of Sicily. The invasion of Normandy took place on June 6, 1944. In this period when the course of war changed, Barth saw no occasion to speak again sharply against Hitler-Germany or to encourage perseverance in the struggle against Germany.

All the more, he continued his theological work. He had already begun a new theme in his lectures on dogmatics in the summer of 1942, the treatment of the doctrine of creation. That theme, with its different facets, would keep him occupied until the beginning of 1951. And he held theological lectures on different occasions at various places.

11.2 "The Teaching of the Church Regarding Baptism"

The lecture he held on May 7, 1943 in Gwatt (Thun) at a conference of theological students from the joint Swiss faculties on the "doctrine of baptism" drew particular attention. In it, he offered his very critical view of the practice of infant baptism. He had made known his reservations already in 1939, in a discussion during his visit to the Netherlands (see 9.6). Now, in 1943, he laid his cards on the table. Here he even called infant baptism "a wound in the body of the church, a weakness of the baptized."[1]

It belongs to the good order in the practice of baptism, he claimed, that the baptized does not undergo baptism purely passively but actively participates in the baptism as a "second principal" and consciously accepts and affirms baptism. He had interpreted that from the New Testament. Along with Calvin he called baptism a "sign and seal" of salvation, thereby distancing himself from the notion that baptism is a magical, self-activating *means* of salvation. From that he could (differently than Calvin himself!) arrive at no other conclusion than that the baptism of children (infants) is unjustified.

In the meantime, he would not absolutely deny that baptism has an objective meaning that applies despite the manner in which it is received by the baptized. Whoever is baptized stands under the sign that says that one *has* oneself died and risen with Christ. Its factual nature, so Barth maintained, does not depend on the worthiness or unworthiness of the minister or the church where the service of baptism takes place; and even less on the pious manner in which baptism is received by the baptized. It is valid, "whether he reflects upon it or not, whether he takes notice of it or not."[2] The baptized is characterized by this sign; it was not under one's control; it has overcome them. Thus, one also cannot, on one's own, cease to be a person so signed.

> He cannot divest himself of his baptism, just as no one else can take it from him. He may become a [Muslim], aesthete or atheist, a National Socialist or a Bolshevik, or—worst of all—a heretic, or a bad or nominal Christian. . . He does not however cease to stand under the sign. The whole teeming, evil humanity of western lands stands under the sign.[3]

That also holds for Hitler and Stalin, Mussolini and the pope. Even the most pious and most convinced Christian cannot get around it, existing together

1. Barth, *The Teaching of the Church Regarding Baptism*, 40.
2. Barth, *The Teaching of the Church Regarding Baptism*, 59.
3. Barth, *The Teaching of the Church Regarding Baptism*, 59–60.

with a variety of strange people. There are differences of opinion on the meaning of baptism and the manner in which it is practiced, but "[t]he very sign, however, as such, stands and remains and has its significance for all these men."[4] Thus, "one should not despise this sign," however insignificant it otherwise is (only a few drops of water that have immediately dried up).[5]

Did not Barth, with this heavy emphasis on the objective meaning of baptism, independently of the subjective attitude of the baptized, contradict his own rejection of infant baptism? No, for Barth's real objection to child baptism was not that the subjective attitude of the baptized was considered too little. His objection was rather that in this practice he saw what he considered the fatal inclination at work in the church to (continue to) posit itself as the center of society. A Reformer like Calvin had also cherished that inclination. Thus, even Calvin, struggling with his own theological insights, had stubbornly continued to practice infant baptism. The Reformation church, too, had retained the ideal of embracing the entire society, as "people's [*volks*] church" or even as the "state Church."[6]

For those who value this ideal, the continuation of the practice of infant baptism is understandable, Barth said. Where infant baptism is rejected and baptism is exclusively for those who come on their own decision and on their own confession, the *volks* church will soon be a thing of the past. After all, more and more people will then renounce baptism. Then the church more clearly becomes a minority. But that must not be contested by continuing to put the health of the church to the test by continuing infant baptism. The church must not be anxious about its position as a minority in society. It must not wish to be so much the "church *of* the people" as "church *for* the people."[7]

Here, a relevant point was at issue for Barth. A position like that of a *volks* church or a state church appears attractive but is in fact dangerous. After all, the church then forsakes its vocation. Barth had seen precisely that happen in Hitler's Germany. That had moved him to distance himself from every effort to allow the church to be coopted by the National Socialistic ideology of the state and instead to engage in that the church would be "confessing church." His rejection of the practice of infant baptism reinforced this engagement.

That becomes clearer for those who see how Barth engaged in discussion with those who justify infant baptism by claiming that baptism takes

---

4. Barth, *The Teaching of the Church Regarding Baptism*, 60.
5. Barth, *The Teaching of the Church Regarding Baptism*, 61.
6. Barth, *The Teaching of the Church Regarding Baptism*, 52–53.
7. Barth, *The Teaching of the Church Regarding Baptism*, 53.

the "place of circumcision." In contradistinction, Barth claimed that baptism must be emphatically distinguished from circumcision. The Jewish rite of circumcision is indeed performed on infants because it is related to natural birth. Circumcision is the sign that in Israel the procession of generations is holy. Every Jewish boy is circumcised because it is valid if only by virtue of his birth, and he belongs to the holy people of the covenant. But now that the Messiah has been born of Israel, this procession of generations has reached its goal. So viewed, circumcision has lost its meaning. With the coming of the Messiah, the people of the new covenant has appeared and one belongs to it *not* by birth or by virtue of national or familial relationship. Here one belongs by faith. A child of Christian parents is thus not per definition a member of the Christian community.

Barth's argument recalls his conviction advanced elsewhere that the church can in no way be viewed as a matter of blood connection, of "blood and soil." In Germany, that had already been seen as a sensitive point. That now appeared to be the case in Switzerland as well. The commotion among the students following the conclusion of Barth's argument, was great. The discussion leader attempted to neutralize it by saying that he himself was "for the moment . . . not completely convinced" by the speaker.[8] Nonetheless, Barth's argument would have its effect when it was publicized as a brochure; following the war, via reprints, also beyond Switzerland. It would not be included as a specific theological lecture in the collection *Eine Schweizer Stimme*. Still, as we have seen, it was concerned with the events of the day.

11.3 The War Changes. What the Church is in a Position to Do Now

In July 1944, Barth broke his silence on the events of the war. On July 23, he lectured at a church gathering in the Swiss region of Oberaargau on "Promise and responsibility of the Christian church in contemporary events." His view of the peculiar character of the church in relation to the people and the state, thus also of what is on the agenda politically, was also expressed here.

Barth offered an account of the situation that had changed in the meantime. The powerful force of Hitler's Germany had been overcome by the force of the opposition "and can now be as good as certain to be seen as lost." "The end is in view."

> There is only one German victory and triumph . . . unceasingly continual: the systematic undertaking and practice of destroying

---

8. Busch, *Karl Barth*, 320.

and eliminating Jewish men and women, children and infants by the millions.⁹

The Christian church has, said Barth, the privilege (the "promise") of a particular perspective on these events. It must be struck by the fact that German National Socialism has made the "Jewish problem" the heart of its effort and that as it approaches its end it has dug in its heels here all the more. It would be odd if the church did not realize that its Lord, Jesus Christ, was himself a Jew, and thus the people of Israel constitute its own root. The defenseless massacre of the Jewish people must remind it immediately of the prophesy of the suffering servant of God (Isaiah 53). "Is it not, in the fate of those countless Jews, killed or buried alive, suffocated in crowded cattle cars or finally killed by poison gas . . . our Lord Jesus Christ who becomes visible?"¹⁰ It is precisely the Christian church that must now know itself called to advocate for the Jews and that not only out of "general human love." Thus, it cannot be surprised that National Socialism has also turned against the church in the form of physical persecution but above all by taking on the church from within and coopting it. That this effort was coupled with brute injustice and inhumanity is also not accidental. Jewish persecution means a battle against the Jew Jesus and thus resistance to the mystery of divine election, thus to the reconciliation of the human with God. Whoever takes this position is becoming demonic and so, by definition, inhumane. Besides, for the church it is also not a surprise that this German project could not succeed. After all, it knows that that God—the God of the Jew Jesus—is not to be trifled with. Between 1938 and 1941 others may have held their breath but already at the time it had no occasion to do so.

And now, said Barth, the Christian church has a particular responsibility. It is its task to witness that God rules over this evil world. And it also must "testify to the divine benefaction and divine necessity of the right and free earthly *state*." It may express gratitude that contrary to the war state "in the events of our time still a piece of earthly human order has always been maintained to be in a position of opposition." After all, in that case it appears that God in his patience "did not will to leave humanity to itself and its foolishness and evil even outside the Christian church and even prior to the coming of the glory of his Kingdom."¹¹ The church's task is to consider that reality, for it is not self-evident that justice and freedom are served in politics. That does not mean that the Christian church must intend to enter politics. But it may not remain indifferent to it. Where matters threaten to

9. Barth, "Verheißung und Verantwortung," 315.
10. Barth, "Verheißung und Verantwortung," 319.
11. Barth, "Verheißung und Verantwortung," 327.

go awry it must be alert. And "better that it stands up three times too often for the weak than one time too few."[12]

Barth referred the Christian church to its particular responsibility in yet another perspective: it is also called to make known the deepest mystery of God and of his Kingdom, namely that he is a *graceful* God, the God who forgives sins. The German people has resisted that God and suffered shipwreck. Hence, it now stands before Jesus Christ, who came for sinners and not for the righteous, and it stands alongside the Jewish people. The Christian church, which knows that the last can become first, can in no case go along with the death sentence that the German people has incurred. Within the foreseeable future the German war state will have harmlessly fallen away, but "then it cannot be our business to sentence again where God has already passed sentence." The German people is in God's hand, "in the severe hand of the *graceful* God."[13] We should let that be established, and say it also to the Germans, as soon as we can again speak with them. What they have done cannot of course be glossed over or minimized. But

> We will also not be able to withhold from them that the great promise "Jesus Christ the atonement for our sins" also applies to them and precisely to them—to every German, including the unhappy man in whose name all the fearful things of these years have been concentrated for us.[14]

11.4 Striking a New Key. "The Germans and Ourselves"

As stated above, Barth held this address on July 23, 1944, three days following the failed attack on the man to whom he had alluded in these last phrases, Adolf Hitler. He struck a tone that he would often sound in the years immediately following the war. Later, he would talk of a "new course" that he had struck here. Previously, he had seen Germany primarily through the National Socialist regime, and thus as a formidable power to be fought against; now he was committed to the fact that despite everything, a new beginning could be possible for the German people in the midst of the community of peoples.

He spoke extensively of that topic in a lecture on "The Germans and Ourselves" that he held in January and February 1945 in many places in Switzerland. We must have no illusions of the contemporary situation in

---

12. Barth, "Verheißung und Verantwortung," 329.
13. Barth, "Verheißung und Verantwortung," 331.
14. Barth, "Verheißung und Verantwortung," 331.

Germany, he said. The greatness and glory of Germany is now completely finished. "The achievement of Frederick the Great and Bismarck could not be brought to a more logical conclusion nor to more complete destruction than it had been done by Adolf Hitler."[15] Enjoyment in their suffering is not appropriate for us Swiss, outsiders; rather empathy, sharing. For this also touches us. The defeat of present Germany shows that there are limits for us humans, and not only for the Germans, and, "which will break man if he does not bend before it." That lightning has struck "so near us" means that it "could easily have struck us as well."[16]

What the Germans need above all, so argued Barth, is friends. After all, they no longer have friends, only enemies. Hence, friendship is what we now owe them. That is something other than instructing them. It is to be unconditionally forgiving, being prepared to make their business our own. That is something new for the Germans. "They know no other politics but power politics." They would now have to discover that forgiving each other is "the deepest wisdom of a strong policy."[17] As Christians, we Swiss should be able to show them that. Then it becomes clear that "in Switzerland we understand Christianity to mean first the Gospel and only after that the Law."[18] Then we are followers of Jesus Christ who has said "Come to me you who are weary and heavy laden" (Matthew 11:28).

> "Come unto me, you unlikeable ones, you wicked Hitler boys and girls, you brutal S.S. soldiers, you evil Gestapo police, you sad compromisers and collaborationists, all you men of the herd who have moved so ling in patient stupidity behind your so-called leader. Come unto me . . . I know you well, but I do not ask who you are and what you have done, I see only that you have reached the end and must start afresh, for good or ill; I will refresh you, I will start afresh from zero with you . . . 'I am for you, I am your friend.'"[19]

Suppose that we Swiss, with all our "Christian" ideas, were to turn away from the Germans, uninterested. Then we would degenerate into the role of the Pharisee vis-à-vis the tax collector (Luke 18:9–14), of whom the parable says that it is not *he* who returned to his house justified. Thus, Jesus' appeal to all the weary and heavy laden, his invitation to come to him, would then pass us by, no longer apply to us.

15. Barth, "The Germans and Ourselves," 83.
16. Barth, "The Germans and Ourselves," 88.
17. Barth, "The Germans and Ourselves," 94.
18. Barth, "The Germans and Ourselves," 96–97.
19. Barth, "The Germans and Ourselves," 98.

Barth emphasized, "It is well known that it is a property of sincere friendship to be able to *contradict* the other and to contradict him in the most definite way, if one sees that he needs it for his own sake."[20] Thus, it cannot be about helping the Germans "to justify and excuse and build up again, under whatever name, the Germany that has been. The more thoroughly that Germany is unbuilt, the better—above all for themselves."[21] No, now it is about building a new Germany. The German people must let go of the pretension of being "lordly people" in order to be a free people. No longer a swastika, but also no proud German eagle either. That also implies, said Barth, a critical attitude toward the German churches. For the leadership of the church and the theological faculties have played a role in the old Germany of the swastika and the eagle. We must *not* help to churches in building themselves anew in the style and spirit that has ruled them up to now.

Moreover, Barth deemed it not self-evident that the Germans themselves understood the necessity of a totally new beginning. Most Germans, he said, have scarcely a clue "in what collective madness they have lived so long . . . what a responsibility they have assumed when they supported first Bismarck, then Wilhelm II, and last of all, Adolf Hitler."[22] Germans are very good at glorifying their own violent past and reacting to accusations indignantly with counter-accusations. They can also claim with religious profundity that for God all persons and peoples are guilty in equal measure and thus to be forgiven, and that would mean that a special German penance is unnecessary and would not be right. It must be patiently made clear to the Germans that these are fallacies, attempts to cling to the past, and that it is down to them to strike a new way forward.

11.5 "How Can the Germans be Cured?"

As so often was the case with Barth's statements, this lecture provoked many reactions. Many Swiss now found Barth's attitude too pro-German. In contrast, German emigrants living in Switzerland found Barth too radical, too critical of the German people. Specifically, they had difficulty with the way in which Barth had set the appearance of Hitler in line with nineteenth-century German history from Bismarck and Wilhelm II, and even the appearance of the eighteenth-century Prussian king, Frederik II ("The Great"). Did evil then not only appear with the swastika but was it also already present with the German eagle?

20. Barth, "The Germans and Ourselves," 101.
21. Barth, "The Germans and Ourselves," 103.
22. Barth, "The Germans and Ourselves," 104.

He was asked in letters whether such a thing as "collective guilt" could really be spoken of in connection with the German people? Is it not rather the case that the great majority of Germans were fashionable citizens, even where one had not actively resisted the injustice of National Socialism? Is not one who is not a hero thereby still innocent? And does the rise of the criminal National Socialist regime in Germany say anything specific of the German people? Has not the same evil also raised its head in other European nations?

In these reactions Barth saw his suspicions of the German lack of understanding of their own German "collective madness" confirmed. He answered: do you think that it is a service to the German people to tell it that its great majority in fact would be innocent of the misdeeds of the Hitler regime? That kind of reasoning presupposes that the population consists of passive citizens and promotes that the situation remains like that. But Germany has a new future only if its citizens themselves take responsibility rather than wanting to shift it onto others. And if the citizens now take responsibility, it cannot be otherwise than they also understand that they have failed in this perspective in the Hitler period. Consider, he responded in another letter, that it was the people itself that chose Hitler. Thereby it had itself also chosen to wage total war and to perish.

Concerning the historical line Frederick the Great—Bismarck—Wilhelm II—Hitler, Barth wrote: In Germany, the National Socialists have claimed this "gallery of forefathers" for themselves—it was not for nothing that one spoke of the "Third Reich" (after the medieval "Holy Roman Empire of the German Nation," and the recent German Kingdom of emperors Wilhelm I and II realized through Bismarck's politics)! And this claim was subsequently acknowledged by authoritative historians, at least silently. Later, in 1946, during his stay in Germany, in response to questions from the press office of the Evangelical Church of the Rhineland, he would again clarify his view of German history from the time of Frederick the Great. Of course, every people, including the Germans, have a claim on a national existence in the form of its own state. Germany may legitimately desire to be strong and free. But not if that is pursued using power at the cost of justice. And moreover, Frederick the Great and Bismarck were power politicians par excellence, out to suppress the citizen's own responsibility. Just so, a tradition of authority originated that could indeed lead without difficulty to the situation in Hitler's "Third Reich." Meanwhile, so he also answered a letter-writer (in April 1945), the German problem lies not in Bismarck and Hitler himself. It lies more in the fact that one has accepted this tradition of authority, the tradition of unthinking obedience. The German intelligentsia was also susceptible to figures like Bismarck and Hitler and had not protested their appearance.

The question "how can the Germans be cured" kept Barth very busy. In April 1945, he wrote an article for an English newspaper. The Germans would, in "Christian realism," have to concentrate for a longer time on their own responsibility; specifically, they would have to keep in mind their own, shared guilt for what had happened under the National Socialist regime, he wrote. Thus, it would not have to be the case that one group of Germans would settle accounts with the other group. Profound changes in the political, societal, and economic structures of the German people will be necessary. That also applies to the German churches. Above all, let people work together and not fall apart again into groups, parties. The allied occupying powers will be able to assist this healing by offering visible education in what real democracy means in their appearance with the Germans. They must prepare the German people as quickly as possible for the public arrangement of joint responsibility. For many years, the Germans have been only "officers" or "soldiers"; now they have received the opportunity to become "citizens," in freedom, for the unfree German is always the sick, dangerous German.

11.6 Direct Contact with Germany Renewed

Germany capitulated on May 8, 1945. On the evening of the same day Barth spoke at a gathering in Spiez on "the spiritual requirements for reconstruction after the war," a lecture that he also held later in other places in Switzerland. He emphasized that it is not about simply *re*building; it is about a *new* building. And that requires a new spirit characterized by accepting responsibility for the sake of humanity (it may no longer be about one or more "higher Goal"—at the cost of the human—for example, the glory of the state), solidarity, soberly doing what is concretely necessary (no longer being carried away by high-profile ideals!). Can that really be expected of humans? Yes, because we may believe in the *Holy* Spirit, who works through the human spirit. The church (which in a short while will again celebrate Pentecost) knows that. It claims, with all its shortcomings, that the appeal for the Holy Spirit is in order. That is, with an eye on the requisite new spirit, more important than contributions from elsewhere.

The end of the war made direct contact with Germany possible again. Barth immediately committed himself to do what he had planned to do for some time. His book, *Eine Schweizer Stimme,* already appeared in June 1945, a collection, in chronological order, of his most important statements (addresses, letters, etc.) from 1938–1945 on Hitler's Germany and the Second World War (see 10.1). The first document included is the text of his lecture "Justification and Justice," from 1938 (see 9.3); the last is the just cited lecture on "the spiritual presuppositions for reconstruction following the war" of May 8, 1945. Altogether, an attempt to concretize the fact that Jesus Christ intends to be and must be confessed as Lord, of the world, politics included. Barth intended to make summarily clear to the Germans how he continually had participated in the German church struggle between 1938 and 1945 from Switzerland, how he had attempted to remain in solidarity with the "confessing Christians" in Germany and with the Protestant churches in Europe in the face of the threat of Hitler's regime.

Barth also gave expression to that solidarity in a letter to German theologians who were prisoners of war. He wrote of the background of the current emergency situation in and for Germany:

> Understand me well, brothers, I too cannot excuse the German people and the German church . . . that under which you have to suffer so painfully today has . . . necessarily become a divine answer to an aberration to which it should never have come to in the land where the Reformation had its origin.[23]

Thus, Barth wrote, you are now in need, "poor as Job, poor as Lazarus, poor as the tax collector in the temple."[24] There is nothing from the previous years to be saved. Germany can now only begin completely anew ("begin from the beginning"), that is, begin again with God. But where that is understood, there too the offer of grace prevails. For does it not stand written just of the tax collector that he, rather than the Pharisee, returns home "as someone who is justified in the eyes of God"? Where is God closer than where he has so awesomely judged and humbled?

In this context, Barth also referred the imprisoned German theologians to their coming task. It is, he wrote, to show and make transparent to your churches, and so also to your entire people, how all these things fit together. Germany has been inculcated with a gospel malformed by human dreams and constructions. Now that those dreams are unmasked, there is an opportunity for you to comfort the people again with the genuine gospel and to call it to a new sense of responsibility. Looked at that way, it is a privilege for you to live in this time. It cannot be about continuing on the old foot. You may open yourself to the Word of God as it speaks to the German

---

23. Barth an die deutschen Theologen in der Kriegsgefangenschaft, in *OB*, 50.
24. Barth an die deutschen Theologen in der Kriegsgefangenschaft, in *OB*, 51.

today. The more you do that, the better you will do your study and the better you will be equipped for your task in the new situation.

Barth wrote this letter on July 8, 1945 at the request of the ecumenical commission for the pastoral care of prisoners of war. This commission, situated in Geneva, had already been installed at the beginning of the war by the Word Council of Churches (in a preparatory state). Among other things, it published a monthly periodical for German chaplains active in French prisoner of war camps. Barth's letter was published in this periodical and later printed separately for German chaplains who worked in the camps in Italy and Great Britain.

11.7 First Post-war Visit to Germany: New Beginnings of the German Church

At the end of August/beginning of September 1945 Barth could visit Germany again for the first time since October 1935 (see 8.1). He received special permission to do so from the American occupying authority. He made the trip by military jeep. He was deeply affected by the ruins he saw. And he witnessed how a new beginning was being pursued in the life of the church, including its organization, in Germany.

In the first place that concerned the Confessing Church, that part of the Evangelical Church that, in line with the Barmen Theses of 1934, had resisted the influence of the (pro-National Socialist) "German Christians" in the church. We already saw that it had formed itself as a separate church body. It had advocated for the freedom of the church and its proclamation and had attempted to protest, even with Hitler himself, "against the systematic violation of justice and humanity of the Third Reich." The organizational leadership was in the hands of "councils of brothers," formed everywhere, in communities, province and regions, centrally coordinated by the "national council of brothers." Where the German Christians had come into power in key positions in the official ecclesiastical apparatus, these 'councils of brothers' had become unofficial counter institutions (see 7.1 and 8.3). They had committed themselves to a better ministerial education, prepared pulpit addresses and public statements, initiated collections for assistance, and to the best of their ability had also extended help to persecuted Jews. In church services of the Confessing Church during the war, prayer for German victory was consciously omitted. In general, these were not impressive acts of resistance. Still, it manifested an unfavorable, critical attitude toward the Hitler regime. So, there had been repeatedly conflicts between the Confessing Church and German authorities. Preachers had been wire tapped, banned from speaking and imprisoned. A prominent number of them, including Dietrich Bonhoeffer, had been executed. The Confessing Church had lived under intense pressure.

Now that the pressure had dissipated, one must resume. That happened at a gathering in Frankfurt am Main. At the invitation of Niemöller, who in the meantime had been freed from prison, Barth was present. He reported on his activities since 1935. And he pressed for a self-critical consideration of the proper German past (that anyway also offered occasion to protest, even in this circle). Barth's meeting with Niemöller was a touching reunion.

A few days later, a gathering took place in Treysa, Hessen, of representatives from all the regional evangelical churches (*Landeskirchen*) that belonged to the German Evangelical Church. There a decision would be taken on a new over-arching structure of the entire German church. The Confessing Church was also invited to participate. A delegation was sent that included Barth.

A contrast manifested itself in Treysa. On one side were reactionaries who put all the emphasis on maintaining the classic confessional writings and deemed talk about a new confession, with attention to current events, unnecessary. On the other side were those who strongly desired new confessional expression in line with the Barmen Theses of 1934. Barth saw the first group as the continuation and extension of the neutral attitude that many in the German church had preferred during the struggle against National Socialism. They themselves had not belonged to the "German Christians," but had not really connected with the movement of the Confessing Church. They reasoned: why take risks and place the church in greater danger? Was it not better to silently accept the power relations that just existed? But such a mentality plays into the hands of restorative, reactionary tendencies. It strengthens the bureaucracy and in fact contributes to a German nationalism that must no longer exist.

What course would the German Evangelical Church now take after Hitler? A split threatened, but that could be avoided. The name "German Evangelical Church" was changed to "Evangelical Church in Germany," a small but still, in Barth's eyes, an important step in the right direction, away from too close an entanglement of church and German nationalism. Even more because all the participating regional churches (*Landeskirchen*) belonging to this Evangelical Church, without giving up their own confessional writings and organizational structures, were now expressly set on the foundation of "Barmen." The councils of brothers of the Confessing Church would remain watchful on this point but need no longer function as (shadow) ecclesiastical administrations. They handed that function over to official institutions of the Evangelical Church. A new, national over-arching administration ("council") was chosen, consisting of members who had not gone along with the German-national camp in the time of Hitler. Niemöller, a representative of the Confessing Church, became vice-moderator. He also got the task of overseeing contact with the churches elsewhere, thus with the international ecumené. All in all, Barth was not unsatisfied with these developments. At least he saw points of connection for progress in the right direction.

11.8 Necessary Steps for a New Way of Being Church

But there was still progress to be made. Back in Switzerland, Barth took part in a conference of the Swiss Protestant "*Hilfswerk für die Bekennende Kirche* (see 9.4) (at the time established with his cooperation) in Wipkingen near Zurich on October 14. In a review of his German trip, under the title "The Evangelical Church in Germany following the collapse of the Third Reich," he identified a few steps that the church would now have to take. It must make an unambiguous *confession of guilt*, an acknowledgment in the name of the German people that it had erred when it gave itself politically into the hands of Hitler in 1933, as well as in the name of the church itself, that, after all, both by its statements and by its silence shared responsibility for this error. The church would also have to become clearer as to the meaning of the state; that belongs to the kingdom of Christ just like every person and thus the just state commits to the free responsibility of every citizen, i.e., to *democracy*. It is also and precisely the church as such that must make that plea, so: not setting itself up as "apolitical."

In that context, Barth said, it would have to be open to possible developments that result from the growing influence of Communist Russia in Central Europe. That influence will probably also be felt in the new Germany. That then means a challenge for the "Christian-civil West." Are its days numbered? Then Christianity can quickly be deprived of its traditional social position. But the church should not represent any particular social class or interest; it has learned anew to be the church of the gospel. Thus, it need not compulsively resist such a development, or, for example, cooperate with attempts to form "Christian democratic" parties to play the West off against the East. It would indeed have to search for a positive involvement, not only in democracy in a formal sense, but also in *social democracy*. Just then it could also advocate for the responsibility and right of human freedom in a socialist or even Communist society vis-à-vis all materialism and mass movements. After all, just then it is clear that its aim is the human and not the defense of economic and power relations of the past.

How the church will be organized is also important, Barth claimed. Is it organized again, as previously in Germany and in parallel to the structure of the state, from the top down? Will it also revolve around the appearance of authoritarian figures in the future? Then the real church—the congregation— would again remain out of sight. Alas, in large part congregations appear to accept that in silence. That is disturbing. For "church" centrally happens where Christians gather around Word and sacraments. So understood, ecclesiastical administrations are nothing other than places where the true existence of the church is now seen as also a living movement of all congregations. The German church could well use a strong shot of *congregationalism*. That then also could be an important preliminary step for the education of the entire German people in political democracy.

Finally, in this review Barth emphatically pointed out the necessity, for the Germans, of *sobriety* in the evaluation of their situation. Germans are repeatedly inclined to take flight into deep, mythical ideas. It had struck him, including within the circles of the Confessing Church, how often he had heard passionate talk about the "demons" and their "tempting power" of which one would have come into contact in Germany during the twelve years of Nazi-rule. "We have looked the demons in the eye," one prominent German theologian had said to him. That would then be about the most important experience that the contemporary German church could say to the other churches. Contrariwise, one had also talked enthusiastically about the deep and strong experiences of Sunday liturgy and in the celebration of the Lord's Supper (that was preferably called the "sacrament of the altar"). That would be an antidote to the "power of the demons."[25] It appears, said Barth, as though many Germans "are at the point of confusing Christian faith with the magic mountain of a magical world-view." That is what they must just not do. Are there, since Christ, really demons that still rule? Is there really still reason to fear demons? And are there, after Christ, still priests, altars, offerings necessary? Has he not sufficed once and for all for us? Is all this talk about "the demons" and "the holy liturgy" not a great flight from the reality of God and thereby also from everyday reality and the concrete demands that obtain? Just here the full possibility of striking the requisite new course is at stake. For if one takes this route one will never end up in a public confession of guilt; it does not come to a positive relation between church and (political and social) democracy and everything will supposedly continue in the old (distorted) relation between the congregation and the leadership of the church.

---

25. Barth, *Die Evangelische Kirche in Deutschland*, 50.

Of course, Barth had also spoken of these matters during his visit to Germany, in Frankfurt and Treysa. Niemöller had also called for confession of guilt, openness to democracy, and building the church from the bottom up at the gathering in Trysa. In Wipkingen, Barth made known his conviction that only when the above-mentioned points became concrete steps may the church in Germany really be called an "evangelical church"; and then its presence alone would be hope for Germany.

11.9 The Stuttgart Confession of Guilt, a Compromise Text

That a confession of guilt from the German church was necessary, was also advanced from another side, namely from the (secretariat of) the World Council of Churches. Only then, so it was said, could the first thing happen that was necessary following the war: reconciliation between the church in Germany and the churches beyond Germany. Based on particular contacts, it was hoped that that was understood in Germany itself.

On October 18–19, 1945, a gathering of the newly elected council of the Evangelical Church in Germany took place in Stuttgart. Representatives of the World Council of Churches were also present. The discussion with these ecumenical guests, together with a fiery plea from Niemöller, led to a decision to prepare a public declaration. That in fact happened during the gathering and the declaration was gratefully received by the delegation from the World Council. It was deemed that this "Stuttgart confession of guilt" had done what was necessary. Now the Evangelical Church in Germany could again be welcomed into the ecumenical community. That was also pursued from the German side. It was also decided in Stuttgart that the Evangelical Church in Germany would become a member of the World Council.

But was the Stuttgart declaration really a telling witness? It was instead inwardly contradictory, a typical compromise. It was certainly intended as a confession of guilt. See the opening statement: "With great sorrow we say: unending suffering to many peoples and nations was brought about by us." However, this is not made concrete. The following sentence strikes a different tone:

> What we have often said to our churches we now express in the name of the entire church: True, we have for many years fought in the name of Jesus Christ against the spirit that was fearfully expressed in the National Socialist violent regime; but we blame ourselves that we have not confessed more courageously, not

prayed more faithfully, not believed more joyfully, not loved more passionately.[26]

This is not about the guilt of the German church but about its own ecclesiastical resistance to National Socialism, as a positive point of course, not a negative. This sounds like the opposite of a confession of guilt. True, it is stated that the resistance lacked sufficient courage, faithfulness, passion; but that is not so much a confession of guilt as it is a concession.

Apparently, there was a difference of opinion in Stuttgart between the drafters and in the gathering of the council. The text attempted to bridge this difference. But in the following years, there would be intense internal discussions in Germany on the correct interpretation of the text. Those who found that Germany's guilt, including that of the German churches, was overdrawn opposed men like Niemöller who emphasized just this shared guilt. Both sides appealed to the text of Stuttgart. The council of the Evangelical Church did not take an unambiguous position. They preferred to emphasize that the declaration was purely theological and thus may not be considered political. Niemöller was one of those who took just the opposite position and resisted a spiritualized interpretation.

11.10 Again in Germany: "A Word to the Germans"

Barth did not want to dissociate himself from "Stuttgart." In the publication of his review of his experiences in his trip to Germany given in Wipkingen, to which the Stuttgart declaration was appended, he indicated his gratitude "that in any case so much could be accomplished under current circumstances."

He reported this same gratitude in a speech that he held, again on a short visit to Germany, on November 2 in the same Stuttgart, not at a church gathering but a public meeting in the city theater of Württemberg. He spoke before an audience of 1500 at the invitation of the regional authorities. It was the first time following the war that someone from outside Germany publicly addressed a large German public.

Barth sketched the course of events in 1933 as having emerged from the inclination of the German people to be carried away by the tempting dream of the new power and so in one blow to rise above all the after-effects of the First World War. And he called the German people to wake up from that dream. Here, too, he encouraged sobriety, a sober understanding of their own responsibility for the unnamable suffering of war under which now

---

26. Barth, *Die Evangelische Kirche in Deutschland*, 60.

primarily the German people themselves suffer. It was in this connection that he referred to the "Stuttgart confession of guilt" of two weeks previous. That the German Protestant church leadership had come to that confession he now called "a great matter, greeted gratefully by us outside Germany." So it would also have to be discussed in other sectors in Germany, he said. "The entire outside world would take a breath as they . . . in hearing this, would receive it as the voice of the German people." And the German people itself may take a breath; it could stand with a free conscience in all poverty "honorably before God and humanity."[27]

Barth called on his audience to stop longing for the past. One must no longer give in to the inclination to leave all decisions to "higher institutions" and consider it sufficient to obey orders "from above." One would, in freedom, have to take responsibility for decisions that must now be taken.

Barth subsequently held the same speech before a still larger audience at the University of Tübingen.

11.11 Further with the *Dogmatics*. The Doctrine of Creation

In the meantime, in October 1945 a new part of Barth's *Church Dogmatics* appeared: the first part of the doctrine of creation (*CD* III/1) on God the Creator and the work of creation. Barth had dedicated his lectures between the summer of 1942 and December 1943 to that topic. From December 1943 he had gone further with lectures on the human as creature (anthropology). Originally, he had intended to publish the content of these two series of lectures together. But on further reflection Barth deemed it necessary first to reflect further on the content of his lectures on "the human as creature." Thus, he had decided to have the contents of his lectures on God the Creator and the work of creation appear first.

In the latter years of the war, when the world stood in fire and flame, Barth kept himself theologically busy with the question of the good creation. He conceived talk about the creation of the world as talk about its destiny, the destiny that is given in that God is the Lord of reality. It is from this reflection that he has been able to take on and persevere in his position in the fearful events of those years.

Often faith in God is seen as an inference from existing, "created," reality. That there is a "God who exists" is then argued by reference to reality; the more tenaciously as the discussion partner is considered more atheistic or indifferent. But Barth reasoned in the other direction; faith in God does not rest on faith in the creation; it precedes it and just so the world also

---

27. Barth, "Ein wort an die Deutschen," 94.

comes into view as creation. This faith in God is first of all and centrally, faith in Jesus Christ. So Barth understood the witness of the Bible. We know God in and through Jesus Christ, namely, as God-with-us. It is from that that we know well that God is not alone, for he does not *will* to be alone. There is also a world, a reality, a humanity, a church, alongside him; the world in which the Word became flesh (John 1:14). So from that we know equally well that the human, too, and his world are not alone; they are present to and destined for God's goodness. That we learn to *understand* that only from Christ led Barth to the further claim that this world also has its ground of its existence in Christ, in what has happened in Christ. In other words, the world exists because Christ exists.

Faith in God the Creator is thus, according to Barth, not a piece of general philosophy or worldview. It is an assertion that the reality in which we live and in which we share exists as a workplace and as material available to God, the God and Father of Jesus Christ. Thus, an assertion that it is its destiny to serve to that end.

Barth works these thoughts out in a discussion of the relation of creation and covenant. He argues that the creation as an action of God must be seen in inextricable coherence with God's further acts in salvation and consummation. The creation and its results, the created reality, so understood, has no other meaning and destiny than to make the covenant of God with the human in Christ possible. It is the space in which the covenant history can now and indeed does take place.

From that Barth shows that it is understandable that the Bible talks about creation in story form. It is also already history, the pre-history of Israel and of Jesus Christ. Or better, *pre*history. As such it is not susceptible to ordinary "historical" description and perception. The biblical stories of creation, Genesis 1 and 2, then are not historical reports but rather sagas, poetic images.

Thus, Barth further unpacks his doctrine of creation in the form of a careful exegesis of these creation stories. The creation is the "external ... basis of the covenant," oriented to the covenant; Barth sees that as the tenor of the first story. And the covenant is the "inner basis of creation"; that is the tenor of the second story. The creation already appears to be good, testimony to God's goodness. God speaks his word of "yes" already in his creative action; the creation may exist, God is well-pleased with it, it is good in his eyes. Even in his creating act God gives himself to be known as the one who he will appear to be in his covenant with Israel and in Jesus Christ.[28]

---

28. Barth, *CD*, III/1, 97.

One could also expect that in a view of faith in God the Creator, the relation between faith and natural science would be discussed. But Barth leaves that theme undiscussed. After all, going into that reflexively would mean attempting to defend faith in God over and against the insights of natural science. As we saw, Barth deemed that as arising from a fundamental misunderstanding. Faith in God need not be defended over and against the claims of natural science, he claimed. By definition, it is not threatened by the developments of natural science. Even less need natural science be anxious of being curtailed in its development and activity by biblical faith in God the Creator, at least when it is genuine science, thus, a description of what it perceives and does not secretly cherish religious pretension.

The world as created reality stands under God's word of "yes." It may exist. Knowing that, from faith in Christ, offers the possibility of maintaining hope for a world plagued by war. So, we may gather, that obtained for Barth himself.

12

Guest Professor in Post-war Germany

12.1 Summer, 1946: Guest Professor at Bonn

BARTH'S INVOLVEMENT WITH POST-WAR Germany did not remain limited to the fall of 1945. He felt involved with the necessary reconstruction in Germany in such a way that in the spring of 1946 he considered whether he should not have to return to Germany to commit all his efforts there. He would have to resign his position as professor in Basel and cease work on the *Church Dogmatics*.

During his stay in Germany in August 1945, he had been approached whether he would not be professor again in Bonn. That was too much, but he later accepted an invitation to come as a guest professor for a few months in the summer of 1946. Basel granted him paid leave for that period, until the end of August; Emil Brunner was appointed as his replacement; Barth would have had mixed feelings about that (see 6.7)

On May 10, shortly after his arrival in Bonn, he celebrated his sixtieth birthday with a small circle of friends. He received greetings from England and France as well as from various (ecclesiastical and societal) sectors in Germany itself.

Bonn, the city and university, had changed radically from the one he had left behind in 1935. Already during his trip there, from Basel by boat on the Rhine, he had seen the devastation: sunken ships, burned bridges, bombed out cities. Bonn had also been heavily damaged. The university building (originally the castle of the elector) where Barth had previously lectured was largely in ruins. He now had to lecture in the midst of debris, in a chemistry lab, between ampules and retorts, with the rattling of machines busy with reconstruction in the background.

The students he encountered were also different from those of the 1930s. They had, Barth wrote later, "grave faces." Many of them had been in military service or had been prisoners of war. It looked as though they "had still to learn how to smile again." Barth had the strong impression that he could not be an ordinary docent under these conditions. For the first time in his life he "lectured without a manuscript," improvising, by means of theses.[1] He sometimes saw himself in the role of a Sunday School teacher who has "something to say which a mere four-year-old can really understand. 'The world was lost, but Christ was born, rejoice, O Christendom!'"[2] Besides, was that, to Barth's understanding, not the heart of theology, to hand on the story so that the message is passed on? There were also non-theologians among his audience. He was repeatedly asked, "'Are you not aware that many are sitting in this class who are not Christians?' I have always laughed and said: 'That makes no difference to me.'"[3]

Despite—or better by virtue of—the special circumstances, he experienced the semester as a special time. "And when it was past, my impression was that for me it was the best ever."[4] It was also something of a jubilee; this was Barth's fiftieth semester as a professor—after all, he had begun twenty-five years before, in 1921.

12.2 "Dogmatics in Outline"

In his lectures, Barth aimed for a "dogmatics in outline" ("Dogmatik im Grundriss"). Just as in 1935 in Utrecht (see 7.7) he did so by using the Apostles' Creed. He advanced the same main ideas. Recent events and changed circumstances come through in particular accents, as in a particular perspective on "believing" as "confessing." You confess, he said, not only within the church and in the peculiar language of the church, but also in the midst of the world. After all, the church exists for the sake of the world. The way in which Christians position themselves in the world and take part in world history, for example in politics, also is a form of confessing. The confession of the church must be translated into political choices. It should already have led to a radical "no" to National Socialism in 1933 in Germany. Alas, that had not happened in the German Evangelical Church at the time with disastrous consequences, although an upright, deep and living Christianity continued to exist as did a Christian confession within the church. And the same danger threatens today, said Barth. There is within the churches a great longing for the Word of God, but there is again an inclination, primarily among

1. Barth, *Dogmatics in Outline*, 7.
2. Barth, *Dogmatics in Outline*, 67.
3. Barth, *Dogmatics in Outline*, 93.
4. Barth, *Dogmatics in Outline*, 7.

Christians themselves, to gather with and for each other within a separate ecclesiastical space. While just now it is about expressing itself as church on the question of guilt; thus, not to withdraw from a shared responsibility for what had happened in Germany in the previous years. He did not name the Stuttgart confession (see 11.8) in that connection. As we saw, he had not intended to publicly distance himself from that confession. Privately, however, he had let it be known that he was not pleased with it and that he did not see it as the confessing word that was required in Germany.

Barth also dedicated a separate look at the confession of God as "the almighty," "the omnipotent." That "omnipotence," so he argued, is to be strictly distinguished from "power in itself," power as brute fact. He recalled how Hitler preferred to refer to "God" as "the almighty." But this "power in itself" is demonic per definition. Where it is honored as divine, justice is set aside, and nihilism boasts its victory. God's power is just the contrary. It is the power of Love, the power in which he displays himself as Father.[5]

Speaking of Jesus as "Christ," Barth underscored that he is a "man of Israel," the one "who reveals and sets forth, in a definitive function, the nature and mission of Israel." He "would not be what He is, were He not the Christ, the commissioner who comes out of *Israel*, who is the *Jew* Jesus."[6] "Israel is nothing apart from Jesus Christ; but we also have to say that Jesus Christ would not be Jesus Christ apart from Israel."[7] The meaning of the people of Israel must be seen first in order to see who Jesus Christ is. God has made a covenant with that people; that is not a philosophical idea, but a fact. So has God begun and so he is God of the entire world. Israel lives from God's free grace; and thus, free grace is valid for all. "If as Christians we thought that Church and Synagogue no longer affected one another, everything would be lost." Where the church has separated itself from the Jewish people it has already denied the reality of God's revelation. The Christianity that remains then would probably be self-made on a Greek or Germanic model. Frederick the Great's doctor could, when asked for a proof for the existence of God, answer, "'Your Majesty, the Jews.'" Indeed, "in the person of the Jew there stands a witness . . . of God's covenant with Abraham, Isaac and Jacob and in that way with us all!"[8] Thus here too, Barth spoke of the "radically anti-Semitic" character of National Socialism. That anti-Semitism was no accident. In National Socialism it was "realized with a simply demonic clarity, that *the*

---

5. Barth, *Dogmatics in Outline*, 46–49.
6. Barth, *Dogmatics in Outline*, 72.
7. Barth, *Dogmatics in Outline*, 74.
8. Barth, *Dogmatics in Outline*, 75.

enemy is the *Jew*. Yes, the enemy in this matter had to be a Jew."[9] For National Socialism meant that a people—the German people—posited themselves as elect and the basis and measure of all things. Such a self-positing people "*must* sooner or later collide with the truly chosen people of God." And in this collision it *must* run aground and collapse as that happened to Hitler's Germany. "For the mission, the prophetic, priestly and kingly mission of the nation Israel is identical with God's will and work, as surely as it has been set forth and revealed in Jesus Christ."[10]—A similar focus on the meaning of the Jewish nature of Jesus and the particularity of Israel had been lacking in Barth's Utrecht lectures of 1935. The subsequent events in Hitler's Germany had increased his awareness here.

In the interpretation of the statement in the Apostles' Creed that Jesus was crucified "under Pontius Pilate," given in Utrecht in 1935, Barth had already noted that with that the passion of Christ is characterized as historical, set in a concrete, historical moment. Now, in 1946, in Bonn, he offered a detailed perspective on the meaning of the state within the perspective of the Kingdom of God represented by Jesus Christ. Thus, he continued the theme that he had already developed shortly before and during the war under the pressure of the events of that time. What he had elaborated there in his lecture on "Justification and Justice" ("Church and State" see 9.3), he now put forward again in Bonn. The meaning of the state must also be considered in post-war Germany. Pilate functioned as a statesman and politician. In the gospel, and thus in the creed, he represents the Roman emperor. What is to be said of authority as such and what Jesus says by saying to Pilate that his power is "given to him from above" (John 19:11) holds for him (Pilate). Jesus did not protest but accepted it. That in Pilate's appearance light is thrown on the power of the state in its negative form, namely as an unjust state, does not change things. Pilate abuses his power by declaring Jesus innocent and nonetheless handing him over. But he just so unknowingly executes God's justice: the just dies in the place of the unjust. Pilate functions here as a bad and yet (despite himself) a good statesman. He functions unknowingly, carrying out God's salvific intention with Jesus and humanity. The state serves God and thus the church cannot be indifferent to it; Christians pray for the authority and see themselves as sharing responsibility for the maintenance of (just) authority.

Barth's lectures in Bonn quickly appeared (in 1947) in book form under the title *Dogmatik im Grundriss* [*Dogmatics in Outline*]. They were published by Chr. Kaiser in München, the earlier publisher of many of Barth's writings.

---

9. Barth, *Dogmatics in Outline*, 76.
10. Barth, *Dogmatics in Outline*, 77.

After Barth had been banned from speaking and publishing by the Hitler administration, another publisher had to be found, Evangelischer Verlag Zollikon, Zürich. From that point on, that would remain Barth's publisher. But his work could now again appear from Chr. Kaiser in München. *Dogmatik im Grundriss* was the first piece, after a long while, for which that was the case. It found many readers in Germany and was a clear introduction to Barth's thought for many non-theologians. That was also the case in the Netherlands. It appeared in a Dutch translation (by A.D. Dekker) in 1949 with the title *Hoofdsom der heilige leer* ["Summary of holy doctrine"]

12.3 "Christian Community and Civil Community"

Barth did not limit his activities in the summer of 1946 to guest lectures in Bonn. He received many visitors and maintained an active correspondence. From time to time he led church services. And he lectured in various places in Germany. One of these lectures was on the theme "Christian community and civil community." The relation of church and state was again the topic, a subject with which Barth was continually and intensely involved in these years.

A comparison of this lecture with the one just noted on the same theme, on "Justification and justice" of 1938, is interesting. In both texts he pointed out the positive significance of the state, functioning in service of God, called to maintain justice and to eliminate chaos and to guarantee for the church freedom to proclaim the gospel, a calling and function to be acknowledged and supported by the church. But in 1938 the argument ended in an appeal for vigilance against the possibility that the state can degenerate into an unjust state. Where that happens, so Barth had said then, the church may not shy away from voicing its criticism and so advocating for the true, just state. In the extreme case the church must even appeal for resistance against the unjust state. A consideration that was simply all too relevant with the emergence of the Hitler administration in Germany.

Now, in 1946, the immediate threat of the unjust state was past with the fall of Hitler. Now for Barth it was primarily about a meaningful cooperation between state and church in the new relations within Germany. He referred to what is said positively about that in the Barmen Declaration of 1934 (see 1.2). Thesis 5 of this declaration begins:

> The Bible tells us that according to divine arrangement the state has the responsibility to provide for justice and peace in the yet unredeemed world, in which the church also stands, according

> to the measure of human insight and human possibility, by the threat and use of force.
>
> The church recognizes with thanks and reverence toward God the benevolence of this, his provision. She reminds men of God's Kingdom, God's commandment and righteousness, and thereby the responsibility of rulers and ruled. She trusts and obeys the power of the word, through which God maintains all things.[11]

Barth now underscored that where the church fulfills its own task it also participates in the state's task. It knows that it shares responsibility for a well-functioning state, considering that that is also God's business. By this, it does not work for a specific "Christian" state. The state exists for the defense and furtherance of justice and peace, thus of an (outward, relative, provisional) humanization of human existence. The church offers its assistance, of course, from its own orientation, oriented to the coming kingdom of God. It is from that perspective that it has its expectations and its questions concerning all political concepts and critically follows governmental policy.

It is not thereby about the retention and promotion of its own societal influence of course. And it can even less be its efforts to shape the state on the model of the kingdom of God; after all, it would thus anticipate what is yet to come. But because the state too, already, falls under the lordship of Christ, a certain analogy must exist between how things happen in the state and how they will happen in the kingdom of God. The justice that is maintained by the state must display a similarity with the justice of the kingdom of God. Things may be led to that in the state. The church alone can do that, for the state neither believes nor confesses (it is not about that) and thus knows nothing of the mystery of God's kingdom. The church does. Thus it must plea for political decisions that can clarify the lordship of Jesus Christ.

For what decisions then? Barth identified a few examples to indicate the direction. As far as the church is concerned, it will always have to be about humans and not about one or another "important" matter (for God in Christ is also about humans). The state must be a just state and may not degenerate into anarchy or tyranny (for God has justified the human in Christ). Politics, in the opinion of the church, has to concern itself with the weak, the poor, those at the bottom; hence, politics must be about social justice (for Christ also came to save the lost). The state must eliminate discrimination (of class or race or women), (so says the church, that is, with all its divisions, one communion, living under one Lord, on the basis of one baptism, in one Spirit, in one faith). Legislative, executive and judicial

---

11. "The Barmen Declaration," 521.

power must be separate (says the church, that embraces a variety of gifts in its own circle, given by one Spirit). According to the church, power cannot be executed other than as service; thus the state cannot be established from top down (for Christ too came not to be served but to serve). In politics it may never be about the absolutization of national (or regional or local) interests, one will always have to look beyond its own walls (says the church that is "catholic," oriented to the whole).

This all comes down to a plea for democracy, indeed for social democracy (although, said Barth, the good state can have the form of a dictatorship—albeit never in a principle sense for that then degenerates into tyranny). Before, Barth had already entered a similar plea (see 11.8) but here he inferred it directly from the content of the gospel as the message of the Kingdom of God. However, one need not be Christian to enter this plea. Barth himself was conscious that one could also arrive at such political choices from considerations of a sound understanding (or "natural law") and does so in fact. But, he claimed, that only confirms that even where its representatives are not conscious of it, the state falls under the lordship of Christ.

However that may be, the church has its own motivation and responsibility. Is a separate Christian political party necessary to that end? A party like that had already been established in Germany—with an eye on the first upcoming election following the capitulation—the CDU (Christian Democratic Union). Barth had seen that happen and had held his breath. In his review of his first travel experiences in Germany following the war (see 11.8), he had expressed his concern about such a coalition of Protestants and Catholics. Are Catholics not reactionary-minded when it comes to social questions? Does the formation of a "Christian-democratic" bloc not necessary mean that Protestants have also given themselves over to social reaction? Now, speaking of the relation between the Christian community and the civil community as such, Barth stated principle reasons to be critical of the formation of separate Christian parties. That leads, he claimed, to Christians setting themselves up against others and engaging in political power plays while they must, as Christians, exist for the sake of others—all. If the church arrives at a political position from the gospel, it must not intend to argue "Christianly" (thus in the manner of a "Christian" party) then to attempt to gain success for that position. After all, in the political discussion it is about making clear to all that it is good in practice, beneficial for society. The church must be the "salt of the earth," including for the state, for the society; if it allows itself to be represented by a political party (in the midst of and over and against other parties) then it can no longer be that. And further, other ("non-Christian") parties exist; Christians cannot get around it. But it would be best if they, also as party members (and putting the party in perspective) always advocate for the whole.

Barth closed with the consideration that the decisive contribution of the church to the state and the society is that it seriously work first of all on its own existence, its own order and organization. It is sad if in a nation and people that must again learn the meaning of justice, freedom, responsibility, democracy and openness to other peoples the church would remain caught in hierarchy, bureaucracy, and nationalist sentiment.

12.4 Frustrations with the German Church

These last words explicitly referred to the situation in Germany and in the German church. Previously, he had privately let it be known that he was not very happy with developments in the German church. That also concerned the readiness of the German church to confess its guilt. On various occasions he had publicly called the appearance of the Stuttgart confession in this church an important matter, something for which to be thankful (see 11.10). Still, the declaration was not sufficiently concrete as a confession of guilt. He was not pleased that it was interpreted in a weakened manner in later church commentaries. Barth found statements of "guilt of the others" (specifically of the occupying powers) toward the German people an inappropriate avoidance maneuver. He deemed the political course of the church that the new leadership of the German church had hammered out to be too much that of restoration.

In June 1946, during his guest professorship at Bonn, he expressed his frustration in a long letter to his friend, Martin Niemöller. Niemöller had complained in a letter—also widely distributed—to Hans Asmussen, leader of the new ecclesiastical office of the Evangelical Church of Germany, that he felt ecclesiastically set on a dead-end course. Although in August 1945, at the meeting in Treysa, chosen as vice-moderator of the new council (administration) of the Evangelical Church (see 11.7), he had remarked that a number of important decisions and letters had been formulated without him. Saddened by the reactionary course that he perceived everywhere, including in the regional churches, he had concluded that his position in the official church had become untenable and he had announced his resignation. Niemöller had sent a copy of this letter to Barth. It gave Barth the occasion for a heartfelt response.

He recalled that already before the war, shortly after the synods of Barmen and Dahlem in 1934, in the German church and even within the council of brothers (the national representative of the Confessing Church), it had gone wrong (see 7.6); that one had already then begun to retreat from the principal agreement witnessed in Barmen against National Socialism (in all formal respect for it) and had withdrawn to a more careful, conservative course. That tendency had occurred everywhere in the German church. One had hoped to find the right course in faithfulness to the classic confession, or in a new focus on mystery, liturgy, the celebration of the Lord's Supper. The new, post-war beginning had in fact consisted in something like a "coalition government" being formed ecclesiastically that included representatives of the Confessing Church but this as only one of the participating groups, with little real influence. Barth had initially drawn hope for progress in the right direction from this involvement of the Confessing Church (see 11.7), but in the meantime he had lost that hope. He did not see things ending up well in Germany according to the principle views he had developed on the attitude of the church (the Christian community) over against the state (civil community.)

Or had he still clung to hope? Yes, apparently. Barth encouraged Niemöller to persevere and not to angrily withdraw into a corner. He also called on him to be a biting louse in the "thick fur of this animal." "Who knows whether or not a door may suddenly open through which an unexpected light will enter in our stuffy room."[12]

In his turn, Barth sent a copy of his letter to Asmussen. And as with Niemöller's letter, Barth's letter became broadly known in church circles. There were indignant reactions from church authorities, specifically from Asmussen (still Barth's comrade in 1934, in Barmen). Barth had not taken great pains to avoid this. Rather, his closing sentence had thrown gas on the flames:

> I feel very much at home among today's German students and also—more or less—among the preachers, but when a church leader shows up my voice falters and my heart is unsettled.[13]

12.5 A Contribution to the Ecumenical Reflection on the Church

At the end of August 1946, Barth returned to Switzerland. There he resumed his regular activities. He also became involved in the preparation for the 1948 assembly of the World Council of Churches. Thus far he had skeptically kept his distance from the official movement (growing since the 1920s).

12. Barth an Pfarrer Martin Niemöller, 1946, in *OB*, 92–93.
13. Barth an Pfarrer Martin Niemöller, 1946, in *OB*, 94.

Would anything more result than the bridging of church differences and water be added to the wine? But now he went by request to offer assistance to an ecumenical reflection on the church. The text that he wrote on "the church—the living community of the living Lord Jesus Christ" appeared as a brochure in the beginning of 1947, and was included, somewhat emended, in the preparatory materials for the assembly.

This task gave him the opportunity, following his German experiences, to think through what the church essentially is, as well as how it must be structured. The church, so he argued, does not "exist," it "happens" where Jesus Christ calls people together and gives himself to be known as the living Lord so that they may now respond to it in free obedience. It would be better to speak of "community" rather than of "church"; that makes it clearer that it is not about a body that transcends the human, but about humans themselves.

Because it exists in God's intention, it may be confident that it will continue into the future. But as a human matter, the church is continually under threat. The faith by which it lives can dissipate. People can still acknowledge the Bible as authoritative, but it no longer touches them. They can continue to utter the traditional confession of faith, but faith has become for them an abstract theory. Or, worse, without noticing it, they have confused the Word of God with a particular form of Christianity or with a particular, traditional vision of the relation of church and state. They can also disappear into a world of self-made dreams whereby the Bible offers only building blocks for their own thoughts. That the human is by nature locked up before God can also look "Christian." Then what perhaps is still called "church" ceases to be church. And so too the unity of the church that is confessed has become problematic.

Thus, the church is dependent on renewal, reformation; renewal that must come from Jesus Christ. But that has consequences for how the church is organized, its church order. It must be such that it does not hinder Jesus Christ's work of renewal. A bishop or a synod or church council all too easily become human authorities that impede the course of God's Word and Spirit. It is said then that one is anxious about human arbitrariness in faith and biblical interpretation, but in fact one intends to close the door on the living Lord.

Hence Barth deemed discussions between champions of an episcopal—or even papal—church structure and advocates for a church structure with elders, councils and synods to be senseless. He pled for a congregational church structure, a church order from the bottom up that begins with the local congregation as the most concrete form of church. There are different ministries in the congregation (among which the "ministry of the

Word") without there being talk of hierarchy or subordination (thus it is preferable not to call them "offices"). It is primarily the congregation that is called to act. Naturally a connection with other local congregations exists. And leading organs are necessary for the sake of a broad connection of congregations, so a synod consisting of representatives of the diverse local congregations. But a synod does not stand above the congregations. It coordinates. And it is itself a form of congregation.

A church with bishops or a hierarchy above the congregation, wrote Barth, only shows that it distrusts the freedom of the congregations. At best, in such a church restoration is possible, not reformation. And then any genuine input into politics, in the political debate cannot come about. But where the church essentially has the form of the congregation, it not only has, but already is a message to politics in its exemplary way of existing. There it contributes to "the political recovery so necessary in every country today."[14]

A congregational church order as developed in England and America also has its weak points; Barth would not deny that. The question of the unity of the church is not very much in view there. Nevertheless, he set himself squarely behind the principle of congregationalism; the free community of the free Word of God. Previously, in the view of the postwar reorganization of the German church, he had pled for a "strong dash of congregationalism" (see 11.8). But here, for the first time, he offered a principled and detailed plea for it.

12.6 Summer 1947. Again in Bonn

In the summer of 1947 Barth was back in Bonn. Again, over the course of four months, he gave guest lectures. The conditions were unchanged. Again, he stood early in the morning in the chemistry lab, between ampules and retorts. By virtue of special permission from the British occupying authority more students could participate than in the previous year. Their preparatory education was inadequate due to the war. Entrance exams produced insufficient results. But Barth discounted the exams and allowed all candidates to participate. Again, his lectures were improvised, organized around theses.

This time he chose the *Heidelberg Catechism* as the starting- and reference-point for his lectures. This old book of doctrine from the Reformed tradition, arranged as questions and answers, discusses Christian faith under three aspects. The first is about human sin and misery and the

---

14. Barth, "The Church: The Living Congregation," 102.

way by which in that situation God maintains his justice in and through Jesus Christ in such a way that he also appears for the salvation (justice) of the human. The catechism subsequently lays out the human share in salvation by faith. The content of this faith ("all that is promised us in the gospel") is elaborated by means of the articles of the Apostles' Creed.[15] And the sacraments, baptism and the Lord's Supper, are dealt with as means, by which use the Holy Spirit strengthens faith that had been effected in the heart by preaching. Finally, the catechism goes into the question of how the human, having received salvation, justified by faith through Christ, can be thankful. It is there subsequently about command (Ten Commandments) and prayer (Lord's Prayer).

These lectures were also published later in book form, this time based on stenographic notes from his auditors, each chapter introduced by the text of a thesis prepared by Barth. They appeared in 1948 under the title *Die christliche Lehre nach dem Heidelberger Katechismus* ["Christian Doctrine According to the Heidelberg Catechism"] and offer an interesting picture of his engagement with the Reformed tradition. For Barth it was not, of course, about an historical exegesis of the old document. His field was not the history of dogmatics but rather reflection on "Christian doctrine." And by "according to the Heidelberg Catechism" he did not intend to indicate that it was about inducting his students into "Heidelberg orthodoxy":

> there is no point in staring spellbound at the sixteenth century and holding on to what was said then and there as unmovable and unchangeably as possible. Such a procedure would be inconsistent with the Reformation.[16]

The confession of the sixteenth century is no anchor whereby we may be held fast, he said. The confession deserves respect and gratitude; we can learn from it, but we have the freedom to confess today as must be confessed now. In his lectures, Barth carefully followed the train of thought of the Catechism but at the same time allowed his own accents and objections to surface where necessary. In the meantime, he presented them, so far as possible, as the extension of what was said in the Catechism itself. It was the engagement with the Reformed tradition as he had applied it from the beginning of his professorship in Göttingen (see 4.3 and 4.4). So too he found the occasion here to offer a complete picture of his thought. The time appeared too short to discuss everything. He did not get to a commentary on Catechism's passages on the Ten Commandments and the Lord's Prayer.

---

15. Heidelberg Catechism, Q&A 22, in Barth, *The Heidelberg Catechism for Today*, 53.

16. Barth, *The Heidelberg Catechism For Today*, 21.

The book, containing Barth's lectures includes here only the theses that Barth had already prepared.

12.7 The Christian Doctrine According to the Heidelberg Catechism

As a whole, Barth could find himself in the Catechism. It particularly seemed to him that, with a few exceptions, no particular Calvinist hobby horses were ridden here. Even the doctrine of election is hardly mentioned. He found that Lutherans too could feel at home in Christian doctrine as unpacked here. It is true that the Catechism is primarily oriented around faith that is about human salvation. It says a lot that it begins with the question of what the "only comfort" is for the human "in life and in death." It seems as though the human, human experience, is central. Barth understood that danger but pointed out that the Catechism also talks primarily about God as distinguished from all creatures, as free and sovereign vis-à-vis the human. After all, immediately, already in the answer to the question about the "only comfort," it says that that "comfort" also implies that the human is made "wholeheartedly willing and ready" (by the Holy Spirit) "to live for him" (Christ); an orientation (to Christ, to God) takes place in human lives. Moreover, in the Catechism, God is not an abstract, absolute, hidden divinity, but continually, consequently, God in Jesus Christ; God as he has revealed himself in his Word. The most important thing is not that we are saved but that God is praised by us.[17]

On one point Barth thought that a correction must be made to the entire Catechism. In its (proper!) talk about Christ as the One in whom the complete salvation of the human is summarized, the Catechism displays a tendency that salvation is to be limited to Christianity, the church. That thought is too limited. God's kingdom extends beyond the church. For God, it is about the world. Hence, the church does not exist only for itself; it exists for the world as it also exists first before God.

Here the Calvinist doctrine of election again raises its head. Speaking of the coming Last Judgment (on the occasion of the passage on faith in the "second coming" of Christ) Barth claimed that here the Catechism incorrectly gives the impression that there would be (and is made) an absolute separation between "us" (the "elect") who may gladly expect the coming Judge and may enter "the heavenly joy and glory," and "all his enemies and

---

17. Heidelberg Catechism Q&A 1, in Barth *The Heidelberg Catechism for Today*, 29–30.

mine" who will be cast into "everlasting condemnation."[18] He found that these matters must be talked about with greater reserve. We must hold on to the fact that "all people, including ourselves" are "enemies" but that all prepare to meet this same Judge who has placed himself before God's judgment on our behalf:

> Would it not be better in the time of grace in which we still live to proclaim to men this good news, to tell them who our Judge is, rather than to reflect on whether there is an eternal damnation? We Christians are called to confess and bear witness that Christ died for all men. He is *the* Lord, beside whom there is no other. We may *believe* that—*for* his enemies also. We certainly should not weaken the seriousness of condemnation, but we should hold fast to the fact that Christ *suffered also for them*. Then the contrast between the elect (us) and the damned (them) can continue to concern us only humorously. For the elect who await his Judge with head held high there can be no alternative but to proclaim this Judge to those who do not yet know him and thus to remain in solidarity with all men.[19]

Barth's commentary on the passage from the Catechism on the law of God that accuses us and gives us to know our misery expresses a similar approach. There he accentuated that this law, as included in the Bible (first given to Israel) is the law of the covenant of grace. It is the law that Christ has fulfilled in his own person and that thus, also in its accusatory function, is full of mysterious comfort of the gospel. Here too and not just when it is about God's grace, we already have to do with Christ. The three-fold division, misery-salvation-gratitude, treated in the Catechism cannot, so viewed, thus be conceived as a description of three consecutive phases; more as a description of three aspects that must be simultaneously kept in view. It is not the case that the human must first be conscious of his sin and misery to be able subsequently to hear the message of salvation and grace. The human described as sinner and miserable is not the unbeliever who has not yet been reached by the gospel; it is the human to whom the gospel has addressed, who is overcome by grace, the human of whom it was previously said that the "only comfort, in life and in death" obtains for him. That human can now, as such, know one's true misery.[20]

---

18. Heidelberg Catechism, Q&A 52 in Barth, *The Heidelberg Catechism for Today*, 81.

19. Barth, *The Heidelberg Catechism for Today*, 82.

20. Heidelberg Catechism, Q&A 29 in Barth *The Heidelberg Catechism for Today*, 29.

12.8 Again with the Apostles' Creed

That the Catechism elaborates the content of the Christian faith by means of the Apostles' Creed gave Barth the occasion to follow these articles of faith yet again—just as he had done the previous year in Bonn. He deemed the passage on belief in "God the Father, the almighty, Creator of heaven and earth" to be theologically one of the most beautiful parts of the Catechism. Here he rediscovered what was on his heart, that the Creator is none other than the Father of Jesus Christ. The meaning, ground and origin of Jesus Christ is also the meaning, ground, and origin of all that exists. Thus, living in this world we may already feel at home with the God who is not against us but for us. That gives courage to live! Where God, in his grace, lays his hand on us, nothing supernatural or particular overcomes us but just the natural, that to which we as creatures are destined for from the outset. Based on this notion Barth could unreservedly support the elaboration in the Catechism on God's "providence"—as the "almighty and ever-present power" by which God sustains and rules everything. To critical questions like that proposed by the Dutch theologian O. Noordmans whether it speaks too easily in the sense of a natural (pagan) concept of God, Barth appeared to have seen no particular issue:

> Everything is very good because everything is created and destined and therefore also suitable, whether we see it or not, for *his* [God's] service . . . Because of this government of his, the whole realm of being becomes the theater and instrument of his righteous action, the mirror and echo of his living Word, the parable of the kingdom of heaven. . . also on its dark and evil side.[21]

In his commentary on the passage in the Catechism on belief in "Jesus Christ his only-begotten Son," Barth summarily emphasized what he had said in his lectures of the previous year:

> The eternal Word of the Father was a Jewish man who realized the election and calling of this people [Israel] in his threefold office . . . Old and New Testaments, Jews and Christians, belong inextricably together.[22]

The passages in the Catechism on Christ's passion, death, and resurrection had brought Barth to comment that in the crucified Christ we may see *God himself* who has made the business of the human his own and that in the resurrected Christ we may see *the human* who has come to new life.

---

21. Barth, *The Heidelberg Catechism for Today*, 61–62.
22. Barth, *The Heidelberg Catechism for Today*, 65.

In summary: "In reestablishing God's right and thus the triumph of God's grace by his death, he has also reestablished our right."[23] Just so he also illuminated the meaning of the traditional confession of Christ as "God" and "man." It is not so much about two "natures" precisely distinguished as it is of two aspects by which the one, complete, Christ can and may be viewed. Thus, he deemed it a "theological disaster" that the Catechism still makes such a distinction in the passage on Christ's ascension. That happens in the sense that Christ would no longer (since the ascension) be on earth "according to his human nature," but would always be with us "according to his divinity, majesty, grace and Spirit." But one cannot separate these two, said Barth, as if there would be a presence of Christ "in the Spirit" in which his human nature is not involved![24]

However that may be, the cross and resurrection must be seen as side and counter-side. That implies that the reality of Christ's resurrection also matters. This was the topic of a good deal of discussion in post-war Germany. The New Testament theologian Rudolf Bultmann, originally a comrade of Barth (see 3.7), had proposed a program of "demythologizing" in his approach to the New Testament. He would thereby distinguish in New Testament texts the real message (the "kerygma") on the one hand, and the way in which the message is framed on the other. The framing consists of a number of "mythological" images, of miracles, demons, etc. Mythological images have become unbelievable for the modern human but that need not stand in the way of the acceptance of the message (the address coming from God), said Bultmann. He also viewed the resurrection of Christ as such a mythological image that need not be believed by those who want to hear the Easter message. The meaning of Easter would not be that somewhere a miracle happened to a dead person (by which he has again come to life) but that Jesus' disciples had learned to see *the meaning of the cross in a new light*, and thus had come to a new faith.

Barth would later, in another connection, go into Bultmann's claim, but this discussion reverberated already in his commentary here on the passage in the Catechism on the resurrection of Christ. Certainly, the Easter stories are not a historical description of the way in which reporters have written their reports and chronicles; they are qualified rather as "saga" or "legend"; to that extent he supported Bultmann. But that does not mean that it would not be about real events, about something that has taken place once in time! "His (Christ's) exaltation is history just as his humiliation is history," he maintained to his students. It is not the new faith of Jesus' disciples that is primary

---

23. Barth, *The Heidelberg Catechism for Today*, 74.
24. Barth, *The Heidelberg Catechism for Today*, 77.

but the "resurrection" as an objective event (so unique that it can be spoken of in no other way than in the genre of saga) that has taken place outside ourselves, for our own need. It is this objective event that led to the Easter message and from that could become Easter faith.[25]

Barth paraphrased belief in the Holy Spirit as the belief "that *I* may exist, that God the Father-Creator and God the Son-Redeemer is also *my* Creator and Redeemer." Here it is not about faith "in my faith," but about the third form of faith in the one God. From this point, said Barth, a number of separate Christian streams, such as mysticism, pietism, liberalism, can be seen as legitimate. Here (but then here alone) the nineteenth-century Neo-Protestantism of Schleiermacher gets it right (see 2.1).[26]

12.9 On the Sacraments

That alongside the content of Christian faith, the Catechism discusses the sacraments as means that serve to strengthen faith gave Barth the occasion to discuss the sacraments. Sacraments are "visible, holy signs and seals," that "more fully disclose and seal to us the promise of the gospel," so the Catechism.[27] Barth subscribed to this. He maintained that the sacraments are about a particular form of proclamation. And he appended the question whether, so understood, the (theologically heavily laden) concept "sacrament" had not been better avoided.

The two "sacraments," baptism and the Lord's Supper cohere and are yet to be distinguished. Barth put it as follows: the one, baptism, is concerned particularly with the death of Christ. The Lord's Supper (as foretaste of the marriage of the Lamb) with his resurrection (the Lord's Supper may not be drawn too much into the atmosphere of Good Friday—as happened in the sixteenth century). In baptism faith finds its foundation, in the Lord's Supper it is renewed and sustained. Baptism assures me that I *am* Christian (namely, taken up in the communion of the death of Christ). The Lord's Supper assures me that I *remain* Christian (namely, taken up in the communion of Christ's resurrection), for that I am held fast as such.

In the passage on baptism the Catechism separately asks about the justification of infant baptism. The question is answered by referring to God's covenant to which young children belong no less than adults and to circumcision (as sign of the covenant) which was already performed

---

25. Barth, *The Heidelberg Catechism for Today*, 75–76.
26. Barth, *The Heidelberg Catechism for Today*, 84.
27. Heidelberg Catechism, Q&A 66 in Barth, *The Heidelberg Catechism for Today*, 95.

on children "in the Old Covenant."[28] We heard that Barth had expressed himself earlier on this subject and had advanced serious objections to the practice of infant baptism (see 9.6 and 11.2). He repeated them in his Bonn lectures in the summer of 1947.

According to the Catechism, baptism (like the Lord's Supper) presupposes the presence of the faith (wakened by the proclamation of the gospel) of the recipient. That, follows Barth, appears remarkably to have been forgotten here, with infant baptism. Moreover, reference to circumcision makes it appear as though there could be a covenant of God with "Christian peoples" as with the people of Israel. But that misunderstands the unique place of Israel as the one people from which the Messiah must come. Now the Messiah has come. Thus, the history of this people has come to an end. "Holy peoples" no longer exist today. And in any case, the church is something different than the people of Israel. Israel is a people on the basis of blood relationship but in the church one is gathered in on the basis of faith, by the Holy Spirit. Clinging to infant baptism by arguing that Israel has (had) circumcision means a hyper-Jewish conception of the church; that is to say, an error.

Besides, this argumentation is not the real reason for maintaining the practice of infant baptism. That lies more in the tendency of sustaining the church as a *volkskerk*, thus as a church of the masses. In fact, said Barth, here one is and becomes led by anxiety. One is anxious about the loss of the central position in society that the church has occupied for centuries. Understandable, but fatal, for it turns out that there are "church members" who are never asked about what it means to be Christian and who thus do not know the comfort of baptism.

12.10 "Protestant Theology in the Nineteenth Century"

While Barth was in Germany as guest professor the texts of his lectures given in 1932 and 1933 on Protestant theology in the nineteenth century were published in Switzerland. His son Christoph, who recently had received the degree of doctor of theology on an Old Testament study and was preparing to leave for missionary service in Indonesia, did the preparatory work. So they appeared as a book (see 6.4). In each of the chapters, a particular philosopher or theologian was discussed, from the eighteenth century from Rousseau through Hegel, and from the nineteenth century beginning with Schleiermacher and ending with Ritschl. It was not a complete treatment.

---

28. Heidelberg Catechism Q&A 74 in Barth, *The Heidelberg Catechism for Today*, 102.

Specifically missing were chapters on Goethe (in the "prehistory") and Troeltsch (in the "history" of nineteenth-century protestant theology). In those days he had had no time for that within the scope of the academic program. Barth himself was conscious of the incomplete character of his presentation. Still he stuck to having this book appear in this form.

Thereby he granted that it was not about him being "objective," but was about a "theological" history. Thus, not about going on record with historical facts perceived from a distance but a description of his relation to those he wrote about. The theologians at issue could only be described as really influential by whoever today faces the task of giving theological account, thus the task of critical reflection on how and what the proclamation of the church must be. How did the theologians of that time hear the Word of God? Whoever has to proclaim that Word today will not be able to do so without listening to the theological reflection from earlier times. That will not be possible without expressing critique, but the critique can never be easy. As if the peculiar insight of the contemporary evaluator would be exempt from criticism per se!

The relevance was now certainly different than it was in the Germany of the 1930s when these matters were originally advanced in the lecture hall. But Barth deemed it important that the young generation of Protestant theologians not forget this pre-history. He would gladly contribute to that effort. He still viewed his criticism of Protestant theology of the nineteenth century as relevant. We already heard (see 12.4) of his concern in connection with the post-war developments in the German church. But, more than in criticism, it comes down to good exegesis and dogmatics, of that he was impressed more strongly that before.

13

Further with the *Dogmatics*. On the human

13.1 A Critical Look at the German Church

DURING HIS SECOND STAY as guest professor in Bonn, in the summer of 1947, Barth remained intensively involved with the German situation, above all with the church. We already spoke of his dissatisfaction with the "Stuttgart confession of guilt" of October 1945 that for him was an insufficiently concrete confession. In his opinion, the German church could not stop with that even though a delegation of the World Council of Churches that was present at Stuttgart was satisfied (see 11.9–10 and 12.4). A more unambiguous acknowledgment by the German church of its shared responsibility for the wrongdoings of National Socialism would have to be confessed. Otherwise, a genuinely new beginning would not be possible for this church.

As in the previous summer, Barth also held lectures in many other places in Germany besides holding lectures in Bonn. He did not keep his dissatisfaction with "Stuttgart" quiet. He often advanced his ideas on "the church" that he developed in preparation for the assembly of the World Council of Churches to be held in Amsterdam in 1948—on the church as living from Christ's gathering of humans, but with its own particularity threatened at the same time when it forgets that. Among the threats to church that Barth identified was a solely formal attachment to the Bible and tradition; allowing itself to be determined by interests and conceptions of its surrounding society; or being captive to a particular combination of church and state. Where that happens, the church in fact ceased to exist (see 12.5).

In another lecture, held for the first time at a Reformed conference of preachers at Barmen on July 30, 1947, Barth explicitly harkened back to the Barmen Theses accepted there in 1934. At the time they were directed to the

"German Christians" within the Evangelical Church and their efforts to reconcile Christianity and National Socialism. But Barth deemed them just as applicable to the church in post-war Germany. He also deemed it a present danger that the church would offer itself up to political powers. It may not do so under any condition, he said; its task is and remains the proclamation of "the message of God's free grace" in Christ's name. It is also now the case that the church's freedom resides in that task.

13.2 The Darmstadt Declaration

One of those who felt addressed by Barth was the Lutheran theologian Hans Joachim Iwand. He was convinced that everything must be done to stop the church (as he said) from "functioning as a haven for repressed nationalism." To Barth's joy, he sparked a discussion on this question in circles of the council of brothers.

Hence, discussions began that same summer in preparation for a new ecclesiastical declaration on the political stance the German people would have to take. At a meeting of the council of brothers, held on July 5, Iwand was asked to prepare such a declaration. He presented a first draft already on July 6. Barth and Niemöller were also involved. The council of brothers gathered again in Darmstadt on August 8. The definitive text (largely based on Iwand's draft) was unanimously accepted, what henceforth would be called the "Darmstadt declaration."

This declaration breathes a completely different spirit than that of Stuttgart. Four times it is said that "we have erred." Erred in that "we have dreamed the dream of a particular German vocation, as if the world could be healed by the German essence (German national character)" (so "we have prepared the limitless use of political power and set our nation on God's throne"). Erred in that "we have established a Christian front over and against necessary societal changes" (so we have cooperated in the apparently necessary "covenant of the church with conservative powers"). Erred in that "we were of the opinion that we needed to form a front of good against evil . . . just against unjust in politics and by means of political means (so we have obscured "the free offer of God's grace" by the formation of political fronts). Erred in that "we did not see that the economic materialism of the Marxist doctrine admonishingly reminded the church of the task and promise of the church for the life and society of people here and now" (so we have "neglected to make the cause of the poor and the disabused to be Christianity's cause in agreement with the gospel of God's coming kingdom").

"With that we acknowledge and confess this," so it is stated, "we know ourselves as the church of Jesus Christ freed to a new, better service to the honor of God and the eternal and temporal salvation of humans. We must not allow ourselves to be led by the motto 'Christianity and Western culture!'" "Turning back to God and turning to the neighbor in the power of the death and resurrection of Jesus Christ," that is "what is necessary for our people as well as for ourselves as Christians in the midst of our people." Thus, "let yourself not be seduced by dreams of a better past or speculation of a coming war, but become . . . conscious of the responsibility that all and every one of us separately bear for the building up of the German state that is in service to justice, well-being and peace and reconciliation among the peoples."[1]

It is not surprising that Barth, involved with the production of the document, heartily agreed with this text. We heard how following his first post-war contact with the Germany and the German church, he had already entered a plea not only for democracy but also for social democracy and in that for an openness toward communism (see 11.8). The plea for openness is expressed here with reference to "the economic materialism of Marxist doctrine," that can (must) be a beneficial reminder for the church of its peculiar task in relation to the cause of the "poor and the abused."[2]

Attempts to reach agreement first on this text with the council of (the official administration) of the Evangelical Church in Germany were turned aside. The declaration was published on August 12 as a text "of the Confessing Church." It was distributed to all Protestant ("evangelical") churches, local and regional church administrations.

13.3 Reactions

Strong protests quickly appeared. They came primarily from the conservative Lutheran quarter but some representatives from the Confessing Church, from the council of brothers, registered also their criticism. It was at precisely this time that tensions between East and West increased and the first contours of the "cold war" became visible. That also found its way into the church.

Following the capitulation, Germany was divided into four zones of occupation, three in the west, one in the east, but soon a tendency to a more definitive governance had become manifest; a tendency by which the three western zones were joined. The intention, apparently, was eventually to

---

1. "Darmstädter Wort."
2. "Darmstädter Wort."

form one new West German state. It would come into existence in 1949. In reaction, that year the Russian, eastern zone of occupation, would also be formed as a "state," called the "German Democratic Republic" (DDR), under Communist rule, of course. Things had not yet gotten so far in 1947 but the growing tension already became all the more palpable.

The church of course was not immune to the sentiments accompanying these events. The Darmstadt Declaration attempted to transcend them but was deemed unacceptable on all sides for just that reason. In West Germany, Marxism held as the great threat and there was thus no openness for an appeal to see Marxism as a valuable reminder of the church's peculiar task in relation to the "poor and abused." In the eastern zone one was confronted with the practice of Communism and talk of building a just state was experienced as unrealistic; after all, the dictatorial regime allowed for that no possibility at all! The Darmstadt Declaration was not accepted by the council of the Evangelical Church in Germany.

13.4 Dogmatic Reflection on Human Existence: Jesus as the True Human

Back in Basel, Barth resumed his regular activity. That included primarily the continuation of his lectures on dogmatics. Since 1942 they had been dedicated to the doctrine of creation, in particular to God the Creator and the work of creation. The discussion of that theme was published as a separate part of the *Church Dogmatics* (*CD* III/1) in 1945 (see 11.11). At that time, he had already begun to lecture on the human as creature (anthropology). But the treatment of that theme was still incomplete. The business now was to continue and complete it. The relevant part (*CD* III/2) appeared in the summer of 1948.

Reflection on human existence was a relevant matter in the post-war years. With the terrors of war and the millions of human victims fresh in mind, broad circles reflected on the value of the human being. At the end of 1948 the "universal declaration of human rights" was accepted in the context of the United Nations. That Barth had just now arrived at this theme was not only a happy accident; it was very much to the point. We briefly review the main lines of this—again very thick (800 pages)—part.

In the light of God's Word, Barth said, the human appears as sinner. But then assuredly, as *graced* sinner. Thus, despite one's sin the human remains human. God's grace is not only the last but also the first word spoken of the human. And the human shares in that grace *in the human Jesus*. It is (we heard this from Barth earlier, see 10.12) *in Jesus*, the elected one, that we humans are co-elected. Thinking along this line, Barth now claimed that what it is to be human as intended by God the Creator, is to be derived from Jesus. This human is *the* human. According to the Gospel of John (19:5), when confronted with the scourged Jesus, Pilate said "Behold, the man!" That was, Barth said, more than an expression of sympathy. It expressed a deep truth.

Dogmatic views of the human have always traditionally begun with a conception of the general human nature. In that connection it is emphasized that Jesus had *also* become human ("for our salvation"). Reflection on Jesus' human nature (as part of Christology) was thus based on what human nature as such (anthropology) includes. Here too one was of the opinion that Christian faith could intersect with what is already (by nature) present (in view of human nature). This traditional way of thinking was reversed by Barth. As always, he rejected every intersection with natural concepts. Being human nature, he said, is by definition being co-human with Jesus. The human nature of Jesus was the point of departure for Barth. It is from that perspective that Barth saw what human nature in general includes illuminated.

Barth distinguished four aspects in the human nature of Jesus: 1) he was (and is) the human before God, 2) the human before the fellow humans, 3) the total human (in the unity of soul and body, and 4) the Lord of time. He subsequently inferred a characteristic of our human nature from each of these aspects. Jesus' human nature was (is) certainly unique. But an agreement must also exist between Him as human and ourselves as humans (otherwise Jesus would not have become genuinely human).

13.5 Human Nature: In Relation to God and the Fellow Human.

What makes a person human? What distinguishes him from other creatures? Is it his capacity to reason? His capacity to speak? His free will? His capacity to act, to decide, to accept challenges? Natural science, psychology or philosophy propose such characteristics. Theology also works that way sometimes as a defense against evolutionary ideas that view the human as no more than a kind of animal. That defense was a good thing. Except that in Barth's opinion the identified characteristics, phenomena, do not get to the heart of the matter. They presuppose human nature as existing but do not describe it. That can happen only via the human nature of Jesus.

Jesus was (is) first and centrally the human "for God."[3] He is not first (neutrally) human subsequently to become Savior; his human nature was already as such, by definition, being Savior, in God's name, to God's honor. Apart from that work as Savior there could be no talk of a "human Jesus." So too, then, for every human, for the human as such, relation with God is not secondary, a particular filling out of human existence but the heart of it, that which makes him to be human.

In that connection human nature must likewise be described as essentially co-human nature. That is not self-evident. Does the modern age not see the human as just the being that says, "I am"? Oriented to develop himself? Barth finds that illustrated in particular in the thought of the nineteenth-century philosopher Friedrich Nietzsche. He described the true human being as characterized by the will to power, by the effort to become the "Übermensch," "beyond good and evil." In that connection he sharply rejected a Christianity that he saw as representing a "slave morality" in which not the strong but the weak, the suffering were made central. Nietzsche had seen that clearly, better than many Christians. It is time for Christianity itself clearly to realize that, with all its consequences.

Jesus, the human "for God," was (is) also "man for other men"[4] His "being before God," "standing in God's service," implies after all that he has committed himself to humans, his fellow humans, even unto death. So too human nature as such appears as fellow human nature; an existence "in meeting," whereby the one looks the other in the eye, whereby humans express themselves to each other and stand alongside one another; and that: readily, considering that humans continually need each other to exist as human. That is still not what is intended in the New Testament with "love," but it also does not stand apart from it: in "love" the true (co-human) human nature is fulfilled. Barth sees the extent to which this is an essential determination of human nature confirmed in the fact that a human is always man or woman; as man always relying on the woman, as woman always relying on the man as partner. The other is preeminently the woman for the man, the man for the woman. As Barth sees it, its primary form is found in marriage (here the phenomenon of homosexuality in 1948, as well as homosexual partnership, is not in view; although it would not necessarily have contradicted his view of human nature as essentially co-humanity, indeed!).

---

3. Barth, *CD*, III/2, 55–71
4. Barth, *CD*, III/2, 203–22

13.6 The Human as Soul and Body

When speaking of human nature, one unavoidably stumbles on the duality of "soul" and "body." One has always been conscious of the fact that the human is more than one's body and at the same time that one not only "has" a body but "is" one. But how are the two aspects related? Historically, the notion is that soul and body are two separate substances, the soul spiritual and immortal and the body material and mortal. That dualistic notion already existed in Greek antiquity and was taken over by Christianity. That led by itself to the devaluation of the body as simply a material shell and the over-valuation of the soul as the immortal core of human nature.

Materialism, that reckoned only with a material reality and thus with bodyliness, emerged in reaction and would know nothing of a "soul" as separate, let alone as something immortal. That was advanced especially in the nineteenth century; feelings, images, thoughts were reduced to products of chemical processes in the nervous system. These ideas betray the effects of the rise of natural scientific thinking of that era, like that of the industrial revolution and the economization of life that accompanied it. The human became a robot, either as the director of a factory or as a worker in the factory. There was very little inquiry into the human soul in that climate. It was a one-sided but understandable reaction. Confronted with that, the church at least should have been open to critical questions over the tenability of its own dualistic (and thus spiritualizing) view of the human. Against that notion a kernel of truth lies hidden within materialism!

It was in this connection that Barth spoke of Marxism/Communism (that had become an influential power in Eastern Europe following the Second World War). Marxism, so he analyzed, sees all of life materially (economically) determined, that is to say, ruled by the opposition between "bourgeoisie" (rich factory owners, "capital") and "proletariat" (exploited workers). According to Marxism, the proletariat must bring that opposition to an end (violently, via class struggle) so that every human can obtain justice in the "classless society" (a vision that, by the way, means a confirmation of the image of the human as a robotic, soulless essence). The church is considered here as the henchman of the rich, capitalist class; it also stands squarely under attack of Marxist polemic.

But the church must not complain about this, Barth said. It has always in fact stood on the side of the dominant class. And for centuries it was fixed on the idea of the immortality of the soul. Hence, it has never really dealt with the problem of material, bodily, economic life. It is not surprising that that problem has led to a massive abandonment of the church. With its spiritualization of the image of the human it has been defenseless against the massive emergence of the materialistic image of the human that received extra encouragement from Marxism.

Here, too, it must be led by the biblical witness to the human nature of Jesus. We read of Jesus that he, in is relation to God and (thus) to his fellow-human, is one. He is *totally* present in that (double) relation. There is thereby no division between inward and outward, between soul and body. He is, says John 1:14, the "word" that has "become flesh." True, that says more than that it has become 'body'. "Flesh" in the Bible indicates human nature as a whole, in particular human nature as stamped by sin and contradiction and thus by weakness and under the threat of death. But in that bodyliness is presupposed. Jesus shared in that human nature. Just so he has become our Savior. He has committed his whole human nature, including his bodyliness, to that end. "Flesh," in itself fallen into disobedience and sin, here has become obedient, appropriate instrument of his salvific activity. Soul, i.e. he himself, and body form a unity in him, but that an ordered unity: the soul precedes, the body follows. Jesus' bodyliness is in what he does, in the way he lives and is human, always included, although never playing an independent role.

So viewed, not only the materialist image of the human (including Marxism's image) but also the Greek (and Christian) dualistic image of the human appear untenable. The human is not only simply one's bodyliness (for example, one's brain!); one is both body and soul. The body cannot exist without the soul, without the "I"; but, contrariwise, the soul cannot exist without the body. In that the soul precedes and the body follows the soul, the human is a reasonable being. That one is so in this order, that one perceives and thinks, desires and wills, is decisively to be inferred from the fact that God addresses and treats one as such, which again means that God has created the human as such.

13.7 The Human, Living in Time

Constituent to human nature is also that it is existence in time. Time is the sequence of yesterday—today—tomorrow; past—present—future. That sequence applies to all creatures: to the human as well as all living beings. The Christian tradition has always known that. It has also carefully distinguished between time (as a form of existence of the creature) and eternity (as a form of existence of God). But Barth specified eternity as not equivalent to timelessness (which would mean rigidity): it consists in that yesterday, today, and tomorrow do not follow each other but coincide. However, that does not apply to human existence, as created existence. The human lives in time; and for him time is limited by definition; time has a beginning and an end. Just as each human is born once, one also will die once.

But is there not more to be said about the human? Is there no future for the human beyond death? Does not a promise of eternal life hold for him? That question has historically been answered in the affirmative. With that it intersected with the idea of the immortality of the soul that came from classic Greek philosophy. Is there not support for that idea in the biblical witness? Is there not the promise that the human soul, the human "I," is sustained, even in death, even beyond death? Barth does not agree. We already heard that he indeed maintained the distinction between soul and body, but at the same time firmly holds to the notion of the unity of soul and body. He cannot think of a soul that would (continue to) exist apart from the body. He deemed the notion that "something" of the human would still escape death to be illegitimate, unbiblical, avoidance of the temporal and thus the limits of human existence as created existence. He saw that limitation as part of the good creation.

Again, Barth oriented himself to the human nature of Jesus. Jesus' life too moved from birth to death, not as a timeless myth but as genuine history, sequence of days, limited. Of course the New Testament narrates a second (likewise limited) history of Jesus that follows (accompanies): the Easter history, the forty days between resurrection and ascension. Barth would not avoid the reality of that second history. He engaged in a lively discussion with his old comrade Bultmann, who interpreted what the New Testament calls "Jesus' resurrection" as the "dawning of the meaning of Jesus' cross." What in itself was meaningless (the cross), Jesus' followers would later have understood as meaningful; "a light" would have appeared to them (in them) and they would have described this inner event as if something had happened, objectively, factually, outwardly. Barth saw this interpretation as a misunderstanding of what the New Testament proclaims and as coming from a pre-judgment; as though the real history of God and the human occurs in humanly experienced inwardness ("existentially") and not in concrete history. But on the other hand, as he understood it, Easter history is not about a piece of extra, ordinary, time, as a kind of prolongation. Barth infers from the New Testament that Easter history is the history of Jesus' revelation. Indeed, a "Light" has gone on here! But that not by means of human creativity; rather, by what really happened, beyond and despite human considerations. What previously had been hidden appears, that it was God himself who has come to dwell in the midst of humanity in him. So he, a human living in his (limited!) time, has appeared, to be the Lord of time—of all time. With that, Barth intended that the time (the history) before Jesus' coming was already the time of Jesus, and that applies also for the time following him. All history, pointing forward as well as backward, is oriented to the events of and in Jesus, determined by him. Jesus' time, as limited time, appears to be the time of all times—that is the meaning of the forty days between resurrection and ascension. So the New Testament can place Jesus' beginning back even before the creation; the "Word" that "had become flesh" was already present as the creating Word "in the beginning" (John 1:1, 14). And the New Testament sees the future consisting in that Jesus himself will come; the future time will also be His time.

For us life-in-time is fleeting; our past is really past, our future is uncertain, our present is nothing other than the ever shifting, instantaneous border between past and future. Properly seen, we "have" no time. But it is different with the one man, Jesus. His present is not something fleeing and instantaneous but filled time; his past is not just past but as such is present today; his future is more than an (uncertain) "not yet," namely, already filling the present. Well now, Barth said, so human existence-in-time is originally intended. And so is it still realized, for God sees us all in this One and sets our being-in-time in the light and under the promise of his time. With and through Jesus' being-in-time we are guaranteed that our being-in-time is reality and not a fleeing (fleeting) dream. We may experience time as a form of existence given to us by God. In the human Jesus God himself has taken time for us; with that he has really given the time of life. Now being-in-time means for us being together with God and our fellow human. For us too, that fills all dimensions of time; in the present we live under God's address and appeal; we know our past as established and so sustained under God's graceful judgment; in the future God will be there for us, and so we will also then exist.

But not endlessly! Happily not, said Barth. Precisely the limitation, finitude of our life tells us that we cannot and need not ourselves reach the fulfillment of our lives. That limitation reminds us that the time of our life is limited by God and thus confirms that our time is given to us by God. Seen like that, the limits of the time of our lives are not oppressive threats but protective walls. In essence, it is God himself who gracefully surrounds and limits us.

Of course, we experience death, approaching us at the end of our lives, as a threat, as an enemy. Death often also appears in the Bible as a threatening enemy power. That has to do, said Barth, with the way in which we humans live, inadequate, in conflict with our destiny. It is no doubt possible that we stand guilty at the end of our life. So death can be called "the wages of sin" (Romans 6:23). The death that Jesus died (on the cross) had the grim character of the judgment of sin par excellence. Our death does not itself bear that character (Jesus' death was unique), but it certainly points to it. That makes it shocking. But that shocking character is thus not part of death in itself. It is given with that in our death we are confronted with God our Judge. However, just this is full of promise, for this Judge is graceful to us; as Judge he takes it on for us! That that is so, he has proven for us in Jesus of Nazareth, the one who has undergone judgment in our place. By his dying the character of judgment in our death is taken away. Even in death God is gracefully with us.

In that context, the Old Testament talks of God who "saved" from death, who "leads out" of the kingdom of death. With that it is essentially said that the human "has existed" once but is also then in God's hand. That during their lifetime the dead have shared in the covenant with God, is not over, although their life now has ended. The New Testament says basically the same thing. That Jesus was raised from the dead stands here as confirmation that death as the enemy, as judgment, is also really overcome for us.

Is there then still not a difference between the Old and New Testaments in that the Old Testament does not yet, and the New Testament assuredly does, speak of a coming "resurrection" of the dead? After all, that seems to indicate that the New Testament, differently than the Old, knows a continuation of human life in a time that follows dying. Still, Barth said, that is a misunderstanding. For us humans, the "resurrection of the dead" means just as little for us, as Jesus' resurrection was for Him, an extended existence in time; it rather seals the fact that time will come to an end: "time shall be no more" (Revelation 10:6 according to a literal translation cited by Barth). According to Barth, what is called "resurrection of the dead" in the New Testament can best be interpreted as "eternalizing" of this, our finite life. That is also what, to his understanding, Paul has intended when in 1 Corinthians 15:53 he wrote, in his argument on the resurrection, "the perishable body must put on imperishability." It is our ex-life that as such becomes "new," receives eternal significance (becomes "eternal life"), because it is taken up into communion with God.

Following Jesus' death our death no longer has the character of judgment. Thus, we can now distinguish between death as judgment and death as limit. And, Barth claimed, it must indeed be said of death as limit that it belongs as such to the good creation. After all, when we die, what we can achieve ourselves is over and we are absolutely left to God in Christ as our Savior. Thus, death as limit is not a loss or threat but gain. Certainly, death means the end of our existence; there is no hereafter; but such a hereafter is not necessary, for *God himself is our hereafter, our future.*

These last statements again provoked critical reactions. The idea that the limitation of human existence, death, of itself belongs to the good creation and that there is no hereafter to be expected "beyond death" stood at cross-purposes to what for many was the traditional conviction. Does not biblical talk about a coming "resurrection of the dead" still imply the promise of a new existence beyond death? Moreover, what did Barth really intend, it was asked, when he said that our finite life is "eternalized," as he would not say in this wording that we ourselves will still exist, as new persons in a new creation? That our contemporary, earthly existence will be "taken up in communion with God," that we humans as those who have died will also be "in God's hand," will we ourselves recognize something of that?

But Barth himself rejected the notion that he would have excluded this last consideration. Contemporary, earthly human life will, he said, then be renewed, glorified in God's eyes "*and so also for our own and all eyes.*" Does that not imply that there will still be a continuity of our existence, also after death? No, for "continuity" would mean that then, following death (and thus into infinity) time, ordinary time, would continue. We just heard Barth reject that thought. After all, he argued that time (history) has principally come to an end with Christ, in his resurrection. Since then, and later perfectly, there is only eternity in which we may exist together with God.

14

Between East and West

14.1 Continuing to Live and Work in Basel

IN THE SPRING OF 1948 Barth was asked for the third time to fill the guest lectureship for the summer semester. He was even extended an invitation to become rector of the University of Bonn. That would mean that he would have to abandon Basel and return to Germany. Barth decided not to accept this invitation. One of his considerations was that he did not have a particularly positive impression of the course of events in the German church. He detected too strong a tendency of an (evangelical-national) restoration and too little openness to a course of renewal like one he himself had advocated; so, he would not be able joyfully to rediscover a place there where he could do all his work. Basel remained his residence and his workplace.

Many students came to Basel in the post-war years including students from foreign lands. The frontiers were open once again. Barth lectured in dogmatics; he continued with an eye on further work in his *Church Dogmatics*. And he held seminars in which he read and discussed important texts from church and theological history with his students. In doing so he continually kept in mind that theology is done in view of preaching, of ecclesiastical practice. If that is forgotten, theology soon becomes a sterile academic matter, he found.

14.2 Visit to Hungary, March-April, 1948

While Germany had not become his travel destination again in 1948, he undertook another foreign trip, to Hungary, in March and April of that year. He had been invited by the Hungarian Reformed Church and he remained for two weeks.

This visit took place at a sensitive moment in history. Since the end of the Second World War, tensions had grown between East and West. In February 1948, shortly before Barth's trip to Hungary, a Communist take-over had taken place in Czechoslovakia; so it was that that nation, like others that had been liberated by the Red Army from Nazi rule, had come under Communist domination. There were also developments in Germany. In March 1948, a conversation among the occupying powers in Germany went wrong; the Russian negotiators announced that they did not agree with Western plans for an economic reformation in the various occupied areas in Germany and even viewed those as an act of aggression. By way of reprisal, on April 1, Russian patrols began to impede traffic between West Germany, occupied by the Western powers, and West Berlin (located in East Germany but according to a special arrangement under Western occupation as well). Shortly thereafter, the narrow connecting corridor between West Germany and West Berlin was completely closed by Russian troops. This blockade continued for more than a year and the West was forced to construct and maintain an intensive air lift. It was in this atmosphere that the dividing wall between West and East was dubbed "the iron curtain." In fact, both parts of Europe were hermetically sealed off from each other.

These developments influenced the position of the churches in the East and in the West. In the East they were confronted with a new regime that viewed religion as a reactionary phenomenon that at best it would tolerate as a symptom of the longing for a better social life but certainly would neither support nor assist it. Churches there, accustomed as they were earlier to a favorable political and social climate, were confronted with the task of defining their position in society anew. Would they be called to oppose the new Communist power, to be faced with all the difficult risks? Or would they have to opt for an attitude of patient, accepting silence, thereby retaining as much space as possible for its own existence and activity? Or—a third possibility—would their way have to be one of critical-loyal cooperation in the construction of a new, communist society? In the latter case there would have to be an equal accent on both aspects, loyalty and criticism, and to make it clear that they did not exclude but rather include each other.

The developments in Eastern Europe also presented a challenge to the churches in the West. Did one need to view the churches behind the "iron curtain" as churches in need, under persecution, reliant on "our" help in order to survive in a new, difficult situation? Or could (must) one see the new situation in the East as a positive challenge and opportunity for the churches there to take up a more independent position in society and no longer be (or desire to) be dependent on the support of the government? In that case, would the West perhaps have something to learn from the Eastern churches?

Public opinion in the West was dominated more and more by anti-communist feelings. The events from the beginning of 1948 in East Germany and Czechoslovakia gave a strong impetus to such feelings. In these circumstances, Barth's visit to Hungary, to the Hungarian Reformed Church, was a tense affair. How would it go with him in that nation, behind the "iron curtain"?

It was not in Barth's nature to avoid these tensions. Already, directly following the end of the war, he had let it be known that he did not view the growing influence of Russian Communism in Eastern Europe only as something negative. The church, including in Western Europe, would have to look for a positive relation to social democracy. We saw that Barth was involved with the drafting of the "Darmstadt Declaration" in August 1947, in which the drafters, speaking for the German church, noted as an error, that it had no ear for the message of Marxism, that could (should) have been a reminder to see the "affairs of the poor and the disabused" as the "business of Christianity" (see 11.8 and 13.2). So Barth accepted the invitation to visit a Hungary that had in the meantime come under Communist domination. He must have undertaken his trip with a great deal of interest and anticipation. Just as, conversely, in Hungary one must have been full of expectation of what Barth would have to say in a situation like that of the church in post-war Hungary.

These weeks were hectic weeks for Barth. He lectured in various places. He presided in some church services. And there were meetings in which he engaged questions that were set before him. He also met with the Hungarian state president. A Hungarian pastor, whose mother had roots in Basel, functioned as interpreter for all occasions. Following his return home, Barth wrote of his experiences in various Swiss church periodicals. The text of this reportage, along with the texts of Barth's sermon in Hungary, lectures held there, and responses to questions is included in a brochure, published under the title *Christliche Gemeinde im Wechsel der Staatsordnungen* [The Christian community in the midst of political change].

14.3 The Church and the Changing Structures in the State

Speaking to a number of youth gatherings, he called on them not to continue relying on a nostalgia for the past but to keep the new situation in mind, open to their own responsibility. There can no longer be a reversion to old traditions. But it is also not advisable to escape to the pleasures of sport, art, or technology. That could lead to the loss of spirit in which one easily falls prey to the slogans of charlatans and dictators (consider the Germans of the 1930s!). Even less must one seek salvation in "strong leaders" who lie ready with recipes for how things must proceed (Germany has also experienced something like that). Finally, Barth warned of escape into an attitude of skepticism and nihilism like "we in Western Europe" know at the moment, an attitude nurtured by a philosophy that proclaims the message that nothing else is to be expected from life than to sit out a blasé and boring time. Besides, this is perhaps the woodworm that was active eating away the beams of the earlier house; away with it! Consider your responsibility! And in that sense experience your freedom! Then you can honor what is valuable from the past, including that which is morally valuable. And it would not be good if there would no longer be a place in the future for a just state, freely configured, based on the freely expressed will of the people, one in which the gospel of Jesus Christ can be proclaimed and heard (that above all!).

The question of how the church must respond in view of structural changes of the state (concretely, the replacement of a democratic state on the Western model by a Communist state) was the theme of Barth's most important Hungarian speech, given in various places (Budapest, among others). In fact, this speech was a focus of his earlier publications on the relation of state and church (see 9.3. and 12.3) dating from 1938 and 1946.

Barth began to put the importance of the change in the structures of the state into perspective. Much more important than such changes, he said, is the change (the reversal) that had taken place in the death and resurrection of Jesus Christ the effect of which will become manifest in his return. In the light of that it obtains that the church sees the state, however structured, as an institution given by God, the God and Father of Jesus Christ, a beneficial institution that serves to defuse chaos and make human society possible in this time between Easter and the Second Coming. Thanks to the state there is a space—also for faith, and thus for the Christian church to fulfill its task. The Christian church in particular is thankfully conscious for that. The state is never perfect; there will always be reasons for the church to be critical. But the state also will never be purely bad, purely the work of the devil. And Christians will always know themselves called to a shared political responsibility, a responsibility that takes primary form in their intercessory prayers for those in governmental authority, but also in active cooperation, critically of course, where necessary, but also constructively.

Even as the structures of state change, that happens under the lordship of Christ. Christians will never unrestrainedly rejoice over such reversals but even less be extremely upset by them. At the same time, they will, for Christ's sake, be fully interested and involved in them. Where a system of state collapses and gives way to a new structure, they will see that as an indication of the imperfection, the injustice, of what humans bring about in this world, a reference, thus, to that kingdom—the kingdom of Christ—that will have no end. And at the same time, they will see the coming of a new system of state as a sign that God's care for all humans is present anew. Is the new system not a possibility for a new, perhaps better, arrangement of human society? For the church, co-responsible for the state in its old and its new configuration, a change in the system of state means an occasion for penitence and a new beginning, thus, by definition, also an occasion for a renewed study of the Word of God.

In any case, such a change may never tempt it to forget its own task. That could happen by clinging principally to the old order, or just as principally by opting for the new order. In both cases alien gods would be served. No, the church must proclaim God's Word and that Word is bound neither to the one system of state nor to the other. Of course, it can happen that the church, on the basis of God's Word, must say "no" in the one concrete case and "yes" in another concrete case. Anyway, it must stand against injustice and for justice whether or not that pleases the new administration. The Christian church cannot take a neutral position when it comes to such political questions. For the church, it will have to be about people by virtue of the Word of God. Hence, it can also arrive at a prophetic judgment of the earlier regime and of the consequences of the regime change. It will not be able to propose great policy agendas, but can surely plea for small, first steps in what it sees as a good direction, as advice to the new administration. But that too may not be interpreted as a principle choice for (or against) that new administration as such. The church is bound absolutely only to the Word of God. Thus, the Christian community can never become a political power, a political party (alongside or over and against other parties).

14.4 Concrete Questions

Thus far the main line of Barth's argument. It poses the question whether Barth did not talk here too easily about the "change in the structures of the state" in general. Does it make no difference whether the change presents itself as a matter of course or as a conscious, ideological power play? Did Barth not miss what had concretely played itself out in the Hungary of 1948 (as in other nations in the developing "Eastern bloc") with his general, perspectival remarks?

His argument offered the occasion for questions to be put to him at a special gathering in Budapest. They required him to express himself more concretely. If a Christian has to do with a state that does not maintain justice and that presents itself as a friend of the church but will sooner or later appear to be the enemy of the church based on its own world view, what then? Suppose that the state allows the church space but only provisionally and for tactical reasons, by which it is clear that that space will not exist on the long term, what must the attitude of the church then be?

Yes, said Barth, if the state appears as these questions presuppose, then the biblical word absolutely applies, "One must serve God rather than men" (Acts 5:29). But, he added, again by way of perspective, do not begin too quickly from the worst! Do not lose your composure or your humor! Consider: no state can escape being placed under the lordship of God. In any case, begin with respecting the state, even where it presents itself as threatening, and addressing what it is instituted to be about: the beneficent maintenance of order. In no case be driven by anxiety. Anxiety (of the East) is far too prevalent in the West.

Other questions related to membership in political parties, this of course against the background of the position, in the new system of state, of the Communist Party. Can a Christian be a member of any party, even if it is non-Christian? Barth answered that one can talk of a "Christian party" as little as one can talk about a "Christian state." In the matter of party membership, a Christian will adhere to the party in which he sees the greatest effort for a just state realized without thereby absolutizing the party. Moreover, a party that factually (secretly) presents as "church," thus, that absolutizes itself by longing for humans to take their place under party ideals even where it concerns their relation to God and their fellow human, cannot of course be acceptable to Christians, members of the church of Christ.

In Barth's judgement there can and may be no talk of state compulsion to a particular party membership; a state that would practice such compulsion would thereby foundationally undermine itself. In any case, citizens must not acknowledge such compulsion. They also should not become a member of a party solely to make their societal position secure. Naturally, Barth wanted to state as best he could that it is understandable when people here give in to great societal pressure or their own security needs. But to the question whether such is legitimate, he was still of the opinion that principally it can only be answered in the negative. Whoever still does so acts against his own conscience, he said. At the time, in Nazi Germany, many did that; they walked around as broken people. Such a thing is good for no one. Even less for the state that tries to maintain its authority in this way; in the long run that must fail. One need not be a Christian to see that. Every state, including the new Hungary, needs citizens who stand behind their own conviction.

14.5 Reportage to the Swiss Homefront

Barth offered an extremely positive image of his experiences in his reportage, published following his return to Switzerland. Seen politically, he wrote, things are not the best in Hungary, but my discussion partners were also of that opinion. It is not easy and not pleasant to have to live behind the iron curtain. "Curiously enough, however, I came across more calm and serene people there than in Basel." The nervousness that afflicts many in the West is absent there. "I came across much impressive humility and patience, alertness and bravery, a faith that holds out and a closeness to the eternal things such as one does not meet here."[1] In Hungary, one has had to put up with the lordship of Turks and subsequently of the Habsburgs. Perhaps that experience helps the Hungarians now to endure the contemporary situation without despair.

Barth specifically stated that he valued the leadership of the Reformed Church. This was Barth's second visit to Hungary. His first visit to that nation took place in the fall of 1936. Then he had stumbled on a very nationalistic mood, including in the Reformed church. There was still the dream of the Great-Hungarian kingdom of the past (dismantled following the First World War). Now, nothing is left of the nationalism of the past (that had even led Hungary to have chosen Hitler's Germany's side in the Second World War) at least among the leadership of the church and theology, he wrote in 1948. Indeed, Barth wrote, one has learned to accept that the pro-Hitler course during the Second World War has subsequently led to Russian domination and the engrafting into the Eastern Bloc as a judgment of God. One sees the matter realistically and has understood that it now comes down to the current system of state choosing its course.

Not that the Hungarian Reformed Church would have principally united with the system of state that now rules. The current Hungarian government has tried thus far to lure it with a variety of tempting invitations but without result. The church has expressly affirmed certain measures from the new state, primarily the radical reclassification of the ground (the land). But it retained the freedom to reject and criticize other measures, without thereby opting for a principle opposition. That it did not opt for the latter made for the reproach from its own circle of lukewarmness and cowardice, but that did not move the leadership of the church. One is too conscious of the faults of the Hungarian past that one would now defend oneself against the consequences. And one is too open to the social question and knows the weakness of the West on this point too well that one

---

1. Barth, "The Christian Community in the Midst of Political Change," 102.

would now permit a fervent, pro-Western anticommunism. The Hungarian church is on a good path, Barth wrote, with its avoidance of the choice between a pro- and anticommunist course. He also saw that manifest in that the Hungarian church was not mesmerized by the East-West conflict or by questions of justice and injustice in the current Hungarian government, but with the more ordinary question of what possibilities exist for the positive task of the church in the new situation; thus, with the question of possibilities for the new proclamation of the old Word of God.

14.6 The Critical Reaction of Emil Brunner

Had Barth evaluated the situation in Hungary with rose-colored glasses and the attitude of the Hungarian church too positively? On April 5 he was back in Basel but soon heard of new developments in Hungary; negotiations had begun on an agreement (concordat) of the church with the new Hungarian state and the leadership of the church (the synod) had expressed its principle agreement. That report provoked a critical letter from Barth, directed "to my friends in the Reformed Church of Hungary." He sent this letter on May 23.

In this letter to the church he brought up as an appeal what he had identified as the positive point in his reportage on the Hungarian church, that in the new situation it desired to be free, faithful to its essence as the church of Jesus Christ. Factual and juridical acknowledgment of the new authority of the state is obvious but, Barth wrote, it would not be good to go beyond that by declaring solidarity with the particular ideology of that new authority. In the practice of its freedom (to the fulfillment of its real task, the building up of its congregations, the strengthening of the faith), the church must not only not allow itself to be hindered, but neither to be helped by the state. Concessions to the state cannot always be avoided, but it may never be the case that the church allows itself to be "synchronized" and so to become again a state church. Finally, its position must not be determined by political or diplomatic considerations but by the gospel. Meanwhile, that must not mean that they withdraw from the political and social domain and henceforth concentrate only on "internal" matters. Indeed, it is precisely from the gospel that the church's task is also to be politically and socially alert. On this point, Barth stated that he was not completely satisfied. The synodical declaration of agreement with the new government in the matter of the position of the church in Hungary was for him several steps too far in the direction of resignation to what had been determined by the state.

This critical note from Barth may have been distributed as an open letter to Hungary, but Barth did not let it be known in Western Europe. He did not desire to throw oil on the Western fire of anticommunism. In the meantime, that anticommunism was expressed in many negative reactions to his reportage. At the end of May/beginning of June a public correspondence with his Swiss colleague (and former comrade) Emil Brunner began. Already earlier, in 1933/34, Barth and Brunner had come into serious conflict (on the idea of a connection point within human nature for the reception God's revelation, developed by Brunner and rejected by Barth; see 6.8); and now it happened again. Brunner made himself the spokesperson for "not a few, including some of your own theological associates"[2] who absolutely did not understand Barth's positive attitude toward the Communist regime behind the iron curtain.

Did Barth have no eye for the fact, so asked Brunner, that the Communist regime, just like the National Socialist regime, was totalitarian? Of course there is a difference; unlike "brown" totalitarianism, "red" totalitarianism claims to advocate for social justice. But still, can the Christian church ever say anything but a straightforward and passionate "no" to any sort of totalitarianism, "brown" or "red"? Does totalitarianism of whatever sort by definition not mean, injustice and inhumanity? Was not the real offensive, the essentially atheistic, or even anti-theistic nature of the National Socialist regime just as now too of the Communist regime, the total subjection of the human, of all of life, to the state?

Brunner could not get over the fact that Barth, who during the Hitler years had condemned every ecclesiastical collaboration with the regime, now suddenly would be the spokesperson for those in the church, living behind the iron curtain, who would condemn every form of resistance against the regime. Did this not come down with Barth to a plea for a retreat to the "inward," for a concentration on theology and the proclamation of the Word apart from any concern with questions of justice and injustice? In this connection he alluded to Barth's famous brochure *Theologische Existenz heute*, from 1933. There Barth had explicitly turned against the effort of the "German Christians" who would allow their policy and organization to be determined by political considerations of National Socialism. But, with hindsight, was what he had strongly opposed at the time so strong? Barth had claimed that for the church and theology it was about continuing with the particular task of theology and not engaging in politics. Yes, he really had called church and theology, called them back, to "theological existence today," to continue as ordinary "as though nothing

---

2. Barth, "The Christian Community in the Midst of Political Change," 106.

has happened" (see 6.6). Was that then an appeal to passive unconcern? Of course, Brunner readily acknowledged that later Barth had actively participated in the fight against National Socialism. But still, the original attitude of passive unconcern gave Brunner, in 1948, occasion to reflect. Had Barth now fallen back into the old passivity? Why did he not call the church today to resistance and confession against Communism as he himself had, later, in the case of National Socialism?

Would Brunner have set this open letter aside if he had been aware of Barth's critical reaction to the most recent events in Hungary cited above? Surely not. He would also have found that reaction much too soft and have missed an unambiguous rejection of the totalitarian Communist regime.

14.7 Again: Theological Existence Today

Barth did not leave Brunner's letter unanswered. He made his reflections public under the title that is a direct reminder of his 1933 brochure, "Theological Existence 'Today'" (see 6.6 and 6.7).

The church is only called to speak on political questions, he claimed, where necessary. That was certainly the case in the years following 1933. Hitler had admirers everywhere in Europe. Swiss authorities did everything to maintain correct, friendly relations with this powerful neighbor. In that situation, Barth wrote, I have committed myself to mobilize against the present danger of National Socialism. That danger was not seen by many at the time. But today the situation with Communism is completely different. Apart from a few Communists in Western Europe, public opinion does not view life under the Communist regime as attractive. The church needs add nothing to this from its side. It is not the church's vocation to say something theologically based that everyone can read daily in his newspaper. "No, when the Church witnesses it moves in fear and trembling, not with the stream but against it."[3] That totalitarianism is a bad thing is blatantly true. Saying that again here in the West is easy enough and it is not much help to the churches behind the iron curtain.

The church (that is: we, as the church in the West) can better be silent in this situation and speak again where necessary—and it then also costs us something. And then the church cannot suffice with delivering timeless, general truths (like "the objectionableness of 'totalitarianism'"[4]) but will have to say something essential. As an example, Barth identified the Barmen Declaration of 1934, specifically the first thesis on Jesus Christ as the one

---

3. Barth, "The Christian Community in the Midst of Political Change," 116.
4. Barth, "The Christian Community in the Midst of Political Change," 117.

Word of God alongside which "other happenings and powers, images and truths" cannot be acknowledged (see 1.2); a thesis, so he wrote to Brunner, "that alas was not much to your taste at the time."[5]

Finally, Barth could not allow Brunner's remark that he would have originally, in 1933, have appealed for a "passive resistance" toward the threat of National Socialism to remain unanswered. He described the idea as though he had been advocating such an attitude of passive unconcern at the time as "a tale without historical basis." He stipulated that if one in the church had followed his appeal to continue with theology and proclamation "as though nothing had happened," thus, absolutely ignoring the so-called revelation of God in Adolf Hitler, then just that would have meant a political fact of the first order.[6] So the church now, including the church in Hungary, has to mind its own task, bound not by principles but by the Lord. It must not allow itself to be confused by a law that is not the law of the gospel. Just then would it now be of significance to the Hungarian society.

14.8 Amsterdam, Summer 1948: Founding Assembly of the World Council of Churches

Barth's answer to Brunner was dated June 6, 1948. Shortly thereafter, the (first) general assembly of the World Council of Churches in Amsterdam (in which Brunner also participated) required his entire attention. It took place from August 22 to September 4 of that year with its theme: "Man's Despair and God's Design." He had already become involved, despite his reluctance, in the preparation for the assembly (see 12.5). Moreover, he had now been asked to offer the introductory lecture on the main theme. This lecture took place on August 23, at which Princess Juliana (who a few days after the assembly would be inaugurated queen of the Netherlands in the same Amsterdam) was present, along with Prince Bernhard, as guest of the assembly.

The theme gave the assembly every occasion to speak on current events. The "despair of man" would particularly be on the agenda of the sections (sub-commissions) that were busy with social questions and international politics. These two sections extensively discussed the relation between Communism and capitalism; this all the more lively because representatives from both systems and power blocs were present at the assembly. The Czech Hromádka was an articulate representative of the churches behind the iron curtain. American representatives Reinhold Niebuhr and John Foster Dulles (later American Secretary of State) spoke. Barth did not

---

5. Barth an Prof. Dr. Emil Brunner, 1948, in *OB*, 165.
6. Barth, "The Christian Community in the Midst of Political Change," 118.

take part in the social and political discussions; he was involved in the section on specific theological questions. That was primarily concerned with the nature of the church (after all, he had offered his own contribution to the preparatory material for that discussion, see 12.5). But in his lecture held at the beginning of the assembly on the main theme, social-political matters were of course also addressed.

Indirectly, in a typically Barthian manner. He began with the question whether the theme "Man's Despair and God's Plan" should not be reversed. Does it not say: "Seek first the kingdom of God and his righteousness" (Matthew 6:33)? If we begin with man's despair in all its aspects we never get to God's design. Then we remain caught in care and anxiety, or we seek comfort in illusions. Then we orient ourselves to a number of problems and try to reach solutions while we forget that we ourselves are part of the problem. Our situation, the nature of our "despair," becomes genuinely visible in the light of God's design. In this context, we must consider that God's design is really God's business, his kingdom that after all, has already been established in Jesus Christ. Above all, let us not think that "God's design" would coincide with the churches and what the churches do in the world, proclamation, Christianizing, promoting peace and justice. God's design is determinatively something other than a Christian Marshall Plan!

If we view the church as if it were a sort of continuation of the incarnation of God's Word (which, the gospel says, has happened in Jesus Christ himself), then it indeed appears as if the lordship of Jesus Christ, who sits on God's right hand, thus God's own providential rule, would have transitioned in the direction of Christianity. But do we really think that God no longer takes his own business to heart? Then it is likely that we, seeing "Man's Despair" become nervous like Peter when he saw the wind and the waves and threatened to drown.

But no, the world and the church are not our care. Barth called the notion as if the human would have the task to bear the entire vault of the heavens on his shoulders like the giant Atlas of ancient mythology "fearful, godless, ridiculous." It comes down to jointly placing our trust in God who will perform his work.

From this perspective he closed with a review of the various subjects that were on the assembly's agenda. On church unity we then do not cling tightly to our ecumenical ideals but are oriented to him who alone has the power to call his holy catholic church together. On the church's task of preaching and mission we then do not think that we ourselves could/must bring the world's population to faith but that we consider that that is God's own work and that besides, all in all it applies to our all fellow humans that Jesus Christ has also died and raised for them. And on the social and international "Man's Despair" we then do not jump on a number of our own "Christian" undertakings but we give ourselves over to God alone who himself brings about his Kingdom of justice and peace so that we as church have nothing other to do than to proclaim and to point to that Kingdom.

It was here that Barth briefly went into the questions that had come up already in his visit to Hungary and following, in his correspondence with Brunner. In our involvement with social and political questions we must, he said, allow ourselves to be determined by the gospel and not by particular Christian principles. It had occurred to him that the preparatory material was completely silent on current questions of ownership, property, capital, etc., while this theme is emphasized in the New Testament where the choice is set before us between "God and mammon" (money). This alternative is held before us from Eastern Europe by the synod of the Orthodox Church in Moscow or their political advisors, whereby we non-communists are accused of anti-democratic inclinations. Is there not something to that? "I fear that we will not be able to give a worse, but also not better, reply to Communism, so viewed, than most of our Western contemporaries." However that may be, for us it must be in our prophetic vocation concerning society and politics about God's kingdom and not about "a future political state to be set up with Christian assistance, whether of liberal or authoritarian character."[7]

It remains a question whether Barth saw his considerations concerning the main theme later in the results of the assembly. Still, his ultimate impressions of "Amsterdam" were not negative. Later, in an autobiographical look back, he wrote that he had experienced the assembly not only as interesting but as important. He specifically thought of his involvement in the discussions on "the church": it was good to sit at table with representatives from other traditions and confessions, not to formulate new dogma or to make compromises but to obtain clarity on differences of understanding within Christianity. Among other things, he identified as encouraging elements the presence of the "young churches" from the "third world" and the unity whereby the assembly had come to decision despite clear differences of understanding. That the assembly had not allowed itself to be tempted to partisan choice in the East-West conflict he also saw as a positive experience. In February 1949, speaking in Switzerland (Thun, Bern; later in Geneva) on "The Church Between East and West" he referred to it again with agreement thereby mentioning how much, because of that, the "Amsterdam Church Conference" had come under criticism in the West.

---

7. Barth, "No Christian Marshall Plan," 1332.

14.9 The Church between East and West

In the lecture just noted, Barth again elaborated foundationally, more broadly than in his letter to Brunner, on considerations that had led him to his position on the East-West conflict. He held the lecture on invitation of the ecclesiastical administration of the Bern Region that had put the matter on the agenda because the uproar in Switzerland on the occasion of his report on Hungary would not recede.

The starting point of his considerations was that the relation between the East and the West was a conflict of power. Russia and the United States of America both in a certain way (adult) children of old Europe stand over and against each other. Both are allied with a number of smaller, friendly satellite states; both are out to dominate old Europe. And on both sides of the dividing line (the "iron curtain") one claims to advocate for freedom and peace, although it is not completely clear what one understands as "freedom" and "peace" on either side. It is clear that they are anxious about each other. There is the feeling of being threatened by the other.

What must the Christian attitude now be in view of this power conflict? Barth advanced three things. First, do not be anxious for Christ rules; his promise remains valid. Secondly, do not participate; we can only warn of the inclination of allowing this conflict to result in a third world war (at least here, said Barth, I hope not to thwart Swiss foreign policy!). Third, stay sober, do not choose between East and West; the Christian church must go a third way, its own way.

But, said Barth, there is more at issue than a power conflict. The opposition between East and West is also one of principle against principle, of ideology against ideology. Reproaches, accusations echo again and again. The West says: you in the East hold a mistaken image of the human—the human is only defined economically, by one's material conditions. You think you can solve everything through the dictatorial introduction of a socialist order of society. In it the individual is only "free" to produce and consume. He is nothing more than a cog in a machine, the mass man. You in the East hold a false belief, namely a belief in which God is replaced by the demon of "social progress." Inhuman!

But the East tosses the ball back: your so-called spiritual, moral image of the human is a masquerade. Life for you in essence equally turns on production and consumption. In fact, with you everything is defined by money. Humans end up under the wheels of the carriage on which capital sits enthroned as divine. Just so the mass human is really created! Your democracy is purely formal. It appears as though there are independent political parties but in reality with you the big banks pull all the strings.

As to your faith, sand is being thrown in your eyes; you speak of "God" and "heaven" to keep real life out of view and to make sure that everything remains as it was. That is really inhuman!

Must the church, in view of these ideological opponents choose sides? That is what in the West is expected of us as the (western) church at the moment. The church must be pro-western. In the East it is just the converse; there the church is expected to opt for the Eastern way of thinking and acting. We in the West, observe closely whether the church there, in Prague and Budapest, offers sufficient resistance to that expectation, that it not collaborate. While it is now just the question, Barth said, whether we ourselves, in the West, do not end up collaborating, namely where we allow ourselves to be drawn into a pro-western anti-communism. In any case, we must be conscious that the western standpoint is not simply the Christian standpoint (just like the eastern is not). For the Christian church it comes down to refusing to choose sides. Here, too, it has to go a third way, namely its own way.

14.10 "Now No Choice of Parties!"

This time as well, as in his correspondence with Brunner, Barth could not avoid going into the question of how his plea, now in the conflict between East and West, to forgo choosing sides, as Christians or church, was consistent with his plea ten years previously for a church to do just that, to choose sides. In his answer, Barth underscored the difference between the situation of the past and the present. Then it was a choice for or against National Socialism, "a mixture of madness and crime in which there was no trace of reason," one that, note well, presented itself as a sort of pseudo-Christianity and had, moreover, adherents within the church itself.[8] There existed everywhere in Europe a remarkable inclination to adapt to this phenomenon and with an appeal to Christian love to disqualify all clear protests against it as fanaticism. The danger and reprehensibility of National Socialism was simply not seen through by many, certainly not originally. Thus it was necessary then, and it also cost something, to say "no" against it (what happily also happened, by or at least from the church). But, Barth said, what is at issue today in the East, in the Soviet Union and behind the iron curtain, cannot simply be put in the same category as the events in Hitler's Germany. Certainly, it is about a questionable totalitarianism there. But in any case, today's Communism cannot be lumped together with National Socialism of the past.

8. Barth, "The Church between East and West," 136.

First, Communism is not only madness and error; it attempts to offer a solution to the social question. Our Western "no" to it would only be justified when we ourselves would as energetically try to answer that question. Second, differently than National Socialism, Communism does not drape itself in Christian dress and does not replace the true Christ with a national Jesus; it is roundly godless. To that the church can only answer with a positive witness in the matter of the gospel. It must thereby consider that that is not the same as the world view or morality of the West and may not be confused with an appeal to an inward or heavenly faith. That it would thus be about such in the Christian faith is alas the impression that one has received of Orthodox, Roman Catholics and Protestants together in the Communist East. And that is also precisely that against which one has so fiercely resisted. Do we really have the right to call our Western society "Christian"? Do we ourselves stand in the true, Christian faith? The church, including that of the West, must not appeal to a crusade against the "godless" East, but proclaim the Word of the Cross in the East and the West and above all be newly edified by the Word itself.

Thus it remained Barth's position; differently than in the 1930s, when the church, confessing (Barmen, 1934) against National Socialism, had to choose sides, the church today would in the East -West conflict (also ideological) have to expressly refrain from choosing sides. The true Christian confession must today consist in just this refusal to choose sides. Whereby Barth underscored that that does not mean that the church would no longer interest itself in politics and would no longer be conscious of its responsibility for the entirety of society. Only, society and politics today is not so much about battle as about building.

It is striking to see how one in East and West claims to advocate for freedom, justice, and peace. The church can only join. It then comes down to making good distinctions. In the East one commits to a "justice" whereby freedom appears to be compromised. And in the West one advocates a "freedom" that does not appear to comport with justice. And the "peace" for which one constantly claims to advocate is in fact, on both sides of the iron curtain, filled with threats of war. The church has its own task to fulfill here. It proclaims God's righteousness which does not remove human freedom but founds it. It proclaims God's freedom (the freedom of his grace!), whereby human justice is not superfluous exertion but is pressingly required. It proclaims God's peace that includes human reason and cares that we not stumble by virtue of any number of quarrels, that thus cares also for peace among humans.

So understood, the church can only take a position between West and East. Here in the West it will then advocate for that which threatens to be forgotten, as it (hopefully) advocates in the East for what threatens to be missed there. So, as a free church, it will appeal for true humanity in the service of East and West. And so it shall have something of Israel of which the prophet Isaiah declared that it would stand as a third alongside (between) the great powers of Isaiah's time, Egypt and Assyria, as a blessing for the whole world: "The LORD of hosts has blessed: Blessed is Egypt, my people, and Assyria, work of my hands, and Israel, my heritage." (Isaiah 19:25).

15

Does Life Stand under God's Leading? The Doctrine of Providence

15.1 *Church Dogmatics* Continued

AT THE SAME TIME that Barth was so deeply involved with current tensions between East and West, he also continued his work on the *Church Dogmatics*—his main task. What he wrote was always the result of what he had said in his lectures. Because he did not follow well-worn paths, the lectures demanded thorough preparation.

He certainly followed tradition as much as possible in the choice of his themes and the order of their treatment. After having treated the doctrine of creation following the doctrine of God, he came to the doctrine of providence, the consideration of the question whether and how divine leading of life and society, of human life and world events, may also be believed. Traditionally, this theme is treated in connection with creation. The belief that the world owes its existence to God who has called it into being leads by itself, after all, to the question of the nature of the relation between this Creator and his creation following the creation. Has the Creator left the creation to its fate or does He continue to be involved? The tradition begins from the latter. Barth followed this tradition of a continuing relation between Creator and creature.

We have seen earlier that Barth originally had no intention of developing a "new" theology. He had initially characterized his undertaking as really nothing more than adding a "footnote" *next to* what already existed theologically. Of course, as a "correcting" footnote. But the real aim was attending that theological reflection is in service of proclamation. And proclamation is about the Word of God itself coming to articulation in and through human words. That means that theology must take the living reality of God seriously as unique, a reality revealing himself to us.

But only that? Now yes, Barth had himself experienced that a great deal of existing theology, primarily in its effort to modernize (in service of the "modern man"), came up short in precisely this respect. Theology often disappears into scientific reflection on religion, on human piety. There exists an intersection with human logic and philosophy in order to be able to present the truths of faith as self-evident insights. With that, theology appears completely inadequate to its orientation to the task of proclamation. In that respect the theological task must be corrected (see 3.3, 3.4, and 4.1).

That looks like a small matter, but it is not. As professor, Barth had quickly perceived that his "footnote" could not leave theology substantially untouched. In fact, the entire traditional content of the Christian faith must be reconsidered. So, following an earlier attempted start, the project "Church Dogmatics" had begun. In that context, Barth would also have to go his own way in many respects in considering belief in God's providence.

15.2 The "Christological Thread" of Belief in Providence

Barth had begun his lectures on the doctrine of providence in the summer of 1948. A year later he could conclude his treatment and the manuscript for a new part of the *Church Dogmatics* was ready, *CD* III/3. The book appeared in the summer of 1950. In the preface Barth again indicated what was new in his approach. Taking seriously the living reality of God as a reality who reveals himself to us concretely meant for Barth starting from the appearance of Jesus Christ as the revelation of God. He also intended to do that by considering God's providence. It was his real intention, so he wrote, "to hold fast at all costs and at every point to the Christological thread."[1] Besides, it was precisely the "Christological thread" that required him to remain faithful to the traditional idea of a "providence" of God in respect of his creation.

How does the human come to believe that life is not an arbitrary play of chance in which everything is determined by "blind chance" but stands under divine guidance? In any case, one found that self-evident in the theology of the foregoing centuries. One found that this can be believed much more easily than, for example, such dogmas as that of God's tri-unity or the divinity of Christ. One was happy to point out that one need not be a Christian to conceive of a good God who exists and cares for everyone and everything in a "fatherly" way; after all, every right-minded person already comes to that thought! Right-thinking person? Barth recalls that even Hitler gladly appealed to "the Providence" in explanation of his successes or of the failures of attacks against him.

1. Barth, *CD*, III/3, xi.

Such a "belief in providence," said Barth, is factually a question of self-projected world views, a philosophy of history. It does not have a real basis. It is no wonder that just in our time it cannot cope with the crisis, with the shocks of life (consider the terrors of the war!). And that the earlier "self-evident" belief of a "divine guidance" in life has mostly disappeared.

But if a Christian, despite everything, still believes in God's providence, that does have a basis. The basis is the proclamation that God in Jesus Christ has chosen sides for the human and the world; he has entered his covenant with them. We saw how Barth had argued that belief in God the Creator must be inferred from belief in Jesus Christ. The creation exists with the history of the covenant of God with the human in Christ in view; it is the space in which this covenant history takes place. Barth had summarized that insight in the thesis: the creation is the "outward ground of the covenant" (as conversely the covenant is the "inner ground of the creation," see 11.11). Barth now continues this train of thought. Not only does a covenant history exist (or: salvation history), a general history of humanity and the world, a history of creation, also exists. Covenant history is part of that. But one should thereby maintain that covenant history is what really matters. General world events exist with covenant history *in view*, it makes that covenant history possible. For that, the God of the covenant also allows general events to happen. Just as the covenant from the beginning had its outward ground in the creation, so covenant history has its outward ground in the history of creation. There is a relationship of creation history to covenant history thanks to God's faithfulness, that here can be called "providence."

Thus, believing in that is not simply a question of worldview, of philosophy of history, or of experience, it is truly an expression of Christian faith, or better, included in Christian faith as such. At the outset of the Reformation this was, differently than later, a living idea. Barth referred to the Heidelberg Catechism, to the passage in it on the belief "in God the Father, the Almighty, Creator of heaven and earth." We heard how in his guest lectures in Bonn in the summer of 1947 he had positively evaluated the way in which it is worded, that the Creator is none other than the Father of Jesus Christ, and he therefore could unreservedly acclaim the elaboration given there concerning God's providence (see 12.8). Barth also cites the same Catechism now, extensively, as one of the few theological texts in and since the sixteenth century in which he sees the Christological content of providential faith respected.

15.3 The King of Israel is the King of the World

How must we think of the substance of God's providence? Older, orthodox theology here uses three complementary concepts: God cares for his creation by *sustaining, accompanying* and *governing* it. Barth takes over these concepts. Not, of course, without filling them out in his own way. It must not be imagined, he said, that this is said about an arbitrary "Highest Essence" but about the God and Father of Jesus Christ.

That God "sustains" means that he guarantees that the creature can continue, held in position against all threats. Barth notes that that means that the power by which God holds the creature in position is the power of his mercy having appeared in Jesus Christ. That must and will come into its own as the creature (the human) participates in it. But if that were to happen, then the creature must exist, be sustained in his existence. Sustenance thus may be believed as presupposition and consequence of belief that God's mercy extends to the creature. The creature is *sustained* in his existence in order that it also can be *preserved* in Christ. Note well: this "sustenance," "holding in position," does not mean that the creature is guaranteed endless continuation. Here Barth takes up what he had argued in the foregoing part of his dogmatics: that the human lives as creature within the limits of birth and death (see 13.6). That must also be considered in the doctrine of providence. God's sustenance does not erase the creaturely limit of death. It concerns the human in one's finitude. The promise that he may participate in the kingdom and salvation of Christ obtains for this human: "Praise the LORD, for he is good—his faithfulness endures forever" (Psalm 136).

In order to properly understand this "sustaining" work of God, the fact that God "accompanies" his creature must be considered at the same time. That means that God leaves space for the freedom and peculiar activity of the creature. God's lordship does not restrict the freedom of the creature; it creates it. Here too Barth adds his own footnote: this partnership between God and the creature comes into view where one considers that the creation does not stand apart from the covenant. The tradition has too often conceived "God" as nothing other than "Highest Essence." Thereby Reformed orthodoxy particularly inadvertently came thus to the idea as if God's dominance were sovereign arbitrariness. The obedience of faith then all too soon becomes slavish subjection. But that the God of providence is the God and Father of Jesus Christ implies that his power is at its core the power of his grace and as such the power in general history. Thus, it is power that does not slash and burn, but—indeed accompanies, namely as the power of God's Word and Spirit. Here with providence in mind,

"Immanuel," "God with us," already applies. That does not stand apart from the great "Immanuel," realized in Christ.

And that God "sustains" and "accompanies" his creatures also implies what the Bible calls God's "kingship": that he "governs" his creatures. He directs and orders them toward the goal he has determined for his creatures. Thus, too, he directs and orders the entirety of world events, just as he does the life of his creatures, so that it responds to his plan. That is to say, it ultimately serves the salvation of his creatures and thereby his own honor. The tradition has seen that but left unclear the ground on which that could be said. Barth now advances what he had previously seen as underexposed: the King of the world is none other than the King of Israel, thus, the God of the covenant. It again applies that divine power is the power of God's grace and mercy. That also asserts itself in general world events. World history does not stand apart from salvation history. So God's "plan" and "goal" are seen in relief. We do not simply have a general concept of God in mind when we think of the meaning of world events; we see a shape, a face: *this* God.

15.4 The Jews as Sign

We learn to believe that world events are oriented toward a goal, have meaning and coherence, from the covenant and salvation history witnessed in the Bible. It comes in view from nowhere else, that is, than from Christ. Still, in Barth's opinion, that does not exclude the fact that in this general world history particular matters are to be noted that for unprejudiced observers can also point in this direction. One of those matters is the (post-biblical) history of the Jews. It is said of the doctor of the Prussian king, Frederick the Great, that to the question from the king whether there could be a proof for the existence of God (or of God's rule), he answered: "The Jews, Sire!" Barth would not go so far. One can ordinarily view the history of the Jewish people as one of the many events in world history. Still, whoever sees this clearly has something to consider. Powerful peoples and nations of the past have long since disappeared. How is it possible that just this people, despite persecution and oppression, has always existed and is still there?

Barth had earlier given an account of the separate meaning of the Jewish people. We saw that in his dogmatic volume on the doctrine of election (*CD* II/2), published in 1942, thus during the persecution of the Jews by National Socialism, he had given thought to Israel as the elect people of God; in that context the relation between Israel and the church was of course discussed. We also saw that at the same time, lectures expounding Paul's Letter to the Romans showed how, differently than in his earlier publications on this letter, the relation between Jews and Christians is a central theme—and not only in chapters 9–11 (see 10.13).

He had also continued to work on this topic following the war. That the Jewish people had survived the terrors of the Second World War and had even begun to establish their own political independence in Palestine (the state of Israel!) set him thinking further. On December 13, 1949 he held an address for Swiss radio on "the Jewish Problem and the Christian Answer." He claimed that to this "question" there is not yet done justice when the Jews are approached from the "general commandment" of neighbor love that "naturally" also applies to the Jews. Whoever rejects anti-Semitism as a barbaric affront of "our [Christian] culture" is not wrong, but nonetheless disposes of the matter too easily.[2]

One must begin, said Barth, by realizing how surprising the continued existence of the Jews is. Would the Bible be right then with its declaration that just this people has always been the chosen people of God despite its apparent repeated unfaithfulness to God? Would what we hear there be true, that this God in the person and death of the one Jew, Jesus, has radically settled with the unfaithfulness of his people so to make a new start with this people and with all of humanity? Would the continued existence of the Jews have to do with that?

This continued existence of the Jews is all the more surprising for whoever realizes that it is really impossible to indicate precisely who the "Jews" are. Despite all the Nazi propaganda, they do not form a separate race; there can be no talk of a specific "Jewish race." They also do not have their own common language; biblical Hebrew has long since become a theological learned tongue and the "Hebrew" of the contemporary state of Israel is only an artificial language, a sort of Esperanto. A specific Jewish culture has not developed over the centuries. There is no common religion for all Jews; only a small portion of Jews belong to a (orthodox or liberal) synagogue, and a Jew can also be a pantheist, atheist, skeptic, or even Christian. And it is even less the case that there is (since the diaspora following the fall of Jerusalem in 70) a common Jewish "national history." In short, it cannot even be said that the Jews would be a "people." In any case, they are something totally different than all other peoples. This people appears to have its peculiarity in that it has nothing at all of its own. Earlier it did indeed have that, when it existed as a people by virtue of its election by God. That was then its particularity. But it had itself rejected that when it allowed the Jew born in its midst to die on the cross before the gates of Jerusalem. And still this people lives by virtue of God's continuing

---

2. Barth, "The Jewish Problem and the Christian Answer," 195.

election and mercy; as a shadow form but under the continuing promise: they, the Jews, will once again really become a people.[3]

Once this is seen then, according to Barth, it is clear from whence anti-Semitism exists. The Jews do not have a special "unpleasant characteristic."[4] They are not worse or less acceptable than others. But to us others all our faults and our lack of faith are held up in their existence as in a mirror. After all, it is God's grace that brings to light that the human does not deserve it. That appears in particular with the Jews, but it applies to us all. And we do not hear that gladly. That is why there is a continuing hatred of the Jews; we prefer to shatter the mirror that displays our own faults to us. And with that it appears that the continued existence of the Jews, living so unrooted and in the shadows, but still living, under God's grace, shows us that the grace of God is not simply for all. In the first instance, God's election appears to pass us by and to concern another; it concerns us only via that other. Again: we do not hear that gladly. That we share in salvation in and through Jesus we know well; only we must thereby realize the Jewish nature of Jesus. Then it becomes clear to us that he regards us in the lost and yet continuing existence of the Jewish people. That insults our honor; we reject that. Thus, we are already in fact on the way to becoming anti-Semitic (however much we as "cultured people" officially turn up our nose at anti-Semitism).

What does this mean now for our attitude toward the Jews? Barth claimed that what divides us Christians from the Jews is the same as that which connects us with them, the one Jew, the crucified. The Jews, proud as they are, do not acknowledge him as the fulfillment of Israel's promise; they do not want to be dependent on God's grace. But Christians coming from paganism also cannot acknowledge this one Jew, Jesus, if they do not know themselves in utmost solidarity with the Jews. We recognize in their pride our own feelings and inclinations and we know him who has already overcome all divisions between humans, including between Jews and non-Jews. Thus, we cannot but be connected at heart with the Jews.

These are the considerations that Barth advanced in his radio address. He also included them in his doctrine of providence. As we saw, he speaks of the continued existence of the Jews here as one of the noteworthy matters that are a sign for those who are open to it that God in his providence rules the world and history. Indeed, one must be open to see it, in order to note it as such. We are given a glimpse of what is unique to the Jews only from the Old and New Testaments. But whoever has heard this can no longer keep the enigma of Jewish identity at arm's length. He discovers in it the

---

3. Barth, "The Jewish Problem and the Christian Answer," 197.
4. Barth, "The Jewish Problem and the Christian Answer," 198.

confirmation of his belief in God's providence and rule, namely, that the King of *Israel* is the King of the world.

15.5 Reactions. Questions

Barth's vision of the Jewish people elaborated here is a continuation of what he had put forward in the context of his doctrine of election (*CD* II/2). Here again, we are struck by his conception that Israel (the Jewish people), in its rejection of God's grace and election at the decisive moment represents the human, all humanity. And again, like there we hear him argue that nonetheless God's electing grace of specifically this people is not undone and that now everyone, all peoples, are reliant on it, on God's continuing faithfulness. Still, Barth's thought continues to be determined by what he has heard in Paul's Letter to the Romans, chapters 9–11 (although that is not discussed in detail any more here). According to Barth, there can be no talk of playing off the position of "the others" (the non-Jews) vis-à-vis that of the Jews.

But differently than before (that also coheres with his theme, the doctrine of providence) he now explicitly offers an account of the *history* of the Jews, the way that they *have concretely continued to exist* in the centuries following the destruction of Jerusalem in 70 to the present. More sharply than before (in 1942, the year of the publication of his doctrine of election) he is deeply touched by the real problematic of Jewish existence. Already earlier, he had shown that he was conscious of the reality of what one calls the "holocaust," the Jewish persecution, with as its aim the total elimination of the Jews by the Nazis (see 11.3). That also comes through now in his dogmatics. He talks about anti-Semitism, not just as an ideology but as a fact, puzzling in the persistence with which it has manifest itself through the centuries up to the most recent time. He sees his theological vision of Israel as standing under God's judgment as now confirmed by what he signals as the uprooted, shadowy existence of the Jews following their diaspora. Just as he sees his insight confirmed that Israel has not fallen from God's electing grace despite its unfaithfulness, by the fact that the Jews continue to exist, even following the holocaust ("the worst catastrophe in their history").

In the meantime, here Jewish existence, Jewish life is determinatively viewed through a theological lens. Barth's starting point means that he must characterize it as "shadowy." Did he go too far? Questions, reactions, specifically to his radio address, came primarily from the Jewish side. Is it to be maintained that the Jews would not be (in the general meaning of the term) a genuine "people?" A Jewish "race" may not exist but is there still not talk of a blood relation, a family relationship? Is Hebrew as a common heritage not more important for Jewish identity than Barth presupposes? So that it is not surprising that in the formation of the state of Israel one reverted to Hebrew in a modern form? Has a Jewish culture really not developed nor been maintained? No Jewish way of life in that which has been handed on from the old holy writings? No notion of a common history, of a common historical origin? Despite his foundational idea that God's electing grace continues to hold for Israel, Barth begins from the fact that an entirely new existence of the Jews has begun following the fall of Jerusalem in 70; but must not a continuing line, an historic continuity, also according to Jewish understanding, be taken into account? Finally, it is true that there is not one religion confessed by all Jews, but why would that be required to be able to talk of a "people"?

In his dogmatics, Barth does not speak *with*, but *about* the Jews. They are not his discussion partners but an object of his perspective (that could not be otherwise in a dogmatics). His radio address of December 13, 1949 offered an occasion for a meeting with a Jewish youth group in Basel. Twice, in January and March 1950, a sort of "religious discussion" took place in a packed hall. But it was a difficult discussion, as Barth himself would also recall later. It continued the repetition of positions already taken. Barth would not, even later, engage in a real discussion with Jewish thinkers, with Jewish thought. What if he had? We can ask ourselves whether that would have at least given his discussion "of" "the Jews" a different tone.

Objections brought against Barth's view of the Jews rather often concern his analysis of anti-Semitism. He also saw that in a theological light, namely as in its ineradicable nature as equally enigmatic as the Jews in their continued existence. He posited that a connection exists between the two; that Jewish existence in itself continues to evoke anti-Semitism. Therewith he offers (against his own intention?) an explanation of anti-Semitism (he himself speaks of a "sense in the great nonsense" of anti-Semitism). Does that not come horribly close to a justification? That indeed was not Barth's intention. On the contrary, he would make clear how objectionable anti-Semitism is. But must then not a great reserve be exercised in the search for an explanation? Barth seems to posit that where there are Jews, there anti-Semitism will (must!) by definition always emerge. Can that be said?

The search for phenomena in reality that confirm that God governs world history is a perilous undertaking. Indeed, Barth himself is aware of that. On the other hand, his reference, in this connection, to the enigma of the continued existence of the Jewish people is striking. The Jews have indeed lived through a continual history (!) of persecution and oppression; that just they are still recognizably present in the world community is thus far from self-evident. Whoever, by virtue of the person of Christ, believes

God's provident rule of world events is aware that this is not self-evident. That Barth has attended to that contributed in the churches, specifically in Germany, to a greater positive openness to the presence of the Jews.

15.6 The Reality of Evil

There are matters in world events to be noted that for those who as Christians believe in God's providence can support this belief; Barth was convinced of that. But are there not also matters that attack that belief or even undermine it? How must we think about evil in the world? How can belief in God's providence stand up against, for example, the terrors of the Second World War?

In post-war Germany, one exhausted oneself, specifically in Protestant circles, in emphasizing that the unheard-of had occurred, particularly in and around Germany, in the past few years. "Demons" and their "tempting power," with which one had been confronted in Germany during the Nazi rule were talked about with a certain passion and eagerness. We saw earlier that during his first post-war visit to Germany, in the summer of 1945, Barth had heard a prominent German theologian say, "we have looked the demons in the eye" (see 11.8). That way of speaking had irritated him; he had characterized it as a lack of sobriety. On one occasion, he had not been able to resist critically asking his discussion partners, "Why do you keep talking only about demons? Why don't you say outright that you were political fools?"[5]

Would Barth then minimize the "demonic," the reality of evil? Of course not. The question of how that reality relates to belief in God the Father of Jesus Christ already kept him busy in 1945. In his dogmatic volume on creation that appeared that year, this question was already discussed. We have seen (11.11) that Barth elaborated his doctrine of creation in the form of an exegesis of the biblical creation narratives, Genesis 1 and 2. In them he found expressed what lay at his heart: that the creation exists for the sake of the covenant (of God with the human in Israel, in Christ), thus is oriented to the covenant. In that context he had also stumbled on that remarkable second verse of Genesis 1, "the earth was a formless void and darkness covered the face of the deep." That is said following the statement, "In the beginning God created the heavens and the earth." The "void" and the "formless" and the dark "deep," typifying chaos par excellence, have not been viewed by the biblical writer, so Barth argued, as a stage preceding God's action. But also not as a first (provisional) result of it. For what follows in Genesis 1 says that

5. Quoted in Busch, *Karl Barth*, 328.

the void and darkness are *overcome* by God's action. After all, it is said of God's creative act there (in verse 3) that it brings *light* and where the light shines the darkness disappears. The condition of chaos thus is here seen exclusively as *that which God in his creative work has passed by*; as that which God the Creator has not willed from the beginning, thus as rejected by God. It is only as such, that the condition of chaos "exists." It "exists" as the negative converse of the real world created by God. Already in 1945, Barth saw evil represented in this chaos/non-world portrayed in Genesis 1:2; thus, as what "is" because it really may *not* exist for God's sake. This chaotic world, Barth said, can only exist "behind God's back." But let the human not think that he easily escapes it! The human can live passing by God's word and reality and cling to what God as Creator has rejected. Where that happens— and it happens over and again!—the deep, the darkness, the "formless void" of Genesis 1:2 is an acute ever-threatening danger; the story of the flood (Genesis 6-8) metaphorically shows that. Then it appears that the world in itself, apart from God's gracious creative will, is absolutely not secured from degeneration into chaos. But thanks be to God's gracious creative will it is secured. God will not allow a definitive demonization, chaotization of the world. He remains faithful to his creative will in that in Christ he takes the ultimate destruction on himself. "The old is past, the new has come," says 2 Corinthians 5:17, referring to the death and resurrection of Christ. Barth read that as confirmation of what in essence was already intended in Genesis 1:2.

Barth must have had the "demonic" reality of the Second World War in view here. The dogmatic volume on creation (*CD* III/1) that included these views appeared in 1945. His "forward" included in this part is dated October 1945. This was precisely the time that he was confronted in Germany with the discussion that flared up on "the demons" of which someone said that one "has looked them in the eye" in the war years. He must have been all the more motivated to give a theological account of the reality of the "demonic," the chaotic, evil in the world, albeit that he did so at that time still only in passing.

In the part of the dogmatics we discuss here, *CD* III/3, on providence, Barth went back to this issue, expressly and in detail. Here he calls evil, the "demonic," using a not easily translatable German word, the *Nichtige*. That is to say, that which certainly "exists"—and decidedly not as something insignificant—but has not part in genuine existence as intended by God the Creator. It certainly exists but without having a right to exist or a future of existing. We can infer that that is so, said Barth, from the coming of Jesus Christ. From ourselves we could at best note that alongside its light side life has a shadow side, but with that the real "*Nichtige*" is still not understood.

Just where Jesus appeared and God's saving intentions have thereby been definitively made clear, real evil, the demonic, has also been lured out of its tent. After all, it is precisely in conflict with these saving intentions and wants to block them. However, in Jesus God himself, by making himself in solidarity with the human, has entered the conflict and has in principle defeated it. Afterwards, because that has happened, we humans discover the reality of real evil as that which has brought Jesus Christ to the cross and what he has overcome on the cross. And from just that we get eyes to see what words like "devil" and "hell" mean. Moreover, what the deepest "sin" is, turning away from God's grace and command, the presumption to will to be our own boss. Because it is said of us that our sin is forgiven and borne away we learn to see that we are indeed sinners and with that given over to ourselves, given up to the "Nichtige." However, it must also be considered that the "Nichtige" does not reside exclusively in human sin. It is also a power to which we are subjected. It also manifests itself where created existence is threatened, where it is confronted with death-as-the-enemy. Jesus Christ has come to unmask and defeat the "Nichtige" including in this guise. He is the Savior, also in this inclusive sense. The gospel stories of Jesus' healing miracles are witness to this.

Evil exists with that (and because) God does not will it—as he has made clear in Jesus Christ. In him God has begun the battle against it and in principle already overcome it. So, in this sense, Barth claimed, it can be said that this evil also happens under God's providence. He is also Lord over that. That he has condemned evil by his mercy that appeared in Jesus Christ means that he decides where and how, and how far it may obtain and still serve his work. This, up to the moment in which it will be generally manifest what in essence already obtains: that it is set aside and overcome. We must, so Barth argued in closing, not make too much of the "demons":

> It has never been good for anyone . . . to look too frequently or lengthily or seriously, or systematically at demons . . . It does not make the slightest impression on the demons if we do so, and there is imminent danger that in so doing we ourselves might become just a little or more than a little demonic. The very thing which the demons are waiting for, especially in theology, is that we should find them dreadfully interesting and give them our serious and perhaps systematic attention.[6]

We must not allow the demons that pleasure. For those who believe in Christ there can be and may be no talk of "belief" in (of) the devil or demons.

---

6. Barth, *CD*, III/3, 519.

16

Swimming against the Tide

16.1 The 1950s. Discussion of German Rearmament

CURRENT EVENTS CONTINUED TO engage Barth's thought in the 1950s; he could not simply withdraw, neither as a Christian nor as a theologian. The opposition between East and West, the "Cold War" only grew sharper. Political developments had continued since 1948. In 1949 NATO was established, a Western military alliance in opposition to the threat from the East. It quickly appeared that following the United States of America the Soviet Union had the atomic bomb. Also in 1949, the three western occupation zones in German were consolidated into a new, West German state (federal republic). In response, the Russian occupation zone was formed into a state on its own, that same year, the "German Democratic Republic." From that point, the reunion of Germany looked to be more distant than ever. Elsewhere in the world divisions became sharper. China had come under Communist domination. In June 1950 the Korean war broke out; a coalition under the leadership of the United States committed itself to keep Communism from gaining a wider grip. The Cold War atmosphere deepened everywhere through these events. How must one respond as a Christian in the midst of these developments?

Barth certainly did not feel attracted by Communism. Life under oppressive Communist domination did not seem to him a recommendable an existence. But he did not hide the fact that he was even less inclined to join in principled anti-Communism as was acclaimed in the West; he deemed that a still greater evil than Communism itself. After all, have we forgotten, he asked, how much the Soviet Union had contributed to the victory over National Socialism? That the Soviet Union would cling to the power it had obtained in Eastern Europe following the Second World War, naturally coheres with the need for its own security; that may be over the top but still not incomprehensible. Must the West in its turn thereby feel threatened?

In the fall of 1950, the new West German chancellor, Konrad Adenauer, developed plans for the rearmament of West Germany and for the participation of German soldiers in a joint Western army. These plans were highly contested in West Germany itself. Gustav Heinemann, minister of homeland affairs (and leading member of the Evangelical Church in Germany) resigned his cabinet office in protest. Church representatives, among them Niemöller (who in the meantime had become president of the Evangelical Church in Hessen-Nassau), expressed their protest in critical letters to the chancellor. But this protest did not find general support, including within the Evangelical Church. Church leaders like Otto Dibelius, bishop of the Evangelical Church of Berlin-Brandenburg, thought it best to applaud a rearming of Germany because of the threatening "demonic" danger from the East.

One appealed to Barth's letter of September 1938 to Hromádka. In it, Barth had called the Czechs to resistance, if necessary: armed resistance to the aggression of National Socialism. Christians must not remain aloof, he had written. Indeed, such resistance is itself service to Jesus Christ (see 9.1). This appeal, then against Hitler, applies now, it was said, even more against Stalin. Freedom is again in the balance. A defense by all means is more necessary than the rejection of resistance for the sake of a cherished peace.

As in 1948 in Switzerland with Brunner (see 14.6) so now in Germany an earlier statement of Barth was offered as an argument for a policy to which Barth absolutely could not agree in the current situation. From his side, Barth could not allow that. In a letter to Wolf-Dieter Zimmermann, written in October 1950, he elaborated why in his opinion the situation of 1950 was different than that of 1938. In 1938 Europe and European Christians were not at all conscious of the threatening danger from Hitler. Thus, there had to be a call to wakefulness. Now, in 1950, everyone in the West is overconscious of the threat of Stalinist Communism. There need be no Christian word to enforce that. Indeed, it now comes down to not being carried away by nervousness and anxiety. At the time, in 1938, Hitler's aggression could not be resisted other than with violence. War was unavoidable then. Now, in 1950, that is not yet the case in relation to Russia. Now it obtains that our own war footing is a bad thing; war is only to be justified as a last resort. And the best defense against Communism is the creation of just social relations. Barth wrote that "whoever does not want Communism—and none of us wants it—must advocate for a true socialism!"[1]

1. Barth an Pfarrer Wolf-Dieter Zimmermann, 1950, in *OB* 210.

Moreover, Barth saw particular reasons to reject a *German* rearmament. Germany is, of itself, always inclined to militarism, he said. When a German dons a military uniform, he too easily becomes a "total soldier." Germany has had to do with a great deal of mischief with such "total soldiers" in the past. There would still have to be a great deal of change in Germany itself. Not much of the recent past has yet been processed. So long as that has not yet happened, we can only shudder at the thought of a fresh appearance of a German army. Barth claimed to be squarely behind the position of Heinemann and Niemöller in the German political and ecclesiastical discussions on this question.

16.2 Rumor in the Swiss Media

With Barth's agreement, the letter was published in a magazine from the circles of the Confessing Church under the title "Fear Not!" The title nicely typifies the intention. That theme was close to Barth's heart in those years. In 1949 he had published a collection of sermons (1934–1948) with the same title. And in May 1952, in a radio address for Swiss radio (on the question "what must we then do," (that is, what can we ordinary folk do to contribute to world peace?), the same elementary appeal would echo, "we should not be so anxious." He would say there that whoever is anxious already desires war; and then the other becomes anxious in return and also then desires war. Hence, peace is served when we remove anxiety.

Barth's position unleashed many reactions. He received a lot of criticism. He was seen, if not as a crypto-communist, then as a fellow traveler of the Communists. Or one disposed of him as too old to talk sensibly about political affairs, or too gullible to be capable of evaluating real threats. He later wrote of this period, "In the leading political and ecclesiastical circles of West Germany I have become still more unpopular than I always was even in the best of times."[2]

But Barth also had to endure heavy criticism in his own country, Switzerland, specifically from authorities. Markus Feldmann, politician and member of the government of the canton Bern with special responsibility for church affairs, had for a long time felt offended by the attitude of the Evangelical-Reformed church council of Bern. In his report on the year 1949, accepted by the Council (the canton government), he had mentioned the "statements of leading persons in the church," that, noting the acclaim they had received, according to him, showed that "in certain church

---

2. Barth, "Recapitulation Number Three," 73.

circles, little interest is devoted to our democratic form of government."³ In a speech, before the Council in September 1949, he explained that. He had, he said, "certain representatives of dialectical theology" in mind, who evidenced an attitude of "expressed benevolent neutrality toward Communism," and displayed "an even greater lack of interest" in the "free, democratic foundation of our state." He thereby identified Karl Barth, referring to his lecture given in Bonn, among other places, in February 1949 on "The Church Between East and West" (see 14.9 and 10) in which Barth, so he said, had taken a "surprising bow toward Stalin."⁴

The matter had become public and Barth heard of it via the press. He did not recognize himself in what emerged from the press reports on his person and work. It gave him the occasion to write to Feldmann requesting a personal meeting in the hope that the misunderstanding could be cleared up. In the same month, Feldmann announced that he was ready for such a discussion. However, he deemed it necessary that written questions should be prepared prior to a mutual discussion.

Barth responded in the returning post. He asked Feldmann to indicate concretely where he could base his judgment that he (Barth) was inclined to undemocratic and pro-communist (Stalinist) thought, a judgment of which Barth himself found that it, in fact, had no basis, including in his lecture of February 1949 cited by Feldmann. He also stated that the Evangelical-Reformed church of Bern (as with every other Christian church) could not, as a church of Jesus Christ, simply walk on the leash of the state and that tensions between church and state could not be excluded ahead of time and he further asked whether Feldmann could yield to that understanding. Barth included a copy of his brochure *Christian Community and Civil Community* from 1946 (see 12.3) as an appendix, asking Feldmann to engage with this document in his expected questions in response.

16.3 The Accusation of Politician Markus Feldmann

An answer to Barth's letter, written at the end of September 1950, arrived in February 1951. However, it did not consist of questions to further the conversation. Indeed, Feldmann gave a more precise account of what he had reported earlier about Barth (and his supporters); it was, in fact, a sharp accusation.

He expressed his indignation over the disdain for the Swiss army and pleas for an attitude opposed to the military and of defenselessness

---

3. Barth an Regierungsrat Dr. Markus Feldmann, 1950, in *OB*, 217.
4. Barth an Regierungsrat Dr. Markus Feldmann, 1950, in *OB*, 219–20.

that he had met among some "Barthians." This coupled with statements in which Communism was typified as "seen ecclesiastically nothing other than a threatening judgment of a Christianity that posits itself as cultural Christianity."[5] He thereby also identified the reserve coming from the same circles with the national- and *volkskerk* position of the Evangelical-Reformed church of Bern. That church must not, so it was claimed, rely on outward guaranties from the state and must not shrink, eventually, if necessary, from speaking against the political will of a people in its proclamation. Feldmann stated his anger with all that.

The statements cited were not from Barth himself, but they were from his followers, and so Feldmann thought he could because of these statements address Barth directly. Was one, was Barth, really of the opinion that it must be about an a-cultural Christianity or a non-cultural Christianity or even an anti-cultural Christianity? Did he really think that a free state like Switzerland (or Bern) would simply accept an eventual Communist attack characterized in church pulpits as a "just judgment" that one must simply allow? That Barth's followers appeared to present his political positions as beyond criticism strengthened his aversion, he said.

Moreover, he said he was disturbed by the inclination that he detected with Barth and his compatriots to authoritatively determine what can rightly call itself a "Christian church"; as though all who are not with Barth and his theology must therefore already be thrown out of the Evangelical-Reformed church! He accused Barth of intolerance; an intolerance that does not apply within a *volkskerk* (people's church) in a free state like the Swiss state or the canton Bern. He saw here again, as so often and so fatally in earlier centuries, religious fanaticism raising its head in conflict with the constitutionally guaranteed freedom of belief in Switzerland and Bern. The state must defend against that, Feldmann claimed. So he did not shy away, as politician and political authority, from calling Barth out, "The gospel is not identical with theology, even if it is yours."[6]

He emphatically maintained his sense that Barth, specifically in his lecture on "The Church Between East and West," had disclosed a pro-Communist disposition. In that lecture Barth had called for a distinction between Communist (totalitarian) practice and what Communism "positively intends," the effort to solve the social question.[7] So long as the West (with its

---

5. Barth an Regierungsrat Dr. Markus Feldmann, (Zweiter Brief), September 26, 1950, in *OB*, 238.

6. Barth an Regierungsrat Dr. Markus Feldmann, (Zweiter Brief), September 26, 1950, in *OB*, 245.

7. Barth an Regierungsrat Dr. Markus Feldmann, (Zweiter Brief), September 26, 1950, in *OB*, 250.

defense of economic freedom) fails here, it must abandon its unconditional "no" against the Communist East. It must rather stand open to the reproach of inhumanity (in an economic regard) that it is to hear from the East. Feldmann cited extensively from Barth's lecture and offered his critical commentary. Is it really so much more social in the East than in the West? Besides, can the West be lumped together as Barth allows? Does Switzerland not deserve to be judged more fairly? And in any case, in the West there is the freedom to express social criticism including criticism of one's own state. Barth unjustly overlooks the fact that freedom is repressed in the East. In short, Feldmann deemed Barth's critique of the West one-sided and thus unacceptable, including for those who are well-disposed to the church and would gladly listen seriously to its voice in social-political matters.

Another point from Barth's lecture was his claim that Communism, in contrast to National Socialism, had not wrapped itself in Christian garb. Here too, Feldmann added his critical notes. He brought up the fact that in the "Communist total state" the Russian Orthodox Church in fact functions as an instrument of the state, just as that had previously been the case in tsarist Russia. He called it also noteworthy that the Bolshevik state had also established a special "regulation" with the churches in general. Had the Communist state thus not also wrapped itself in Christian garb? Moreover, Communism eagerly responds, said Feldmann, to all the praise that it gets in the West from church circles. Preachers who speak positively on the position of the churches of the East—note well, these are preachers from "your church orientation!"—are gladly cited in the Communist press; their statements are interpreted as in seeming agreement with Communist dictatorship![8] That this happens in an officially recognized church that as such is closely connected with our free state makes it particularly delicate. Our state and our people must and will, of course, resist any tendency to undermine our own will to self-maintenance, certainly including such tendencies coming from the church. Eventually voting church members in church elections must be informed by the authorities of what is at issue here. Thus it will appear how church people *really* think of the questions that affect the independence of our state and the freedom of our people.

On Barth's question whether Feldmann could conceive that tensions could emerge between the (Evangelical-Reformed) church of Bern (as the church of Jesus Christ) and the state (Switzerland/Bern) Feldmann underscored that the state decisively does not view the church as the servant or creature of the state and that the church of course can and must fulfill its own

---

8. Barth an Regierungsrat Dr. Markus Feldmann, (Zweiter Brief), September 26, 1950, in *OB*, 254.

task in conflicts around social justice. There is no talk, he said, that the state would erect a barrier to the church here; the church must speak, including on public matters; it must call for reflection and practice criticism where it deems necessary, provided that happens in the spirit of understanding of love and based on facts.

16.4 Again on "Christian Community and Civil Community"

At the conclusion of his argument Feldmann again went into detail in response to the brochure appended to Barth's letter on "Christian Community and Civil Community." He found in this letter arguments for his view of Barth's lack of enthusiasm for democracy. He said that he found it questionable that Barth did not rank any particular political system, including democracy, as "Christian" par excellence. Barth himself even said that it is also possible to deem a monarchy or even a dictatorship a good state. While at the same time he reckoned with the converse possibility, that what is formally a "democracy," in fact, turns out to be tyranny and thus becomes an unjust state. Here Feldmann was thrown off track and he could no longer follow Barth. It was clear to him that Barth rejected tyranny, but how can such a rejection comport with the acceptance of dictatorship under certain conditions? That Barth was only half-heartedly disposed to democracy Feldmann saw confirmed in Barth's reserve in respect to the importance of political parties. In "Christian Community and Civil Community" Barth argued that Christians must not seek politics in the formation of their own "Christian" parties over and against other parties that are thereby forced to profile themselves as *non*-Christian. As though Christians must not be about general welfare rather than the interest of a particular party! In that connection, he noted that political parties in themselves are already "dubious phenomena" in political life, not constitutive for the functioning of the state, at best of secondary importance. Just this incidental remark had stuck in Feldmann's throat. He let fly: how can a democracy function without the existence of parties?

That Barth's compatriots presented his political claims as practically beyond criticism (based on his "subjection to God's Word") again strengthened Feldmann's aversion. He again addressed Barth directly on what his compatriots had credited him with. He said that in Switzerland, in Bern, we must be conscious, certainly in the twentieth century, of the "total impossibility of such a church-political conception." For our state is "a democracy, not a theocracy, let alone a theologian-ocracy."[9]

9. Barth an Regierungsrat Dr. Markus Feldmann, (Zweiter Brief), September 26,

16.5 A Short Retrospect: Democracy or Theocracy?

The entire argument was anything but an opening to a discussion yet to be held. In fact, with this, for Feldmann, the discussion had already ended before it had begun. Barth felt himself not so much queried by his opponent as attacked, or even already condemned. He was not pleased to be addressed in such a way; "I hear badly with this ear." Under these circumstances a personal meeting between the two no longer made sense. A few days after receiving Feldmann's letter Barth let him know that he withdrew his proposal. "I sincerely regret that I must view my attempt as a failure."[10] Feldmann again replied to have taken notice of that and now to have ended the correspondence from his side as well.

A short time later, the entire correspondence was published without Barth's knowledge as a brochure as an official publication of the canton Bern by Feldmann. It provided the occasion for an intense months-long debate in the Swiss press. The question "whether it was not time that the Herr Professor of Theology should at last be hauled before the courts." was bandied about in all seriousness. It is true, not all newspapers expressed themselves so critically on Barth. And he received supporting testimonials; among others in the name of sixty-three Bernese preachers and a tart with the subscription in frosting, "*Multorum corda non Agricolae sed Barbae sunt!*" "The hearts of many are not for Feldmann but for Barth!"[11]

Was there a misunderstanding in this collision between Feldmann and Barth? In any case there was a difference of perspective; where Barth spoke as a theologian and related to the church, Feldmann spoke as a politician and an administrator of a canton. Differently than Barth, Feldmann had a particular interest to defend, that of the ordered rule of law. Of course, Barth was not one to misunderstand that interest. For him too, even as a theologian, the rule of law represented a great good. Only, not the greatest good. For Barth, democracy was not, as such, an "article of faith." His approach from the Word of God brought with it the fact that he relativized the importance of democracy as a system of governance. And from that his relativization of the importance of political parties. For Feldmann that led to the notion—indeed, a misunderstanding, directly opposed to Barth's own argument—that Barth would prefer dictatorship to democracy.

It is remarkable that Feldmann was of the opinion that he had to accuse Barth of theocratic (or even "theologian-ocratic") dispositions. That

---

1950, in *OB*, 268.

10. Barth an Regierungsrat Dr. Markus Feldmann, (Dritter Brief), February 10, 1951, in *OB*, 271.

11. Quoted in Busch, *Karl Barth*, 384.

also appears to be a misunderstanding. After all, Barth himself had, in his "Christian Community and Civil Community," pled that Christians (and church) not profile themselves as Christians in political matters. He had even used the word "anonymous" in that connection: "There will be no lack of individual Christians who will enter the political arena anonymously."[12] For, he had said, for them it may and can thereby not be about a defense of the interests of the church itself. After all, in their political engagement they will commit to what they deem good and beneficial for the entire society; that can be the case only when they work with arguments that are (hopefully) understandable by everyone. Or is the anonymity intended by Barth an attitude behind which a theocratic fire is befitting? Barth decidedly did not intend that Christian would leave their faith behind in the political lists. After all, in his "Christian Community and Civil Community" he had attempted to lay out the connections between Christian faith and political orientation (on the basis of the analogy that must exist between the kingdom of God and the state). That God rules, including over and in politics, is according to Barth a non-negotiable starting point for Christians. But this theocratic approach, he argued, opens the Christian to the importance of democracy. After all, God's governance need not be specially realized by Christian efforts! That already obtains; it is the fore-sign, and by virtue of that Christians can work together politically with others, pragmatically, soberly, including where one is not aware of this fore-sign.

16.6 Distance from Pro-Communist Standpoints. Letter to Albert Bereczky

At the same time that Feldmann's question was at issue, Barth saw himself required to clarify his critical reservation regarding pro-Communist standpoints. He was approached in May 1950 by the Russian writer Ilya Ehrenburg, one of the initiators of a "peace council" established from Moscow. Ehrenburg had, with a number of other involved parties, attempted to use the occasion to get Barth to agree with the Moscow-initiative and to sign this peace council's "protest against the atom bomb." Barth had not answered that. However much he, himself, opposed the emerging nuclear arms race, he had not wanted to be listed as a kindred spirit of the Moscow activists. In the course of the discussion he made it clear to Ehrenburg, "what you understand as peace is completely different from what I understand as such."[13]

---

12. Barth, "The Christian Community and the Civil Community," 187.
13. Barth an Dr. Rudolf Rübesam, May 1, 1952, in *OB*, 314.

In August 1951 he had a meeting in Zurich with the Hungarian Reformed bishop Albert Bereczky. That month, Bereczky had participated in a meeting in Switzerland of the Central Committee of the World Council of Churches and there, as a church leader from one of the nations from the Eastern bloc, he had unsuccessfully attempted to move the World Council to a more anti-Western course. He had opposed a declaration of the Central Committee, in his eyes too pro-American, on the occasion of the Korean war (begun in 1950), and the decision to hold the following assembly of the World Council in America (Evanston). He had complained to Barth that he had not found a hearing for his opposition in the Central Committee. Barth had said in that discussion that he too had his reservations, at least with the latter, the plans regarding the coming assembly of the World Council. But at the same time he had said that what he had read from and about church developments in Hungary did not please him.

When Bereczky later, from Budapest, again presented Barth with his objections to what was to him the pro-Western course of the World Council, requesting express approval, Barth saw himself required to react critically. He did so in a fairly extensive, principally stated letter. Already in 1948, as a follow-up of his visit to Hungary that year, he had found the occasion to express his criticism on the position of the Hungarian Reformed Church toward the state (see 14.6). Now that was even more the case.

For me, Barth wrote to Bereczky, it is not so much that you apparently accept Communism as a political system as something good (although I also cannot share that political position). My question to you is much more whether you have not ended up in a serious theological error. "I have the impression that you stand at the point of making your acceptance of Communism a part of the Christian message, an article of faith."[14] And when something like that happens, then the inclination naturally originates to (re)interpret all Christian faith from this strange, new understanding. But that means to ideologize in the same way that the "German Christians" had committed themselves in Germany in the past. With all their "good intentions," their outcome was with the claim that a particular revelation of God lurks within world-historical events (at the time that meant in the "great acts" of Hitler); a "particular revelation" that they intended to combine with the Word of God in Jesus Christ. In essence, said Barth, I see you doing the same thing, when I hear you speaking of "the great things" that "the God of world history brings about on earth by means of socialism."[15] You apparently use completely other sources alongside God's revelation in

---

14. Barth an Bischof Albert Bereczky, September 1951, in *OB*, 279.
15. Barth an Bischof Albert Bereczky, September 1951, in *OB*, 281.

Jesus Christ for this understanding. Barth's conclusion was straightforward: "Here is something wrong in the theologically fundamental presupposition of the entirety of your church politics."[16]

In discussing church politics, Barth asked Bereczky, how can it still be that the Hungarian Reformed Church (according to reports that I get) has no problem being in step with the Hungarian regime? It appears as though contemporary Hungary is a true paradise where the prophecy that the wolves will dwell with the lambs (Isaiah 11:6) already has been fulfilled! Thereby it is taken for granted that we here in the West "would live under the dominance of an unambiguous capitalism and imperialism." Naturally Eastern propaganda happily presents matters as such, as black and white. But how is it that you go along with that so unreservedly? "Would it really work out that we—your friends!—swim *against our stream*, but that you so unconcernedly swim *with your stream*?"[17] In any case, you must be conscious that you, by so positioning yourself, offend us in the West and provide the occasion for a strengthened anti-Communism. Basic self-examination is necessary for you, Barth said.

Finally returning to Bereczky's criticism of the World Council, Barth said that he could not share in it. That behind the entire policy of the World Council there was nothing other than "an ocean of 'Western' ill will"[18] could not stick, he found, and must decidedly not be said. The decisions regarding Korea and the following assembly may be regrettable, but there is no reason to withdraw confidence in the World Council on that basis alone.

Barth's critical position in regard to Eastern propaganda or defended positions was not intended for Western publicity. Here again Barth did not desire to pour oil on the Western fire of anti-Communism. Still some of it leaked out; core parts of the letter to Bereczky in specific were published in German, and later Swiss, French, Dutch and American newspapers.

16.7 "Political Decisions in the Unity of Faith"

The question of West German rearmament— and of accepting West Germany into NATO, the Western military alliance—remained on the table. Opinions were divided, including in the German church. How can one come to a concrete standpoint regarding burning political questions and still maintain the unity of faith? That became a central question within the church, specifically in Germany. Barth dedicated a short study to the matter. It appeared in the

16. Barth an Bischof Albert Bereczky, September 1951, in *OB*, 282.
17. Barth an Bischof Albert Bereczky, September 1951, in *OB*, 283.
18. Barth an Bischof Albert Bereczky, September 1951, in *OB*, 84.

summer of 1952. In it he also implicitly gave an account of his own concrete political position as a Christian, as a theologian.

We now must realize that the Christian, that the church, is politically co-responsible, thus, has its own word to add in regard to political questions, Barth wrote. But with burning questions it often takes time before official ecclesiastical assemblies can make official statements. Usually such an official statement falls flat. In practice, it will always be individuals who as pioneers, at the moment, take over the task of the church.

How does a Christian now personally come to determine a standpoint regarding a political question? It is necessary of course that one weigh all arguments and counter arguments. But one cannot leave one's faith out of view. Indeed one must do so before the face of the God of Jesus Christ, thus inquiring of God's command. Behind all substantial arguments there always lurks a particular train of thoughts, a particular spirit. Exactly here, a Christian will be alert; one must "discern the spirits" led by the Holy Spirit. If he thus makes choice, a decision, then he cannot decline to defend this decision openly and calling on other Christians.

However, among the Christians concrete decisions can diverge, even where they all take this route (as with the question of West German rearmament). Yes, that threatens the unity of the faith and the church. The blame for that automatically goes to those who have executed and propagated their political standpoint most expressly as a decision of faith, with the reproach that they would lay a law on others in the church and would even deny their Christianity. Precisely that, Barth wrote (and he could do so from his own experience!) happens today to those within the church who oppose West German rearmament (the advocates have never appealed to Christian faith or to the Word of God to support their standpoint.)

But this reproach is a misunderstanding. In general, it is already true that we in the church never have the one truth of the faith at our disposal; it must ever be sought anew, be found again. And that is always first the venture of individuals. They come with "bold" versions or statements. They are all too happily accused of wanting to force consciences or to put the unity of the church on the line. As though this pioneering work would not help the entire church to newly understand the truth!

Well now, this also is at play in political questions. Whoever means that he or she must take and defend a political standpoint with an appeal to faith, undertakes an adventure. Yes, he thereby places himself under God's judgment; has he evaluated problematic clearly? Does he have pure intentions? Indeed, such questions stand before every Christian, who thereby cannot escape having to make his own decisions. And indeed, whoever as a Christian defends a particular political standpoint, his political standpoint soon comes in conflict with that of fellow Christians who think differently. With that, as a matter of course they already stand before the question whether or not they must weigh the same political decision from the same faith. And so now, how it then stands with the correctness of their own faith. But is it not normal when people in the church ask themselves such questions? Is such principled disquiet not characteristic for the Christian church on the way to its Lord?

When Christians, as Christians, take a political standpoint, that happens by definition in the unity of faith. After all, the unity must always be renewed because the faith as well, as faith in Jesus Christ, is not a rigid formula. The political standpoint of some must not call for offense (with others); indeed, it must be conceived as an appeal or invitation to the reconsideration of one's own position. Even with the maintenance of one's own position one has himself given account of his own faith afresh. Everyone is responsible for his own faith and faith decisions. But everyone is also called to testify to his own faith and decision of faith to others and to be open to the consequent witness of other to himself. Yes, the unity of the church is thereby placed in crisis. But the church that would practice its political responsibility cannot escape the risk of this crisis.

17

Ethical Reflection: The Command of God the Creator

17.1 Ethics as Part of Dogmatics

CONCRETE DECISIONS AND STANDPOINTS can (must) be an expression of the Christian faith. Or said conversely, faith is not separate from life, it comes to expression in life itself. Barth's intensive involvement with the events of his day in the years before, during and after the Second World War already give witness to that perspective. But he also worked this understanding into the design of his dogmatics. In his opinion, ethics as reflection on life's questions separate from the content of the Christian faith would be unthinkable. Hence, he also wanted to put ethics expressly on the agenda within the framework of his *Church Dogmatics*. Not as one complete "separate section" but variously observed from particular aspects in connection with what was first considered dogmatically here, then there, then again elsewhere.

Besides, he had been busy with ethics earlier. He had lectured on it in 1928 and 1929 in Münster. He had been criticized as someone whose theology had very little to do with everyday life. He would not have that said. At the same time, he wanted to be careful that theology would not be completely absorbed in ethics. So, he had come to put ethics on the agenda of his lectures. He had already defined ethics as an "auxiliary discipline . . . to dogmatics," with the task of reflecting "that this Word of God which is to be proclaimed and received in Christian preaching claims man in a very peculiar way."[1] But in the course of his further development, after 1930 (his book on Anselm in 1931, the start of his *Church Dogmatics* in 1932, see 5), he had also come to a still clearer understandings in his view of ethics.

---

1. Barth, *Ethics*, 18.

We have seen how Barth in 1935, following his release from German service and his departure to Switzerland once back in Germany, had put the theme "Gospel and Law" on the agenda (see 8.1). He had learned to see the order, first gospel and then law, as essential. With that alone he already wanted to state that we do not simply know the law as God's will for human life from ourselves, for example, from the course of events or from natural law or from human nature. No, the gospel as the message of grace, precedes, and the law is the way in which that takes hold of human life. It was this claim that Barth wanted to think through further in his dogmatics.

He had already begun with that when, following the discussion of the "doctrine of the Word of God" (as reflection on the criterion for all dogmatic work), he had placed the "doctrine of God" on the table as the first subject of his further, substantial reflection. We have seen how he had also spoken of "election" in that context: God is the electing God; he had gracefully said yes to us humans in Christ (see 10.12). Barth already had added a chapter of ethical reflection in *CD* II/2 (1942). He had done so from the conviction that the doctrine of God must also be about human life, human action. For that God is gracious to us, elects us, means that he takes our life in tow, wills to "sanctify" it, claims us for himself. In sanctification, the renewal of our life, election becomes concrete! That it is what becomes clear to us from the law. Thus, in 1942, Barth had freshly and more broadly worked out the foundational thought that he had advanced already in 1935 on the relation between gospel and law: "the law is the shape of the gospel."

In that connection, Barth had also discussed the Ten Commandments (Exodus 10:1–17) and the "Sermon on the Mount" (Matthew 5–7), biblical passages that appear to summarize the heart of the law in a series of commandments or ethical guidelines. But, he claimed, that is not the way to deal with these biblical passages. They cannot, as individual commandments, be separated from the context in which they stand, the biblical proclamation of God's liberating deeds. It is not for nothing that the Ten Commandments begin with a proclamation: "I am the LORD your God who liberated you from Egypt, from slavery." And Jesus begins the Sermon on the Mount blessing the poor, the grieving, the merciful, those who search for righteousness, because God's kingdom has come for them. The Ten Commandments and the Sermon on the Mount, each in its own way, are both first of all proclamation to the listeners: that they are God's elect people, the community of Jesus Christ. And we, who read that today, may know ourselves partners with those first hearers of God's gracious election. Thus, we ourselves are also addressed. And from that we also may live.

What then must we do? What is God's concrete command for us? That, so Barth had argued in that context, cannot simply be stated in general, because of necessity of concreteness. Nowhere does the Bible give general rules. What various biblical passages show is that particular attitudes and deeds were required then and there. But that does not mean that the same attitudes and actions must simply be copied at another time, today for example. It is always about hearing what God, God's self!, asks of me, of us, now. The good that he commands us to do is never "good" in and of itself; it is always the answer that we may give to the good, gracious decision that God in Christ has taken of our life.

17.2 The Human as Creature under God's Command

These views, given in the framework of the doctrine of election (as a focus of the doctrine of God), were still primarily formal in nature. Barth had intended to get to more substantial ethical considerations in the following parts of his dogmatics. In traditional dogmatic reflection the doctrine of creation, the doctrine of Jesus Christ and redemption of the human (one's reconciliation with God; thereby also the work of the Holy Spirit) and the doctrine of consummation and salvation (the doctrine of "last things") always followed the doctrine of God. Barth intended to join this, in order to show in that context how ethics is also substantially affected by the notion of God's absolute alterity—knowable only in Christ. The command of God must thus be specified as the command, in turn, of God the Creator, God the Reconciler and God the Savior. Three times the same command, from the same God, but thus thrice seen in a different light.

Barth had not been able to work this scheme out fully. He did not get to the doctrine of salvation within the framework of the *Church Dogmatics* and could not complete the doctrine of reconciliation. But in any case, he was able to complete his doctrine of creation with a separate part of the dogmatics, *CD* III/4, dedicated to ethics from the viewpoint of creation: "The command of God the Creator." Since the spring of 1950 Barth had, also again along with all his other activities, dedicated his lectures to this theme. The book appeared in May 1951.

So, already as creature the human is under God's command. We have seen above how Barth, thinking from Jesus, the true Human, typified the true human nature in four ways: the human is human in that he lives 1) in relation to God; 2) in relation to his fellow human; 3) as "soul" of his "body" (thus participant in earthly reality as "body," and at the same time, as such, as a responsible subject, i.e., "soul"; 4) in time, thus in limited time (see 13.5–7). Accordingly, he also divided his creation ethic into four paragraphs. He set the command regarding the relation to God first in order;

subsequently the command concerning the relation to the fellow human; then the command regarding life as such (as "soul" and "body"); finally, the command concerning life within its temporal limits.

17.3 Called to Freedom Before God. Sabbath

Leading Christian ethicists have argued that the relation of the human to God is a subject in itself that does not belong to real ethics. To the contrary, Barth emphatically claimed, the biblical witness also knows of a vocation, a call, a human duty in view of God alongside his vocation in view of his fellow human. It is not for nothing that there are two love commandments in the summary of the law in the New Testament that may not be reduced to one. As, after all, in the Old Testament, in the Ten Commandments, the first commandments are expressly related to the relation with God and following that, in the second half, the subject is the relation to the fellow human.

Barth begins his creation ethic with a discussion of one of the first commandments: the fourth, regarding the day of rest ("Sabbath," Exodus 20:8–11). He elaborated: it is this command in which a limit is placed on human action. It says that the human must repeatedly allow a pause in his work, and this "in deference to God and to the heart and meaning of His work," because exactly in this way human work can also consciously participate in God's coming salvation.[2] In submitting to this regular pause, concretely keeping the day of rest, the human accepts "that God has taken his case into His own hands and therefore out of those of man." "The Sabbath commandment requires of man that he understand and live his life on this basis."[3] Said otherwise: it requires that the human believe in God and no longer make his own plans and work an object of faith. Belief in God may be expressed in the celebration of the day of rest as a feast day. And where the feast is celebrated, there humans are together. Thus, it is obvious that on this day the congregation, as a communion of believers, gathers.

It is not arbitrary that Barth began his creation ethic in this way. In his own mind, he could not do it otherwise. For, he claimed, the command concerning the day of rest "explains all the other commandments." It is specifically this command that makes it clear that the commanding God "is the God who is gracious to man in Jesus Christ."[4] Knowing that is fundamental. It is here that the human may learn to be free. Freedom is the central concept in Barth's creation ethic. Barth used it to characterize each of the four

2. Barth, *CD*, III/4, 50.
3. Barth, *CD*, III/4, 58.
4. Barth, *CD*, III/4, 53.

parts (that he distinguished). The command, he said, calls the human to "*freedom* before God," and to "*freedom* in communion"; to "*freedom* to live" and to "*freedom* within limits." But Barth saw it becoming clear from the command regarding the relation to God and so in the command regarding the day of rest that it is about freedom in all its aspects.

The fourth commandment calls the Sabbath the seventh day. That corresponds with the "seventh day" in which, as it is said, God himself "rested" (when he had completed his work of creation). Barth commented: God himself then took time to delight in his completed creation and to dedicate himself to it (with which salvation history really began). The command to the human to rest is to participate in God's rest. This is not a "contemplation of accomplished work" for the human. Indeed, one may begin with Sabbath before one has done anything else:

> The first divine action which man is allowed to witness is that God rested on the seventh day and blessed and hallowed it. And the first word said to him, the first obligation brought to his notice, is that without any works or merits he himself may rest with God and then go to his work.[5]

But thus it is a bond "to be free." In other words, "the history of the human under God's command indeed begins with the gospel and not with the law." It is to be noted from the New Testament that the first Christians, already early on, had made a transition to celebrate their weekly day of rest on the first day of the week. That seems to conflict with the fourth commandment that calls the seventh day (the last day of the week) as the day of rest, but in fact it agrees with the intention of this commandment. The "first day"— namely the day after Sabbath (Mark 16:2)—is after all also the day of the resurrection of Jesus Christ and the congregation

> saw and understood that in the resurrection of Jesus Christ it was concerned with the revelation of the truth and faithfulness of God in His blessing and hallowing of the seventh day . . . In the resurrection it recognized the fulfilment of the covenant between God and man which was established in creation.[6]

In short: with the fact that the first Christians had celebrated their weekly day of rest on the first day of the week, they expressed the signal idea that human life, where it is oriented to God's commands, may begin with the memory of God's goodness to the human. The first thing to which

---

5. Barth, *CD*, III/4, 52.
6. Barth, *CD*, III/4, 53.

the human is called in the commandments is, in fact, to remember that. Everything else is derived from it.

17.4 Called to Freedom in Co-humanity. Man and Woman

For Barth, co-humanity is one of the essential characteristics of human nature. And he realizes that the human is also addressed by God's command in this aspect of his existence. Here Barth goes into various connections and contexts in which human life is lived out: the family and family relations, people and nation, as well as humanity as a whole. Whoever hears God's command knows that this commanding God is the Lord of all peoples, who in the covenant history, fulfilled in Christ, has given general world history one, common center and goal. Every human is part of a particular people and in that connection finds one's task identified by God's command, but where he is led by the command of the God of the covenant at the same time he sees the importance of his nationality relativized. Here Barth finds the occasion again to illuminate how badly things have gone awry in this regard, specifically in Germany since the beginning of the twentieth century. Christians have much too easily let themselves be carried away by the inclination to the idolatrous honor of blood and soil. That comes about when one views the existing (national) reality as an "order of creation," from which norms and guidelines from God could plainly be inferred. It is precisely this reasoning that is impossible for those who learn to understand that the reality of creation comes into view only from and in view of the covenant; thus, from and in view of Christ.

In speaking of the command of co-humanity, Barth specifically arrived at the discussion of the fact that the human is always man or woman; as man always in a particular measure relying on the woman-, as woman always in particular measure relying on the man as partner. That is, so he argued, also the case outside the special relationship of marriage. From that he inferred that the man must also really desire to be total man, the woman to be fully woman; the pursuit of sexual neutrality is against the intention of God's creation. According to Barth, that also holds for the establishment of specific communities (for example of cloisters) of men or of women. The phenomenon of homosexuality is still completely alien to him (1950/51!); he can only view that as a sickness, namely as a tendency to a humanity without the fellow human. Here he shows that he, with all his systematic aim to derive the ethics from dogmatics, is unmistakably a man of his time. That also appears in his views of an "order" in the relation between husband and wife that would be from God; the husband leads, the wife follows. There he appeals to biblical passages in which the relation between husband and wife is compared with that between Christ and the church. By the way, it is just from that comparison that he immediately corrects a possible misunderstanding: the male leadership given here is by definition not a tyrannical rule just as the female following intended here is equally not a slavish subjection.

Naturally, Barth also talks about marriage as "the exemplary form" of the encounter of man and woman.[7] With that he would not say that every man and every woman should (if possible) enter marriage. Here he points out a difference between the Old and New Testaments. The Old Testament still waits for the one Son; an eventual unmarried state is still not in view. But the expectation is fulfilled in the New Testament; a salvation-history necessity to beget children is no longer in order; consequently, there is also the conscious refusal to marry as a possible way of life. Moreover, where a marriage does take place it does not mean per se that it must lead to the begetting and birth of children. Barth sees marriage as something that already in itself, as communion of life, has value, not as only serving reproduction. In passing, we again note that he does not have the possibility of a marriage as communion of life for partners of the same sex in view.

Marriage is intended as a durable, life-long communion of love. Here too Barth sees a distinction between the Old and New Testaments. Specifically, the indissolubility of marriage is powerfully underscored in the New Testament. That has to do, Barth said, with the fact that the reality of the covenant between God and the human (of which marriage is a reflection) has become fully revealed. Marriage is as unbreakable as this covenant. "What God has bound together no one may rend asunder" (Mark 10:9). But this word must be understood as gospel, an offer of freedom; not as a formal rule or abstract prohibition. Here too it must be considered that the Bible does not give general rules; after all, the living God repeatedly gives his own command. In particular situations, divorce may be necessary, where it appears that the marriage in question is not based on a covenantal existence given by God but on purely human arbitrariness. Where Christians set divorce in motion, they do not do so lightly, but knowing that they bow to God's judgment of their failed marriage. Just so is healing then possible for new obedience and space opens for a new beginning, eventually to entering a new marriage as well. The church should not condemn such a second marriage and may not categorically refuse a request that it be blessed—with an

---

7. Barth, *CD*, III/4, 182.

appeal to principles and rules. When something like that still occurs, Barth deemed it nothing less than "scandalous."

Marriage, however much (hopefully) sealed by both partners in freedom and love, has an institutional side. Its occurrence is an official event: the formal wedding ceremony, the wedding day. Barth points out its importance. Where two people marry that after all touches the community (the family, and the congregation) of which they are a part; that must also be publicly registered in order that they can now be addressed as married. At the same time, Barth desires that this importance not be over-accented. The essential reality of marriage does not depend on it. Marriage is not constituted by the formal act of marriage, only confirmed (to the outside world).

> Two people may be formally married and fail to live a life which can seriously be regarded as married life. And it may happen that two people are not married and yet in their precarious way live under the law of marriage.

Barth deemed the notion that marriage would be the same as the situation of being formally married as "a dreadful and deep-rooted error."[8]

It is not to be assumed that with these considerations Barth would not also have thought about his own situation. We spoke above (see 4.12) of his close relation with his coworker Charlotte von Kirschbaum, that had more and more overlapped with the relation with his wife, Nelly Hoffmann. Was his marriage with Nelly "seriously . . . regarded as married life"? Or did he live with Charlotte, however not formally married to her, still "under the law of marriage"? And how did the triangle in the Barth house relate to what he himself brought to this connection: that marriage is firmly intended as an *exclusive* life-communion of *two* people? After all, that too is not something incidental for Barth. In his opinion, it coheres with the exclusivity of the covenant of the one God with his one people. Again, Barth points out the distinction between the Old and New Testaments. That monogamous marriage appears in the New Testament more unambiguously than in the Old, he said, is because only there can be talk of the full reality of the covenant in Jesus Christ.

17.5 Called to Freedom to Live

The human is soul and body. So one lives, as part of earthly reality ("body") but as responsible subject, as "I" ("soul"). As such, one is addressed by God; one's existence rests on that. And the address is also a command. God the

---

8. Barth, *CD*, III/4, 225.

Creator not only gives us life. He also gives us life as a task. He commands us; that is, He calls us to freedom, to live. Barth dedicates an extensive paragraph to reflection on that topic.

It is usual in ethics to treat this theme by interpreting the sixth commandment, "Do not murder" (or in the old translation, "Thou shalt not kill" (Exodus 20:13). This wording is negative; something is forbidden. But that prohibition has a positive background: the human is called to live and thus to a positive valuation of life. In this connection, Barth talks of "honor for life." He derived this wording from the theologian and medical doctor Albert Schweitzer, but with a correction. For Schweitzer, "life" is the highest good and thus the criterion for all good action. Barth does not take over the latter. Life as such cannot be the criterion, he said; we have received it on loan from God. He himself is the one who calls us to honor life.

That he does so is included in the gospel of the birth of Jesus Christ. After all, in and with that birth, Barth said, it is decided that it is a privilege, a good, a value, for the human to live. The consequence of the command to honor life is the support of good health. Barth does not fail to point out that real health also has to do with good social relations. Supporting good health thus also includes supporting a healthy society. In any case, the reality of illness may not be minimized or hidden. The connection that is laid in the New Testament between the Kingdom of God that has come nearby and the healing of the sick is telling here. In this connection, Barth names Johann Christoph Blumhardt, whose son he had met in 1915, with honor (see 2.4).

Called to live includes being called to *will* to live. Rather boldly (as he also found himself!) Barth further identifies this will to live as the human "will to power." Derived from the German philosopher Friedrich Nietzsche, this is dangerous terminology, ripe for misunderstanding, as though it is about power itself. That is not what Barth intended of course. No, the "power" at issue here is, as life itself, given for God's sake. That "power" is what is necessary for the human to be able to live, to be used in gratitude and humility. That immediately suggests that there are limits. A human can will to do more than is necessary. One tries to expand one's power, one's ability. So modern technology has developed. And where something succeeds technically the human wills to go further. After all, new needs then are always created that again want to be satisfied. So, technology becomes a goal in itself. At a given moment, things then go amiss. Technology can lead to interference, destruction, war. That does not lie at the feet of technology; it lies at the feet of the human, to one's exaggerated will to power. The human must realize that one stands in *service*. Then one knows which "power," which capability, is necessary to that end and which capability one must forgo. This latter,

17.6 Called to the Protection of Life: Limit Cases

The sixth commandment, "Thou shalt not kill," must also be taken seriously as a literal text. The human is also forbidden to lay hands on the life of another. So, said Barth, human life is taken into protection against arbitrary assault. Barth also dedicated a number of reflections to that. First of all, he warned, here life itself is not elevated to the greatest good. He applied to that notion the correction that he earlier had applied to Albert Schweitzer's concept of "honor for life." Human life is a gift from God and thus something relative. It is always about the protection of life as God wills and commands. Thus, a moment (a situation) can arise in which life must be given up, handed over. "In certain circumstances, should the commanding God so will it, it may have to break and discontinue the defence of life."[9] Such a situation is certainly a limit case. One can only conclude with the greatest caution that such a thing is an issue. But even with the Bible in hand (think of biblical stories of men who are killed, and of law texts that even prescribe that those who go wrong must be killed) it cannot be excluded in advance that such limit cases present themselves. For example, not every suicide is an unjustified assault on (one's own) life. And not every abortion is to be condemned; after all a limit situation can present itself in which—with an appeal to the gospel of God's grace that obtains for both mother and unborn child—it must be decided to end the unborn life.

Barth dedicated a few reflections to a number of situations in which one is attacked or threatened. Must the life of the attacker also be protected? Or may (must) precisely this attacker eventually, in the most extreme case, by necessity, be killed? Barth warned against easy, readily available conclusions. He offers for consideration: whoever strikes back as one attacked lowers himself. Moreover, what do I know of my attacker? Perhaps he is disappointed, frustrated. Of course, that does not justify his attacking me. But my violent resistance intensifies his misery. Is that then really a just reaction? And is my killing him to be excused? Jesus' word, "I say to you, do not resist those who do evil to you but whoever strikes you on the right cheek, turn the left cheek" (Matthew 5:39) cannot simply be rejected as unrealistic.

Still, said Barth, limit situations can also present themselves here. The command to the protection of life is not a standing law in itself. After

9. Barth, *CD*, III/4, 398,

all, we do not have to follow this command so much as to obey the One who himself commands, in what He commands us here and now. As humans who live from God's grace, it can be borne on us to resist evil for God's sake because God himself also and first does so. It cannot be God's will that human life under attack simply be harmed or wiped out; whoever, if necessary, resists commits himself to God's affairs if with that the attacker is eliminated.

The threat, the attack, can also be directed against the state, against the legal order of the state. Then it is the state that must defend itself. Right must be maintained, the attacker punished. Can, may, the death penalty be applied in such a case? Where that happens, said Barth, that is not beyond the personal responsibility of every citizen; after all, citizens are also involved with the introduction of a system of laws. The executioner appears in the name of the entire civil community. Hence every citizen is confronted with the question: can, may the death penalty exist? Again, Barth sees himself, by virtue of the gospel, pressed to resist easy conclusions. He sees none of the general arguments advanced in favor of the death penalty as valid. By definition, it cannot serve the re-education, the life-betterment of the criminal. With the application of the death penalty the state appears (irrevocably) to want to sit on the judgment seat of God and thereby transcend its power. Moreover, the state exists, even as a community of law, not for destruction but just for the maintenance of life; the death penalty goes directly against that. It would, as a generally possible means of punishment, have to be abolished.

But Barth also reckons with the possibility of a limit situation here. The existence of state itself can be attacked. Then a powerful action is required. After all, the maintenance of order by the state exists as God's good gift to make life and society possible. Thus it cannot be excluded that in the case of a fundamental threat—Barth thinks by way of example of attempted treason in a situation of war—the application of the death penalty is God's concrete command, not as a regular possibility but as an exception.

Another fundamental threat can present itself where a ruler emerges as a tyrant who abuses his position of power to annul the law. If there is then no authority that can (or will) appear to stand in the way, may (or must) the initiative to do so not come from society itself? Someone would, at the commitment of his own life, be able to eliminate the "tyrant." Is that then murder, or is it an act of faithfulness to the state? Formally, such a "murder of the tyrant," of course, is not the execution of the death penalty. There is no judicial sentence that provides the foundation for it. It is (eventually) an act of one courageous individual, based on his own judgment. However perilous, it can be necessary and thus commanded.

This last instance recalls what Barth had advanced already in 1938, in a lecture held in Scotland on the Scots Confession. There he had said, among other things, that where the state absolutizes its own ends and thus degenerates into "tyranny," resistance, even violent resistance, against this state is commanded. In that context he had referred to the Scots Confession itself that calls the "resistance" of tyranny as belonging to the fulfillment of the command "thou shalt not kill" (see 9.2). Here, in his creation ethic, we see Barth focus on the eventual possibility or necessity of resistance against an unjust state, on resistance against the "tyrant" as the personal representative of the power of the state, a resistance that can mean even the eventual elimination of the "tyrant." If Barth had the Hitler regime concretely in mind in speaking of a state that degenerated into "tyranny" in 1938 in Scotland, he specifically named Adolf Hitler here, looking back on the 1930s and 1940s. And he referred to the plans that, between 1938 and 1944, had existed to remove Hitler; plans in which Dietrich Bonhoeffer had been involved. That the execution of the plans had not come about (and also was not successful on July 20, 1944), had nothing to do with religious or moral considerations. There was a lack of decisiveness. Apparently, the realization was lacking among the plotters and planners that it could be God's command to remove this "tyrant."

17.7 War: Not Normal, but Sometimes Necessary

In the preceding, we saw Barth already touching on the problem of war. Of course, he could not leave it undiscussed in this context. War and the threat of war determined his existence, as a man and as a theologian. We saw how he had intensely sympathized with the struggle against Hitler's Germany in the years before and during the Second World War, and how in the years following 1945 he equally intensively warned against the overwhelming inclination in the West to come up against Soviet Russia combatively and with arms, as one had done with Hitler. There were those who reproached Barth with inconsistency. It cost Barth a great deal of effort to bring his conception that Communist Russia was simply not the same as National Socialist Germany into the open. In his creation ethic, speaking of the command to the protection of life, he gave a principle elaboration of his thoughts on war and the conduct of war.

He began by bringing reality to the attention. A war means that human life stands in the balance and is offered up. A fighting army is directed to make as many victims as possible among the enemy. How can that be excused in regard to the command to the protection of life? In the past, one gladly spoke of the "honor" of one's own nation that must be defended. But in fact, it was mostly about nothing other than economic interests that one wanted to protect at the cost of the competitors. That is a mentality that makes a person, even a nation, warlike, even in "peace time." The old Romans honored the precept, *si vis pacem, para bellum,* "if you want peace, be prepared for war." But, said Barth, that reasoning must be the other way around: *si non vis bellum, para pacem,* "If you do not want war, then prepare the peace."[10] More than war, peace is something that requires commitment and preparation. If a "right" to conduct war can be talked about, then that can be only with extreme caution.

After what we have heard in the forgoing of Barth's attitude before and during the Second World War, it does not surprise us to see here that he does not agree with pacifism, with its rigorous rejection of every conduct of war. He certainly cannot avoid recognizing with reference to the book *De zondeval van het christendom* [The Sin of Christianity] by the Dutchman G.J. Heering that there is "infinitely much" to say for it. Christianity has indeed, said Barth, made a wonderful turn from aloofness toward war and the conduct of war to a self-evident support of what (since Constantine) is called "just war." The fault was not that one reckoned with war as a possibility; that cohered with the acknowledgment of the state as such. The fault was that one viewed war as something normal (because the inclination was seen as belonging to human nature) and that one thus gave the state a blank check to conduct war. Still up to the twentieth century, German Protestant theologians have expressed themselves on war in this sense. So not only the world but also Christianity landed squarely in the First World War, and so one could from 1938 lead up to the Second World War. "And only a few years after its termination the question of German remilitarisation has given rise to similar pernicious nonsense."[11]

Barth claimed (what he had already advanced in his discussion of the problem of the death penalty) that the normal task of the state is not the destruction of human life but to sustain and assist it. That also means not conducting war but serving peace. Concretely that includes advocating for democracy, namely for *social* democracy, thus, the establishment of a sensible and just order of life for all (not only militarists but also pacifists unjustly see that as of secondary importance). A state that sees itself pressed into the conduct of war is in general a state that does not fulfill its normal task. Certainly, the church is called to commit first of all to peace, and thus to (social!) democracy *within* the state. Doing so, it can also advocate for

---

10. Barth, *CD*, III/4, 452.
11. Barth, *CD*, III/4, 457.

(the maintenance) of peace *between* peoples, *between* states. Again, Barth placed a critical note to pacifism where he said that the church recognizes our world as not yet saved, still imperfect, and that it is thus not its task to proclaim that war should be "principally" avoided. But he added that "also in this world" it has the task to turn against the converse namely the "satanic doctrine as though war is principally unavoidable and thus principally justified." Against that and also against all war fever, the church must consider each case, requesting attention for the voice of quiet reflection that looks for every practical possibility to avoid war.

Only after this has been said, the other must be said also, that here too a limit situation can present itself, a situation in which the conduct of war must be engaged. The existence of a people, of the state itself, can be threatened. Thereby something cherished can stand in the balance. Then it can be God's command to defend this existence even if that costs human life (in one's own circle or with the attacking party). And this apart from the question whether this defense has a chance of succeeding. A war can thus be a just war. It may and must then be conducted in obedience, and thus with good conscience, in faith. And the church will then stand comfortingly and encouragingly and calling to conversion alongside the affected people, involved in the war (which is different than howling with the warring wolves).

We recognize in these reflections Barth's particular standpoint during the Second World War, just like his position at the time he wrote this, the 1950s, the era of the "Cold War," of the growing tension between East and West. There is indeed no talk of inconsistency. It becomes ever clearer to us that Barth's sympathy with the war against Hitler is to be understood from his judgment of the evil, the injustice, that manifested itself in the appearance of the Hitler regime. Even in the years between 1938 and 1945 he was not someone who gladly agitated for war. But he saw that, in the confrontation with Hitler, there had been no other choice than engagement in armed conflict. He had experienced that situation as exceptional.

17.8 Called to Active Life: The Meaning of Work

God calls us humans to live. What is the content of that life? Barth answers: we are called to *active* life, to activity. That is to say, to service as God's covenant partner, namely in response to and in participation in what God does (in Jesus Christ, and with an eye on him in all the events of the world). That applies for every human whether one is conscious of it or not. With God having made human business his own, God has made his own business that of the human, of every human. This participation in

God's work must not be too highly spoken of; it is only about the human being *active with*. But it is about that.

Of what does this activity, this service, concretely consist? Barth said: its foundational form, its center is cooperation in the task of the Christian community. It is precisely in the community (as already prior to Christ's birth, in Israel) that one knows, after all, when it is good, of God's covenant, and of human vocation, to be God's covenant partner. It is true that most people still have no knowledge of that. Still it is everyone's destiny that is realized just in the community, the small minority, the separate "people."

But God, the God who acts in and to his community, is also the King of the world, the Lord of the universe. He extends his provident care over the entire creation. So, too the human has to serve, i.e. not only to work within the community but also beyond it, in the world. In one's work, the human is not only an object of God's provident care, but also, in that context, subject. Of course, one's (everyone's!) destiny is to be "Christian" (community member); but to be able to be that one must also be "human." That is precisely the meaning of work. Barth further describes work as the humanly active affirmation of his existence as creature. In that active affirmation the human is something other than a stone or a plant. He is present in it as a unity of body and soul. Again Barth underscores that only the Christian recognizes this meaning of work but it obtains equally for the non-Christian. He (she), too, is factually in the service of the God of Jesus Christ.

In work it is primarily, simply, about the sustenance of life, in which things then should go humanly. That means, said Barth, first of all, simply enough, goal-oriented, substantial work, not make-work. And that is worthy of the human in that it genuinely means something for human existence. Meaningless, dumb work is unworthy of the human. Further, shared work belongs to the human character of work, thus acting in cooperation and level-headedly; after all, the human is not a machine even in his work; one is a subject. Finally, the human must also keep the limit of his work in mind; alongside work there is also rest; if that is neglected the human becomes contorted in his work. This latter recalls how he began his creation ethic: his reflection regarding the meaning of the command to a day of rest (see 17.3).

17.9 The Social Question

In the context of his remarks on the co-human character that work must have, Barth goes further into the social question. People must work alongside and with each other. The reality is different. Competition exists. Everyone wants to achieve his own advantage at the cost of the other. One certainly tries to justify that. It is said that that's the way it is in nature, among humans as well as among animals. This is *the survival of the fittest*. But it is precisely this mentality that is at the root of the social wrongdoing. Moreover, it appears as though this wrongdoing is not as bad as it seems. In the process of work, agreements on work and pay are being made. That sounds positive. But in practice it means class struggle. The owners of the means of production (raw materials, machines, capital) stand over and against those who have only their own labor to offer. The latter are thus dependent on the arbitrary will of the former. Of course, not all employers behave as exploiters. And is it not positive that in this competition the strongest and best surface? Has this competition also not provided a number of technical developments? Still, the principle of the exploitation of one man by another rules here. That really means social injustice. There are counter-movements of course. Social laws have been implemented. The free play of the market is somewhat restrained. Some employers install a sort of collective policy in their business in which employer and employees work together. That has happened primarily under the influence of a powerful workers' movement that has risen in the meantime, partially inspired by Marxism. But however disguised, a class struggle always exists. Is it different in the socialist states of Eastern Europe? There, ownership of the means of production has gone over to the hands of the state. But if that means in practice that all economic power now rests with a ruling state elite, what has been accomplished?

Barth said that here par excellence God's command calls for a countermovement, to humanity, and thus to the choice for the weak against the strong. The Christian community, certainly in the West, was late realizing that. Thus, it must not prefer to point accusingly at wrongdoings within state socialism of the Eastern bloc. It has enough to do in its own, Western, house. As it advances God's command over and against social wrongdoing, it must position itself on the "left," although it will not identify with a particular counter-movement. State socialism is also not the panacea against social injustice, and like other attempts to bring competition and class struggle to an end, it has at best a relative significance. The root of evil goes deeper, namely in that the human does not see that he can be human precisely in his co-humanity. If God in his providential rule would have no patience with us, then things would be much worse than they now in fact are. And

> If the kingdom of God had not come on earth to be manifested one day in power and glory as His kingdom, there would be no hope at all in the social question . . . The Christian community both can and should espouse the cause of this or that branch of

social progress or even socialism . . . But its decisive word . . . can consist only in the proclamation of the revolution of God against "all ungodliness and unrighteousness of man" (Rom 1:18), i.e., in the proclamation of His kingdom as it has already come and comes.[12]

17.10 Affinity with Socialism

In the views articulated above on the social question, Barth's affinity with socialism again appears along with his refusal to completely identify himself (and the vocation of the Christian community) with it. We met this attitude with Barth from his earliest days. We briefly review it here.

We saw how as a preacher in Safenwil Barth came into contact with the social question and committed himself to the rights of the factory workers in his congregation and how he still had critical questions for socialism. Those reservations did not prevent him from becoming a member (in 1915 albeit for a short period) of the Swiss Socialist party. With that he openly declared himself to be in solidarity with the Socialists and gave himself the possibility of criticizing the party from within where he did not consider it sufficiently radical.

We also heard how Barth further elaborated both his affinity with socialism and his principle reservations on that in his controversial speech at Tambach (1919): God's Kingdom is not laid in the extension of our protest; nor can social democracy organize that; the real revolution must come of God, and comes from God (see. 2.2 and 2.6).

Later, in 1931, during his sojourn as professor in Germany, he saw himself pressed again to express his sympathy with Socialism; he became a member of the German Socialist Party, the SPD (see 6.1). This was not a principal step for Barth; nor was Socialism a sort of new "confession of faith" for him. He saw this choice of party rather as a way to protest the emergence of Hitler's National Socialism; he saw the SPD as a party that committed itself in a sensible way on behalf of the German people. Moreover, especially after Hitler's acceptance of power in January 1933, he remained a party member against the advice of the party leadership. In that same year the SPD was banned by the new authorities. With that Barth's membership in the party came to a ("natural") end.

That following the war Barth could not join in Western anti-Communism, but in fact repeatedly pointed to Communism as something that those

---

12. Barth, *CD*, III/4, 545.

in the West could learn from regarding the social question (see 11.8, 14.9 and 10) is along the same line. We have seen that that definitely did not mean a principal choice for Communism. He decidedly did not want to idealize the course of affairs in the Eastern bloc and in Soviet Russia.

We find this all now again in Barth's views just articulated on the social question. Here, in his ethics, developed within the framework of his dogmatic reflection on the doctrine of creation, he systematically elaborated what drove him in his performance in practical church and political action through the years.

17.11 Called to Freedom within Limits

Alongside the relation of the human to God, one's involvement with one's fellow human and one's identity as subject (as soul-and-body), there is according to Barth still a fourth characteristic of created human nature: the human lives in time, hence between the limits of birth and death. We saw that he also deemed that aspect as belonging to the good creation. So, Barth comes in his ethics of creation to a closing paragraph on the question of what God's command (that calls to freedom) has to say about this fourth aspect of human existence.

In this paragraph the limits of human nature are again on the agenda in a different way, that is, where Barth goes into the fact that every human lives within concrete circumstances and in a concrete phase of life in which he receives his vocation and has to carry out his profession. Barth argued that God's command reaches the human where one stands such as one is, thereby emphasizing that this does not mean that the circumstances themselves, as such, would constitute the content of that command. God's command does not simply coincide with the circumstances! Here (and elsewhere) Barth turns against the notion (still somewhat adhered to by himself in his ethics lectures of 1928 and 1929) that "orders of creation" exist from which we ourselves could derive Gods command. The human must not simply identify oneself with his circumstances or just accept them as they are; one must indeed relate to them to hear in that context what God's command has to say to one, to oneself. He dedicated a separate section to the claim that this does not weigh the human down, but rather lifts up and brings to freedom, yes, to honor. But in the most direct connection with his dogmatic reflection on human nature (his anthropology) his thought extends here to the human limit in time, between birth and death.

That limitation, he said, is not something negative. Indeed, it is just the limits that determine the individuality of every human. It is through one's limitation that one is this specific human. And precisely so one may know oneself wholly and completely accepted by God. The temporal nature of one's existence makes one's life, everyone's lives, a unique, unrepeatable affair. Indeed, we live but once. And in his command, God calls us to grasp that unique affair and to use it. Thereby Barth points out that God's self has also become human in this uniqueness and unrepeatability. Jesus too lived once, between the limits of his birth and death. The confession that Jesus will come again does not contradict that. On the contrary, the expected second coming will be the definitive revelation of the meaning of his short life, lived there and then (see 13.7).

That the limited nature of (everyone's) life is something positive is also understandable from the human themselves. If the human was an infinitely continuous essence, then there would be no talk of history. Just as the generations follow each other, as new people are born and old people die, something old comes to a close and something new begins. Just as living in his limited time, between birth and death, the human, every human, stands in history as an (indispensable) link in a great, long chain. And is thus oriented and set toward God who calls him to his covenant and to participation in the salvific events that proceed from this covenant.

Not that every human factually shares in this covenant and these salvific events. One is not by definition already "in Christ." Thus, it is also necessary that God's Word opens for (this) human and that the human answer in faith. But as a unique, limited human one is destined, elected, to that end. For it obtains of every human that Jesus Christ is his fellow human. Thus we have the time of our life *in order that* what has happened in Christ *for* us can also happen *to* and *in* us. He is the real limit of our existence, this Jesus Christ. His birth and death are the presupposition of ours. We do not come by our birth from an empty place but from him; we do not go in our death into darkness but to meet Him.

The time in which the (each) human lives is the limited place assigned to him. So understood, God's command has a pressing character. It is that the human must be actively concerned with one's place, must actively make use of it. His one lifetime is his unique, unrepeatable affair to the participation in history and to the Kingdom of God come in Christ. That matter can pass a human by, but it wants to be grasped. Thus it is that God's command calls.

A human who responds to this appeal is to be recognized by various characteristics. Barth names three. First, one lives both open and determined at the same time. Open for what one can learn from others, but without becoming a cliché of a human, thus, without simply clinging to what "one" says and finds. One goes one's own way with all its risks, to be precisely that what one alone can be, between one's birth and one's death.—Further, one has no time to lose but still knows to take time. One is addressed from all sides and has much to do but does not allow oneself to be hurried because ultimately in everything it is God's command itself that addresses him; so one can and must choose and determine that with which one will not and with which he will have to be active.—Finally and above all, one is conscious of the fact that one will die (when?) and does not repress that; and (for) one is not anxious about that coming death. In itself the thought that one must die, that one then will no longer exist and that then it is thus too late for anything, is anxiety producing. No wonder that one runs away from it. One seeks comfort, for example, in the idea of the "immortal soul" or of the surviving events of nature into which one can disappear as a small part. It is only with God (who in Jesus Christ himself has said "yes" to mortal human existence) that we can really accept our mortality and so accept ourselves, our own existence, knowing that he, God himself, is our beginning and our end. So, conscious, going to meet our death does not paralyze us, but gives our lives importance here and now. It makes us watchful. It is to that watchfulness that we, as mortal humans, are called by God's command.

18

The Heart of the *Dogmatics*: The Doctrine of Reconciliation

18.1 Still not Retired

WHEN, IN MAY 1951, Barth had completed his doctrine of creation with the publication of his ethics (*CD* III/4, on the command of God the Creator), he had just reached the age of 65. Still he would not rest on his laurels. Indeed, in his mind the central part of the Christian faith had still not fully been addressed in his *Church Dogmatics*. For him, the doctrine of reconciliation was at the center.

In fact, all that he had developed in the preceding parts of his dogmatics (on the doctrine of God, on election, on creation) had already been determined by the idea of reconciliation. In traditional dogmatics, Jesus Christ is in order at a particular point, as one theme following and alongside other. It is about the salvation that this Jesus had come to bring to us humans; not for nothing is he called the "savior" (Luke 2:8). But for Barth there can be no sensible talk of God and, for example, of God as Creator, or of human existence as such if Jesus Christ is not immediately spoken of. His foundational idea was that we can see who and how God is only in and through Jesus Christ. In that, that God has brought about salvation (reconciliation) for us humans, God has revealed himself to us! That was the presupposition of all Barth's dogmatic reflections. Still, the event of reconciliation itself had not yet been considered in the preceding parts of the dogmatics. That must now happen. That was the task to which Barth now set himself: the working out of a doctrine of reconciliation in a real sense.

He added a "foreword" to the part of the dogmatics in which he had concluded his doctrine of creation, the part on ethics as a reflection on the command of God the Creator (*CD* III/4); there, he looked already ahead to what he still had to do. In it he revealed that he was impressed with the importance of the task. He felt the weight of his responsibility:

> *Vita nostra brevis est* . . . It makes me think when I notice how my contemporaries, my former colleagues and fellow-students are now one by one beginning to retire from their life's work. I can visualise what it means to spend forty years in giving instruction to first communicants, in seeking the right spiritual word at a graveside or for young married couples, in being pastor to every conceivable kind of folk, and above all in expounding the Gospel Sunday by Sunday and proclaiming the Word of salvation for the community and world . . . I greet all those who have already these forty years behind them, because I am as firmly convinced to-day as ever I was that in this work—in the future it will no doubt be performed even more than in the past through the co-operation of ministers with as many other members of the parish as possible—there is accomplished the decisive part of what can be done by human effort in the Church . . . May some of them at least spare a kind thought for me, who being a late starter am still not in a position to seek a well-earned retirement, because I am only just facing my main task. How far all of us will still have opportunity for one or the other does not lie in our hands.[1]

18.2 Reconciliation as a Dogmatic Theme? Rudolf Bultmann

Can reconciliation really be talked about as a dogmatic theme? Or broader yet, is a substantial dogmatics, as a doctrine of faith, really possible? Is the Christian faith not essentially more, something other, than agreement with a number of doctrinal theses? We heard that Barth himself, in his beginning years as professor, had wrestled with that question. Then he had emphatically rejected the thought that he would propose his "own theology." God, the living God, cannot be captured in dogmas. He would emphasize especially that, as a sort of "footnote" to all doctrinal dogmatics. Still he felt pressured to consider that, just that "footnote," further (see 4.1 and 2). So, gradually, the parts of his *Church Dogmatics* had emerged. Barth had still taken the path of doctrinal dogmatics. Had he thereby become unfaithful to his own starting point? And would an elaborated doctrine of reconciliation definitely confirm that Barth ultimately, "completely ordinarily," was active developing an ("orthodox") theology alongside others?

1. Barth, *CD*, III/4, xi-xii

At just that time, at the beginning of the 1950s, the question whether dogmatics, as the doctrine of faith, is possible became newly urgent, specifically in Germany. The discussion was primarily fueled by Rudolf Bultmann. We met him earlier as one of Barth's earlier compatriots (see 3.7). Barth and Bultmann were contemporaries (Bultmann was two years older). They had had the same teachers as students. But both had gone their own way.

Differently than Barth, Bultmann had never felt pressed to give a systemic account of "the content of the Christian faith." Indeed, he was, as researcher and interpreter of the New Testament (that was his area), more and more convinced that such a systematic, substantial account is, in fact, principally impossible.

Already in the 1940s, he had made a sensation in Germany with his plea for "demythologizing" the New Testament. That was for him to (help) distinguish between what the writers of the New Testament *intended* to say (the message, the *kerygma*) and the *form* (the mythic representations) in which they have, in fact, done so. The New Testament presupposes, he said, a mythic image of the world; the earth with the heaven above (where God and the angels dwell) and the underworld (hell, as a place of torment). It speaks of "God" and "Satan" as supernatural essences that are active on earth. It tells of "God's Son," come from "above," appearing as a man on earth, who died "for our sins" and later is "raised" from the dead and "went up to heaven" ultimately "to return triumphally." That too, said Bultmann, is mythology.

He emphasized that modern humans can no longer accept such mythological representations as true even if they are packaged in dogmas. It is likely that they can have nothing to do with the doctrine of a "substitutionary suffering and death of Christ." Even less can they still believe in Jesus' resurrection as an event whereby a life power would have become active so that the human can now appropriate it to oneself by means of "sacraments." But to be a Christian, you need not believe all that. Above all, you must not build a dogmatics, a "doctrine of reconciliation" around it. Because it is not about the mythological representations as such. It is much more about the message that is packaged in the mythology. It comes down to that which is read through the packaging.

What is that message then? Bultmann argued that it is simple: Word—Word of God—that addresses and appeals to us humans. In the philosophy of the time one claimed that human nature is existing, that is, designating your future responsibly, and so realizing your own existence again, here and now. Bultmann rediscovered this concept of existence in the Bible. It is about what human nature is and is intended to be; as disclosed, illuminated by the Word of God. As Christians we know that it is that Word that on the one hand discloses our "sin and misery," or the unreality of our contemporary existence, and on the other hand calls us to a new existence in "faith," that is to say, oriented to a future that we do not have in hand. So that Word has a double effect on our existence.

Bultmann saw that the Word has that double effect given in that it speaks to us of Jesus Christ, of the cross and resurrection. He did not see the cross essential as an event in itself, but rather the *proclamation* of the cross, as an appeal to also undergo, "with Christ," the judgment of our inauthentic existence and so to come to a new existence, that we have to orient ourselves in faith to what is invisible and is not at our disposal; just that, Bultmann argued, is said to us in the proclamation of the cross. Hearing that proclamation, so seeing the *meaning* of the cross can also be called believing in Christ's "resurrection." The resurrection of Christ, no less than his cross, must not be made into mythology. For again, it is not about the events (Easter events) as something in itself. Bultmann saw the real "Easter events" as the fact that the meaning of the cross (as described above) has become revealed to us. In other words, it is in the proclamation of the meaning of the cross and in the faith wakened thereby that what the New Testament calls "the resurrection of Christ" has taken place (and still takes place).

18.3 Critical Questions to Bultmann

Barth had followed the progress of Bultmann's work, his plea for "demythologizing" the New Testament and for an existential interpretation of its content, with mixed feelings. On the one hand he recognized with Bultmann what was also important for himself, the conviction that theology is more than the elaboration of purely "objective truths," as though such "objective truths" were simply at our disposal. On the other hand, he had felt more and more uncomfortable with the manner by which Bultmann made the existential character of the message the one and all. Is it about human existence as such? Must not the basis for the biblical appeal to exist, to new life, hence where it comes from, be considered? In other words, must not the objective substance also (and first!) be talked about? Otherwise, does not the Appeal, the Word, hang in the air?

Bultmann was a controversial figure in post-war Germany. His views were contested in orthodox circles. There were even those who pressed for ecclesiastical discipline against him. But he also had many followers, especially among the youth and students. In any case, his views were intensely discussed. That also happened in Switzerland. There, Barth had to deal with it directly. He felt pressured to give further account. He dedicated a separate series of seminars to Bultmann's views in the winter semester of 1951/52. Many of his students had come from Germany. The seminars were jam-packed.

Still in the same year, 1952, he published a summary of what he had brought to attention in a brochure entitled *Rudolf Bultmann. Ein Versuch, ihn zu verstehen* ["Rudolf Bultmann. An Attempt to Understand Him"]. Here he elaborated his critical questions of Bultmann. With these questions, he also made clear what was important for himself.

Bultmann sees everything oriented to human self-understanding, even in the New Testament. But, Barth asked, is the New Testament not much more about the human learning to understand God—and thereby learning to forgo learning about one's self? Bultmann offers a modern translation of "sin": the "inauthenticity" of our existence, as fixed on what is "visible" and "measurable," on what is "at our disposal." But does not this remain abstract, Platonic? And is it in the "new existence," to which we, according to Bultmann, are called by the Word, really centrally about letting go of old certainties in order to turn ourselves to the invisible, unknown, new? Does this articulation of the biblical message not wind up cold and legalistic? Above all, must it not be discounted that that "new existence" is an existence in gratitude, in answer to God's grace?

Bultmann called what takes place in the proclamation of the message, the transition of the human from one's old to one's new existence, the Christ event. But, asked Barth, is not the real Christ event Christ's cross and resurrection, namely event that precedes all proclamation and forms the foundation thereof?

18.4 The Doctrine of Reconciliation: Incomplete, Last Great Undertaking

The discussion around and with Bultmann made the development of a doctrine of reconciliation all the more a pressing matter for Barth. The question of how he would have to structure it kept him intensely busy in the summer of 1951, including during his vacation in the Swiss Tessin. There, in Locarno, he must have seen it for himself at once, as in a flash. He related it in a letter to his son Christoph. About two o'clock in the morning he woke and wrote down his fleeting thoughts in notes. That became the starting point of the lectures that he would give beginning that summer. Naturally they were the continuation of his dogmatic lectures he had already given, beginning in 1931, first in Bonn, later in Basel. But at the same time it was a new beginning.

Barth would remain active developing his doctrine of reconciliation for the remaining years of his life. It became his last great undertaking. And the result of his thinking would find its result in a series of new parts of the *Church Dogmatics*. In total, four parts (IV/1–4) would be dedicated to the doctrine of reconciliation. The first would appear in 1953, the second in 1955, the third (in two volumes) in 1959. Barth could not complete the fourth and final part.

It was his intention of bringing the doctrine of reconciliation to completion with a part dedicated to ethics as seen from the viewpoint of the doctrine of reconciliation, (thus as the unpacking of the "Command of God the Reconciler") just as he had completed his doctrine of creation with a part on ethics as seen from the viewpoint of creation (thus as unpacking "the command of God the Creator"). But Barth could realize only a fragment of this last, fourth part. That fragment was released by Barth for publication in 1967, one year prior to his death and so forms the closing volume of the *Church Dogmatics*. Other later texts were found in his estate, also intended for inclusion in the ethics of reconciliation although Barth had apparently desired to do further work on them. They were posthumously published. But even accounting for these texts, the ethics of reconciliation Barth had in mind did not come to a definitive conclusion.

18.5 Reconciliation as Fulfillment of the Covenant

We will speak of Barth's ethics-fragment later. In the following we view the complete doctrine of reconciliation as Barth had been able to elaborate it (in CD IV/1,2, and 3). He had given an overview of the whole at the beginning of the first part, a sketch of what he could see from that point. (Is that sketch perhaps the first elaboration of his thoughts in the night?)

The first thing that stands out in Barth's arrangement is that he does not begin with a reflection on human sin. Traditional (and contemporary) dogmatics often commits a separate "doctrine of sin" to precede Christology and a doctrine of reconciliation. Indeed, that appears to be logical. "Reconciliation" is usually conceived as the reestablishment of what has gone wrong (between God and the human). Is it not obvious first to analyze what has gone wrong (sin) in order to lay the basis for a view of how reestablishment is to work? Is the nature and necessity of reconciliation not determined by the misstep, the sin, of which it is the answer, and which must have preceded it? No, not according to Barth. He turned the order around and began with speaking of Jesus Christ and his work, thus immediately about reconciliation. Against that background, so he claimed, it becomes really clear what "sin" is. He gives his views about that in a second instance.

Barth emphasized that reconciliation is not an abrupt, new event. That there can be talk of reconciliation presupposes that a relation already existed between God and the human. The Bible calls that the covenant (we have seen how Barth had already spoken of that in the context of his doctrine of creation, see 11.11). Of course, that covenant was broken from the human side and thus threatened with cancellation. Reconciliation is eliminating that malfunction and thus fulfilling the conditions of the covenantal partnership; the covenant between God and the human is always—or, now anew, now all the more—reality. But it was and is, ultimately, about the covenant.

It is, Barth argued, established by God. He himself has decided to be the Covenantal Partner of the human (and therewith now also calls the human to be the covenantal partner of God from the human side). So we have learned to know God in Jesus Christ. Stronger: it is *reality* in Jesus Christ. He himself *is* in person "Immanuel," "God with us," (Matthew 1:23). And indeed, that includes the message of reconciliation. But Barth argued, reconciliation is more than an action of reestablishment, it is the *fulfillment* of the covenant. It is in essence the execution and continuation of God's original intention, the further description of what it implies that God has revealed himself to the human. Sin, however serious, cannot have made that undone. It is at most incidental.

By so positing Jesus Christ as himself, in person, the reality of reconciliation, Barth already chooses (silently) a position vis-à-vis Bultmann. Here he said already that it is not the proclamation of Jesus Christ as the decisive moment in the victory over the chasm between God and the human (as though the decision thus must take place ever anew), the decision *is* taken. It indeed precedes all proclamation and makes proclamation possible.

18.6 Jesus Christ, the Mediator

That Barth talks about Jesus Christ and his work in his doctrine of reconciliation is not surprising. What is certainly surprising—that is the second striking thing here—is how he does so. In fact, for him, the entire Christology, all reflection on the meaning of Christ, is *nothing other than the doctrine of reconciliation*. And conversely, the doctrine of reconciliation itself is *nothing other than Christology*.

Traditionally, a great deal of theologizing about Christ also preceded the real doctrine of reconciliation. It was (and is) then specifically about the person of Christ, on the question of who he was (is): God? Or human?

Or both? And how does the one relate to the other? The tradition of the church is anchored in the doctrinal decree (dogma, executed in 451 in the Council of Chalcedon) that Jesus Christ is "God and man," that he has "two *natures*," a divine and a human nature, clearly to be distinguished from each other and still not to be seen as separate from each other, both peculiar to one and the same person.

After discussing this, traditional dogmatics then gives specific thought to the work that this Christ has done. Thereby one pauses on the various stages of the way that one has gone, as they were identified in the classic confession of faith: first downward (his suffering, death, descent into hell, the realm of the dead), then upward (his resurrection and ascension). Thus, one speaks successively of the "state of humiliation" and of the "state of exaltation," and the salvific significance of each is considered.

Differently than many today, Barth retained the above-named dogma of the "two natures" of the "one person" Jesus Christ. But at the same time, he set it in a new light. Talk of the,"divine" and "human nature," of Christ as separate objects means, according to Barth, fruitless speculation. For talk about who and how Christ is can only be sensible from reflection on the *work* that he has done.

Barth claimed that we must begin to see Jesus Christ as the "Mediator," as the one in whom God and the human are together. God and the human together, that is reconciliation. In him God has turned to the human in utmost grace as in him as well the graced human has turned to God. Barth emphasized that so he exists, as Mediator between God and the human; not apart from that. Thus, Christology can be nothing other than the doctrine of reconciliation and the doctrine of reconciliation nothing other than Christology.

Here we stumble across the reason why Barth clung to the old church dogma of Jesus Christ as "God and man." That dogma is dear to him because he hears in it, however static it sounds, of the *events* happening in Christ of the reconciliation between God and the human. Saying who (what) he *is* (dogma does that by talking of his "natures") is, according to Barth, nothing other than saying what he *does*. Jesus "is God," that is to say, He *acts* in the name of God, in God's sovereignty, as the one sent by God, as God's representative. And, he "is human," that is to say, he stands *indeed* between humans, really takes their place. It is precisely the latter that is the work he performs (in the name of God). His "human nature" is not something extra alongside his "divine nature"; it is the counter-side, the expression, the concretization of it. Hence, two manners of the identity of Jesus Christ can and must be talked about, according to Barth. First, we have to do with the graceful God in what happened in him (that is his "divine nature"). And in the second place, we see in him the reality of the human reconciled with God (that is his "human nature").

18.7 Christ's Humiliation and Exaltation

In this context Barth also set the above-named traditional talk of the two "states" (humiliation and exaltation) in Christ's life in a new light. Traditionally, the "states" have been conceived as two *subsequent stages*, first that of humiliation followed by that of his exaltation. With that, Christ's humiliation is considered in the doctrine of reconciliation, but Christ's exaltation is a topic of the following chapter. Barth, however, sees these two "states"—this is the third thing that stands out here—as *aspects or configurations* of the one that has taken place in Christ for the reconciliation of the human, *to be considered alongside each other*. And Barth connects the two aspects with what we also heard him argue concerning Christ's "divine" and "human" nature.

He said that what happened in Christ is indeed on the one hand *humiliation*, to the cross and into death. It was for that that he appeared as a human. But just now the fact that in him, in this humiliation, we *have to do with God himself,* must be illuminated. Thus, where Christ is humiliated, *God himself is humiliated*. God himself is the one who in Christ has given himself into the bondedness and misery of the human and so has taken the human cause (the human fallen away from Him!) in hand. *Here the Lord has become servant*. And note well: that does not mean that God would have thereby taken leave of his own divine status or his divine power. Indeed, *this is the way in which God, this God, is "God."* Just so, and not otherwise, he apparently uses his majesty, his freedom: by committing himself in love for the human. What Barth had said earlier, speaking of God's "perfections" (see 9.7), he repeated here; we will have to radically let go of our own concepts of "God," "Almighty," etc. We will have to allow ourselves to hear in the suffering, humiliated Christ that "the One . . . whose omnipotence is so great that He can be weak and indeed impotent, as a man is weak and impotent."[2]

This on the one hand. On the other hand, the gospel proclaims to us Christ's *exaltation*: his resurrection, his ascension, his "sitting on the right hand of God." Apparently, said Barth, it is not about yet again acquiring the glory that is his "as God," as appearing in God's power. After all, he has not lost that glory on his way into the depths, that he need not be granted "again." Just here it must be considered *that Christ is human,* just as we are human. Thus, where Christ is exalted *he goes before us humans, to God's glory*. The

---

2. Barth, *CD*, IV/1, 129.

exaltation of us all is grasped in Christ's exaltation, namely, that we are all turned to God, and so "human nature getting real."

And we heard Barth already argue that this second aspect (exaltation) is not something that "follows"; it is the counter-side of the first-named (humiliation). The one is true with the other:

> As in Him God became like man, so too in Him man has become like God. As in Him God was bound, so too in Him man is made free. As in Him the Lord became a servant, so too in Him the servant has become a Lord,[3]

raised above servanthood, lifted to glory. In Christ God is with the human and the human is bound to God. Reconciliation between God and the human includes both these aspects. The one may not be seen apart from the other.

Here we see Barth connecting with the traditional talk of the "offices" fulfilled by Christ. Barth sees the fact that he, as the Lord, has become servant as the "priestly office" of Christ. And he recognizes what the tradition has called the "royal office" of Christ in the fact that he, as servant, is raised above servanthood, lifted to glory.

18.8 A Different Doctrine of Reconciliation than that of Anselm

This all means that Barth saw it as his task to unpack and think through the doctrine of reconciliation in more than one way. That would have to happen from the viewpoint of both Christ's humiliation and exaltation. *CD* IV/1 went further into Christ's humiliation as his reconciling work. The second aspect, Christ's exaltation as reconciling work, is the subject of the subsequent part, *CD* IV/2.

Over the course of centuries, the significance of Christ's humiliation (his crucifixion) for the reconciliation of God and the human was often reflected on. The train of thought as developed in the eleventh century by Anselm of Canterbury (see chapter 5) has greatly influenced Western Christianity, specifically among Protestants. Anselm's starting point was that God's honor is assaulted by human sin and God's wrath is provoked; that therefore God cannot simply allow sin, or, that satisfaction must be given him. But, claimed Anselm, the human as creature cannot supply the required satisfaction (beyond that which the human as creature is already to do to meet God's requirement). Thus, God's Son must become human to be

---

3. Barth, *CD*, IV/1, 131.

able to offer this satisfaction in our place. That is what happened in Christ's crucifixion. In it, he bore the wrath and judgment of God, the punishment that we had deserved and that we now need no longer undergo. So, God's wrath is now appeased and his honor rescued; we no longer stand under judgment; reconciliation is a fact.

Barth's treatment of this train of thought is very short. It is clear that he harbors great reservations about it. The "God" that Anselm talks about here is in the first instance an offended Majesty who appears to wait for satisfaction to be capable of letting go of his wrath and being able to let the sinner go free. This image of God is reinforced in the presupposition that God's Son "became human" to be able as such "again" to give (give back) the honor taken from God, as if he would thereby have been God's counterpart. According to Barth, this reasoning does violence to the gospel. Here it is as though we can first imagine for ourselves God as God is in himself, apart from Christ. From the beginning of his dogmatics he had emphasized that such is an impossibility. The God whom we know because he comes to us in his Word is from the outset the God and Father of Jesus Christ. That means that this God does not wait, offended, for satisfaction, but takes the initiative just as He had taken the initiative in the establishment of the covenant with the human. This initiative to reconciliation lay in the extension of the initiative of the covenant; it is the covenant initiative redux.

Thus, Christ, the incarnate Son of God, cannot be seen as a party who appears separately in the events of reconciliation vis-à-vis God. We heard Barth claim with emphasis that in Jesus Christ *God has humiliated himself.* Of course, Anselm was right when he pointed out the awesome weight of sin and when he argued that God's honor is assaulted by our sin; God is the Judge before whose judgment the sinner cannot exist. Anselm was also right by advancing that Christ has set himself under judgment "in our place." Only, that in Christ *the Judge himself* stands in our place, thus is "condemned in our place," and that just so God's honor is maintained, was not considered by Anselm. To Barth, that is precisely what really matters.

18.9 The Way of God's Son into the Depths, "Into the Far Country." Jesus, the Jew

In his further reflection, Barth uses the name (the title) for Jesus Christ that had already been applied to him in the New Testament and that had found entry in the tradition of the church, "Son of God." This title denotes the distinction between Jesus and God and at the same time expresses his close connection, his union, with God. Barth would do justice to both.

Barth typified the way that Jesus Christ has gone (with a play on the figure of the "prodigal son," from the parable in Luke 15, who "traveled to a distant land," v. 13) as the way on which "the Son," had left his home, with God, to dwell "in the far country," among us humans. That is what is traditionally called the "incarnation" of the Son. Thus, this meant humiliation for him. It reached its climax in Jesus' crucifixion.

Barth powerfully underscored the reality of Jesus' human nature; Jesus was not simply human-in-general. He was a Jew bound to the people of Israel in the very marrow of his being. The New Testament sees the history of Jesus as the conclusion and summary of God's history with that people. Jesus stands in the place of Israel. In the Old Testament (in Exodus 4:22, Hosea 11:1 for example) that people is called "God's Son," thus, bound to God, just as is the case in the New Testament with Jesus. That, of course, has a further meaning: Jesus is the *unique* Son of God, one with God the Father. However that may be, it is clear that the Christ event was no accident, not arbitrary, but the fulfillment of what God had intended, already in and with Israel and so for all people. As God was manifest in the human Jesus of Nazareth, so he had always been, graceful, prepared and of such condition to descend to the human into the deep and to take their business for his own reckoning.

Moreover, Barth said, the Old Testament also shows how the people of Israel stands before God. Israel, the elect people, appears at the same time to have trespassed God's law and to have turned themselves against God. Over and again, Israel responded to God's faithfulness with unfaithfulness. That God has entered his covenant with just this people and held to that covenant himself means in itself that it is all the more a journey of humiliation for him, a journey "into the far country." Barth warned: do not allow this Old Testament talk about Israel's unfaithfulness to God to bring us to anti-Semitism or hatred of the Jews! Then we would misunderstand the matter. Israel's attitude brings to light how the human as such stands over and against God. Israel is the mirror that is held before all in which they can see how they appear. That just Israel is the mirror is its elected nature; in the light of God's election the true human nature sees the light of day.

Thus, that Jesus was (is) a Jew means that he is directly and without reserve in solidarity with this people, even when it is rebellious and unfaithful. He allows all that can be brought against this people for God's sake to be said of himself. He took Israel's resistance and unfaithfulness on his own shoulders. And he is the Son of God, uniquely connected with God; that means that in him God himself does so in the extension of the graceful way that he has always gone with this people. That solidarity, said Barth, goes even a step further. The Old Testament also shows that the rebellious, unfaithful human stands under God's judgment. Certainly, also under God's grace. But that grace has the form of judgment toward him. Grace does not deny but confirms that he is rejected by God as a sinner. The elect is the one who understands this. Israel stands under God's judgment and receives it as addressed by his prophets. Jesus exists in solidarity with *this* people. Thus, he now stands under God's wrath and judgment and he accepts that. So it is already given with Jesus' Jewish nature that his history can be none other than the history of suffering. The Lord has become servant. Just so, reconciliation has come about.

18.10 The Way of Obedience. The Unity of God

Barth characterized the way of Jesus Christ in yet another way; he typified it (differently than the way of the "prodigal son" from Luke 15) as the "way of obedience." Thus, Jesus does not enter this way of arbitrariness or of self-sufficiency, nor of accident, but in the conscious acknowledgment that it must be so, as God's way. Here the question arises: how does the "obedience" of Jesus "to God" agree with his appearance in the name of God, in the power of God, as the "Son of God"? Must we then really imagine that God is obedient to God's self? How is that thinkable?

Barth does not avoid this question. He calls the notion that the one God commands and obeys difficult to swallow. Still, he deemed it essential also to give way to the witness of the New Testament, that in the man Jesus of Nazareth God himself is present and acts. That Jesus goes the way of obedience, then, does not conflict with his appearance in the name of God. It is just in obedience that he shows that he really is God's Son. When we encounter difficulty in thinking here, it is because we begin from our own representations of "God" and the "divine." The New Testament says to us that "it belongs to God's inner life that this happens in him as well: obedience." Is God then not one? Yes, certainly, but apparently that unity consists in "being one as being obeyed, and being another as obeying." In our minds, this is an internal contradiction. But, said Barth, we must be done with the monotheism that many religions and philosophies honor. That presupposes a unity as a fixed, empty neutrality, "beyond parties." The unity of the God of the Bible is a living unity, a unity that *happens*, namely in the history of the involvement between the different modes of being of the one God.

18.11 Reconciliation: God as the Triune God in Action

With the latter, Barth refers to the doctrine of God's "trinity," formulated already in the first centuries of Christianity by the councils of the church, that God (the one God!) is "Father," "Son," and "Spirit." That too, just as with the dogma of Christ's "two natures," is a doctrine that few today are still able to handle. Barth is convinced that just this doctrine cannot be omitted from the reflection of Christian faith, provided that this also be placed in its proper context.

He had spoken earlier of the doctrine of the trinity, in the first volume of his *Church Dogmatics*, *CD* I/1, in the context of his reflection on the Word of God (see 5.7 and 6.3), on what it means that God "reveals himself." Those who say, "God reveals himself," have, Barth said, already thereby stated something that is to be understood in three ways, with three different accents. It is about God, the subject of revelation (the first aspect). But immediately also about the form, the configuration, in which God reveals himself (the second aspect). In the form of revelation God has become "his own alter ego." Said differently, revelation implies that God distinguishes himself from himself. God is and remains himself but becomes "God once more, in another way." He manifests himself "in a form of what he is himself not." The "form" announces itself already in the Old Testament where sometimes God's "justice," "faithfulness," "goodness," "word," his "face," "arm," "hand," or again God's "name" is talked about as of conditions in which God himself is deemed present. The same trend is described still more directly in the New Testament, less ambiguously, more understandably; here is the man Jesus of Nazareth, "in the form of something He Himself is not"[4] in whom God has revealed himself, thus, *in* whom God is "yet God once in another way," as "God with us." Thus, God's revelation happens par excellence in the form of this Jesus. He is the *Son* of the *Father*. And (the third aspect) this revelation really comes to the human; it happens in part to the human as it touches him. It is that aspect that in the Bible is called *Spirit*. Hence, it can (must!) be said that God exists in three modes of being.

It is not accidental that in his doctrine of reconciliation Barth again brought up what he had talked about in the context of his doctrine of revelation. He saw the one as closely cohering to the other. That God reveals himself means, he said, by definition that he has already entered a covenant with the human; what else could it be directed to? And we heard that Barth sees the essence of God's reconciling work in that he keeps to that covenant despite everything and fulfills it. Said differently, reconciliation is that God

---

4. Barth, *CD*, I/1, 316.

confirms his self-revelation as the God of the covenant. Reconciliation is God's self-revelation to the very end. So both can be said: in Christ God has revealed himself to us and in Christ God has reconciled himself with us humans. That, both, is what is stated in the doctrine of the trinity. Reconciliation is the triune God in action. Moreover, the concept "trinity" is not what matters. That is human terminology, an attempt to indicate what is at stake: the event of revelation and reconciliation.

18.12 The Judge Judged in Our Place

Reconciliation is really effected in Christ's way of humiliation and obedience. Barth interprets that in a further reflection of what we already heard him argue: that Christ has not only placed himself under the judgment of God but that he underwent that judgment *as the Judge himself*. Barth actually said it more strongly: *by placing himself under judgment, he acts as Judge*.

It has been traditionally confessed that Christ has come as Redeemer, as Savior, that God's grace has appeared in him. True, Christ's coming "to judge the living and the dead" is also talked about in the gospel, in the tradition. But that, so it is traditionally said, is future; that obtains at the end of time, it is not yet in order.—Barth also here takes another path. He argued that grace and judgment do not conflict with each other. Real grace is not cheap. Grace means acquittal, and acquittal is always the outcome, the execution of a judgment. Thus, grace through Jesus Christ does not mean the delay (or cancellation) of judgment. It implies that judgment *is* executed over humans, the sentence *is* declared, namely that in it he (Christ) himself as human stands in our place and so the judgement that must obtain for us is allowed to come to him. Standing there, he has taken our sin on his own shoulders. It is forgiven us. And just so we can really see it.

The history of Christ's passion and death is central here. It is traditionally said that he has borne the punishment that we have deserved and that we thus no longer need undergo it. And that thought is often connected with the notion that Christ has so made satisfaction to God, of his wrath. Barth cannot agree with this train of thought, derived from Anselm (see 18.6). He deems it is the purport of the proclamation of the New Testament that Christ has definitively settled accounts by entering death in our place, in his own person, with all us sinners. Thereby he interpreted the "in our place" not only exclusively but also and above all inclusively; in and with Christ *we*, we humans who live in conflict with God, *are nailed to the cross*; as such we no longer exist.

"For this reason the divine judgment in which the Judge was judged, and therefore the passion of Jesus Christ, is as such the divine action of atonement which has taken place for us."[5] This passion was thus no passive, but active, deed, the deed in which the radical evil in the world is attacked and uprooted. Here a divine vengeance or need for retribution need not be satisfied but the radicality of divine love becomes manifest; divine love that fulminates against the sinner and does not rest until he is killed, wiped out, put away. This has happened in the passion of Jesus Christ. So in this passion God's judgment is indeed executed and thereby reconciliation is effected.

Thus, Barth said, Christ has—in our place—"done this before God and has therefore done right"[6] He, God's Son, has been the true, just man among us, as the obedient one in the midst of our disobedience. That he, the Judge, has accepted the judgment of himself, was an act of obedience, an act in contrast to our inclination to want to sit on God's right hand at the cost of others.

18.13 The Judgment of the Father: The Resurrection of Christ.

How can we now know that this is true, that Jesus' crucifixion is not really the end for us (as we were) but also a new beginning? According to Barth, that question finds its answer at the close of the gospels, in the reports of Jesus' resurrection—or better, resuscitation—from the dead. It is with this discussion that Barth concludes his reflection on Jesus' way of humiliation and obedience as the event of reconciliation.

He understood Jesus' resurrection as the "great verdict of God," the affirming judgment by God the Father confirming Jesus' way of the cross; this way was in agreement with God's will and thus for our salvation. Said differently, Jesus' resurrection is the event in which he is rehabilitated, "justified" by God (1 Timothy 3:16).[7] In and through the resurrection, Jesus' way of the cross, trod there and then, is not undone nor turned back, indeed, it is thus made current for us (and for all time). A completed past, so it remains; but it still applies today! The resurrection makes it so that we may confess the Jesus Christ of yesterday as present in our midst, albeit in a hidden way (the gospel speaks of that as Jesus' "ascension"), and thus looking toward his coming in glory, that is, fully revealed.

5. Barth, *CD*, IV/1, 255.
6. Barth, *CD*, IV/1, 256.
7. Barth, *CD*, IV/1, 308–9.

So Barth thus talks of the resurrection of Christ here. He had already done so in that part of his dogmatics on the human, namely in his consideration of human nature as principally being-in-time, as mortal being. That being in-time, temporality, he argued there, also obtains first of all to the human nature of Jesus. The story of Jesus' resurrection and of the short period of his appearances that followed is not in conflict with that. That story does not say that he still continued to live after his death (a special extra time). Certainly, it is more than a fantasy of the imagination that would simply state that the disciples would have *inwardly* come to a new understanding of faith following Jesus' death. Over and against that interpretation, advocated by Bultmann, Barth had already held that the resurrection of Jesus, together with his appearances, must have been a concrete event in time, an event in which God himself has acted in a unique way and has set the preceding, with the life of Jesus ending in crucifixion, in its true light, and has revealed its meaning (see 18.2 and 13.7).

Now, speaking of reconciliation through Christ, he brings it up again. He again underscores that the resurrection (resuscitation) of Christ (according to the New Testament) must be seen as a new event in which God himself acted. And then also as an event that, just as the crucifixion—and coherent with it—has taken place in our world. Thus, historical; though, it is not a fact detectable by historical research, analogous to and in connection with other events (that is not even possible, as it is about a direct, unique act of God himself). This event was the foundation of the faith of the disciples/apostles. That faith did not originate from nothing. It rests in the encounter with God, which they saw concretely at work in this event of Jesus' resurrection.

19

The Doctrine of Reconciliation from Another Perspective

19.1 Continuing Concentration on Reconciliation

RECONCILIATION IS GOD AND the human together. Barth had argued that reconciliation has become a reality in Christ. We have seen how he had worked that out in the first part of his doctrine of reconciliation *CD* IV/1. There he had emphasized that Christ means that God came to us, *God with us*. That is the first thing, the fundamental thing. But it is still not everything. Now it is about considering that reconciliation also means that we turn to God, *we with God*. Reconciliation also implies that we humans have become different. That must also be on the agenda.

Barth quickly set himself to the continuation of his dogmatic work. The first part of his doctrine of reconciliation, *CD* IV/1, had just appeared in the summer of 1953 when he had again begun with his lectures further thinking through the second side of reconciliation. The result came to press two years later, in the fall of 1955, *CD* IV/2. His impatience comes through in the preface to this part. Barth would have gladly been ready earlier. He excused himself to his readers, "I fail to produce with the regularity of clockwork."[1] Meanwhile, those who observe the pace that, even now, the parts of the *Church Dogmatics* follow on each other can only be astonished.

19.2 The Human is also the Subject of Reconciliation

Through the centuries, it is often claimed that reconciliation is complete when the human is involved, renewed, turned to God. Sometimes the human return to God is even highlighted as the decisive moment. Reconciliation is,

---

1. Barth, *CD*, IV/2, ix.

so understood, an event not so much "from above to below," as "from below to above," from the human to God.

Such views are popular. They fit with the way that "religion" is often thought of. Religion is something human, the human effort to contact the "higher," "the divine." Within Protestantism, pietism, with its expansive idea of human piety, has existed in this sense since the seventeenth century. That had, and has, its parallel in the Netherlands in the experiential stream of the Further Reformation (*nadere reformatie*). One may think also at the revival movement, risen especially in the nineteenth century. In another way, Enlightenment thought has had broad influence since the eighteenth century; human reason came to be central and later, relatedly, human feeling and experience. Theology and the church were influenced by those movements. A liberal Protestantism developed that understood and presented orthodox truths in a new way.

This way of thinking "from the human to God," was the world of thought in which Barth had grown up as well. During and following the First World War he had wrestled with it. Since that time, he had emphasized ever more strongly that the orientation of thought must be turned around within theology; the idea must be: from God toward the human. Thus far, he had explicitly justified that. Now, speaking of the reconciliation between God and the human, he felt pressed to reconsider the justification of this other way of thinking. Indeed, in theology, and specifically in the doctrine of reconciliation, it is really about God *and the human*. The human is not only the object of God's actions; he is (as such) also the acting subject! That is what the second part of Barth' doctrine of reconciliation, *CD* IV/2, is about.

Therewith he intended in his own way, not only to do justice to the intentions of pietism but also to offer a Protestant answer to the Roman Catholic doctrines of Mary, the mother of Jesus.

He also writes about the latter in his preface. Only a few years earlier, in 1950, the notion that Mary herself "was taken up into heaven" was declared as a dogma by Pope Pius XII. For Roman Catholics, this proclamation lay in line with what the Roman Catholic tradition earlier, for centuries, had confessed concerning Mary. But the new dogma of Mary provoked an uproar in Protestant circles. Here, a central role was ascribed to the human (for the sake of Christians), namely, Mary, the mother Jesus, a claim that Protestants could not share. In their mind, by that, the central, unique salvific significance of Jesus himself was shortchanged. Barth shared that objection but not without having in mind what he viewed as the element of truth in the Roman Catholic dogma, that the Christian faith is also about the exaltation of the human to God, that God's grace for the human includes not only justification (acquittal), but also effects renewal (as is gladly be said by Roman Catholics), sanctification. Only, he argued, that a special dogma of Mary is not necessary for such an understanding. He saw what is connected with Mary for the Roman Catholics, her role in interceding for us humans with God, as she makes way for us on the way to glorification, as already taken up in (the human) Jesus himself, so that alongside that there is simply no longer a place for a peculiar role for Jesus' mother.

19.3 Jesus Christ: The Exalted Human

With the latter, the heart of what Barth explained in the second part of his doctrine of reconciliation is touched upon. Just as in the first part, Christ remains the starting point. For Barth, here also everything depends on the confession that God in Jesus Christ has become human.

We heard Barth explain that that means that God has humbled himself in Christ, has entered the depths. Now he said (what he had already indicated) that that also means that in Christ (with the coming of Christ) the human is exalted. Christ is, in person, "the Lord as servant," that was the first thing; but as such he is also "servant as lord," that is its counterside, Christ *represents God before us*; in him we have to do with God's self; but that may not lead to the idea that Christ would not be fully human.[2] Indeed, he is the one human who belongs to God, who had lived in absolute obedience to God and in that *represents* and precedes *us humans*. And hence it now also applies to us that we are connected with God, reconciled, are lifted up as humans to new life with God.

Barth also connects with the tradition of the church again, with the dogma of Jesus Christ as "God and man." Something particular is the matter with the human nature of Jesus in that dogma: *God* has become human. Is that intended to say that God would have been changed into a human? No, says the tradition of the church; God has taken up an existence as a human in "His own divine existence."[3] That is difficult for us to imagine, but in any case, this ecclesiastical language intends to give powerful expression to the fact that God has essentially bound himself with the humans.

Barth said: that God has done that must certainly go back to God's own decision. He himself has willed it. It was not too little for him. Again, Barth pointed out that this God does not answer to what we represent for ourselves by "God"; this God is not a prisoner of his own majesty; He can apparently also be humbled and then just so maintain his divine majesty. There is a flexibility in God!

2. Barth, *CD*, IV/1, 135; IV/2, 20.
3. Barth, *CD*, IV/2, 51.

And Barth explained for his readers what this is about: *as a consequence of this action (this self-manifestation, this entrance into the depths) of God*, human life originated: the human Jesus. Here, too, Barth advocates a train of thought that has developed in the tradition of the church in connection with the gospel story. This man did not "ordinarily" originate from humanity, from the normal chain of the generations. Yes, he was born within a concrete people, Israel, and as the son of a concrete mother, Mary. But neither Israel nor even Mary brought about his coming. That it took place is specifically the result of God's own action. The idea is not that the Son of God has bound himself to an already existing human (a certain "Jesus of Nazareth"); no, the human Jesus owes his existence in that God himself has bound himself here with human nature. And now the converse must be said: that the human is firmly taken up and exalted in a unique bondedness with God. And where "human nature" ("the human") is peculiar to us all, we may also realize for ourselves that this one human nature, that of Jesus, includes a promise for all of us humans. That too is the message of reconciliation.

19.4 Again, the Meaning of Easter

As he did following his consideration of the first aspect of reconciliation (see 18.13), Barth now again speaks of the resurrection of Jesus Christ. Then he argued that the resurrection is a mark of the judgment proclaimed by God the Father on Jesus, the crucified, proof of God's concurrence with Jesus' way of the cross. Now he throws new light on it. Barth interpreted Jesus' resurrection here as a mark of his exalted existence as the human into being bound with God. On Easter it became clear that that is really true.

Note well, Barth said, that Jesus' exaltation is not just a fact with Easter. It was already the case throughout his entire life (ending in his passion and death). So understood, the report of Jesus' resurrection does not report anything substantially new. And yet, Barth said, the Easter report is not simply a beautiful conclusion, pure decoration. For that Jesus Christ the crucified is and *as such* the exalted, *that is what is made manifest on Easter*. It is from that, looking back, that we see it already manifest in what went before—the full story of Jesus' way to the cross as described in the gospels. We humans become consciously involved through the Easter events. That, too, is essential. Thus, we cannot do without the Easter message.

19.5 A Paragraph on the Life of Jesus

That Jesus in what went before, in the course of his life on his way to the cross, was already exalted human is the theme of a separate paragraph. In particular, Barth analyzed here the witness of the first three gospels. How are the life, the appearance, the words and actions of Jesus described there? According to that witness, he was a real human in the midst of his contemporaries. And still there was something special with his human nature. It had a royal allure. So the gospels reported. Barth surveyed that and drew a few outlines that together sketched the image of Jesus as "the royal human." With that he did something that does not appear in other dogmatics.

There was, of course, consideration of who Jesus "really" had been, earlier in theology. There was a great deal of discussion of this, specifically in the nineteenth century. But one did not remain confined to biblical texts. Starting from the presupposition that the evangelists, writing about Jesus from their own faith, would certainly have done violence to the historicity, one began looking for historical reality behind the texts. The "historical Jesus" would have looked vastly different than he was described in the Bible. One would orient himself to the "historical Jesus" to be able to finish with the traditional presuppositions of faith.

However, about the beginning of the twentieth century an understanding had emerged that the gospels would have real value by way of their own character as "tendency literature." We come no further than suppositions of a historical reality "behind" the texts, but, so it was argued, that doesn't matter. Ultimately, we have to do with Jesus as he is *proclaimed* to us. It is not about the "historical Jesus," but about the *meaning* of Jesus. Bultmann was prominent in this regard (see 18.2)

But if we know nothing (or need not know anything) of the "real, historical" Jesus, how can something be said about Jesus' "meaning"? That was a pressing question just at the time when Barth was busy with his doctrine of reconciliation. Hence, a new search for the historical Jesus began afresh—and that in the circles of Bultmann's students. The proclamation of Christ of the gospels, and faith in Christ as it had developed in the earliest Christian communities, must still have (had) a basis in reality.

It is within this discussion that Barth, writing of Jesus as the exalted, "royal human," added his own voice. He was also convinced that the gospels are not historical biographies of Jesus but rather witnesses of faith. But for him that faith character is no reason to dismiss the witnesses as "pious fantasy."[4] Indeed, it gives the witnesses a peculiar authenticity; they

---

4. Barth, *CD*, IV/2, 111.

apparently speak of experienced reality. Barth doesn't involve himself in the search for the "historical Jesus" "behind" the text. His objection is that such would start from the notion that Jesus could be considered—and thus he could be "sought"—apart from his resurrection. Just that doesn't work. The evangelists write from the experience of Jesus as the Resurrected; it was that experience (however strange and unimaginable) that had brought them to report all that went before Easter in Jesus' appearance. Those who negate that search for an abstraction. The "real Jesus" can be no other than the Jesus as he is proclaimed in the gospels. It thus comes down to reading the gospel texts themselves.

19.6 Dogmatics as Re-narration of the Gospel Story. Jesus, the Royal Human

It is said that in the paragraph on the life of Jesus, the dogmatician takes on the role of biblical theologian. Indeed, here dogmatics completely becomes the re-narration of the gospel story. So, Barth again takes an unusual path in traditional dogmatics. Or better, he again does what he continually has in mind to do. For him, it was always about dogmatics as thoughtful repetition of the biblical story.

The first thing that Barth extracted from the gospel stories is that Jesus was apparently so present in the human midst that one could neither ignore him nor pass him by. Where Jesus was present, decisions were made; a division began. Jesus' presence must have been unforgettable for those who experienced it. He was experienced not simply as "a" prophet alongside others; no, rather as the one in whom all the prophets had received their conclusion and fulfillment. He was a human among humans and yet royally free, for he was subject to no one besides God the Father. And his presence of that time is later experienced as not past. Later, too, the church had known him as present in its midst; and even as the one still coming. There is no biography to be compiled from the gospel texts of this Jesus. His peculiarity makes that impossible.

Of what, then, did this peculiarity consist? Barth said that his appearance was wholly in agreement with the actions of God. Jesus continually underwent misunderstanding, contempt. He himself alluded to the fact that his "Kingdom" is present in this world only as hidden, like yeast in dough, or tiny as a mustard seed. "The Son of Man has nowhere to lay his head" (Luke 8:20). In his appearance he continually ran into contradiction, resistance (as in his hometown of Nazareth). That finally led to his imprisonment and condemnation whereby all his disciples abandoned him and he received a crown of thorns as "king." That is never glorious to see, indeed. And still, Barth said, we see here the royal nature of the human Jesus. It is *precisely in this unsightliness, in this undergoing of misunderstanding and contempt, that he appears as God!* Even as in that, in passing by all those who were powerful and rich, he orients himself to the small, the weak, the poor, the sinners.

Barth refers further to Jesus' attitude regarding the society of his days. He was no partisan in the sense that he would have committed himself to a particular new order over and against the existing order. He did not advocate a new (political or economic, moral or religious, progressive or conservative) program. In fact, he relativized all programs and principles. He was royally free in relation to the societal order of the day. But just that threw light on the provisional and event nature of the societal order and led to confrontation. Precisely the attitude of freedom regarding the existing order made him a radical revolutionary. In that, too, he was the image of God.

19.7 Jesus' Royal Speech

Jesus' appearance concretely consisted of his words and deeds. Barth dedicated a separate reflection to that topic. He began with the remark that according to the gospels, there can be no contradiction made between Jesus' words and deeds. His words were also deeds, and he spoke through his deeds. Viewed by themselves his words did not involve anything particular. They were just normal, human words. Jesus' use of language was not to be distinguished from others. The later Jesus-community was also unconcernedly engaged with Jesus' words. That appears from a mutual comparison of the varied gospels. One does not shy away from offering different versions. The Jesus of the gospels sometime expresses himself in the thought forms of late Judaism, sometimes in Hellenistic forms. What then is particular, royal, in his words? Apparently, it lay only in the fact that they were *his* words. In whatever version, whatever thought world they were handed on, *they announced God's royal kingship.*

Jesus' speech is typified by different words in the tradition. Jesus *evangelized*, say the gospels; he brought the message that included really *good* news, the report of the dawn of a new age (in his appearance), the age in which all is whole. And he *taught*; he interpreted the law and prophets from the Old Testament, and he did so "with authority, not as the scribes" (Matthew 7:29); it was his appearance in this authority that provoked the conflict with the Jewish rabbinate. And Jesus also *proclaimed*; promising the future from what had already taken place. Apparently only Jesus could evangelize, teach, and proclaim in that way.

19.8 Jesus' Royal Action

Jesus' speech was announcement and manifestation of the coming, the breaking in, of God's Kingdom. That is made clear from Jesus' concrete acts that the gospels report as accompanying his words. Those deeds were often surprising, extra-ordinary. They broke through the "normal" course of affairs. They had the character of miracles. It is repeatedly about driving out demons, often also about healing sick.

Traditionally these miracles are connected with the classic dogma of Jesus Christ, "God and man." That Jesus performed miracles would have to be understood from the notion that God has acted here, in Jesus. But that means a division in the one person of Jesus, as if he were partly human, partly divine. But conversely, Jesus' full human nature is firmly maintained in the dogma. We saw how Barth underscored that. There was not another Jesus than the human Jesus. His miracles were thus also human actions however much they transcended "normal" human action.

In the meantime, it comes down to seeing just in what the miracle character of Jesus' deeds was located. What was peculiar was not that natural laws were broken in those deeds (for example, of healing or driving out demons). As a matter of fact, Jesus' healings have been explained with the help of theories of psychic influence. But that does not get to the heart of the matter. Barth said that we get a clue when we see Jesus' deeds as coherent with his proclamation, with the whole of his appearance. Just as his words, his deeds proclaimed the Kingdom of God. Or more strongly, in his deeds, just as in his words, the Kingdom of God became concrete. That makes them royal deeds.

Jesus' miracles are not about spectacular, supernatural events in themselves. Barth pointed out a few characteristics of Jesus' miracles that show that, characteristics as they appear from their descriptions in the gospels. Generally, Jesus did not do them on his own initiative, planned. Rather, they appear to be pressed upon him. The story of the healing in which he noticed "that power had flowed out of him" (Mark 5:30) is illustrative. Jesus also used no special therapeutic technique in his healings. And he did not perform them in his own interest. Even less did he present himself as one come to make the world better or as an organizer of human well-being. He did not have in mind the establishment of an institution of health. His miracles stood in service of his proclamation. Jesus apparently could and would not perform them apart from that, purely to draw attention.

Jesus' miracles were kingdom miracles. They could be typified as deeds of power, but here too we must be precise; it was not about brute power ("omnipotence") in itself. No, here qualified power (God's power!)

was expressed (via Jesus' appearance); execution of power that meant that a new light fell on the human situation. Seen in that light, it appears to be a situation of need and anxiety. Jesus entered that situation, saw humans in their deadly need, rescued them, liberated them, made them to be human again. That these sufferers were also guilty apparently did not play a role, or scarcely did so, appears from the gospel stories. Jesus did not confront them with their (guilty) past but created for them a new future. So the God, in whose name Jesus appeared, appears to be interested in the human, to remain faithful to the human. God certainly takes human sin, but primarily the human oneself, seriously (and in that himself as the Covenant partner of this human). Thus, God's powerful hold of earth, a powerful hold that shows that God himself is concerned with the suffering of the human. God himself fights against that suffering. Stronger still, it is his first and real business. That was what was on order in Jesus' deeds. They are deeds of warfare. There is the battle against death, against demons. That is what makes these deeds "miracles," royals deeds.

In a reflection that followed this analysis, Barth expressed his surprise that Western Christianity, in particular Protestantism has blundered here. Differently than in the East (Eastern Orthodoxy) one in the West (apart from a few exceptions) has had no eye for the meaning of Jesus' miracles. One has strongly concentrated on the human, human experience, the realization of his guilt and penance, instead of being oriented to the radiant coming of the Kingdom of God. Christianity thus became a one-sided moralistic, lackluster matter. What in Barth's view mattered in this connection had remained out of view, the gospel as the message of God's grace that liberates from the power of death.

19.9 The Cross as Coronation

Barth adds one more thing to his overview of the story of Jesus from the gospels. That is that Jesus' entire appearance stood under the sign of the cross. We already heard Barth say that Jesus underwent misunderstanding, contempt. He again underscores that. Jesus was not welcome in the world in which he manifested himself royally. He was rejected and discarded. The gospels did not disguise that fact but explicitly illuminated it. Thereby they made it clear that this was neither tragedy nor fate. They have seen Jesus' entire history, including that of his passion, as a whole.

Barth said that Jesus' crucifixion does not compromise the witness to him as the royal human. Indeed, just this ending of his life is described as confirmation and coronation of his royal way of life. As appears from that description it was not an abrupt, unexpected end, but the goal that Jesus accepted as ordained by God for him. He was handed over by representatives of Israel to the representative of Roman power, Pilate, and so, as Israel's Messiah, he became the savior of the world.

19.10 Jesus' Human Nature and Ours

We are aware that this entire view of Jesus' human nature is part of Barth's doctrine of reconciliation. It is not only about Jesus himself here. In that it is about the human nature of us all. Barth argued that a decision has been made about us in Jesus' royal human nature. With Jesus, we too are destined to a new, royal human nature!

Is that only a theory, edifying words that have no purchase in our reality? Barth spent a new paragraph in refuting this skepticism. He again pointed out the meaning of Jesus' resurrection. We already heard that it was on Easter that Jesus had become manifest to us as the royal human. So, we ourselves are actively involved in that. And there is in the message of Jesus' resurrection from the dead a power that affects us, draws us along. It is said to us that we ourselves have, in Christ, become new humans; now it comes down to us allowing this be said to us. We are called to that, challenged, in the New Testament. Where we hear that, we are no longer the same as we were. We are thereby grasped, taken in hand. That such happens is the work of the Holy Spirit. So, we are shown how we actively may and can live as new humans. That such happens is also reconciliation!

19.11 Sin as Pride and as Sloth

We have already noted that Barth does not offer a separate doctrine of sin that precedes the doctrine of reconciliation (see 18.5). Of course, he spoke of sin but did so only secondarily. He began by speaking of Jesus Christ and his (reconciling) work. It is from that point, against that background, that it can become clear, he said, what "sin" is—and how God responds.

Is that indeed the case? Traditionally, that the human is 'sinner' is one of the matters which one agreed was self-evident. Is sin not disobedience to God? Transgression of God's law? Well, one was of the opinion that God's law embraces not only what is in the Bible (the Ten Commandments) but also what can be inferred from nature. In other words, humans know, if they but observe and reflect (and listen to their conscience!), God's will, understand what (measured against God's will) is good and evil. And you need no clarity of sight to grasp that humans invariably transgress the (known) will of God. Anyway, again and again, this exactly is *not* sensed. How can a human then stand open to God's grace? In order to receive that, in order to be reconciled with God, you must first sense that you are a sinner and are in need of grace, of reconciliation. It is from that notion that the emphasis is placed on "sin" in many orthodox circles. A separate doctrine of sin has been developed, subsequently to give grace, reconciliation, its proper place in theology. That order was (is) also often retained in sermons in these circles. The measure to which that happens thereby obtains as a characteristic of "orthodoxy."

Barth also found that sin is a turning against God. But he resists the presupposition, obtaining here, as though we humans would know who and how "God" is on our own. He argued here what he consistently claimed in his dogmatics, that we know God in no other way than in Christ, thus as the gracious God. The knowledge of God's grace toward us humans is not something secondary but comes first. The human is grasped from without by God's goodness and grace, taken up in the covenant with God. Sin consists in that the human turns against that, would free oneself from it. It is seen precisely in this light that the true seriousness of sin comes into view.

In the preceding, we saw how Barth further characterizes God's gracious, reconciling actions to us in two ways. On the one hand, God has come to us in Jesus. He has humbled himself before us; the Lord became servant. On the other hand (its counter-side) God has exalted, renewed us in and with Jesus. Thereby he has taken us humans into real covenant partnership with him; the servant became lord.—That means that sin must now be spoken of in (at least) two ways. On the one hand, we do not want to know of a God who has humbled himself; that is too little for us. Where God humbled himself (to us humans) we would climb upward, to be "as God" and so be able to save ourselves. That is sin as *pride*. And on the other hand, we humans would not allow ourselves to be taken along in God's exalting, renewing work. We also resist that. We prefer to remain where we are. We refuse to be human as God has intended us to be. That is sin as *sloth*.

By the way, that in both regards, in both cases, we really have to do with "sin," becomes clear to us where we are confronted with the configuration, the existence of Jesus Christ. In that confrontation the difference between him and us appears. God continues to say "yes" to us, He remains the God of the covenant. Just that, Barth said, immediately implies our unmasking. God appears to be a forgiving God over and against our sin and thereby, in that, a judging God.

19.12 Reconciliation Focused: Justification, Sanctification

In the meantime, human sin can be no more than an incident (certainly, a great incident!) It did not have the first word in the relation between God and the human. And thus even less so does it have the last word. Despite everything, we humans are held firmly by God. His gracious covenant will remain in power against our sin. The reconciliation that has taken place in Christ also means that God has definitively finished with sin. A decision has been made concerning sin. We humans have said "no" to God, but God's "yes" spoken in Christ has made our "no" obsolete, set it aside, abolished it. It perseveres, sustains itself and overcomes.

Thus, it is about God's reconciliation reaching us humans; that just so we are actively saved. That is a separate point of faith in traditional Protestantism, that the human is "justified" for Christ's sake, or, is acquitted of his guilt and thus may stand as a free and just human before God. A separate "doctrine of justification" exists to explain that. Justification is also a theme for Barth. But he does not make it a separate point of faith. He viewed it as an application, focus, of what is already said in the doctrine of reconciliation. To his understanding, this theme cannot be spoken of other than in the context of the doctrine of reconciliation itself.

Traditionally, reconciliation (the coming of Jesus Christ) is often seen as that which makes justification (the forgiveness of sins) *possible*. In contradistinction, Barth claimed that Jesus Christ, his journey to the depths ("the Lord as servant"), is, as answer to human sin-as-pride, not simply the possibility; he is the full reality of God's grace and forgiveness. Reconciliation itself is/means justification.

But reconciliation, oriented to the human, is more than this. Again, Barth considers that the coming of Jesus Christ also implies that he is himself exalted ("the servant as lord") and now the human with him as well; we humans are exalted. In that is the response to human sin in its other form, sin as sloth. In its focus on the human, reconciliation here means that the human indeed may (will) rise from his sloth to new life.

That is traditionally called the "sanctification" of human existence. That had also become a separate theme in Protestantism. In it, that and how human life can (and must) be renewed is considered, so that it is actively lived to God's honor. A great deal of emphasis is laid on it in certain circles, for example in Reformed Protestantism and currently in revival movements. The gospel is then primarily conceived as an appeal to obedience, as a salvific bond and duty. It is then said that where that appeal is heard and followed, "justification" attains its goal. Thus it appears to come down to this "sanctification."

Barth only partially affirms that. Indeed, he deals with the theme of sanctification. But again it is true that he does not make it a separate point of faith; he also makes his treatment of sanctification a paragraph as part of his doctrine of reconciliation. And even less does he hold to a strict, chronological, order as though a human would "first" be justified (receive the forgiveness of sins) and just "afterward" could reach the "stage" of sanctification. That could even lead to the thought that humans must lay out an entire "way of salvation" whereby some would already have advanced further than others. Barth would know nothing of such thoughts. He sees sanctification, like justification, as the focus of the same reconciliation given in Christ; another aspect of the same matter, of the same salvation. Just as the coming of Christ on the one hand is descent and on the other hand (at the same time! and as such!) exaltation (see 18.7).

So viewed, sanctification is thus not a counter-response following (vis-à-vis) God's grace to be expected from the human. It is, like justification, itself a gift of grace. As such it obtains for all humans. Concretely, it is present where humans are bound with Christ in faith. He himself is the Holy One, and he calls us to follow him. That call reaches us where we hear the gospel. Called to follow, we ourselves may also be called "holy." And from that we will also come actively to live as new humans, as "holy," as "saints."

20

Other Activities. Current Discussions

20.1 Lecture on "Freedom," September 1953

IN THE TWO PREVIOUS chapters we reviewed the main points of the first parts of Barth's doctrine of reconciliation. Barth must have worked in a very concentrated way in these years, between 1951 and 1955. All that has appeared in the *Church Dogmatics* had previously been delivered in his dogmatic lectures. He gave four hours of lecture per week, year in and year out. There was always pressure for further elaboration, preparation, formulation. All in all, it must have taken an immense effort for Barth as he aged and in a fragile health that afflicted him from time to time.

There were also still seminars in which classic or current theological texts were discussed and commented on. As with the lectures, they drew many interested participants, primarily from Germany.

He accepted fewer invitations to offer lectures or readings than before. Meanwhile, he still drew on a theme that interested him. Thus, in September 1953 he held a lecture in Bielefeld in the context of a conference of the German Society for Evangelical Theology on the theme of "freedom." That this was a meeting in Germany was all the more reason for Barth to accept this invitation. He had not appeared as a speaker in Germany since his guest professorship in Bonn in 1947 (see 12.6).

There was great interest in the meeting in Bielefeld. Many old acquaintances, friends, and students, from Germany and environs, would not allow the occasion pass without hearing and meeting Barth again. He spoke before a jam-packed hall of a thousand. Theologians from East Germany (the GDR) were also present. The theme, "freedom," was a hot topic in a world dominated by the East-West conflict. In the West, people saw themselves as the guardian of the "free" world, vis-à-vis the threat from the East. In the East, ruled by Communist ideology, Western "freedom" was criticized as a cover for Western capitalism, a societal system of egoism and lack of social justice. How should the position be chosen here? How should the Christian, the church, choose a position?

These questions had played a part in the organization of this conference. Barth was asked to speak on the theme "freedom" in such a way that the basis of a (Christian) ethic would be in order.

Barth did not go directly into the East-West conflict as such. But he let his criticism on the use of "freedom" as a Western slogan appear indirectly. Freedom, he said, is not a self-evident human right. It is not something that we can demand or secure for ourselves. Freedom is a gift. This theme gave him the occasion to advance thoughts that he had already developed in his doctrine of God in the context of his *Church Dogmatics* (see 9.7). Freedom primarily belongs to God's self. And it does not exist in that God, with unlimited power "can" or "may do everything." God has used his freedom and impressed it in such a way that he himself has made a choice and has confirmed himself in that choice. He has, as the triune God, chosen to bind himself to the human. God's freedom is thus not freedom *from*, separate from everything and everybody, but freedom *to*, that realizes itself in being: being for others, freedom to say "yes" against all that stands in the way of his covenant with the human.

With that God has bound himself to us humans, He also gives us freedom. That, too, is not freedom in the sense of having unlimited possibilities or to do what you have (accidentally) in mind. It is freedom to respond, gladly, to God's choice for us, thus to be human, in relation to God and then also to our fellow human.

This gift of freedom is the basis for ethics, for reflection on what is good and evil in human action. It cannot consist in the establishment of general rules or norms. We must continue to sense that we, we humans together, are set by God in freedom in order to seek in that what must be done here and now. Unconditional commands can come from God only in the concrete situation, although people can, carefully and provisionally, speaking in the sense of given freedom, offer each other ethical advice, as Barth himself had attempted in the context of his dogmatics (*CD* III/4; see 17).

20.2 "In theology, begin at the beginning, with God"

Barth concluded his argument in Bielefeld with a short reflection of the ethics of theological practice. The theologian too can only exist as a free human, living in the freedom given by God, he said. Of course, in theology too one begins at the beginning, with God, who has entered a relation with the human. That the human from his side stands in relation to God will follow, will be in order from that beginning. That means concretely that the theologian acknowledges the resurrection of Jesus Christ as guideline for his reasoning. Alas, it is often otherwise:

> There is an abundance of serious, pious, learned, and ingenious theological undertaking. But lacking the sky-light and hence serenity the theologian remains a gloomy visitor upon this earth of darkness, and unpleasant instructor of his brethren.[1]

It is rumored that these closing remarks on the ethics of theological practices evoked a lively reaction among the audience. Barth apparently struck a sensitive nerve.

In any case, he alluded to current theological discussions. Begin at the beginning, with the acknowledgment of the resurrection of Christ and behind that, with God himself, to whom freedom belongs in the original sense; that is just what he did not see his eminent colleagues doing. He already had them in mind when he had ironically asked them at the outset of his argument whether his commitment with God's own freedom needed special defense:

> I, too, have heard the news that we can speak about *God* only by speaking about *man*. I do not contest this claim. Rightly interpreted, it may be an expression of the true insight that God is not without man . . . But this claim, correctly understood, calls for a counterclaim. We can speak about man only by speaking about God. This general statement is hardly disputed among Christian theologians. There is, however, sharp disagreement as to the priority of the two claims. It is my firm conviction that what I have just called the counterclaim is the true claim and must come first.[2]

Those who honor the contrary conception, thus begin not with God but with the human, go even so far as to claim that human freedom means first of all that the humans are free from themselves. "God" must thereby then, as a limit concept, be called to help the human understand what human existence is. Barth maintained that that thus presupposes that we already know from ourselves what human existence is and that God is the Great Unknown. But that turns matters on its head!

The name Bultmann did not appear in Barth's argument, but it was evident that Barth had him and his kindred spirits particularly in mind.

---

1. Barth, "The Gift of Freedom," 89.
2. Barth, "The Gift of Freedom," 69–70.

We saw how much Barth had to do with Bultmann in these years—the years in which he also worked on his doctrine of reconciliation—and how he expressed himself critically with him in direct discussion on Bultmann's presupposition that the Bible, particularly the New Testament, was about human self-understanding. As though it is not central to the biblical witness that it is about the human learning to understand God and therewith turning away from one's self (see 18.3). No wonder that that discussion could be heard here as well.

20.3 Wiesbaden, November 1954: Speech in Memory of Victims of War

About a year later, in November 1954, Barth again accepted an invitation for a visit to Germany. The invitation this time came from the government of the German province Hessen. There was a gathering there at Wiesbaden "in memory of the victims of the war and of National Socialism." Barth was asked to deliver the official memorial address at the gathering. That it was him, as a Swiss, who was asked, provoked some consternation among the media. But in response the organizers pointed to Barth's status as an "eminent theologian," and to his long connection with Germany and with the developments in the German church. He had, so it was said, himself suffered under National Socialism. After all, as a German-speaking Swiss he also belonged to the greater German culture.

Barth began his address by also pointing out his connection with the German people. Of course, he made it immediately clear that it was not just something about himself personally; in the events of the time it was also about Switzerland as a whole. "We come with you from those events and we accompany you into the future; a future that is most deeply determined by history. So it is not strange to us, to remember the events of that time and its victims with you."[3] For all else he emphatically stated that he did not speak as the mouthpiece of "the" Swiss public opinion. He would, in review and perspective, unpack his personal vision, a vision to which no one other than himself could be addressed.

Barth's appearance on this public occasion is a reminder of the address that he had held in November 1945 in Stuttgart, then too in a public meeting (see 11.10). As he did then, he described the Second World War as not simply the work of one man. Barth emphasized (more than his audience would have preferred) the shared responsibility of Hitler's contemporaries. Hitler could not have taken his course if the outside world, East and West, had

3. Barth, "Volkstrauertag," 165.

not allowed him to get so far, and above all if he had not received massive support in Germany. Thus, the war could begin that in its reach and destructive effect, including the number of victims (among them both soldiers and civilians) was to be compared with no earlier war. In particular, Barth recalled "the dead or those condemned to the life-long wasting of Hiroshima and Nagasaki."[4]—The latter was a point that the organizers and many present surely would not have directly had in mind.

But it was not only the war that was to be considered, but also National Socialism itself. That, said Barth, was a revolutionary movement of human contempt and nihilism, that as such must lead to war. It spread like an epidemic among ever more people. In the leading circles of state, society, culture and faith (church) one irresistibly allowed the rising power of chaos; indeed, one was inclined to adapt and cooperate. Not only bad people, but also fashionable, well-intentioned, intellectual highly cultured and educated citizens did not understand what was going on, but were of the opinion that National Socialism "still had good aspects," or even that here the characteristics of a new, better world were to be detected.[5] A real spirit of enthusiasm originated, a readiness to participate, to submit selflessly to this cause. It was for just that reason that National Socialism could become so great and powerful.

Moreover, one was also affected in surrounding nations, Switzerland included, by the imposition of National Socialism. The alarms of those who had fled from Germany were heard with only half an ear. That a resistance movement still existed in Germany, as took shape in the Confessing Church, for example, was known outside Germany only in passing or was met with disinterest. When many finally became conscious of the true, demonic nature of National Socialism, it had become too late for an effective resistance. All in all, said Barth, no one, in Germany or elsewhere, has reason to point to others as especially guilty of the rise and triumph of National Socialism, as if one would himself be sinless.

Barth had already spoken of the victims of war. But he gave special thought to the victims of National Socialism as such. With that he, "as Christian and a theologian," first named the six million Jews

> because the real darkness of the matter, its character as rebellion against the God-given order (that after all is the presupposition of all human relations, of peace on earth) became nowhere so clear as in the deadly enmity of National Socialism against the people of the revelation of the covenant, the

4. Barth, "Volkstrauertag," 166.
5. Barth, "Volkstrauertag," 167.

people of the Old Testament, the people whose Son and Lord is named Jesus Christ.[6]

The National Socialists knew, said Barth, what they were doing when they calculatedly intended to eliminate the Jews. From here on out a free pass to all their other inhuman activities was given. The torture and killing of all the others in Gestapo cellars and concentration camps, were simply the consequence of the persecution of the Jews.

The victims of National Socialism also included those who, for the sake of their conscience or as witnesses of the Christian faith, had resisted and therefore paid with their lives. The fallen Communist resistance fighters thereby deserve particular thought, said Barth, "whether we today like it or not."[7] Whatever one thinks of their ideals or intentions, they stood on the good side, they would "liberate the city from tyranny." They too deserve to be remembered.

Remembering, that means seeing what really has happened. Realizing our shared responsibility. We cannot really be done with it with a "let's forget about it!"[8] Not remaining stuck in profound reflections on "why?" or in principles about God, good and evil. Above all not remaining stuck in an appeal to "inward renewal," or for example to a "new European spirit." Such appeals suffer from being non-committal. No, said Barth, it comes down to concrete deeds. This, above all, must stand firm: what happened then may not happen again. Thus, not agitating for a third world war. Indeed, avoiding everything that would lead to that.

In other words, it may not come to the reestablishment of an authoritarian German state old-style, in which the citizens may only be yes-men and even less to the rearmament of West Germany "in the framework of a military alliance directed against the East under American leadership" (after all, the opposition would easily experience that as threat!).[9] We must, said Barth, turn aside from the illusions as though Communism could be overcome or resisted with panzer divisions and atomic weapons, instead of achieving new social relations by ourselves. Barth articulated notions here that he had advanced earlier. (see 11.10, 14.9, and 16.1).

It was primarily these last, concrete statements that led to a strong reaction. That Barth had placed the Communist resistance fighters on the same line with others who had died in the resistance was the occasion for many to distance themselves from the entire address. The government of

6. Barth, "Volkstrauertag," 168.
7. Barth, "Volkstrauertag," 169.
8. Barth, "Volkstrauertag," 169.
9. Barth, "Volkstrauertag," 173.

the province of Hessen (socialists) also did so. Church circles reproached Barth as a churchman and theologian for getting involved in politics. Repercussions continued long afterward

20.4 Involvement in Ecumenical Work. "Continental" vis-à-vis "Anglo-Saxon" Theology

At this time, the beginning of the 1950s, Barth became involved again in the work of the World Council of Churches. We already heard that he had participated in the first general assembly of the World Council in 1948 in Amsterdam (see 14.8). This time he was asked to assist in preparations for the second general assembly. This would take place in 1954 in the American city of Evanston, with "Christ, the Hope of the World" as its main theme. In Amsterdam, the (constituting) World Council had defined itself as a "fellowship of churches that confess Jesus Christ as God and Savior."[10] In Evanston it would have to be about thinking through what that means, specifically the hope that this confession implies and how it relates to the expectations and convictions alive in the world. A relevant theme, then, in the face of a society of ever grimmer contradictions. An advisory commission of theologians and scholars was installed in preparation for the discussion. They would have to prepare a report on this theme. After some hesitation, Barth accepted the invitation to participate in this advisory commission.

The hesitations had to do with, among other things, the proposed personal composition of the commission. In the past, Barth had had differences of opinion with various other invitees. He foresaw big problems within the commission. One of those whom he would again encounter in the commission was the American theologian Reinhold Niebuhr. Shortly after the meeting in Amsterdam, a sharp discussion had taken place between him and Barth. It had to do with Barth's lecture in Amsterdam to the plenary meeting on the main theme at Amsterdam, "The Despair of Man and the Salvific Plan of God."

In it, Barth had pled to giving God's "salvific plan" priority and thereafter speaking of the "despair of man," because, as he saw it, just so the "despair" really becomes visible. We must, he had said, not do as though the idea of God's salvific plan would emerge by itself from our experience of human despair. We would then easily think that God's salvific plan would coincide with what we Christians, we humans, do. As though the human, like the giant Atlas from ancient mythology would have to carry the entire firmament of heaven on his own shoulders. No, we must begin by placing

---

10. World Council of Churches, "Constitution," Art. I.

our trust in God who will perform the work himself. God does not need us as his advocates and agents. We may, we can, only be witnesses. We must begin by sensing that God's salvific plan is his own cause, his kingdom, that is already established in Jesus Christ (see 14.8).

It was against this argument that Niebuhr had registered serious reservations; he underscored them in a journal article published in October 1948. He found that Barth had made light of human co-responsibility. Are we not called to be God's co-workers? The threat of war and tyranny exists. Against that, Christians cannot afford simply to point to God's coming and already arrived kingdom in an appeal to holy unconcern. They may not leave it to non-Christians concretely work for peace and justice today. Barth appeared to set Christians at God's level by inviting them to view the contemporary world as through the eyes of God. As if the great consummation had already dawned today! Niebuhr called that the mistake of what he called "continental theology" (which he saw represented in Barth), over and against which he set "Anglo-Saxon theology" (advocated by himself) with its practical impact, summarized in the title of his article, "We are men and not God."

A month later, Barth had responded, surprised by so much misunderstanding, as if he would ever deny that "we are men and not God."[11] As if he would have downplayed the Christian vocation to engage in the problems of the world. He had warned against the depression with which Christians often conceived their Christian task in the world. By pleading that they must first realize that Gods salvific plan is really God's own cause he would remove that depression so that the Christians are able to take hold of what it is for them to do in freedom and joy.

Was it then only a simple misunderstanding between Niebuhr and Barth? No, that was still not it. Barth too had himself experienced in Amsterdam, he wrote, an opposition between "continental" and "Anglo-Saxon" theology. Not on the point where Niebuhr had laid his finger, but in the engagement with the Bible. What had struck him with the "Anglo-Saxon" friends was a remarkable carelessness, an inclination to use random citations from the Bible to support their own conceptions instead of beginning really, foundationally, from texts and contexts of the Bible itself. From that it had appeared to him as though a complete dimension was lacking in the thinking of "Anglo-Saxon" theologians. They know the opposition between "good" and "evil," between "freedom" and "necessity," also between God and world. They reckon with the opposition between fundamentalism and liberalism. Of course, these and similar oppositions exist. But alongside these two dimensions, the Bible knows still a third dimension, the sovereign

---

11. Barth, in Daniélou, Niebuhr, and Barth, *Gespräche nach Amsterdam*, 25.

actions of God's self in which the mystery of God is manifest. Viewed in that light the oppositions come into view in a different way. "Continental" theology takes just that seriously, while "Anglo-Saxon" theology appears to have no eye for it. It is remarkably "mystery-less." Thus, Barth wrote, I can never really find it interesting. They would have to read the Bible a bit more naively and with greater attention.

Those who read this discussion between Niebuhr and Barth can imagine that it must have caused sparks at the World Council assembly at Amsterdam. We have heard that Barth had left no negative impressions at "Amsterdam." But the memory of this sharp discussion, the opposition between "continental" and "Anglo-Saxon" theology that emerged, had remained with him. The fact that he would again have to do with Niebuhr (and his kindred spirits) in the preparatory advisory commission for Evanston did not make it easier to promise his participation in this commission. In a letter to Visser 't Hooft he named Niebuhr a "hopeless discussion partner following the postlude to Amsterdam."[12] Still, he accepted the challenge. He would not become entrenched in his own right. In his reply to Niebuhr from 1948 he had also kept the door open for a further "genuine" discussion; had he himself perhaps caricaturized "Anglo-Saxon" theology? That consideration must have played a role for him in his decision to participate in the Evanston commission.

20.5 The Discussion of Christian Hope

There were three commission meetings—in 1951, 1952, and 1953—each time in the summer. Barth participated in all three meetings. Despite some sharp differences of opinion among the participants, it was possible to make progress. One succeeded in preparing a common text. It was further amended following reactions from member churches. Barth continued to think ever more positively of the performance and results of the commission.

In the meantime, the discussion of Christian hope required a great deal of thought, including from Barth himself. Must all the emphasis fall on the expectation of Christ's return? Or may, must, hope also concern the work of the Spirit in the world here and now? Said differently, is Christian hope apocalyptic, namely oriented on a sudden Consummation, breaking in from Above? Or may the consummation be expected as the crowning of a maturing and continuing renewal already today? American commission members (representatives of "Anglo-Saxon" theology) pled for the latter. In that connection, they feared a too one-sided notion of the decisive meaning of Jesus

12. Barth an Visser 't Hooft, June 11, 1951 in *BV*, 243.

Christ, something that in their opinion they could see specifically in Barth (in "continental" theology). The core question was how the ultimate salvation of the entire created world must be considered and what that then means for our task in the world and for our view of the meaning of history.

However, Barth did not feel at home with either of the two positions. In March 1953, a few months before the third and final commission meeting, he briefly elaborated his own thoughts on the matter in a letter to W.A. Visser 't Hooft (secretary-general of the World Council and also himself a commission member). In short, he wrote that the "old" and "new" world are indirectly identical; the new, expected world, is already present in the old, namely, insofar as reconciliation in Jesus Christ has already happened. What is still outstanding is its manifestation *as* realized in Christ; in that sense: *his* coming in glory: "so, that is still 'apocalyptic' eschatology!"[13] Barth himself had still not thought these matters out. He hoped to be able to develop his insights further, to be able to advance them in its time—"if I still get so far"—in the final part of the *Church Dogmatics* (*CD* V). But he would hold himself in reserve in the commission. Otherwise it could lead to heavy conflict.

20.6 The Commission Report on Christian Hope

Whatever the reservation, it must have turned out well. The final report as it came to fruition (by a unanimous vote!) included core ideas that fit well with what Barth himself had already formulated. That obtained specifically with the fundamental opening chapter. There it was claimed

> Our hope is not the projection of our desires upon an unknown future, but the product in us of God's acts in history and above all of His act in raising Jesus Christ from the dead.[14]

an event that does not stand apart from the Cross,

> that place at the center of the world's history where the Lord of history has finally exposed the sin of the world and taken that sin upon Himself, the place where all men and all nations . . . stand revealed as enemies of God.[15]

The content of our hope is spoken of as of God's Kingdom that already exists and that is yet to come. We see "the gracious power of the Kingdom already

---

13. Barth an Visser 't Hooft, March 8, 1953 in *BV*, 273.
14. World Council of Churches Advisory Commission, "Report," 431.
15. World Council of Churches Advisory Commission, "Report," 432.

at work among men" in Jesus' ministry on earth, and the Spirit who was in Jesus Christ was, after His exaltation and ascension, poured out upon His people." So today we see the victorious Lord "carrying on His warfare against every ruler of darkness," and we, "as we walk by the Spirit . . . participate in His warfare, and participate also in His victory."[16] Thus, we live already in the new world, although it is still not fully manifest. The complete realization of it is still to come. But we can read the scope of the Kingdom from what has already happened:

> Christ came . . . to the lost . . . ; how much more will His return demonstrate the triumph of His descent . . . At the Cross God condemned the world . . . In the coming Day this condemnation will be revealed. At the same Cross God accepted the world and disclosed how much He loves it. In the coming Day this loving acceptance will be revealed.

Two misunderstandings are expressly rejected. Confidence in this consummation does not mean that the history of this world is pushed aside as irrelevant. And this consummation does not mean "that our efforts will be finally crowned with success"; the Kingdom is not "the final outcome of this world's history. There is no straight line from the labours of men to the Kingdom of God."[17]

Barth was asked by the commission to write a concluding paragraph. His draft text was unanimously accepted by the commission and added to the report. It is said in this "sum of the matter" that the report should have been better—"the mystery of Christian Hope deserves altogether more adequate expression than we have been able to give it"—but that the drafters were still thankful to God for what they together, with one voice, had been able to state. And the question is briefly discussed to whom the report was directed. "In the first place simply to the world, whose hope—whether it be a Christian or a non-Christian, a believing or an unbelieving world—Jesus Christ is."[18] But then also "to ourselves and to the Christian congregations throughout the whole world whom we here represent."[19] The right of the church to exist lies in that it witnesses this hope to the world. But does it do that? Do we Christians ourselves live from this hope? Here the church is called to self-examination:

---

16. World Council of Churches Advisory Commission, "Report," 434.
17. World Council of Churches Advisory Commission, "Report," 439.
18. World Council of Churches Advisory Commission, "Report," 463.
19. World Council of Churches Advisory Commission, "Report," 464.

Is the Church the authentic witness of its Lord and Head . . . ?
Is it the pilgrim people who have here no continuing city but
seek one to come . . . ? Is it the company of watchmen who,
because they have seen light in the east, know that the new day
has already broken . . . ? Is it the fellowship of those who now
in this very time are able to recognize the coming King in His
hungry, thirsty, naked, sick, captive and refugee brethren . . . ? Is
it a confessing rather than a denying Church?[20]

Ultimately, so the text closes, we can do nothing other than to pray

> That God, the Father, the Son, and the Holy Ghost may have
> mercy upon the Church in all lands, making it through His Word
> to be the Church of hope and thus His Tabernacle among men.[21]

20.7 Missing: Hope for Israel

The entire report became the subject of a foundational discussion at the second general assembly of the Word Council of Churches in August 1954. Barth was not present. He had, of course, been officially invited to participate in an advisory role and would gladly have come. He could have combined it with a visit to other parts of America. There had been plans to deliver a number of lectures at various American universities. But on further reflection he had passed on it and also had signed off on the meeting in Evanston. He expressly had excused himself in a letter to Visser 't Hooft. The American trip would require too much of his energy. An absolute priority must be given to work of the dogmatics at present.

In the meantime, he had again read through the entire commission report and declared himself to be surprised "on the *good* impression I have of the entire report."[22] He gave speeches about it in various places in Switzerland. He also made the report the subject of discussions in his seminars with students in the summer of 1954. Although he was not in Evanston that summer, he still had an ecumenical field in his seminary; there were students from all parts of the world, including America.

The commission report was not received without criticism in Evanston but was nonetheless received with gratitude as "a creative and provocative ecumenical statement." It was decided to offer it to the churches

---

20. World Council of Churches Advisory Commission, "Report," 464–65.
21. World Council of Churches Advisory Commission, "Report," 465.
22. Barth an Visser 't Hooft, September 15, 1953 in *BV,* 276.

with the recommendation "for their study, prayer, and encouragement."[23] One point of criticism received particular thought; that nothing was said in the report about "hope for Israel." In a letter to Visser 't Hooft shortly after the third commission meeting, Barth had himself already, on further reflection, noted that as a "serious omission."[24] Afterwards he had himself realized that the perspective on the salvation for "all Israel" (Romans 11:26) should not have been left undiscussed. Visser 't Hooft had written back that he in principle agreed with him but feared that on this subject the commission could simply not have come to a common view. This question also became a topic of discussion in Barth's seminars dedicated to the commission report. That had led to a draft of a text that was submitted to the leadership of the assembly in Evanston. It had no effect. It was certainly discussed in Evanston, but representatives of the churches from the Middle East in particular feared "political misunderstandings" through the confusion of the Jewish people with the state of Israel. The proposal to add a passage on "the hope for Israel" to the report did not succeed; it was rejected (by a relatively small majority).

20.8 Critical Voices. Dietrich Bonhoeffer on Barth's "Revelation Positivism"

The above-mentioned distinction, treated by Niebuhr and by Barth (albeit with different substance), between "continental" and "Anglo-Saxon" theology suggests that it is about two uniform blocs (within Protestantism) standing over and against each other. In reality, that was not the case. In any case, there was no theological uniformity on the (European) continent. Here, at the beginning of the fifties, Barth had grown into an influential and respected thinker but there were other voices as well, including those critical of Barth's theologizing, as, of course, there had been from the outset of his appearance.

It is not strange that intense discussions have taken place around and with Barth.

We have seen that it was often he himself, who had criticized his theological colleagues, church administrators, and developments in society. But he was often the target of criticism for his political positions as much as for his theology; the one not apart from the other.

With his new theological approach, his peculiar theological foundational thought, he had, from the beginning of his career, distanced himself

---

23. World Council of Churches, *The Evanston Report*, 72.
24. Barth an Visser 't Hooft, September 15, 1953 in *BV*, 277.

from liberal Protestantism that had flown the flag for the amalgamation of Christian faith and modern culture. But he had done so without presenting himself as a member of the party of Protestant orthodoxy. He had also put his critical questions to that side. He was to be classified as neither with the "liberals" nor with the "orthodox." The result was that he was under fire from both sides (see 3.6).

His waywardness was written off from the liberal side. He did his theology without bothering with the question of the scientific nature of his insights. It was said that he simply posited. With Barth, theological practice in fact came down to preaching. But does that not mean in fact a new form of orthodoxy? In any case, you cannot stop there! You would at least have to ask whether and how far your theological insights are acceptable to reason, are plausible.

This criticism, dating from the onset of his theological appearance, had played a role in all the discussions in which over the years Barth had been involved in church and society. It echoed again in criticism that emerged at just this time when Barth was busy producing his doctrine of reconciliation, the heart of his theological thought. This criticism was articulated by the German theologian Dietrich Bonhoeffer.

He, just as Barth and along with him, had been involved in the German church struggle in the Hitler era. Living and working in Germany in the war years (Barth had already been expelled from Germany), he was also in contact with circles that had plotted to violently eliminate Hitler. That had been exposed. It led to his arrest. In April 1945, a few weeks prior to German capitulation, he was executed (at the age of thirty-nine). But during his two years of imprisonment, he still could remain in contact with the outside world through correspondence. In letters that he had been able to write while in prison, he tried to articulate how things must (can) unfold after the war. The era of traditional religion was past; that was clear to him. People must be taken seriously in their (a-religious) maturity. The question then becomes, "[h]ow can Christ become the Lord of the religionless as well?"[25] With that, he named Barth; with respect (because of his critical attitude toward religion), but also critically. He reproached Barth for not having taken up the question of the a-religious maturity of the modern human and instead having remained stuck in a "positivist doctrine of revelation" that was nothing more than restoration, a positing of truths of the faith under the motto "like it or lump it."[26]

---

25. Bonhoeffer to Eberhard Bethge, April 30, 1944 in *Letters and Papers*, 280.
26. Bonhoeffer to Eberhard Bethge, May 5, 1944, in *Letters and Papers*, 286.

Bonhoeffer's relevant letters dated from April and May 1944. They were published posthumously in 1951. Barth was stricken. In 1952, he wrote to a German theological friend (who had asked for his advice in the matter), that he neither understood nor recognized the reproach of "revelation positivism." He supposed that a misunderstanding lay beneath it. In the meantime, others took up Bonhoeffer's criticism. In a particular regard, it meant a repeat of the old liberal criticism from the beginning of Barth's career.

Bonhoeffer's short critical remarks on Barth also found echoes in the Netherlands. In the sixties, the Dutch theologian J. Sperna Weiland characterized Barth's *Church Dogmatics* as "an awesome building—without a door." Subtly alluding to the title of Barth's brochure aimed at Brunner from 1934 (see 6.8), he would write: "You can walk all around it, can marvel at it and the architecture, and ask why 'No' stands with capital letters where you expect the door." Barth has "certainly given one of the greatest elaborations of the Christian faith, but no authentic account." Barth has failed "to build a bridge between gospel and culture."[27] He has neglected to bother with the accessibility of the Christian faith for the modern human. He has limited himself "to announcing" the gospel massif. With that, so went the judgment, he has neglected, with all his honorable reflection, an essential element of the theological task.

Is that the case? Does the theologian, in fact, have as his task building a "bridge" between gospel and culture? Barth's entire theology was born precisely from the conviction that that must not and cannot be the case; that if you attempt to do that, you are by definition doing violence to the gospel; that of course it need not be done because the gospel itself *has* already come "over the bridge." But the question whether one can start from there "just like that" in theology is precisely the point over which opinions have continued to clash up to the present.

20.9 The Dutch Neo-Calvinists. The New Barth Interpretation of G.C. Berkouwer

Through the years, Barth had not only a great deal of criticism to process from the liberal side, but also from particular Protestant-orthodox side. In the Netherlands, this primarily came from the "Neo-Calvinist" circle. There, under the inspiration of Abraham Kuyper, a revival of Calvinism had originated that had also led to the formation of a real, well-defined church-communion. Here, great emphasis was laid on the real, realizable Christian existence as a genuine manifestation of God's work of renewal. People saw themselves as an

27. Sperna Weiland, "Er is iets aan het gerbeuren," 622.

elite corps, including in culture and society advocating "Christian principles" (derived from the Bible) and thereby doing battle for the "kingship of Jesus Christ" in the contemporary world. It is understandable that in this circle one could produce little valuation for a theology like Barth's, that, after all, from the outset emphasized the radical distinction between God and the human (every human effort) (see 2.5–6 and 4.9).

One of those from this circle who had criticized Barth was the professor from the Free University of Amsterdam, G.C. Berkouwer. In the thirties, he had pointed out in various publications the foundational motif in Barth's theology: that here God's sovereignty and hiddenness (his "other"-nature, his "absolute freedom") were over-accentuated, arbitrary as it were. Thereby, he had argued, God's faithfulness disappears from view. There is no longer any room for the notion that God has "given" us his revelation (as that comes to us in the Bible). Barth focuses so much on God's own, sovereign action that he no longer sees that God continues to walk with his people "in the horizontal line of history." According to Berkouwer, that was the background of Barth's absolute concentration on Jesus Christ as fully and exclusively God's revelation. Berkouwer did not see how from this position one could principally offer concrete clues for political and social action for Christians.— Berkouwer had written this in 1936. Developments in Barth's position had later apparently shown this evaluation to be unjust.

In the meantime, it was he, Berkouwer, who published a completely different book on Barth in 1954, *The Triumph of Grace in the Theology of Karl Barth*. He appeared to have distanced himself from his earlier criticism of Barth. He no longer saw God's "sovereignty" (as hiddenness) as Barth's foundational motif; it became clear to him that he had done Barth an injustice. Barth would rather have to be typified as the theologian of God's grace triumphant over everything. Not that Berkouwer no longer criticized Barth's theology, but the criticism now set a different tone; it consisted at heart in the question whether Barth presented the "triumph" of God's grace as not all too triumphant, so that it degenerated to something self-evident.

Over the course of years, Barth had been the target of fierce criticism from the Dutch neo-Calvinists. It had given him the occasion in 1951, in the Preface of his *CD* III/4 for a fierce attack on them. But in the Preface of *CD* IV/2, appearing in 1955, on the occasion of Berkouwer's new book, he came back to the matter. "The wrath of man seldom does that which is right in the sight of God." He names Berkouwer's book as

> For all its reservations and criticisms this work is written with such care and goodwill and Christian *aequietas* that—in the hope that there are others [i.e. among the Dutch Neo-Calvinists]

like its author—I should like to withdraw entirely the generalised and therefore ill-founded words which after many years of provocation I then suddenly unleashed.[28]

Barth would later expressly respond to Berkouwer's new book. Now already he commented in a personal communication to Berkouwer. He was not completely happy with the title "the triumph of grace" as typifying his theology. It sounded to him too much like a closed system. He would himself have preferred to have spoken of the triumph of Jesus Christ. He wrote:

> My intention, at any rate, has been that all my systematic theology should be as exact a development as possible of the significance of this "name" (in the biblical sense of the term) and to that extent should be the telling of a *story* which develops through individual events—the story of a struggle, but a victorious one.[29]

---

28. Barth, *CD*, IV/2, xii.
29. Quoted in Busch, *Karl Barth*, 381.

21

New Accent on the Humanity of God

21.1 The Doctrine of Reconciliation: Still Incomplete

WITH THE CONCLUSION OF the second part of his doctrine of reconciliation in 1955, Barth was still not finished with this doctrine. Already in the summer of 1951 he must have foreseen that there was still a third aspect of reconciliation to be distinguished. The first part had treated reconciliation as having been effected because *God in Christ* had humbled himself to being among humans. The second part had treated reconciliation as realized because *we humans* are exalted *in Christ* to new life with God. Thus, in turn, the divine nature and the human nature of Jesus Christ had received all the emphasis in Barth's elaboration. But now what still had to be considered was that in the two aspects together *the one Jesus Christ* appears for us, and that thus he himself is the guarantee of the realized reconciliation. Already at the beginning of the first part of his doctrine of reconciliation, Barth had put it this way: "Jesus Christ is the actuality of the atonement, and as such the truth of it which speaks for itself."[1] It must be stated in talking about Jesus Christ as the "truthful witness." In other words, the reconciliation is reality in Christ also in that it manifests itself, *reveals* itself in and through the appearance of Jesus Christ.—This would have to be worked out in the not yet written third part of Barth's doctrine of reconciliation.

In the meantime, it took a while before Barth here could be well on his way. With the publication of the second part of his doctrine of reconciliation, he had reached the age of sixty-nine. According to official regulations in Basel he would automatically be retired on his seventieth birthday. Thus, it became a question whether he would still be able to give his lectures in dogmatics following this date (as always, the first presentation of what later would find written form in the *Church Dogmatics*). Following a few months

---

1. Barth, *CD*, IV/1, 136.

of uncertainty—in the course of 1955—the official decision was made that Barth's position at the University of Basel would continue, provisionally and by way of exception. It was the acknowledgment not only of Barth's ecclesiastical but also societal, not only national (Swiss) but also international significance, that had led to this decision. Still, that did not mean that everything would be "ordinary."

In October 1955, Barth moved with his household to a new, smaller house, closer to the edge of Basel. The move cost the required effort and energy. Despite the extension of his appointment, he didn't deliver his weekly lectures in the summer of 1956 because of a serious illness. He had earlier reduced the number of weekly lectures from four to three. That would remain the case going forward. One thing and another resulted in a slower pace in the further development of his doctrine of reconciliation.

21.2 Seventieth Birthday. The Festschrift *Answer*

He had nothing to complain about involving interest in his work. The number of subscribers for the *Church Dogmatics* in German, primarily in Germany itself, grew at just this time. Moreover, there was an English as well as a French translation of the entire *Church Dogmatics* in preparation. There was even thought of a possible translation into Japanese. In the preface of the second part of the doctrine of reconciliation Barth made thankful mention of that. That weighed for him against the fact that certain theological circles and journals continually decided to overlook his work.—Thereby it still happened that on the attainment of his seventieth birthday he himself was made the center of attention in a special way.

Already at his fiftieth birthday, in 1936, Barth was presented a hefty festschrift with contributions from students, friends and kindred spirits (see 8.2). Now, in May 1956, on the occasion of his seventieth birthday, that happened again. This new festschrift, entitled *Antwort* [English: *Answer*], could in size (960 pages!) compete with the thickest parts of the *CD*. It included not less than seventy-eight contributions. Most were from Germany and other European nations (such as Switzerland, Czechoslovakia, France), but there were also a few contributions from outside Europe (the United States, Latin America, Japan). All in all, an impressive range.

It is surprising that the name of Bultmann is missing in the list of coworkers. He had cooperated in the 1936 Festschrift. That this time he no longer appeared among the writers may have to do with the sharp difference of opinion that had arisen between Barth and Bultmann just at the beginning of the fifties (see 18.2 and 3). Also, according to the correspondence between the two preserved there was hardly any contact between them during just these years.

Some authors wrote of personal memories. A particular contribution of this sort is that of Eduard Thurneysen. He had pulled together with Barth from 1913. Over the years, they had exchanged countless letters. Thurneysen now published parts of letters and postcards that Barth had sent him in the first years, up to 1922. From that emerged a fascinating picture of the beginning of Barth's theologizing. It makes clear how much everything had come for him from his work as a preacher, from the task of preaching the gospel Sunday to Sunday to his congregation. Two years later, in 1958, Barth would conversely (and much more expansively!) publish parts of both their letters (now also from Thurneysen's letters) from the years 1921–1925 in the Festschrift that would then be presented to Thurneysen on the occasion of his seventieth birthday. Still later, in the context of the planned publication of Barth's collected works, a beginning would be made with a complete publication of the entire correspondence between the two. (Thurneysen himself would, in the last years of his life, set that ball rolling). This correspondence is an important source of information on the development of Barth's thought.

Among the contributors to the 1956 Festschrift were two Dutchmen: Miskotte and Visser 't Hooft (perhaps Berkouwer still stood too far outside the circle around Barth to appear as a contributor of note). Miskotte argued in detail how much Barth's theology had emerged from listening to the witness (the story) of the Bible, and thus how much the extended passages of biblical interpretation (excurses in small print!) are fundamental in the *Church Dogmatics* for a good understanding of the rationale for what is written. Visser 't Hooft had to limit himself to a short word of thanks, a "greeting from the ecumenè," including a few fundamental remarks on Barth's relation to the ecumene. He memorialized Barth's growing involvement in the work of the World Council of Churches. "The contemporary ecumenical movement cannot be understood if the theology of Karl Barth disappears from view."[2]

21.3 "The Humanity of God"

At this time Barth came to the point to give a full account of the manner in which he had traversed his life and work. In September 1956 he delivered a lecture for the Swiss preacher's union on "The Humanity of God." He offered a summary characterization of his entire theology. He thereby brought out

---

2. Visser 't Hooft in *Antwort*, 14.

how his thought—in its continuity—had changed over the course of years, specifically, the shifts in accent that had been executed.

The title of this lecture already gave witness to that shift. The use of the title as a superscription above one of Barth's early publications would have been unthinkable. As he himself described it: Not so much God's "humanity," as God's nature as God was his great theme at the outset. That God is of an entirely peculiar sort, the Strange, the totally Other, that was his central theme then (see 2.3 and 2.5). With that he positioned himself critically-polemically over and against the then dominant (liberal Protestant) theology. That was a theology that developed its thinking completely from the perspective of the (religious, Christian) human. By definition, what was unique, sovereign, of God could not be considered here. That must then be contradicted. And, Barth said in his lecture to the Swiss preachers, I still, now in 1956, stand behind that commitment. Only, that is not sufficient. For as little as the human can be elevated to the cost of God (that was the fault of the then dominant theology), conversely God may be elevated to the cost of the human. With that would the one-sidedness of the one be simply exchanged for the other. No, it comes down to seeing and emphasizing that God is just God *in his* companionship with the human; thus, God's nature as God *includes his humanity*! That becomes clear when we take seriously that we can talk about God and the human only from Jesus Christ. We are reminded of the first two parts of Barth's doctrine of reconciliation, as we hear Barth say here:

> Jesus Christ is in His one person, as true *God*, *man's* loyal partner and as true *man*, *God's*. He is the Lord, humbled for communion with the man and likewise the Servant exalted to communion with God . . . Thus in this oneness, Jesus Christ is the Mediator, the Reconciler, between God and man. Thus He comes forward to *man* on behalf of *God* . . . and to *God* on behalf of *man*. Thus He attests and guarantees to man God's free *grace* and at the same time attests and guarantees to God man's *gratitude* . . . Moreover, exactly in this way Jesus Christ, as this Mediator and Reconciler between God and man, is also the *Revealer* of them both . . . We do not need to engage in a free-ranging investigation to seek out and construct who and what *God* truly is, and who and what man truly is, but only to read the truth about both where it resides, namely, in the fullness of their togetherness, their covenant which proclaims itself in Jesus Christ.[3]

---

3. Barth, "The Humanity of God," 46–47.

We see here how Barth in an extremely short stretch has summarized the train of thought as he had worked it out in the two first parts of his doctrine of reconciliation. At which to the close of the citation the theme of the still to be written third part of already begins to be heard, that Jesus Christ is "Revealer" of the reconciliation, and in that regard also effects reconciliation. At the same time that he held this lecture on the "humanity of God," he was well on the way working out this third part. It is clear that the "new course" in his thought, of which Barth here testifies, was becoming visible specifically in his doctrine of reconciliation.

What is the concrete significance of Barth's "new" insight advanced here? Among other things, he said about it that it follows from God's "humanity" that the human, every human must be highly respected. After all, it applies to every human (whether he knows it or not) that Jesus Christ is also *his* brother, God is also *his* Father and that thus he has a claim on the recognition of his human rights and his human value. And there is no reason to derogate people's humanity, human culture. Of course, it often goes amiss; human culture often leads to catastrophic consequences. But culture belongs to human nature. It must in principle be viewed positively. It can come about in human culture to a parable of what God himself intends. That must be taken into account!

21.4 Protestant Theology in the Nineteenth Century: A Revaluation.

Did Barth's new conception of the humanity of God also mean another look at the Protestant theology of the nineteenth century? In the sense that he felt less inclined than previously to set himself off against that theology? Here we must beware of caricatures. Barth had not only expressed himself critically in his earlier publication on this theme—above all in his great book on it from 1947 (see 12.10). He had also already hinted that he wasn't done with the theology of the nineteenth century (from which he himself had come!). But now he clearly gave that greater emphasis.

He did so in a lecture that he held in January 1957 at a meeting of the Goethe union in the Germany city of Hanover. Protestant theology of the nineteenth century had to do, he said with the heritage of eighteenth-century rationalism. In any case, it had the courage to do its work in this rationalistic climate. It did not shy away from advocating for the meaning of the Christian faith in the face of the then modern human. One emphatically theologized in discussion with the outer world, with the spirit of the age.

That openness to the outside is indeed essential, for a theology that claims to be a genuine living theology.

Of course, that openness can go too far. That is, said Barth, what in fact happened in the theology of the nineteenth century. It allowed itself to be drawn by the spirit of the age. It took the "modern man" too seriously, so much so that it no longer was about its real task, the consideration of the Christian faith, namely of the message of Jesus Christ. It was primarily busy with the question of how the Christian faith could find acknowledgment in society, in general. That such acknowledgment cannot be forced and can only happen in freedom, of that one was—rightly!—convinced. But the solution of the problem was sought in connection with particular, then generally accepted, worldviews. One searched in it what could be for the modern man the connecting point for the acceptance of the Christian message. Thus, one let himself be determined in his theology by one or another generally accepted worldview. And one began from the presupposition that every human has a "religious a priori" somewhere. The question, of course, was: is that the case? And above all, has thus not an injustice been done to the Christian faith already, by definition?

In any case, nineteenth century theology was, in relation to the Christian faith, primarily interested in the believing *human*. But in itself, said Barth (and here we recognize the new accent on the humanity of God!) that was not mistaken per se. After all, the Bible too speaks of relationship of Israelite, of the Christian, of the believer, with God! Christian faith cannot and must not be thought of only from above to below, but also from below to above, from the human to God. The converse way of thinking has its right! That the religious human was placed at the center in the theology of the nineteenth century can be seen as an attempt to do theological justice to the work of the Holy Spirit. That theology would in its way hold tightly to the correct insight that the human cannot speak of the relationship of God with the human without (and immediately) being engaged with the relationship of the human with God. Only, on close examination, nineteenth-century theology was still more a theology of the human (Christian) self-understanding than a theology of the Holy Spirit. That the relationship of the human with God has its foundation in God's engagement with the human and not the converse, was not seen. By the climate of thought of the time one could not view the Christian faith other than a form of the general, human spiritual life and self-consciousness; a faith without ground. With this heritage, the German Evangelical Church was vulnerable to the rising powers in culture and society, specifically to National Socialism.

We see that Barth maintained his critical view of the Protestant theology of the nineteenth century. But we also see how he said more emphatically than before that we are not done with that theology:

> I could not follow the rule, *De mortuis nihil nisi bene* (speak nothing but good of the dead) simply because the theologians of that time are not dead... They will not cease to speak to us. And we cannot cease to listen to them.[4]

21.5 Rising Tensions between East and West. The Hungarian Crisis of 1956

At the time when Barth's activities described above took place, tensions between the East and the West increased. Despite the "iron curtain" that had divided Eastern Europe (under communist rule) from the West, the situation was not stable. There was grumbling in certain nations (satellite states of the Soviet Union), and they expressed dissatisfaction with the harsh regime. That was the case in Hungary in 1956. In October of that year, communist leaders there wanted to implement reforms. Russian-minded hardliners were removed from the government; a new government was formed that also included non-communists. This new Hungarian government, supported by enthusiastic street demonstrations, declared that Hungary would withdraw from the Warsaw Pact, the military alliance that the Soviet Union had formed in 1949 together with its Eastern European vassal states vis-à-vis the Western NATO (see 16.1). The Russian Soviet leader, Nikita Khrushchev, could not allow these developments to take their course. Soviet military power invaded Hungary. After ten days of heavy fighting in the streets of Budapest, the Hungarian resistance was broken. The old status, under the old leaderships, was violently restored.

This was followed with intense sympathy for the Hungarian people in Western Europe and America. Active, military assistance for the Hungarian uprising was not possible. But events in Hungary certainly led to a sharpening of anti-Communist feelings in the West. These feelings also lived within the churches. A new public position in opposition to Communism was called for. Must that now—certainly now!—not be condemned by the churches?

The events in Hungary did not, of course, leave Barth unmoved. In March–April 1948 he had visited the Reformed Church of Hungary and became closely acquainted with its situation and attitude under communist

---

4. Barth, "Evangelical Theology in the 19th Century," 32–33.

rule. He had been positively inclined at the time toward the fact that the church had learned to view the situation realistically and had understood that it had come to it to determine its position in the new system of state (and thus not to remain mired in the protest). He had also reported his sense. True, later, in a letter "to my friends in the Reformed Church of Hungary," he had stated his concern over the inclination of the Hungarian church leadership to declare itself in solidarity with the ideology of the new authority and thereby to hand over its freedom as a church in advance (see 14.5 and 6). But at the time he had not allowed himself to be tempted to a principle anti-communist position. Would there now then, following the events of October 1956, still be an occasion to do so?

But Barth deemed such an anti-communist protest now to be superfluous as well. Communism had blamed itself for the events in Hungary, he found; nothing needs to be added to that. His public silence of this matter provoked a great deal of criticism, in his fatherland and beyond. The criticism even came from America. The American theologian Reinhold Niebuhr (see 20.4) openly put the question, "Why is Karl Barth silent about Hungary?" Later, in a letter written to a few East German preachers (and separately published), Barth said

> I have reacted with not a word. It was clear that it was not a genuine question. It did not come from . . . practical trouble . . . but from the safe fortress of an experienced Western politician who wants to put his opponent on slippery ground, as politicians usually do, and to force me to opt for a primitive anti-communism or certainly to unmask me as a secret proto-communist and in any case thus to bring me as a theologian to discredit. What did I have to answer to that?[5]

The nuclear weapons race was also fueled by the events in Hungary. In 1957, Adenauer, the chancellor of West Germany, also pleaded for the West German army to be equipped with (tactical) nuclear weapons (West Germany had already become a member of NATO in 1955). The German atomic expert Carl Friedrich von Weizsäcker had, together with eighteen colleagues, openly opposed this. At the same time, Albert Schweitzer published an appeal to abandon nuclear weapons. Here, Barth was not silent. Asked by a West Berlin newspaper for his opinion, he stood squarely with these declarations. He wrote:

---

5. Barth an einen Pfarrer in der Deutschen Demokratischen Republik, August 1958," in *OB*, 412.

People West and East must resist the madness, that is going on here. They must thereby create a political fact of the first order on which governments and the press must give account. It is not about principles, ideologies and systems. It is not about questions of power. It is about life. It is about themselves, humans. They must help the cause of the most primitive understanding in its right before it is too late.[6]

21.6 Letter to a Preacher in the German Democratic Republic (DDR)

Barth was mindful not only of the situation in Hungary, but also of that in East Germany (DDR). A number of young preachers wrote him a letter requesting his advice over how to act (as Christians, as representatives of the church) in the face of a regime that was more and more aimed at silencing the church and making it impossible for it to function. Barth received the letter in the summer of 1958. In that period, he was just on the point of cancelling a variety of extra obligations; he felt overburdened. But he could not leave the letter from the DDR unanswered.

The letter writers had made it clear that they did not reject the new, socialist (communist) regime, under which they had to live and work, out of hand. They certainly were not looking for a "liberation in the spirit of Adenauer," thus for a replacement of the East German socialism model by a prosperity model of a Western sort; for them that would be a return to the "fleshpots of Egypt." Still, they saw the danger that this socialism would let its "foundational humanist intention" be more and more overgrown by the inclination to act violently in a direct hate against Christ and his church.[7] The question was, what must our attitude be toward that?

Barth's answer was sent at the end of August 1958. I alluded to the letter already. It can be read as a clear elaboration of Barth's position regarding the political tensions of the time and also as a practical, pastoral, translation of the heart of his theology.

Barth began by pointing out that it is not strange when Christians and the church have to deal with counter-powers. He cited 1 Peter 5:8-9, where it talks of "your enemy," that roams as "a roaring lion, on search of its prey," and where Christians from the first generation hear, "Oppose him!" That situation in East Germany is apparently now acute. Only, Barth

6. Barth an die Öffentlichkeit, April 1957, in *OB*, 392.
7. Barth an einen Pfarrer in der Deutschen Demokratischen Republik, August 1958, in *OB*, 404.

said, it is a misunderstanding to think that the "lion" can simply be identified today with Communism: the devil, the roaring lion is also active in the West.[8] There too one is ready to talk the community out of what makes it a Christian congregation and to make that impossible. If it comes down to it, the message of Christ is at the least equally unacceptable for the West as for the East. If the East has its totalitarianism (the almighty party, propaganda, the police), the West has that as well (its almighty press, its free economy, its public opinion).

Of what does resistance, which may be asked of the Christian vis-à-vis all that, now consist? Barth claimed that it simply comes down to returning to the ABCs of Christian existence. That is to say, believing in God and his coming Kingdom, thus in Jesus Christ as really our Lord and Savior. Christian existence is confessing that He, Christ, is above all things. The socialism in force in the DDR, inspired and directed by Moscow, is also simply an instrument of Christ. Barth asks his correspondents, "has this socialism come as a judgment over you?" That for sure: "this power would not have overcome you without the sin of society, church and state in the past." But then consider that the real judgment is not executed by the instrument but by Him who makes use of it. He, God, is merciful and gracious, who also comes with his judgments where and because He intends to bless and to love. The hope for a favorable development of socialism may not appear to be very realistic; "hoping in God, however, who stands above this socialism . . . will, in the domain of this socialism, not be for naught."[9]

God above all things. That also means, Barth made more precise, that He stands above all the atheism and materialism propagandized by the Communist state. The "god" that is denied in this state-atheism is only a conceptual-idol, well-known to the atheists, not the living God—whom they do not know! But this God indeed knows them. And we Christians may take them as such. It comes down to recognizing no one with you in the Eastern Zone, however unbelieving and stoutly he bears himself as such, as the one who he happily would be. It comes down to meeting his unbelief with your cheerful unbelief in the possibility of his undertaking!

God above all things. That also means that He stands above the legal totalitarianism of the DDR. Totalitarian, demanding the total human, is also the gospel of God's grace. But that rules and overcomes the human from inside out. It neither forces nor oppresses but establishes. The totalitarianism of the state does indeed oppress. But its powerlessness appears from that fact. The church must not concur. It must not intend to posit its

---

8. Barth an einen Pfarrer in der Deutschen Demokratischen Republik, August 1958, in *OB*, 414–15.

9. Barth an einen Pfarrer in der Deutschen Demokratischen Republik, August 1958, in *OB*, 419.

own ideology, its own Christian worldview vis-à-vis the ideology of the regime ("dialectical Marxism"). It also must not intend to set its own episcopal or synodical "power" over against the power of party and police. It comes down to following Jesus before all that, holding fast to God's grace that liberates the human and giving witness to it.

God above all things. That also means that He stands above all that is self-evident by which we Christians have led our lives up to the present. We have gotten used to a situation in which the church was generally accepted; in which Sunday and feast days were still generally observed; in which infant baptism, confirmation (public confession), church marriages, and Christian burials formed the self-evident framework of everyone's life. The influence of the church on education, the respected presence of official church representatives in the public sphere, all still outlined the continuing "Christian" character of the general culture. And we Christians have always thought that the proclamation of the gospel must and can take place in this context. That has always been certainly the case with you. But now, Barth wrote to his correspondents, you witness that this framework is being completely broken apart in the DDR. This will also happen with us in the West, but with you it is already happening. It is the case in the DDR that the church is more and more a suspect phenomenon. Christian existence no longer obtains as something respectable; on the contrary. Over time, Christianity can only exist in a far corner, under continuing threat from without. But is that serious? The first Christian communities, that we read about in the Bible, must have done without such a Christian cultural framework. The church is called to serve God's cause. But the victory of God's cause does not depend on the existence of something like a general Christian culture. Perhaps we now witness that God himself is busy settling accounts with such a Christian culture just so to point us to new ways as the Christian community. Indeed we must unlearn the old manner of being *volkskerk*, church *of* the whole people to be able to be church *for* the people. It could be best, Barth said, that you in the East have the particular vocation to demonstrate and practice that before us in the West!

21.7 The Letter as Theology-in-Action

Barth's "Letter to a Pastor in the DDR" appeared as an "open letter" in October 1958. It quickly received a second, then third, printing. It unleashed many reactions. Among the critics was Reinhold Niebuhr. He found Barth's letter insufficiently practical, floating too much above political reality. Others stumbled over Barth's placing the East and West completely on one line as if Christianity in the West was in the same sort of crisis as in the East; as if there was no essential difference between (Communist) dictatorship and

(Western) democracy. Hans Asmussen, formerly an associate of Barth (see 7.3 and 8.2) who had long since distanced himself from him, denounced Barth's "neutralism"; according to him, Barth's letter came down to advice to Christians in East Germany to adjust to the situation and forgo all resistance. Critical reactions also appeared in the press, in both West Germany and in Switzerland. Barth's letter also did not "sit well" in West German governmental circles. Barth was nominated for the 1958 peace prize of the *German Booktrade* (a prize that was offered yearly since 1950). But the president of West Germany, Theodor Heuss, told the organizers that he could not agree with the extension of the prize to Barth and in that case would not attend the event (the prize was conferred in October 1958 on Barth's colleague in Basel, the philosopher Karl Jaspers). Remarkably, the DDR regime also had not understood Barth's letter; the document could not be bought in bookstores there. But among DDR citizens there certainly was interest in it; it was read "underground" and passed from hand to hand.

In defense of Barth's letter, its pastoral character was pointed out. But then it can equally be noted that the entirety of Barth's theology as proceeding from a quest for an answer to the need of preaching, is pastoral in character (see 2.5, 3.3–5, 4.1). The letter is theology-in-action. It is clear that all the central ideas of Barth's theology can be heard in this letter. That God does not coincide with any "Christian" culture; and also that God's cause cannot be identified with the West's cause (as little as with that of the East); that God is not identical with the "god" that is honored as self-evident in a particular type of society (or denied as such); that God, the God of the Bible, is totally other, all that has been in Barth's mind from the outset of his own theological way. That an ideologically or politically motivated atheism does not affect this God is the consequence of that way. That this God is human, oriented to humans, that his grace overcomes and is even extended to atheists, that is a further elaboration we have ever more emphatically seen Barth make in the course of his theological development. Barth's letter strikes a victorious tone, which was meant to encourage readers in East Germany not to give up hope. The sense of the great victorious grace of God that is extended to every human is the heart of Barth's conviction. That the church must live from that sense and thus should not look for continuing support for its task of proclamation from social or political custom or privilege, that it must want not to be the church *of* but a church *for* the people, flows directly from that conviction. We shall see how Barth worked out these thoughts further in the third part of his doctrine of reconciliation that he worked on in these same years (the second half of the fifties).

22

The Doctrine of Reconciliation as a Theology of Hope

22.1 The Doctrine of Reconciliation Thus Far

THE THIRD PART OF Barth's doctrine of reconciliation, *CD* IV/3, appeared in 1959, four years after the appearance of the preceding part (IV/2). Such a long pause between parts had not occurred in the publication of the *Church Dogmatics* since the forties. We have already heard that there were various reasons for delay beginning in 1955 (see 21.1). But Barth had pushed on. This new part is much longer than the preceding parts. It appeared in two volumes with continuous pagination.

We recall that for Barth reconciliation was the heart of the Christian faith, the core of what can be said about "God" and the "human." For, he claimed, "God" and the "human" cannot be talked about other than from Jesus Christ. And he, this Jesus, is himself the concurrence of God and the human. It essentially holds of God that he is a God of humans. And it essentially holds of the human that he is destined to be God's human. God and the human are oriented to each other. That is not a static state of affairs, let alone self-evident; no, it is the result of an event, the coming of Jesus Christ.

From that we see that a covenant has been concluded; reconciliation is effected. So, in that, it is revealed to us who God is and who the human is.

Revelation. That was the key word of his dogmatics from the outset. He began from the conviction that we cannot consider or sense from ourselves who God is; it must be said to us. But where that happens, where God addresses us in his Word, there he appears as the God of the covenant; thus, there reconciliation is in order. In a certain sense, Barth's entire theology is in fact a doctrine of reconciliation. It is no wonder that the proper doctrine of reconciliation is the heart of the dogmatics, including for Barth's own sense (see 18.1).

Reviewing the main line of Barth's doctrine of reconciliation thus far, we see that reconciliation means God with us. But also, we with God. Reconciliation exists because God in Christ descended to us humans. That is the one aspect, discussed in *CD* IV/1. But there is also another aspect; reconciliation exists because we humans are exalted to new life with God. Barth stated, in *CD* IV/2: that also is to be said, from Christ. In the past, defenders of the second view rather stood opposed to those who defended the first view. But we heard Barth argue that both views are justified and complete each other.

22.2 Reconciliation as a Communicative Event

Now, in IV/3, Barth talks about reconciliation in yet a third way. In it he connects with the church's traditional discussion of the "three-fold" office of Christ, and that primarily in Calvinistic Protestantism. Old Testament Israel knew of three functions, the bearers of which were anointed: that of the priest, of the king, and of the prophet. The name (title) Christ itself means "anointed." So, it became usual to speak of Christ in particular as "priest," "king," and "prophet." The entirety of Christ's work was summarized in these names.

Thus, one saw Christ's "priesthood" primarily expressed in his offering, in his passion and death, hence, in his entrance into the depths. One meant by his "kingship" his resurrection from the dead in particular, hence, his exaltation, his victory over death. It is especially in his priesthood, his offering, that one conceived his real action as reconciler. But we have already seen that Barth connected the "priesthood" and the "kingship" directly to each other. He saw both, Christ's humiliation and his exaltation, as side and counter-side. And he also saw both, each in its own way, as expressing the reality of reconciliation (see 18.7).

The prophetic nature of Christ received less emphasis in the tradition. It was mostly thought of as his preaching, going about proclaiming throughout the Jewish nation as reported in the gospels. So viewed, Christ would first have worked as a prophet and later (in the cross and resurrection) have fulfilled his real office, viz., his priestly and royal office. So understood, the prophetic office would have played only a subsidiary, preparatory role in the entirety of Christ's activity. Here again, Barth takes a different path. He relates Christ's prophetic nature as well to his work of reconciliation. That Christ is "prophet" means, he said, that Christ himself stands as guarantee for the reality of the reconciliation that took place in his appearance. Barth said concisely: "reconciliation also, with all that happened, gives itself to be *known*." Christ himself *testifies* to us that we are reconciled with God. That is the content of his prophetic proclamation. So reconciliation happens:

> Reconciliation is not a dark or dumb event, but a perspicuous and vocal. It is not closed in upon itself, but moves out and communicates itself It is event only as it expresses, discloses, and mediates itself.[1]

In other words, if reconciliation did not reach humans as a message, they would still be on the outside. But they are not outsiders, they need not be, seen from Christ they cannot be, for reconciliation itself is the message, addressed to humans. Christ himself, as Reconciler, is also the messenger, the "prophet," or (as Barth also said), the "true witness" of reconciliation.

Barth recognized what he had in mind here in the words of the introduction (prologue) of the gospel of John. There Jesus Christ is named the incarnate Word of God (John 1:14). Moreover, that Word was already spoken of; it was already there "in the beginning" (as the creating word) "with God," and was itself "God." It is also said that "In the Word was life and the life was the light of people. The light appears in the darkness." (1:1, 4–5).

There are biblical interpreters who strictly distinguish between the "Word become flesh" and the Word "in the beginning." But Barth argued that in both cases it is about the same Word, about Jesus Christ. He is involved already in the beginning, at the creation; it is about him, that it is said "in the Word was life and the life was the light of people"; Barth saw that as an extra indication in the same direction. After all, later in the gospel of John, Jesus calls himself "the life" and "the light" (8:12; 11:25; 14:6). "The light shines in the darkness"; that already points to the communicative event that is peculiar to reconciliation, to Jesus as Reconciler.

22.3 Jesus Christ, the Living, the Resurrected

Barth summarized that Jesus as Reconciler is also himself the messenger, the "prophet" (the "true witness") of reconciliation by beginning with the simple but substantial sentence, "Jesus Christ lives." Here everything is included in what he already had elaborated in the two preceding parts of the doctrine of reconciliation. This "life" of Jesus implies that he exists in the way of the God who intends to be the God-of-the-human; and he exists in the way of the human who may be the human-with-God, God's human. God is not to be seen apart from this Jesus Christ; and that also obtains for every creature, every human. Jesus Christ holds God and the

---

1. Barth, *CD*, IV/3, 8.

human world together. That he "lives" is the definitive confirmation and manifestation of that reality.

How do we now get to saying that Jesus Christ lives? Barth claimed that we have not come to that notion by ourselves. We derive it from the witness of Holy Scripture. That proclaims to us his resurrection from the dead. Here we have to do with the heart of the matter:

> If there is any Christian and theological axiom, it is that Jesus Christ is risen, that He is truly risen. But this is an axiom which no one can invent. It can only be repeated on the basis of the fact that in the enlightening power of the Holy Spirit it has been previously declared to us as the central statement of the biblical witness.[2]

Barth had not previously placed the resurrection of Christ so central to his considerations. We have seen how in the first part of his doctrine of reconciliation, *CD* IV/1, he spoke of the resurrection of Christ as a mark of the "judgment of the Father": namely the judgment of God the Father confirming Jesus' way of the cross (the way of the Son of God into the depths). In other words, at Easter, Jesus the crucified was rehabilitated by God (see 18.13). And we have seen how the second part of Barth's doctrine of reconciliation, *CD* IV/2, that is about Jesus the human who is (already in his passion) exalted, discussed the resurrection of Christ as the event in which Jesus' exalted nature, his belonging with God as human, becomes clear (see 19.4). Both times Barth's point was that at Easter something becomes *manifest*, something that already obtained prior to and apart from Easter. That "something" is the main thing. Nothing substantial was added on Easter. It is true that we cannot do without the events of Easter. Without Easter, we would not have known the meaning of Jesus Christ (his entrance into the depths, his exaltation to being God's human). It is through and after Easter that we are really, ourselves, involved. But that is a subsequent consideration. Barth could indeed come to talk about Easter in the final instance in both preceding parts of his doctrine of reconciliation, with his discussion of the meaning of Jesus Christ.

But now, in the last approach to the doctrine of reconciliation, Easter is the starting point of his considerations. For now it is about the revelatory character that is peculiar to the reconciliation event itself, or even in which it has reached its climax, its goal. Now, Jesus appears to be, as the Risen, the Reconciler. As the Living, and thus as the "true Witness," as the "Prophet," he is its embodiment.

---

2. Barth, *CD*, IV/3, 44.

22.4 Jesus and the Old Testament

So, Jesus' prophetic nature is fully considered alongside his priesthood and royalty in Barth's doctrine of reconciliation. That leads to the question of how that relates to prophecy in the Old Testament. Barth felt pressed to dedicate a separate, concise view to that. In it he emphasized similarity as well as difference.

He identified as an important point of agreement that the Old Testament also appears to be about the relation between God and all peoples. In that regard, Israel was called to be active and visible as God's covenant people among all other peoples. Just as with Jesus, the Old Testament Israel was also a light that could not be hidden.

Subsequently, it is the case that the Old Testament prophets still could not speak from the reality of the fulfilled covenant. They still did not know reconciliation as accomplished, the Kingdom of God as present. Still prophesy as it emerged from Israel's history as a whole speaks unambiguously of promises that already are fulfilled, of the covenantal grace that is now already at work. Here too, just as in Jesus prophecy, God's lordship is proclaimed as reality.

The Old Testament also testifies to events in which God and the human exist together, act together in divine-human unity. In this way, God's will and plan with all peoples comes to light, just as is the case in and through Jesus Christ. "The history of Israel is a paradigm or model for the history of all nations, and to the extent that it is prophecy, and is known as such, it is the key to the understanding of world history."[3]

Barth concluded: the history of Israel (the Old Testament) says already in advance what the history of Jesus Christ says later. In fact, in Israel's history it is already about him. Israel's history is true prophesy because Christ himself is already present in it. That is the way the New Testament community has heard the witness of the Old Testament. With that it had seen itself as bound to the old, distant Israel.

Barth included a clear warning here. A distinction remains, he said. It is only in and with Jesus Christ that the covenant is established and proclaimed in its completed reality. Seen like that, Israel's history (prophesy) can no longer really continue. What presents itself as such, in contemporary Judaism, is only a reminder of the past. The Judaism that still exists leaves a deep impression. That it still exists can even exist as a sort of proof of God. But it remains abstract, ghostly, unfruitful. At its best it is the old prophesy without the new, without fulfillment.

---

3. Barth, *CD*, IV/3, 64.

Not that the Old Testament history of Israel is now old-fashioned or even to be erased. The new that has appeared in Christ does not only *follow* the covenant in its old form but it also arrives *out of* it. The apostles and the New Testament community have again—or even only now really—discovered the Old Testament in their encounter with Jesus Christ. They have found the life and the light of the Messiah already testified in it.—However, where it is about Jesus Christ and his prophetic office, it is about him in his dual form, first hidden, then manifest.

22.5 Note: Judaism Unfruitful?

Here we stumble again across Barth's incapability to relate positively and openly with Judaism. We noted that above in his doctrine of election (*CD* II/2; see 10.13) and in his doctrine of providence (*CD* III/3; see 15.4 and 5). His verdict that there can be no genuine continuation of Israel's history and that contemporary Judaism is only abstract, ghostly, unfruitful sounds particularly crass. That verdict, of course, comes from Barth's concentration on Jesus Christ. His conviction that Christ cannot be seen apart from Israel is the counter-side of the conviction that conversely Israel cannot be seen apart from Christ. For that, Barth could appeal to the witness of the apostles and the New Testament community indeed. But must that really lead to the notion that the concrete, contemporary Israel, outshone by the light of Christ, is practically deprived of its significance and voice?

We shall see how Barth came to a positive attitude regarding other phenomena in created reality in his further consideration of the meaning of Christ. According to Barth, the light of Christ does not manifest itself necessarily in its capacity to outshine all other lights and thus to repress them, but rather in his capacity to be reflected in other lights and thus to bring them to radiate their own light. Should this insight not also have reverberated in his view of Judaism?

Perhaps this remark is too preemptory. Barth would later talk about Judaism again in the context of his considerations of the mission of the Christian community. Concrete, contemporary Judaism apparently continued to puzzle him.

22.6 The Light and Other Lights

We take up the main line of Barth's argument again. Jesus is Reconciler, also as prophet, in the practice of his prophetic office. Here, we saw, it is about reconciliation as communicative event. Barth found this aspect expressed in the prologue of the gospel of John where it is said of the (incarnate) Word: "the light shines in the darkness" (John 1:5).

Jesus Christ is the Light. In his elaboration of that claim, Barth does not shy away from the definite article. The Light, that is to say, the only, perfectly sufficient light. Can that really be sustained? Does that not mean a presumption, an absolutization of the peculiar standpoint, a step in the direction of an untenable pretension of the "absoluteness" of "Christianity"? No, said Barth, it is not about Christian or ecclesiastical pretension of power or truth here. It is about Jesus Christ himself. And whoever confesses that about him does not do so to distance him or herself from others, but because one sees oneself confronted in Jesus Christ with the Truth that also and first of all transcends oneself. Whoever undergoes that confrontation can do nothing more.

Jesus Christ, the Light, the one Word, the one real revelation of God. It is not surprising that Barth took his position here. The concentration on Jesus as the one Word of God had already appeared at the beginning of his theological journey. It was stated, for example, in the first thesis of the Barmen Declaration, prepared by Barth in 1934 for the synod of the Confessing Church held in that year in Barmen (see 1.2). But Barth struck a new path in this latter consideration. He warned against the misunderstanding that the confession of Jesus Christ as the Light, the one, true Word, implied that there could not also be other lights, other true words. There most assuredly are such lights, such words, he claimed. Think of the words of the prophets and apostles in the Old and New Testaments. Or of the prophetic, apostolic, words that are spoken by the church. Moreover, why, Barth asked, could there not also be "prophets" and "apostles" outside the church, in the world? Could true words, clear lights, not also appear and stream from the created reality, that, after all, exists fully under God's lordship? Except that a distinction remains. What obtains of Jesus Christ does not obtain of the other words, the other lights: that they are themselves the Word of God.

22.7 True Words from the Profane World, Recognized in Faith

How are such other words, other lights, to be recognized as genuine? Barth reasoned very carefully here. It cannot, he said, be about letting go of the confession of Jesus Christ as the one Light. Such other words can only be "true" if they agree with the one Word that Jesus Christ speaks and himself is and witness thereto in their way. That they do so, they must have been destined to that by Jesus Christ himself.

Barth identified the parables in the gospels as an example of what he intended. Of themselves, they speak of what occurs in ordinary life. But in Jesus' mouth they become resemblances of the Kingdom. They themselves become "true words," standing alongside the Word of God, pointing to it. The Christian community has traditionally heard such "true words" in the proclamation of the Old and New Testaments. And it was thereby led, even called, to speak such "true words."

But are such "true words" then also spoken outside the Bible, outside the church, words that are completely different, and yet do not overlook the biblical message but enlighten and accentuate it in a special way? Barth answered decisively that such completely different "true words" do indeed exist! They are called from the profane world to the community and they must really be heard by the community. Here it seems as if Barth, contrary to his own fundamental conception, took flight to the notion that something like a natural theology or natural knowledge of God could still exist, outside of Jesus Christ. But no, here too he spoke from his faith in Jesus Christ, who as the Resurrected has become manifest as the Reconciler of the world to God. So the community knows him as not only the Lord of the Church, but as the Lord of the world! It is thereby conscious that not only itself, but that basically every human, even the entire creation, is destined to receive and bear God's Word. So the community must take account that it also gets "parables of the Kingdom" from the profane world! With that it does not betray its confession of Jesus Christ as the Word of God, the Light for the world, but confirms it.

22.8 Reconciliation as Victory

Confessing this does something other than to ascertain a state of affairs. In a new paragraph, Barth discusses reconciliation not so much as an accomplished fact than as a continuing event, an event that must reckon with resistance. "The light shines in the darkness," says John's prologue (John 1:5), and that means that the light must persist against the darkness; a battle must still be fought. True, the outcome of the battle is not uncertain; the darkness, evil, in essence does not have a leg to stand on. But it still exists and still plays its role; its exclusion must (will) still be completed. Thus reconciliation happens.

It is to be noted that Barth began to develop this train of thought (and began to present it in his lectures) in October 1956, precisely the period of the dramatic events of the Hungarian uprising and the subsequent repression by the Soviet military power that invaded Hungary (see 21.5). A more telling illustration of the relevance of his doctrine of reconciliation as a continuing battle is scarcely conceivable.

Above his new paragraph, Barth set the pregnant, challenging title, "Jesus is victor!" This exclamation can be based on many New Testament texts in which Christ's victory is sung. But Barth in fact got it from a report of the nineteenth-century German preacher Johann Christoph Blumhardt, sent at the time to his ecclesiastical authorities. Blumhardt reported that in his chaplaincy with the sick he had witnessed how following years of struggle a patient was liberated from an illness that had been experienced as a demonic power. A nurse had recognized in the healing the saving power of Jesus in much the way that the New Testament speaks about healings. The exclamation, "Jesus is victor!" had resounded at the moment of healing, as a cry of the defeated power of illness. Blumhardt himself was deeply affected by this experience. It determined all further church work, extended by him and by his son, that it came to stand under the sign of a firm confidence in Jesus' victorious power and an intense waiting for the definitive inbreaking of God's Kingdom. This was exceptional in the nineteenth-century German theological climate.

Barth had already made the acquaintance of Blumhardt Jr. in 1915 and recognized the work of father and son Blumhardt as witness of a new understanding of the gospel similar to what he, too, was searching for (see 2.4). Here he referred to it, and in it he found expressed what was important to himself in the elaboration of the notion of reconciliation.

22.9 The Battle Is not Illusory

"Jesus is victor!" But, said Barth, that may not be understood as self-evident; as though the battle still to be waged is simply apparent. That is the reason he did not go along with the tenor of the title of the 1954 book *The Triumph of Grace* (treating Barth's entire theology) by the Dutch neo-Calvinist theologian G. C. Berkouwer (see 20.9). We saw that Barth had greatly valued that book and at the same time had not completely recognized himself in Berkouwer's description of his theological intentions. Here, at precisely this point in his doctrine of reconciliation, this was a crucial issue for him. He went further into the matter.

The heart of Barth's objection to talking about "the triumph of grace" is that it then appears to be about the victory of one principle over another principle (evil). To represent the matter like that gives a sense that the victory to be achieved would be the evident result of a process, just the notion that Barth wanted to avoid. Thus, he argued here against Berkouwer, he was constrained to talk of Jesus, Jesus himself, as victor. So it clearly remains that it is about a real battle that is still to be waged. Reconciliation still goes to meet its completion!

22.10 Reconciliation Intends to Be Acknowledged and Accepted

How does it proceed? According to Barth, it first manifests itself and aims to confront the human. Its aim is that its manifestation be understood and accepted by the human. That does not happen in the first instance. Indeed, this confrontation originally leads to resistance. The parable of the sower (Matthew 13:3–8, 18–23) offers a pictorial image; sowing (the proclamation of the Word) appears to fail; it is anything but self-evident that despite many threats the seed ultimately falls on good earth; that is just what must happen now. Two powers collide.

Everyone has to do with that. Naturally there is a distinction among humans. There are believers and unbelievers; there are those who have an eye for Jesus Christ and there are those for whom that does not apply; there is the Christian community and those who do not belong to the community. But, said Barth, that distinction may not be made absolute. "Believers" are again unbelievers; conversely, "unbelievers" do not stand as far from belief as they think. Revelation, the Word, is directed to all. Seen from that point of view, everyone is in the same boat, on the way to a common destination.

In any case, resistance cannot have the last word. In Christ, God has already reconciled the world to himself; if the world would not allow itself to be so addressed (and so would not accept reconciliation for itself), that is in essence meaningless. Ultimately, the Light will overcome the darkness. Barth showed how the life of Paul, the Pharisee and persecutor of Christians who became an apostle, is a witness thereto.

We heard Barth say that reconciliation as revelational event has as its aim that it be understood and accepted. Where that happens, he said, it brings about a new history, a history of Christian knowledge and confession. In that, reconciliation arrives at its goal. As Barth said, it really presents itself among humans.

22.11 Revelation as Already and Not Yet. The Doctrine of Reconciliation as a Theology of Hope

At this point Barth again talked of Jesus' resurrection. There, he said, what is accomplished in Jesus' life and death has become manifest. Now Jesus' life is really the light that enlightens the entire world, and the world is indeed reconciled with him. Thanks to Easter, we know it and need not doubt it.

Easter was, Barth said, in fact Jesus' return. The word "return" is usually used in the Christian tradition for what is still awaited, Jesus' coming in glory at the end of time. And there is talk of yet a third coming, the coming ("outpouring") of the Holy Spirit. Barth now argued that these three belong together; they are three forms of one and the same event, the one return of Jesus Christ, with the Easter event as the first, the original form. Since Easter, we already live at the end of time! The disciples already saw in the appearances of the Resurrected what holds for the entire world and what will be revealed once and for all, for all eyes to see. Moreover, it was not simply a personal privilege that they saw that; seeing that they received the command to mission.

Easter then may be Jesus' return, but world history continues "as though nothing happened." Indeed, the world is reconciled, but it is not yet saved. In that sense, reconciliation is not yet completed. Evil cuts a wide path in the world among us humans. Suffering still remains. Why is that so? Barth said that it says to us first of all that Jesus Christ himself is still engaged in a battle against evil. Yes, he could have brought an end to the battle with one blow. But then, for humans, there would not have been the possibility to cooperate consciously, actively, with Christ.

> He wills to preserve the world to cause it to persist, in its present and provisional form, in order that it should be the place where He can be perceived and accepted and known and confessed by the creature as the living Word of God. He wills to be invoked and proclaimed in His community in the world as the assembly where this knowledge and confession take place. He wills that each man should exist . . . in order that he may be a witness to the reconciliation accomplished in Him, to the future of salvation already present in Him . . . The way between the commencement and the completion . . . , the distance between Easter Day and the day of the consummation of His return, the ground which He has still to traverse and creation with Him, is the great opportunity which He has given creation freely to enter His service.[4]

---

4. Barth, *CD*, IV/3, 332–33.

Are we humans, living between Easter and the concluding Return, left to ourselves? No, even in this between-time Jesus Christ is our hope and he manifests his presence, his "return": namely, in and through the Holy Spirit. Christians are thereby equipped to live as Christians. And the Spirit is also promised to non-Christians, who still have no eye for the meaning of Jesus Christ but for whom he is also risen. Jesus' coming in the Spirit is his coming as hope for all people. So the event of reconciliation extends over the still continuing history. Here Barth's doctrine of reconciliation becomes a theology of hope.

22.12 Sin as Lie

It is not surprise that following this third elaboration of the doctrine of reconciliation Barth spoke of sin for the third time. We have already seen that Barth expressly refused to offer a separate doctrine of sin that would precede the doctrine of reconciliation. After all, he was of the opinion that what "sin" is becomes clear from the event of reconciliation in Jesus Christ (see 18.5).

Barth had considered what reconciliation is in three, complementary, ways. He always began from the meaning of Jesus Christ as articulated in the New Testament. We briefly review Barth's characterization. The first thing that must be said of Jesus Christ is that he, sent by God as God's Son, has become human, has come to live among us humans. That means humiliation, in Barth's characterization, "Jesus Christ, the Lord as servant." But with that something else has happened: he who has become servant and thereby human among humans is (as has appeared at Easter) exalted by God, the new human, the human in advance of us humans, "Jesus Christ, the servant as lord" (see 18.7). That too is an aspect of the work of reconciliation. And now a third characterization is added: Jesus Christ is the one who himself stands as guarantee for the reconciliation that has taken place in the two ways just mentioned, thus, the one who is its revealer, "prophet," and thereby consummator. In Barth's characterization, "Jesus Christ, the true witness."

Everyone agrees that sin is to turn against God. But Barth fills that in from the various aspects distinguished in "reconciliation." Sin is: not accepting reconciliation. But that concretely means something different every time. It means saying "no" to "the Lord as servant," thus resistance to God who humbled himself in Christ. That is sin as *pride*. It also means saying "no" to "the servant as lord," to the new human nature as that has been highlighted in Christ, thus, resistance to a God who in Christ would take us on the way of renewal. That is sin as *sloth* (see 19.11). And now we hear

Barth say that it also means saying "no" to "the true witness," thus resistance to a God who has spoken his Word, his Truth, in Christ in the world. That is sin as denial or as *lie*.

Hence it is not about lies in general (or about speaking untruths or spreading rumors). No, it is about denial (or down-playing or wanting to add to) this witness, the witness of Jesus Christ. That means that these lies would not exist if Jesus Christ, the true witness, did not exist. What obtains of lies here, obtains of sin in general; it does not exist of itself, it only "is" in its resistance to grace. Barth even claims that the lie as resistance to the *witness* of grace, is the specific *Christian* form of sin.

Why would we humans really hear nothing of the witness of grace? Why do we evade Jesus Christ? It has to do, said Barth, with the fact that it is about the witness of the cross. That gives offense. People evade that truth, for example, by making something beautiful or magic of it. We do not feel at ease with Jesus Christ the crucified. Lying is then remaking him into the "ideal human" according to our own taste. God speaks to us in Christ in his freedom, but the human recoils. He then sees everything of which he was certain fall away. He would rather work "God" into his own system of thought. Again, that is the form of the lie that is at issue. And this lie manifests itself all the more clearly where it really has come to an encounter with the truth of the gospel, simply among Christians.

Here we recognize Barth's critical attitude, an attitude we have often met, regarding established Christianity. It was in the summer of 1957 that Barth arrived at the ideas developed here of "sin as lie" in his lectures. That was the same period in which there was a plea in the Western world for a powerful answer to the threat from the Communist Eastern bloc; a threat that had become more acute in the Hungarian crisis of 1956. It was Christian politicians who took the lead, for example, in their plea that the West German army be provided with nuclear weapons (see 21.5). It was argued that it was about the defense of the "Christian West." It is not inconceivable that Barth has considered this kind of plea in the development of his thoughts of the lie as the specifically Christian form of sin.

This lie, where it is propounded, finally brings the human to ruin. But, Barth said, just when we think that, we give it too much honor. For lies cannot ultimately succeed against the truth. That sin in this form also cannot be talked about otherwise than in connection with reconciliation already says that it cannot triumph. May we not thus assume that history will result in a "reconciliation of everything"? That ultimately everything will turn out well? Traditionally orthodox Christians have often reproached Barth for this. They are of the opinion that this is a necessary consequence of Barth's theology and deem that as a misunderstanding of the seriousness of sin and of the threat (the reality) of God's judgement. But Barth considered playing God's judgment against his forgiving love a completely mistaken misunderstanding. In any case, he refused to accept the notion of a coming "reconciliation of everything" as a consequence of his theology. It would mean that we could count on it; that we could presuppose it as self-evident. We may not do just that in regard to God; we cannot. But on the other hand, why may we not hope that God goes further in his mercy on all humans than we can imagine? A text from the Bible like Lamentations 3:22–23, 31, hints in that direction: "The steadfast love of the LORD never ceases, his mercies never come to an end; they are new every morning; great is your faithfulness . . . the Lord will not reject forever."

22.13 Reconciliation Focused: Call, Mission

Where reconciliation is discussed, how reconciliation reaches the human and what that means for him must also be discussed. Traditional Protestantism gives great deal of thought to that. In certain circles, one even began (begins) from an entire scheme (an "order of salvation") that has different stages that a person must go through to ultimately be fully reconciled. The stages are also seen as psychological experiences. So one thinks that one can characterize "how far" someone has advanced already in the direction of spiritual perfection. But even where one is less inclined to examine the condition of inner experience (with oneself or with others) a distinction is made, a distinction primarily between "justification" and "sanctification." "Justification" is meant to indicate that the human (for Christ's sake) is acquitted of his guilt and thus may stand before God as a free and just human. "Sanctification" obtains as the fruit of "justification." "Sanctification" is another word for the renewal of life so that it is actively lived to the honor of God.

We have seen that Barth had taken up these themes. But he did not make them separate doctrines. He spoke of them in the context of his doctrine of reconciliation. For him, both these themes were applications, foci, of what is already said in the doctrine of reconciliation. Thus, he did not talk about "justification" and "sanctification" as subsequent stages. Here it is about aspects of the same event, corresponding to various aspects that are to be distinguished in the one event of reconciliation. Reconciliation is God in Christ coming to the human ("the Lord as servant"); for the human, that means his justification. But reconciliation is also that the human is exalted in Christ to be God's human ("the servant as lord"); for the human, that means his sanctification (see 19.12). And now, in the context of his third approach to the doctrine of reconciliation, Barth advanced what reconciliation means for the human in yet a third way, his *call*.

In traditional Protestantism as well, "call" exists as something that may (must) come over the human on his way to salvation. Mostly, then, that is located at the beginning of that way. Only as someone is "called" by God, "justification" and "sanctification" are portrayed as following. "Call" then always has something mysterious about it: when and how do you experience something like it? Barth broke with such psychological views. That reconciliation also implies that Christ himself *reveals* the reconciliation that has taken place, that in itself means, according to Barth, that the human, who hears this revelation, is "called."

Called—to what? Barth answered, to being Christian, thus, to following Jesus Christ. And that means to being a witness. For "[i]t is in relation to Him that non-Christians and Christians, for all their differences, are what they are, namely, men who have their calling only before them on the one side, and men who have it both behind and before them on the other."[5] That they have heard it means that they have to hand it on so that others too will hear and obtain the reconciliation that also applies to them. Whoever is called is therewith also sent out!

Moreover, that does not obtain only for the Christian individual. It also and first of all obtains for the community. Christians by definition share in that. One is not a Christian on his or her own; one is a Christian as a member of the community. From this conviction, Barth, in his doctrine of reconciliation, speaking of what reconciliation means for humans, how their life changes as consequence, also got to talk about the Christian community (the church). Elsewhere, in the previous parts of his doctrine of reconciliation, he had elaborated on what, in his opinion, the essence of the community is, that it is the work of Jesus Christ through the Spirit. And he had talked about the life of the community, including how that could be given a concrete form. In the third part of his doctrine of reconciliation discussed in this chapter, Barth placed all the emphasis on: that the congregation (the church) is *sent*. It has, he said, its peculiar place in world events as the "people of God"; it is a "community for the world." The meaning of its existence is bringing to light that Jesus Christ has called all of humanity under God's grace and into his service. It has the task of proclaiming the gospel of God's great "yes" to humanity in the world. Thus the answer to the question whether it comes to that depends on whether the Christian community is really "Christian community."

---

5. Barth, *CD*, IV/3, 497.

At the time that Barth wrote this, the theme of the relation between church and world was a major topic of discussion. In the Netherlands, for example, following the Second World War, a "theology of the apostolate" had developed that dominated the church for a long time, a theology that oriented all thought around the coming Kingdom of God, such that there was hardly a place for the church as a separate entity. That was not undisputed, but in any case one was very conscious of the distance that had grown between church and society and was still growing.

Barth also keenly saw that growing distance. We recall his "letter to a preacher in the German Democratic Republic" from 1958. In that letter we heard him go into the difficult position of the church in a Communist society in which the entire framework of the earlier Christian culture had collapsed, remarking that something similar would also take place in the West (see 21.6). It is not for nothing that at this same time in the third part of his doctrine of reconciliation he brought up this theme broadly and principally. We hear him argue here that the work of mission, of "confessing before humans," is not something at the margins of Christian existence and of the church but belongs at the center of Christian and ecclesiastical life. But it is thereby essential for him to show that this insight is not given with the situation in society as it has now become, rather that it more directly coheres with, emerges from, the insight of faith that Jesus Christ himself is the true Witness and as such the Reconciler.

22.14 Again, the Jews

The Christian community is called to mission, to witness. One particular question still pops up: does that also obtain in regard to the Jews? Barth is again obliged to go into the question of the relation between the church and Israel. He said without hesitation that of course the church owes its witness to the Jews, the synagogue. Only, here that witness must take a certain character. For after all, the God whom the community must proclaim was already the God of Israel before it emerged from this people and he is still this God. Jesus himself has come from the people of Israel! Barth again recalled the witness of Romans 11 (see 15.4); we, Christians from among the peoples, are added to this people as a wild shoot engrafted into the noble olive tree. Here the usual path is not in order for Christians missionizing. Just the opposite is the case, the Jew who has continually been sustained through all the disasters of his history "is the natural historical monument to the love and faithfulness of God." He is, believing or unbelieving, "the epitome of the man freely chosen and blessed by God, who as a living commentary on the Old Testament is the only convincing proof of God outside the Bible."[6]

And there is still another reason for the Christian community not to missionize in regard to the Jews. At the crucial moment, Israel has denied its election and call. It had handed over its King to the heathens when he had appeared in its midst (and by that route he had become the Savior of the world!). True, the synagogue continued, but it is now only the organization of people on their way to an empty future. And the Jew now displays "an existence which . . . is dreadfully empty of grace and blessing," characterized by its rejection of the Messiah, as such the reflection of the same graceless existence of which we poor pagans would have gone to ruin without Jesus Christ. Instead of missionizing, the Christian community is only to view and to fear here "the judgement of God in His love."[7] Here the proclamation of the gospel from person to person can no longer help. And dialogue between Christians and Jews does not have any sense either. After all, the Jew can only return from the rejection of his Messiah by reconsideration of his own roots, there where he understands as yet the salvation intended for him in the first place as a Jew and reads his own holy book again. And that can happen only where God himself intervenes—as it overcame the Jew Paul.

Thus, there is no missionizing the Jews. It can be about only one thing for the Christian community here; it must be about making the synagogue "jealous," "envious" (as Paul calls it in Romans 11:11, 14). That is, it must show in its own existence (its entire existence) what it means to live in the comfort of the fulfilled Word of God, in grateful acceptance of God's election, call, and grace. With that they must confront the synagogue. But just that has not happened. It has dialogued with the Jews. It has tolerated them; then persecuted them, or even without a word of protest, left them to the persecution of others. In other periods it has extended baptism certificates to them as entrance tickets to Western society. It has also seriously attempted to "convert" some Jews. But the only thing it can really do for the Jews is: so to live as the church of Jesus Christ that they would become attracted by that. It has neglected to do exactly that. Thereby the Christian community has in fact remained "completely indebted" to the Jews. That continues to be a wound in the body of the community, an unresolved problem, and a shadow behind and over all its further missionary activity.

Thus far Barth's considerations on the matter. Here once more he laid all his cards on the table in regard to the relation between the church and

---

6. Barth, *CD*, IV/3, 877.
7. Barth, *CD*, IV/3, 877.

Israel. We stumble again on his hard judgment of the synagogue, of contemporary Judaism, as without a future, of Jewish existence as "dreadfully empty of grace." So calculated, would the Jew not be under God's grace? Indeed, Barth still saw the Jew always as "the epitome of the man freely chosen and blessed by God." And he continued, with Paul (Romans 11:25–32), looking for the day in which all of Israel will also be saved (in Christ). It is clear that Barth's vision of contemporary Judaism did not emerge from anti-Semitism. After all, he claimed that the fault is not so much with Israel as with the church. He remained mesmerized by Judaism as a phenomenon. He also saw it now, in its continued existence, as a "monument to the love and faithfulness of God." He even valued the contemporary Jew as "the only convincing proof of God outside the Bible."[8] It is just in his negative qualification that Barth respected the continuing exceptional nature of Judaism. But his own theological position hindered him from understanding the sense of carrying on discussions with the Jewish tradition or even with Jewish thinkers, theologians, and philosophers.

---

8. Barth, *CD*, IV/3, 877.

23

Towards an Ethics of Reconciliation

23.1 Again on the Path of Ethics

ON MAY 10, 1959 Barth turned 73 years old. But he still received permission from the University of Basel to continue giving his lectures. His desire for work continued unabated. As he had concluded his doctrine of creation with a separate reflection on ethics from the viewpoint of creation (*CD* III/4; see 17), he intended to conclude the doctrine of reconciliation in the same way. Now too ethics must be in order, this time from the perspective of reconciliation. It would have to be about the same command, the same God, but from a different angle. Barth had said at the time that God the Creator is none other than the graceful God; and that had been echoed in his creation ethics. But now all thought must be oriented to that reality. The command must now be understood as the command of the graceful God.

His lectures on this topic would begin in the fall. That summer he would have given lectures, but he didn't do so because of the thorough preparation that he had in mind for the new project. As he wrote to his two sons, Markus and Christoph, he spent the summer re-reading through the entire New Testament. It surprised him "still to be so much a beginner at the age of seventy-three."[1]

How must ethics as an ethics of reconciliation begin? Is the command of the graceful God, the God of the covenant entered with humans, to be characterized with a central concept? In the creation ethics, Barth had set "freedom" at the center; the human as creature is called by God's command to freedom. What could correspond to that in the ethics of reconciliation? Barth was originally inclined to choose the concept "faithfulness." God has shown the human his faithfulness in his covenant; is not the human, conversely, in turn called to be faithful to God? That is certainly the heart of the matter.

---

1. Quoted in Busch, *Karl Barth*, 441.

Only, with that it is not yet said what the human concretely must *do*. How will one appear to live one's active faithfulness to God? Barth thought that it must be about an action in which one shows oneself as fully present to God and in which one ventures in confidence with this God. Via these considerations Barth came to the concept "invocation." The human, taken up in covenant with the graceful God, is called to turn to God in prayer.

That sounds strange as a beginning of an ethic. Is praying not asking for God's action, and does that not fall outside the conceptual field of ethics? But according to Barth that is decidedly not the case. Prayer and action are not contradictory. The Reformers already knew that. In their train, the *Heidelberg Catechism* (see 12.6) discusses the meaning of prayer in direct connection with a discussion of God's commands. Obedience to God's commands obtains as life in gratitude for the salvation received from God, and there it is said of prayer that it is "the most important part of thankfulness that God requires of us." Barth would continue in this line in his ethics of reconciliation, with the presupposition that prayer and action are interwoven. If only prayer obtains as the starting point. That must continue to set the tone to action.

With that Barth had the outline of his ethics of reconciliation in mind. He decided to orient it around the prayer that Jesus had taught his disciples, the Lord's Prayer (Matthew 6:9–13), to consider with each petition the action that is concurrently asked of the one praying:

> From this incomparable text, familiar to Christianity in every age, we learn not only that we should pray, but also what we should pray and how we should pray. We also perceive what, as those who may and should pray thus, we have to know about shaping our life as Christians.[2]

But this outline could not do everything. First, Barth thought, the *foundation* of this Christian life must be discussed. How can it be that people live as Christians? How does it really begin? And alongside that, at the conclusion, the question of how the Christian life undergoes (continual) *renewal* still must be discussed. In connection with these two aspects, Barth proposed to go specifically into the meaning of baptism and the Lord's Supper. The two are called "sacraments" in the Christian tradition. This designation is connected with the notion that salvation is mediated via these ecclesiastical actions. Among Protestants, baptism and the Lord's Supper also obtain as vehicles by which God's grace reaches humans or at least as confirmation (seals) of God's Word, thus as something extra beyond the Word. At the time,

---

2. Barth, *The Christian Life*, 44.

Barth himself still held such "sacramental" ideas. But now, at this stage of his life, he had retreated from that perspective. In the preceding parts of his doctrine of reconciliation, baptism and the Lord's Supper had not or had hardly been a topic of discussion. Now, at the concluding, fourth part of his doctrine of reconciliation on the ethics of reconciliation, that discussion can and must take place. Baptism and the Lord's Supper, Barth now noted, are human actions (like all of the Christian life), deeds of human obedience, in response to what God in Christ has done for the human, specific actions whereby the Christian life *begins* (that obtains for baptism) or in which it is (continually) *renewed* and *continues* (that obtains for the Lord's Supper). Thus, Barth would begin his ethics of reconciliation with a discussion of baptism and conclude with a discussion of the Lord's Supper.

23.2 Lectures on "The Christian Life"

Barth confidently began his lectures on the ethics of reconciliation in the fall of 1959. At the time it was only his students who could be informed of his view of baptism as (not a sacrament but) a human answer to God's salvific actions, that is, as the first step of the Christian life in faithfulness to God. They must have been surprised hearing it. This view of baptism signified a radical break with the way in which the tradition of the church had talked about baptism. Did it cause a sensation among the students? In any case, a discussion would follow and that in broad circles. He would later rework the lectures and offer his exposition on baptism separately for publication. We will return to this.

In the discussion of the Lord's Prayer, Barth first considered the salutation, "Our Father who art in heaven!" That Jesus had put this salutation in the mouth of his disciples determined their place in relation to God and also in relation to each other in the world. That is, said Barth, what constitutes their Christian existence and what for the time being distinguishes them from others (although the "our" tends, ultimately, to include everyone). A human cannot so appeal to God as "our Father." We must be empowered to do so, and we *are* so empowered, by Jesus Christ. In his reflections on baptism, Barth had argued that Jesus had pointed his followers to baptism as the beginning of the Christian life by the fact that he allowed himself to be baptized (by John the Baptist, Matthew 3.13–15). Here, speaking of "calling on God as Father," Barth again referred to the connection between Jesus and us; Jesus has made it possible for his own to call on God as Father in that he preceded them as an example. Jesus took his own with him in the movement of his own prayer. His relation to God, as that of the Son to the Father, is unique. But he effects our share in that relation and teaches us to call on God as "our Father too." And the Christian life takes on an active form where we do that. How that happens, in what it results, Barth intended to clear up through a reflection of the following petitions of the Lord's Prayer.

23.3 "Zeal for the Honor of God"

From the first petition, "hallowed be thy name," Barth inferred the notion that the Christian is commanded to be filled with "zeal for the honor of God."[3] God's name, God's honor, must be kept holy in the world, among humans—but that appears repeatedly not to happen, including in the church—and among Christians themselves. Seen objectively, God is known everywhere. He is the origin of everything, everything exists in him. Every human is created to him with an inborn orientation toward him. But no subjective knowledge responds to this objective knowledge. Indeed, humans entrench themselves against the reality of God. They do that, either in a primitive way, in a theoretical or polemical atheism (that is in conflict with itself!), or via adherence to a (self-projected) religion, or via the attempt to make God into their own cause, to further their own interest. The result in any case is that one no longer sees his fellow human (or at best as an object that one can treat or ignore, as one likes it). That a factual ignorance of God also exists in the church is, moreover, all the more disturbing. Does the church not exist because God gave himself to be known in Jesus Christ? But the church appears to have repeatedly forgotten its origin. It makes much of itself and acts as if everything turns about itself. Or, it is lacking in the confidence of faith and is thereby unfaithful to Jesus Christ, the Living. And so it also appears that Christians repeatedly deny their Christianity and devalue their vocation to lead a different life. That all is the profanation of God's name.

What does the petition to hallow God's name mean? Does God's name need hallowing? Yes, apparently so. After all, God's "name" is about the God who has entered the world to make himself known. That entrance into the world means by definition that he has made himself vulnerable to the problematic nature of his self-disclosure; God "goes under." But it cannot remain so. God's name calls out, ultimately, to be known in full. And now, in this petition, the prayer appeals to God that he himself will hallow his name, authentically so. Thus the ambiguity (knowing God and at the same time not knowing him) will radically come to an end, We can come to this petition only because we know Jesus Christ, in Whom God has fully and completely

---

3. Barth, *The Christian Life*, 112–13.

disclosed himself. There, in Christ, God's name is already hallowed. The petition, "hallowed be thy name," is the petition that what has already happened in Christ will see itself through in full, world-wide.

Christians are commanded to pray for this definitive hallowing of God's name. That implies, so Barth reflected, that they may not submit to the current ambiguous situation (of God's objectively being known, but repeatedly not subjectively so). They are called to look forward with passionate longing for the coming, the definitive hallowing of God's name. But that in turn implies (here ethics comes directly into view!) that they also commit themselves as much as they can to the hallowing of God's name, now, already, so in a passion for God's honor today. That means that they must give priority to God's Word (the Word of the living Jesus Christ) above all other factors in their life. Of course, other factors exist as well. Christians participate in society, are involved in the struggle to exist. But as hearers of God's Word, they stand differently in that position. They are no longer simply followers. They will make choices, here rejecting, there advocating. That obtains for them personally, but also for them as church members and world citizens. Hence they will not write off the church (as completely perverted) but even less uncritically acclaim it (as though it were without spot or wrinkle). And they will not judge the world as only perverted (to meet it as knights of the cross or to withdraw from it as monks), and even less view it as only good (reconciled after all), and thus accept it without reserve as it is. The actions of the Christians will let themselves be guided by the acknowledgment (and testimony) of the priority of God's Word. Thus, it will always have something of a resistance movement about it.

The state of ambiguity in which the world traffics (God is objectively known but at the same time subjectively unknown) leads to a continual fluctuation between humanity and inhumanity. When the Christian prays for the hallowing of God's name by God himself, he prays concretely that God would make an end to this ambiguity, this fluctuation. For God's name is unambiguously the name of the One who is for the human. Where the action of the Christian coincides with this petition, that also takes the side of the human. Doing so, the Christian will continue to be passionate for God's honor; he shows himself as a truly *human* person.

23.4 "The Battle for Human Justice"

The second petition of the Lord's Prayer, "thy kingdom come," is of course not separate from the first petition, Barth reflected. One also hears a command of God in this second petition, but it is not a different command; it is another element of one and the same command. The Christian, praying for the coming of God's Kingdom, knows that one is at the same time called to "fight for human justice." Whether, in one's passion for God's honor, one is on the right path, will appear from whether one indeed participates in this fight. Where one does so, one is also involved in an attitude of resistance, that is, against the disorder that dominates human life and that is the consequence of the human turn from God, a disorder that also becomes apparent in that the human turns against fellow humans in mutual enmity. The human has become a wolf to the fellow human. Christians are commanded to resist just this situation. They have heard the proclamation of God's justice and thus know that the human is also destined to live in justice and peace. Where the Christian prays "thy kingdom come," one is, when it is good, already active in the fight against the disorder dominant among humans.

Considering the disorder in which we humans live today (and against which the Christian is commanded to engage in resistance), Barth added yet another reflection. That the human turns away from God leads not only to turning against the fellow human; it also has as a consequence that one is estranged from oneself. One thinks that one has now become "like God" (Genesis 3:5), lord and master of one's own existence, but that is not the case. The possibilities of one's own life continue from that point as spirits that the sorcerer's apprentice no longer has in hand. They become powers that dominate the human rather than the converse. Not being able to describe them precisely, one can only talk about them mythologically. And yet their reality and activity are not to be denied. They appear to set society in movement, to assert themselves in what among humans are a matter of course, in human traditions, institutions. They have their effect in politics and economics, in technology and art, as well as in the personal lives of humans. They are what is denoted in the New Testament as "powers" and "principalities," "rulers" and "authorities in the air," etc., not escaping Christ's ultimate authority but powerfully present nonetheless. What does that mean concretely today? One thinks, for example, of political absolutism; the authority of the state that gets a demonic character and puts power above justice (states that call themselves "democratic" can also reveal themselves as such!). Or also of the power of money (the New Testament talks about "mammon") as symbol of what people everywhere can do and what their "value" is. Barth separately considered the role that ideologies can play. That the human forms ideas and that his action is guided by them is in itself a good thing; but it becomes otherwise when such ideas become a kind of article of faith that as such must be firmly held. That leads unavoidably to the cost of humanity. There are many other matters to be identified in this connection that all cohere with the fact that the human happens to live on earth. The human may inhabit, cultivate, and maintain the earth. But apart from God this human gets, in the shortest time, mad about the earth and is intimidated by it, as is the case in fashion, or in getting caught up in watching sports, or in the desire for travel in which humans carry on without really seeing what they're stumbling across.

The disorder to which the human who has turned against God has fallen prey expresses itself in all this. And against such phenomena the Christian is commanded to pray, "thy kingdom come." This petition already witnesses of itself that another kingdom exists vis-à-vis this kingdom of disorder. Thus, a limit is set to the kingdom of disorder! By God himself, and the Christian may appeal to it! That is already an act of resistance. Whereby, Barth claimed, it must moreover be considered that the coming of God's kingdom will be something totally new. It is not the extension of what we humans, or even we Christians, do. It means that God himself will come and intervene, as he has already come in Jesus Christ.

So, praying, looking forward to the coming of God's Kingdom, we should already today stop submitting (here again the ethics comes directly into view!) to the existing disorder. Whoever prays uprightly, "thy kingdom come" knows to be involved in the fight for human justice. Of course, God's justice transcends that. But human, modest, justice exists in rapport with it. That too is about the human, about the right and value of the human. Where Christians commit themselves to that, they obey the command that is given them along with that they are permitted to pray "thy kingdom come."

23.5 Seventy-fifth Birthday. "The Idol Falters"

Barth had come thus far in his lectures on "the ethics of reconciliation" when he celebrated his seventy-fifth birthday in May 1961. That took place in a small circle of friends (Miskotte among them). An extra tone was provided because Karl Kupisch, church historian at Berlin, on this occasion published (with Barth's agreement) a collection of addresses, essays, and letters of Barth from 1930–1969. Barth had previously published several collections: in 1924 *Das Wort Gottes und die Theologie* [The Word of God and Theology], in 1928 *Die Theologie und die Kirche* [Theology and the Church], and in 1957 *Theologische Fragen und Antworten* [Theological Questions and Answers]. Together these collections offer a good overview of Barth's theological development. Now, Kupisch brought together Barth's texts primarily from the later years and those that specifically involved current affairs.

He gave his collection a remarkable title, *Der Götze wackelt* [The Idol Falters]. He had derived this title from a phrase in a letter from Barth to

Thurneysen from 1920. In it, Barth had related, among other things, a visit that he had made to Harnack, his former teacher (see 3.6). They had not been able to come to agreement. Barth had noted that a (liberal Protestant) theology like Harnack's no longer had a future. Combative and self-assured, Barth had written following his return home, "we must both of us spit on our hands in preparation for new deeds. It is clear that the idol totters."[4]

Whether this statement from the young Barth is representative of the older, post-war Barth is a question. We saw how at end of the fifties he had attended to new accents in his own theology: on God's humanity (as the way in which He is the other, strange), and how he also had come to a re-evaluation of Protestant theology of the nineteenth century (Harnack!); it can no longer simply be characterized as idolatry (see 21.3 and 4).

23.6 Work on the *Church Dogmatics* Broken Off

Barth had carefully written out the texts of his lectures (as he had always done) on the "ethics of reconciliation." He had still intended to interpret the other petitions of the Lord's Prayer deriving from them guidelines for "the Christian life." But here progress came to a halt. He would no longer hold lectures after his seventy-fifth birthday. The end of his regular academic activity had arrived, forty years after he had begun in Göttingen (see 3.1). He also didn't get to the definitive conclusion of the text already presented, with an eye to publication. The texts of the lectures remained in their first, incomplete version. Work on the "Church Dogmatics" was broken off and would not be picked up again.

Thanks to the later, posthumous, publication of Barth's lectures on "the ethics of reconciliation," we have been able to listen in, privately as it were, on these lectures. We can see how much Barth tried here to derive ethical clues from the heart of the Christian faith, where it is expressed in prayer. With the first as well as with the second petition of the Lord's Prayer, he had concluded that the Christian is called to commit himself to "the human," humanity. That coincides with the accent that we have seen him place on the humanity of God (see 21.3). What Barth had been able to write out as his "ethics of reconciliation" is the elaboration of tendencies that were already heralded in his theology as such.

Commitment to "the human," to humanity. Is that not a rule to which everyone self-evidently agrees? It naturally comes down to concretization. Barth himself had shown what he intended. He clearly articulated the way in which he, as theologian, had been concerned with current affairs by

---

4. Barth to Thurneysen, April 30, 1920, in *RT*, 50.

means of addresses, open letters, particularly in the time when Nazism was on the rise and during the Second World War and the following era of the Cold War. Barth's theology was no academic philosophy. It had social and political implications. In his "ethics of reconciliation," as far as that had been developed, he showed how much he indeed deemed dogmatics and ethics, faith and practical action involved with each other.

23.7 Swan Song: Retirement as Professor

Barth had laid down his professorate. The question of who would succeed him, however, appeared to be a hot potato. Barth himself had wanted his student and kindred spirit, Helmut Gollwitzer—in the meantime having become a professor in Berlin—to be his successor. There was resistance to that. There were objections to Gollwitzer's political position. They had also been raised against Barth over the years, but ultimately could not thwart his activities. Now one would apparently grab the chance to bring about a change of course.

One thing or another led to a considerable delay in the appointment of Barth's successor. Finally, after a half a year of fairly distasteful discussions, it was indeed not Gollwitzer but the young Swiss Heinrich Ott who was named to fill the vacancy. In the meantime, Barth was asked to again fill in this half year—from the fall of 1961 to the spring of 1962. Barth appeared to be prepared to do so. But he gave up on the elaboration of the ethics of reconciliation. Instead he gave a series of lectures on "Introduction to Evangelical Theology." The text was also published under that title in the spring of 1962. It was, as Barth himself would call it, his "swan song."

This series of lectures drew unexpectedly great interest from his students. At first, Barth gave a summary in five lectures of what he had wanted to say in all his years as a theologian; a summary of what he had developed from the beginning, from his publication of his *Letter to the Romans* (see 2.5) as his fundamental vision. He argued again that the "God" of Whom theology is about can only be the God of the gospel. That is to say, God in the history of his deeds. Deeds in which he is not the prisoner of his own majesty but exists for the human. Theology that reflects on that simply must not be busy with the question whether it belongs in the university, among the "sciences." It must stick to its own business. Where it does that it realizes that it has been and is (repeatedly) called by the Word of God as he has spoken in the history of Israel and of Jesus Christ. It is thereby referred to the witness of the prophets and apostles, respectively from the Old and New Testaments. Theologians must submit themselves to be corrected by their writings. And they have the task of repeatedly receiving the Word of God (that never is a matter of course) and articulating it. Thus, it is not simply about translating the Bible into contemporary language as if with that everything would have been done, as if the content of the Bible is clear. No, the content must repeatedly be dug up. The modern human is primarily served when coming closer to "what stands there," that is, to the Word of God that is testified here.[5] That is what theology is about.

Barth again also argued that theology's place and function is in and to the service of the community (the church). For that is called to life by the Word. Thereby its faith is wakened and it is called to speak and to witness to it. The question is always: has it understood the Word in a good way? It can never proceed as though that is self-evident. The community can be wrong in its proclamation and thereby hinder God's cause in the world instead of serving it. It will have to pray every day that that not happen. But it will also have to do its own business: in theological reflection. Thus, theology is the business of the entire community, all Christianity. Theologians do their work representatively. They help the community to keep its witness and faith pure.

Barth followed with a short series of lectures on the life of the theologian (who never gets beyond astonishment, who does not escape the sense that he is himself at issue, who knows himself taken into service by what he is reflecting on, in short, who exists in faith) and on the dangers to which the theologian is vulnerable (he goes by definition a lonely way, repeatedly has to battle with doubt and attack, "doesn't God distance himself from my theological work?," at the same time hoping for God under whose judgment grace is hidden). And he concluded with an overview of what the theologian has to do in practice. No study without prayer, but also no prayer without (constant) study! That study is primarily about interpretation of biblical texts, that is as texts in which the community has heard the voice of the original witness of God's work and word. That voice must repeatedly be heard. Theology is not really interested in the facts that may lie hidden behind this message. Whoever looks for that does not do justice to these texts.

Barth had never strived for popularity among theologians who would orient themselves specially to "the modern man" or among modern historical-critical biblical scholars. Nor did he do so now. He deemed that pursuing such popularity offered no service to what theology is about.

He concluded his lectures on March 1, 1962, with a lecture on "love." By way of conclusion, he was addressed—after all, this was his farewell as professor—by the substitute rector of the University of Basel. It was anything

---

5. Barth, *Evangelical Theology*, 35.

but a *laudatio*. The speaker used the occasion to offer critical remarks on Barth's political attitude. That led to a powerful protest from the students present. Barth had imagined his departure very differently. In the meantime, as he later stated himself, his inner peace had not been disturbed.

24

Retired, in a Changing Theological Landscape

24.1 Trip to America

BARTH WAS NOW OFFICIALLY retired. But he had no plans to rest on his laurels. In April 1962 he began a journey that brought him further than ever—to America.

He had previously repeatedly been invited to visit the United States, but he had always turned down such invitations. It would take too much time and keep him from his real work, so he argued. There certainly had been contacts. One had not refrained from asking Barth his opinion and advice and Barth had not left himself without witness. So, in October 1942 he had given an extensive answer to an American church leader to a series of questions concerning the attitude to be expected on the course of the war and what to be expected from the church concerning ecclesiastical and ecumenical policy to be followed following the war. Furthermore, different Americans studied with Barth in the post-war years. The American theological climate, as far as he knew it, did not strike him as generally of a high quality. We recall the difference of opinion that he had with the American theologian, Reinhold Niebuhr on the occasion of his lecture at the World Council Assembly in Amsterdam, 1948. Barth had remarked that American ("Anglo-Saxon") theology appeared to have no eye for the sovereign action of God himself. It was, in his judgment, "mystery-less," and thus, not really interesting (see 20.4).

In any case, Barth's name was well-known in America. The editors of the magazine *The Christian Century* had asked Barth several times for an autobiographical contribution. For Barth that had been an occasion each time to give an account of "how my mind has changed." Three times he wrote a retrospective under that title, every time overseeing a decade. Together, the contributions cover the period 1928-1958. They offer an interesting overview of Barth's course of development.

For a moment it had appeared within in the context of his involvement with the second general assembly of the World Council of Churches, that he would attempt the crossing. Barth had been officially invited to be present as an advisor and was originally inclined to accept the invitation. But on further reflection he thought that he had to decline (see 20.7). In his letter to Visser 't Hooft, Barth had written his regrets first of all "because I must resign myself that, by human measures, I shall see America only from the corner that hopefully will be allocated to me in one of the lowest parts of heaven."[1]

And now, following his retirement, it happened all the same during his lifetime. His son Christoph and Charlotte von Kirschbaum traveled with him. He carried in his luggage the text of his five first lectures on "Introduction to Evangelical Theology," just given in Basel. The lectures had been translated by one of his students into English. He was received and accompanied in the United States by his son Markus who had worked as professor of New Testament in various seminaries there already since 1953. It was a trip filled with impressions and encounters.

He stayed for the first three weeks in Chicago. Among others, he met the American evangelist, Billy Graham, held his five lectures, and received an honorary doctorate. And, in the presence of an audience of thousands, he took part in a panel discussion that extended over two evenings. Among the participants of the discussion were leading Protestant theologians from the entire nation as well as a Roman Catholic theologian and a Jewish rabbi.

Primarily on the agenda were questions about the relation between God's revelation and natural reality. Barth took the occasion to set out his insights on the matter as clearly and as appealingly as possible. He said that he did not intend to deny that worldly matters can display God's presence but underscored that they can do so just because and following the fact that God has revealed himself in his own way, directly, in Christ. He compared it with the way reflectors work along a highway; in themselves the reflectors are dark and become light just by means of the light from the headlights of passing autos. A related question (from the Roman Catholic side) was whether the encounter between God and the human does still not presuppose that the human (the Christian) is in a condition to encounter God. Barth answered: naturally the human as creature is destined to be God's covenant partner; only, the human is like a boy with two broken legs. The legs are still there but they no longer function; they must

---

1. Barth to Visser 't Hooft, October 18, 1953, in *BV*, 278.

be healed first. That is the work of the Holy Spirit. Where that happens, only there is humanity restored.

24.2 Panel Discussion on the Relation Between Jews and Christians

Then there were questions concerning the relation between Jews and Christians. The rabbi on the panel asked Barth whether his idea that God has revealed himself centrally, specifically, in Jesus Christ does not mean, in fact, that an unbridgeable chasm between Jews and Christians exists today. Barth contested that: "We have a point of contact, and a very big one, because we read the same law, the same prophets, and the same writings . . . what we Christians call the Old Testament." He claimed that from that point we must be able to come to a common view of the problematic of these documents. The problematic, namely, that consists in that God's revelation through Moses and the prophets in Israel's history belongs to a particular period, that has now come to an end. Do we, since, live in a sort of vacuum or is the event reported by the New Testament the fulfillment of the law and the prophets?[2] At the conclusion of his doctrine of reconciliation, Barth had not only condemned every attempt of a Christian mission to the Jews, but also characterized continuing discussions between Christians and Jews as meaningless (see 22.14). As concerns the latter, here, in any case, he expressed himself less rigorously; we must discuss with each other the question whether (to what extent) the apostles and prophets of the New Testament confirm the witness of the law and the prophets. Enough to discuss!—The rabbi thanked Barth for his clarifying remarks but noted that "we Jews" exactly do *not* believe that God's revelation would have ended after Moses and the prophets. To his understanding, there could be no talk of a "vacuum" as presupposed by Barth. He apparently did not see a discussion like that intended by Barth as happening any time soon.

As the discussion continued, the question was placed on the table of what the continuing existence of Israel (the Jewish people) after Jesus Christ has to say to Christians. Barth answered that we Christians must learn from that that God's election of Israel, including where Israel resisted God, remains valid. Asked about his view of the modern state of Israel, he stated that he was open to the notion that it can be seen as a sign of God's electing grace toward Israel. Just as the eighteenth-century Prussian king, Frederick the Great, in response to his question whether a proof for the existence of

---

2. Barth, "Podium discussion in Chicago," 183.

God could be found, was answered: "Your majesty, the Jews,"[3] Barth said, so today he could be answered extra: "the state of Israel, Sire!"[4] In his dogmatics, Barth had agreed rather hesitantly with the answer given to Frederick the Great (see 15.4). In this panel discussion he dropped his reserve. It is striking that he gave himself room for the idea of the state of Israel as a proof of God:

> The Jews have always owed their existence to the power of God alone and not to their own force or to the might of their history. And here we have another case of this kind of existence for Israel. God alone can help it exist, and it seems that he will do so.[5]

However, the question of how this theological view relates to the political reality of the state of Israel remained unanswered.

24.3 The Conclusion of the American Trip

The panel discussion drew interest from many quarters. The *New York Times* wrote: "to hear him [Barth] and to see him in the flesh . . . is to ecclesiastics what a personal appearance of Sir Winston Churchill would be in the House of Representatives."[6] Barth concluded with the remark that were he an American theologian he would try to work out a "theology of freedom." He filled out the notion of "freedom" to mean freedom from any inferiority complex toward Europe and from any superiority complex toward Asia and Africa, thus as "freedom for humanity"; this, in contrast to the ideology of the image of freedom in New York, based on the freedom to which Christ makes free.

He visited Princeton, where he also held his lectures at the seminary. There was extensive discussion with students. A number of facets of Barth's theology were discussed. He attended a church service led by Martin Luther King. Alas, there was no occasion for a personal meeting.

His stay in the United States lasted seven weeks. He traveled throughout the nation, visited Washington (where he was received by the Swiss ambassador, among others), New York (Union Theological Seminary), and San Francisco. He was very interested in the pitiful social conditions under which many Americans lived (in Harlem, New York City, for example). He was given detailed information of the conditions in American prisons (in the last years of his life, Barth on a regular basis led church services in the Basel prison). At

---

3. Barth, "Podium discussion in Chicago," 170
4. Barth, "Podium discussion in Chicago," 186.
5. Barth, "Podium discussion in Chicago," 186.
6. Quoted in Barth, "Podium Discussion in Chicago," 161.

his request, an excursion was organized to the battlefields of the American Civil War (1861–1865); that had meant the end of slavery for the American society and with that the birth of modern America.

On his departure from the United States, the president of the theological seminary at Pittsburgh came with a special request. Would Barth not be inclined to give his old writing desk to the seminary as a souvenir? The writing desk had been his father's and Barth had worked on it since 1922. Barth agreed. Later the old piece of furniture was moved from Basel to Pittsburgh and Barth received a modern desk in return. In 1963, a year after Barth's American trip, his son Markus became a professor at this same seminary (where he would remain active until 1972). Today, Barth's old writing desk stands in the seminary building as a small but cherished monument.

24.4 Discussion of Being Church in a Totalitarian State

Having returned from America, Barth enjoyed little free time. Again in June 1962 he responded to the invitation to participate in the annual meeting of the Swiss Protestant book dealers and publishers. There too he answered questions before a large audience among whom were many participants from West Germany.

He went into detail in response to a question of the possibilities for the church in a totalitarian state. The person putting the question, of course, had the Communist state in mind. Barth recalled that Hitler's state was also a totalitarian state. Have those who are now critical of the Communist state themselves shouted "Heil Hitler!" earlier? But Barth did not want to stay with that. Rather, he pointed out, "every state has something of the totalitarian state in it," Switzerland not excepted![7] Barth pointed out that various of his own texts, lectures, and letters had been censured during the war by the Swiss censor because they were too critical of the then-current Swiss politics concerning Hitler (see 10.11). Moreover, totalitarianism does not just begin with the state; it already exists in society. It wants us to do certain things. Whoever does not comply runs into difficulty. And behind that stands a complete totalitarian world in which powers rule that we do not have in hand but that on the contrary control us, the power of ideologies, of fashion, of media, of money. Barth had spoken of this in his lectures on "the Christian life" (see 23.4). Here, in brief, he advanced the same ideas.

What now, in this situation, are "the possibilities" for the church? Barth said that the church has only one possibility: to exist around and to remain with Jesus; to feed on God's Word, and to stand in faith. "It is the circle

---

7. Barth, "Conversation with Protestant Book Dealers," 239.

around [Jesus], and he is the middle—that is its 'possibility.'"[8] So, whatever the totalitarian reality of its environment, the church is itself a bulwark of freedom. It need not, therefore, clench its fists. It can wait. After all, it knows that all totalitarian powers are lies. And it also knows that God rules. So, the church remains with its task. However repressed, it is not anxious for its future. Because the Lord is its future.

In this context, Barth also discussed the East–West relationship. He referred to reports on church life behind the "iron curtain." These show, he said, that there one has a better understanding of what it is to be church than in the "free" West.

In discussion, Barth was reproached that he had represented the situation of the churches behind the "iron curtain" too much with rose-colored glasses. One referred to the situation in Russia: churches destroyed, former church leaders imprisoned, current leaders of the church appear to be collaborators. One referred to East Germany where schools, public life, the education of youth were completely removed from the influence of the churches. Barth did not want to minimize all that. But he pointed out that advocating for the gospel is not the same as advocating for another, better political world order. It would have to be about the first for the churches (in the West and in the East) and not the latter.

24.5 "The Time for Big Lectures Is Past"

In the fall of 1962 Barth again began to arrange seminars for theological students. He did so completely on his own, no longer in the context of the University of Basel (he still remembered his unpleasant departure) but in a room in a restaurant in the neighborhood. There he discussed passages from his *Church Dogmatics* with those interested and answered questions. To his surprise, there was a great deal of interest. Barth himself enjoyed these contacts.

Meanwhile, at this time there were hardly any more public appearances in the form of lectures or the publication of texts. All the more, he wrote letters. And he gladly took part in discussions. He often responded publicly to questions presented to him, just as he had done in America. That gave him a fresh occasion to briefly and clearly set forth his own theological ideas. Often questions were presented to him on the task of the church in relation to political events (the East–West conflict, Western anti-Communism). As always, Barth acquitted himself well.

---

8. Barth, "Conversation with Protestant Book Dealers," 243.

His appearance as a discussion partner, rather than as a speaker, was more and more for him an appropriate point. That did not have to so much do with his advanced age as such. In July 1963 he had a meeting with eighty members of the Church Brotherhood of Württemberg. At the outset he emphatically stated that today it is not about my speaking the entire day; I do intend to speak with you; I also intend to listen to you. And he added a general remark:

> I believe that the day of grand lectures . . . is perhaps, not only for me but perhaps also in general, over and gone. Instead what we need in theology and in the church are . . . "Conversations." What I mean by that is simply that people talk with each other and together try to press forward to answers.[9]

Theological existence is to be on a search. That sounds somewhat extraordinary from the mouth of one who since the beginning of the 1920s had held more lectures than anyone, had published texts and books. Is Barth not the one, par excellence, who had had the desire to tell others "how it sits" with God and the human in extensive elaborations? Today he still has that reputation and that does not contribute to his popularity in the current theological landscape. But it could be that what Barth said here, in discussion with the Württembergers, disclosed precisely what he, in all his texts, always had had in mind. Barth did indeed know one thing for certain from the outset of his own appearance, that it must be different in theology than what had emerged in the nineteenth century, in modern liberal theology. There he had encountered a certainty, a self-evidence in which he himself did not at all feel at home. A God who is bound to human expectations, thoughts, and longings as self-evident—that God cannot be the same as the God who is spoken of in the Bible; God's "being-God" is thereby misunderstood. He found that theologians talk much too easily about God and the divine. It was precisely this that Barth from his side could not allow to continue. It was from the resistance to this that his theology was born, in the hope that what, searchingly, he brought forward (in extensive elaboration indeed) would instigate discussion.

24.6 Confrontation with "God Is Dead" Theology

He also encountered a certainty that deeply repelled him in various new theological tendencies that appeared in these years. In 1963, the same year in which we see Barth involved in many discussions, a book appeared that

---

9. Barth, "Conversation with the Church Brotherhood of Württemberg," 29.

quickly became a best seller, *Honest to God*. The writer was an Anglican bishop, John Robinson. Here, critical questions were put concerning traditional faith in all openness and clarity, questions that apparently lived in the hearts of many people; and that by someone who was, himself, an ecclesiastical authority. Robinson was convinced that the faith must be radically thought through and formulated afresh so that the modern human could affirm and confess it. Specifically, the representation of God as Person, distinguished from humans and the world, who can intervene in this world and has even already done so, must be abandoned. After all, that representation was mythological and is no longer appropriate to the modern image of the world. And it need not be retained in order to believe in God, namely: in a different way. That is, in God as the bearing Ground of our existence.

Robinson's book appeared at the start of a true flood of theological literature, mostly of English and American origin, in which this line of thought was continued. This way of thinking would later be characterized as "God is dead theology." Robinson himself would have had his objections to this characterization. Not "God" as such, only "God" as "God above" or "outside," the God of traditional belief, had he declared as "dead" (that is, not existing). However that may be, this middle way between atheism and Christianity appeared to speak to many.

Robinson had derived his concept of God as the "bearing Ground of our existence" from the ideas of the (German) American theologian Paul Tillich. But he had also been inspired by Bonhoeffer, with his plea for a "religionless Christianity" in his letters from prison (see 20.8). In his way, Bonhoeffer had opposed a belief in God by which "God" is spoken of only in moments of human incapacity, as the superpower who compensates for human weakness. Robinson could have taken that in a superficial way as a point of departure for his own ideas. In doing so, he overlooked the fact that Bonhoeffer himself had not thought of a God as a "bearing Ground." He had said: "God is weak and powerless in the world and just so and only so is he with us and he helps us." It is true; Robinson could appropriately use the first half of this statement. But how the idea that God just so, in his weakness is "helping us," does not fit in Robinson's own train of thought. He had been primarily inspired by Bonhoeffer's criticism of traditional representations of God.

This last also applies to the third inspirator that Robinson identified, Bultmann. His influence is primarily to be recognized in Robinson's distinction between the faith really acceptable at the present, on the one hand, and traditional mythological representations of the faith, on the other hand. After all, Bultmann had already, from the 1940s, in his criticism of a traditional reading of the Bible, pled for a "demythologizing" of the New Testament, a reading-through-the-myths so as to discover the real intention of the text (see 18.2). Robinson felt himself addressed by just that critical aspect.

Barth's theology remained completely out of view in Robinson's book. It could not be otherwise. Barth had clearly distanced himself from Bultmann's theology. Bultmann had ventured the thesis that where it is about "God" in the Bible (the New Testament), it is actually about the human, of what God means for the human, for human existence. Barth could not follow him in that focus on human nature as such, with the omission of all talk about God's self (God in his essence) (see 18.3). So, in Robinson's eyes, Barth was yet another representative of traditional belief in God.

And Barth did not walk away from that. He would not parade as a traditionalist, but did certainly not let himself be packed up by the new theological trend. Indeed, he also perceived precisely the same fatal tendency of focusing on human existence itself with Bultmann in Robinson's *Honest to God* and in the entire boom that was the "God-is-dead theology" that followed. He spoke sharply and critically (and ironically) of "the foolish 'God-is-dead' movement" as "the ultimate and most beautiful fruit of the glorious existential theology." He saw there nothing other than a return to the liberal Protestant theology of the nineteenth century against which he had turned from the outset. Here again he saw that one connected with the human, with human thinking and longing; precisely that of which he had seen in the course of the twentieth century the fatal consequences. In his letters, he spoke repeatedly of his painful surprise that the German translation of Robinson's *Honest to God* was brought to market by the same publisher that at the time had published his *Letter to the Romans*. Would his entire work then have been for nothing? He could not, would not accept that. Ultimately, it would have to appear that the entire "God-is-dead theology," begun with Robinson, just like Bultmann, was without any genuine content. In one of his letters, Barth wrote:

> As I see it, not just in Robinson but already in Bultmann and his disciples it resembles a car whose tires have punctured, so that there is no air left [no pneuma!] and it has to run on the rims. Many people find this a wonderful way to travel. But I do not think it will have any great future.[10]

---

10. Barth to Dean Heinrich Lang," 21 June 1964, in *Letters*, 166.

24.7 Searching a "Top-class" Contradiction

Is this the stubbornness of an old man who would cling to old fashioned insights? Some of Barth's discussion partners did not shy away from alluding to that. That happened in particular during an extensive discussion that Barth had in November 1963 with youth ministers from Rhineland, who held their annual conference in Basel at that time. It was extensively about new developments in theology and in that connection about the growing distance between modern theology and the ordinary congregation. One of the Rhinelanders wore his heart on his sleeve:

> [Y]ou must understand, Professor, that for us you are a part of history . . . You see, it may indeed be that a conversation between us is simply no longer possible. That can simply be the case, can it not? . . . It is not necessary that we maintain a conversation. It may be [the task] for a new generation . . . We come from Rhineland and cannot say anything else but that the fathers of our church owe their existence to you. But please understand that our engagement is elsewhere, and we have departed for new shores.[11]

Barth was stricken:

> Now, that was an interesting statement . . . I haven't heard it put that way before . . . So I "have become history"! Well, well, well. That is very honorable. All the same, I am still here, life size. And now *you* are the one who must excuse *me* . . . that as long as I am still alive on this earth, I feel I am still involved, as a member, if I may say so, of the *communio sanctorum* [communion of saints].[12]

Barth said that polite expressions of respect for what he had done earlier could have carried him away and insisted that certainly the discussion would continue now. Where the discussion is cut off, one is done with things too easily! Barth found it remarkable to have to note that he was apparently seen as a leader of the ordinary congregation (with its traditional faith) vis-à-vis modern theology, vis-à-vis the new generation. He countered his discussion partner:

> But I believe it is not a fruitful enterprise that someone simply announces to me: "we are a different generation and find ourselves in a totally different place." . . . As a rule, things only

---

11. Barth, "Conversation with Rhineland Youth Pastors," 200–01.
12. Barth, "Conversation with Rhineland Youth Pastors," 201.

become interesting when a program is *implemented* . . . I cannot say, however, that the productions of the Bultmann school . . . have so far brought forth anything of which one can say, "*That* is where they are; *this* is what they mean." Rather, they make mere announcements . . . Bring it forth! I actually wanted . . . to hear finally what you are really after, positively, starting with the same presupposition as I did: our place is in a congregation, and in the congregation we want to read the Bible together, and now, how? And what? What comes of it? . . . I never claimed to have spoken the last word with the *Church Dogmatics*. It is very clear to me that on every page the matter could have been done differently and better . . . "I am waiting for an *opponent*, but an opponent who meets me on the *same* ground . . . and overtakes me." I was fully aware, I said, of the transitoriness of my work. But this would have to be *done* and not only *announced*.[13]

24.8 Organized Opposition: "No Other Gospel!"

Barth made no secret of his objections to the new theological stream breached with Robinson. But attempts to react to this new theology by organizing a front in opposition could even less count on his sympathy. It took some time before such a front appeared, but in 1966 the time had come. Then a counter-movement originated in West Germany that had as its slogan, "No other gospel!" Distressed church leaders and members gathered under that slogan with the intention of retreating from all theological modernism to the old confession and the traditional theological positions connected with it.

The alarm was sounded elsewhere as well, in the Netherlands, for example. But Barth had to deal with developments in Germany in particular. On March 6, 1966, a massive meeting took place in the Westphalian Hall in Dortmund. Later, one of the participants appeared unhappy with the proceedings and the outcome. He feared that this new initiative would lead to a split within the Evangelical Church in Germany and turned to Barth for advice. "Do you think that the time is ripe to be able to justify such a step? Can one solve the problem of 'modern theology' by separation?"

Barth wrote back a few days later, a letter that was also extensively published in many newspapers. He made it clear in the letter that at the moment he could answer the question put before him only in the negative. He formulated a question himself that he would put to the organizers and

---

13. Barth, "Conversation with the Rhineland Youth Pastors," 202–03.

participants of the Dortmund demonstration so that he could formulate his answer based on the answer to that question:

> Are you prepared to start such a movement and demonstration, respectively, against the efforts of arming the West Germany army with nuclear weapons? Against the war of the Americans, allies of West Germany, in Vietnam? And against the anti-Semitism repeatedly bursting out in West Germany? And for making peace by West Germany with the Eastern states recognizing the borders existing since 1945? If your confession includes that and states it then it is a right and precious and fruitful confession. If that is not the case, then however orthodox it may be, it is not right, but a dead, cheap, hair-splitting, camel-swallowing, so: Pharisaic confession.[14]

We have often seen how much for Barth faith and life, theology and politics, were closely intertwined. Here again, we see his critical attitude regarding Western post-war politics, specifically his protest against Western anti-Communism and his pleas for an open attitude to what took place behind the "iron curtain" in Eastern Europe, ecclesiastically as well as societally, again becoming evident. Barth remained himself in that attitude to the end of his life.

There was, of course, no answer from the side of "No other gospel!" to the question put by Barth. In September 1966, again asked for his evaluation of "No other gospel!," he straightforwardly expressed his aversion to this movement. "The walls of Jericho will certainly not fall down through the blowing of the thousand trumpets there [in Dortmund]."[15] He would not spend much further time on that. A German preacher encouraged him to publish a specific pamphlet on the controversy between "God is dead" and "No other gospel!": ("as you have done in the thirties in the time of Hitler!"). But Barth wrote back that he did not plan to do so:

> And since the good Lord, in spite of reports to the contrary, is not dead, I am not concerned, let alone do I feel constrained, to act as the defender of his cause in a confessional movement . . . For one thing, I have other and more useful things to do.[16]

---

14. Barth an Adolf Grau, March 6, 1966, in *OB*, 520–21.
15. Barth to Dr. R. Meyendorf, September 2, 1966, in *Letters*, 219.
16. Barth to a Pastor in Germany, December 4, 1966, in *Letters*, 229–30.

24.9 Difficult Years. Eightieth Birthday

In that year, 1966, Barth had again regained his strength. Things had gone badly in the two preceding years. He was hospitalized several times. He also had to undergo several operations. Shortly before Christmas 1964, he suffered a small stroke that left him unable to speak for a few hours. In the fall of 1965, he was again in the hospital for a period of time. He returned home, "thankful to God and man that I am still alive."[17] He could again read and take up his work, although he still required nursing assistance. His wife, Nelly, offered a great deal of help.

But just during this period, he received a new blow. Since 1930, he had Charlotte von Kirschbaum always by his side as a faithful, capable, indispensable co-worker and life companion. She had accompanied Barth in the preparation of his lectures and in the writing of his texts, specifically including those of the *Church Dogmatics*. We have seen that since 1929 she had even been a resident in the Barth family; that had unavoidably led to tensions between Barth and his wife Nelly, but ultimately resulted is a (more or less) accepted situation for all concerned (see 4.12). Now that situation came to an end. Charlotte became an invalid through a brain disease and had to be confined to a nursing home in January 1966 from which she would no longer be free. Barth continued visiting her there, faithfully, weekly. But assisting Barth in his thinking and writing work was not possible for her anymore. So far as Barth still had plans to continue work on his *Church Dogmatics*, they were now definitively thwarted. True, Barth got new help. The young German theologian, Eberhard Busch, one of his students, became his personal assistant. He would continue for the last (nearly) three years of Barth's life.

On May 10, 1966, Barth celebrated his eightieth birthday. He did so together with his wife and in the midst of the family that in the meantime had grown large, a family of children, grandchildren and eight great-grandchildren. Bultmann sent him a birthday wish; that was the last personal contact between the two. At the official feast, May 9, a large Festschrift was presented to him, just as had happened on the occasion of his seventieth and his fiftieth birthdays. The title given to it was the Greek word *Parrhesia*. The editors (among them Busch) had interpreted that in their preface as "cheerful faithfulness." More precisely, this word implies "boldness," "fearlessness"; thus, confidence in opposition and not recoiling. They had meant that Barth's appearance and work as a theologian could not be better characterized than just so. Indeed, Barth had never worried about the question

---

17. Quoted in Busch, *Karl Barth*, 472.

whether what he had to say was acceptable to others in the world; whether it answered, for example, to generally valid scientific or philosophical criteria. He had always, boldly, said what he meant that, at the moment, must be said, in an unconcerned return to Holy Scripture.

In the same preface, the editors had given a short characterization of the current theological situation:

> What began promisingly in the 1920s and powerfully developed in the 30s and 40s appears more and more to come apart in unfruitful polarizations for the Christian church . . . It is understandable that at times Karl Barth asks himself whether his work has been for nothing.[18]

Still, it added, we must beware of interpreting the current situation as "tragic." After all, the Reformation has attempted to break with every overarching and coherent ecclesiastical teaching office. One has dared to trust that God's Word itself would be authoritative in the Christian community. Thereby the position of theology has now become less protected, less secure. It is more likely that disagreements emerge. That is the price that we have to pay for the immediate confrontation with God's Word. If only in theology the center of the gospel is sought! With that the contributors of this Festschrift hope to offer their contribution. Among the thirty-two contributors was one Dutchman, Frans Breukelman. He offered an exegesis of the parable of the unmerciful servant (Matthew 18:23-35), emphasizing how much this text included proclamation in its word use and structure, and thereby indicating, from a biblical perspective, how much Barth was on target in his doctrine of reconciliation.

One of those who attended Barth's eightieth birthday was the rector of the University of Basel. Barth appreciated that. After what had happened at his departure from the university (March 1, 1962), it meant a true rehabilitation for him.

---

18. Busch, Geiger, and Fangmeier, "Vorwort," in *Parrhesia*, vii–viii.

25

In Discussion with Rome

25.1 Visit to the Vatican

BARTH HAD STILL CONSIDERED plans to write an autobiography. He had even begun to do so. But plans ran aground at the beginning stage. More than in the past, even in his own past, current affairs engaged him, particularly what was happening in the Roman Catholic Church and its theology. He rated that considerably higher than what was happening during these years in Protestant theology and church life. The Second Vatican Council took place from 1962 to 1965 in Rome. Barth had intensively followed reports of the Council. Here church renewal was in order! To what extent would that really persevere? He had also received an invitation to attend as an observer of the two final sessions and would gladly have accepted. The condition of his health prevented him. But now that things improved, he sought contact.

He requested and received the opportunity to travel to Rome to be further informed of the results of the council. That visit took place September 22–29, 1965. His wife and his doctor (himself Roman Catholic) traveled with him (happily the doctor was not called into action). Barth reported his experiences in a short publication that appeared in 1967 with the title *Ad Limina Apostolorum*, which means literally, "to the residence of the apostles." Under the same title in the Roman Catholic Church also the official, regular visits of the bishops to the pope take place. By "apostles," one thinks then of the apostles Peter and Paul, who according to tradition both resided in Rome (Peter's grave is supposedly found under St. Peter's). Barth set his own trip to Rome in this same context. With the wink of an eye, of course; he came without episcopal dignity and not as one accountable to the Vatican, but to ask his own critical questions. Still, his visit to Rome was something of a pilgrimage.

25.2 From Early On: Objections to Roman Catholicism

His interest in Roman Catholicism was not new. It had always held his interest. He was very conscious that Catholicism represented a position different than that of liberal Protestantism that had become dominant in the nineteenth century. While there the emphasis lay on the personal aspect of the Christian faith, on one's own experiences, in Roman Catholicism the emphasis traditionally lay on the objective aspect, on faith as a given truth and in that connection on the church as an institute of salvation, on the offices and sacraments. That was, in itself, no objection for Barth. Indeed, he too laid emphasis on the objectivity of God's revelation that he saw as perpendicular to our human feelings and experiences. And while liberal Protestantism did not know what to do with the official, classic dogmas of God's "trinity" and the "two natures" (divine and human) of Christ held in Roman Catholicism, Barth did not shy away from those dogmas. We have seen how much he thought them through anew (see 8.2 and 18.6). In liberal Protestant circles, that had brought some to suspect that Barth was himself really on the way to become Roman Catholic.

Indeed, from early on, Barth had taken Roman Catholicism extremely seriously, more so than many of his contemporary Protestants. In a lecture, held in 1928, he had argued that it puts the critical question to us Protestants of how far we are ourselves really "church." Do we still know what "church" is? Or have we in fact made of it a religious gathering? In any case, the confrontation with Roman Catholicism forces us to a renewed reflection on the question of what again the Reformation was about.

But this serious reflection had not hindered Barth from sharply criticizing "Rome." His criticism was concentrated in his one great objection, that in the Roman Catholic view, God's grace has become a human possession and that that grace can also thus be handled by humans, that is, ecclesiastical organizations. With that, Barth said, it is misunderstood that there is a principle difference between God and the human. It means that God and the human are considered on one level. Barth found that stated technically-theologically in the thesis that an *analogia entis* between God and the human would exist, an "analogy of being." For Barth, there exists no more serious misunderstanding of God's sovereignty than this. Already in the preface of the first volume of his *Church Dogmatics* (1932) he had tellingly remarked, "I regard the *analogia entis* as the invention of Antichrist, and I believe that because of it it is impossible ever to become a Roman Catholic."[1] Barth would himself also talk of an "analogy" between

---

1. Barth, *CD*, I/1, xiii.

God and the human and thus of a human possibility to be in contact with God, but he saw the possibility not as based on "being," a nature that God and the human would share in common. He would know nothing of a natural "knowledge of God"; only of knowing God *in faith*. That is, in the faith that is awakened by the Word of God (and must be repeatedly awakened). There is an analogy between God and the human, but then an *analogia fidei*, an "analogy of faith."

That the Roman Catholic Church is serious about God's revelation can of itself, according to Barth, only be valued positively. Only it does so, in his judgment, in a mistaken way, by functioning as mistress of revelation. The ecclesiastical teaching office sees itself as empowered to articulate and to interpret revelation authentically. With that, according to Barth, it misunderstands that the Word of God stands critically over and against the church, even over and against an ecclesiastical teaching office, and that it repeatedly perdures as authoritative. By nature, we humans have no access to God; God, as he is, is hidden from us; we know him not otherwise than because he reveals himself to us—and even so he remains the Hidden. That was the foundational thought from which Barth at the time had taken up his theological thinking (see 2). It was that insight that he saw misunderstood in the liberal Protestantism of his days. But in another way, he saw it also misunderstood in Roman Catholicism.

25.3 Rome and the Ecumenè:
Discussion with Jean Daniélou

Barth did not disguise his criticism of "Rome," i.a. in his opening address held at the founding assembly of the World Council of Churches in Amsterdam on August 23, 1948 (see 14.8). There he had referred to the theme discussed at the assembly: the church and its unity. In that connection, he had pled for an orientation to Jesus Christ, "who alone has the right and power to call us together and bind us together into his holy universal church." With that he had briefly taken up the fact that the "church of Rome" had not accepted the invitation to participate in the assembly. Not too much should one have to complain about that, he found. Perhaps, so he had mused, God has so kept us "from having partners in discussion with whom we could not be a congregation even in an imperfect sense, because they do not fully put their will . . . into that movement away from every ecclesiasticism toward Jesus Christ." Perhaps God has set us in our place just in that Rome seems to be "wishing to have nothing to do with us." Of course, the non-cooperation of the Roman Catholic Church in Amsterdam means a stymying of the ecumenical ambition of the World Council. But, Barth said, "I propose that we should now praise and thank God that it pleases him to stand so clearly in the way of our plans."[2]

At the time, these words had caused a commotion in Roman Catholic circles. The French theologian Jean Daniélou had published a short article in response. We Catholics, so he wrote, highly esteem Barth. "We have much to thank him for. He has rediscovered the real truths of the Bible . . . We have loved in Barth the victor over a dogmatic liberalism that we value as little as he."[3] But now Barth has deeply injured the Catholic heart. That we have stayed away from Amsterdam was not from a lack of ecumenical interest but, so Daniélou wrote, from the sense that the ecumenical movement must be kept from exaggeration, from rash conclusions. Thus, it has to do with a treasure that is entrusted to us, Catholic Christians, that we have to protect, not only for our own sake but for the sake of all Christians. That we, despite Jesus Christ, (still) are not one is tragic, of course. But Barth dispatches the matter too easily.

Barth had not left this charge go unanswered. He had expressed surprise about it. Had Daniélou himself not referred to the principle impossibility of Roman Catholic cooperation (without denying their own principle) in Amsterdam? The Roman Catholic Church

> cannot after all sit at one table with other "churches" to discuss the question of unity in Jesus Christ on an equal plane, in the same humility and openness with those other "churches." After all, it cannot grant that the question of this unity would not already have been answered, simply by its own existence. And would we others now have to mourn what you yourselves do not mourn, even cannot mourn without being disobedient to your own church? . . . No, we may not complain of the absence of your church in Amsterdam because it has excluded itself . . . by its irreconcilability . . . from the common search for unity in Jesus Christ, exactly that which the ecumenical cause is about . . . Your cooperation in Amsterdam could only have meant that you . . . would have given us the occasion to reverse course, on what is the only possible way. In Amsterdam we inquired about God's kingdom and God's work. But you could only have said to us that this should mean that we would have to convert to the kingdom and human work of your church. So we in Amsterdam have engaged neither with the Lord of the church nor with each

2. Barth, "No Christian Marshall Plan," 1331.

3. Daniélou, "Frage an Karl Barth" in Daniélou, Niebuhr, and Barth, *Gespräche nach Amsterdam*, 4.

other. And thus it was also for us not regrettable but a good thing, recognizable as God's clear will, that you were not with us in Amsterdam. You could only have disturbed us in what we had in mind in obedience of faith there. Your absence spared us an offense and a temptation.[4]

25.4 Ecumenical Approach? Hans Urs von Balthasar

This was a sharp discussion. At the same time, we heard how Daniélou testified to his respect for Barth. Roman Catholics highly valued the fact that in his theology Barth had overcome "theological liberalism." Daniélou was not alone in that regard. Over the course of years, leading Roman Catholic theologians, including those in the Netherlands, had been engaged with Barth's work and had published on it. The Swiss Hans Urs von Balthasar was prominent in this regard. He had published an extensive study in 1951 in which he had broadly discussed and commented on Barth's theology (as developed thus far). His answer, at the beginning of his book, to the question of why he, in his interest in Protestantism, was occupied especially with Barth, was characteristic. "We must choose Karl Barth for our partner because in him Protestantism has found *for the first time* its most completely consistent representative."[5] Thus, it is just Barth who has perfectly consistently considered what the Reformation was about, more consistently than the Reformers themselves had done.

How is it that von Balthasar had seen here no reason to distance himself from Barth but had thereby felt himself attracted to Barth? That had to do with the fact that von Balthasar deemed Barth's view of the relation between God and the human, his emphasis on God's sovereignty, not to be in essential conflict with Roman Catholic doctrine. Roman Catholics too, he said, acknowledge the significance of faith; just like Barth, they see the creation, reality, oriented to the coming of Jesus Christ, not as something that exists apart from him. And conversely, Barth can after all not deny that God's grace is related to reality, to "nature." Is the creature not taken in service here so that it begins to cooperate with grace? Certainly, von Balthasar deemed this latter insight as not sufficiently honored by Barth; he found Barth too one-sidedly oriented to Jesus Christ.

From his side, it was difficult for Barth to place this criticism. But he had positively valued the congenial way in which von Balthasar had been

---

4. Barth, "Antwort an P. Jean Daniélou," in Daniélou, Niebuhr, and Barth, *Gespräche nach Amsterdam*, 7–9.

5. Von Balthasar, *The Theology of Karl Barth*, 22.

involved with his theology. He did not regard himself particularly a victim of misunderstanding here. And he saw that as an apparent sign that "in contemporary Roman Catholic theology" something like a new view of the central meaning of Christ was breaking through.

25.5 Hans Küng, an Ecumenical Mayfly?

Was here then something of an ecumenical rapprochement? Still stronger than with von Balthasar, this question could rise with the appearance of the young Roman Catholic theologian (also Swiss) Hans Küng. He earned his doctorate in 1956 (in Paris) on a study of Barth's doctrine of justification. Under that theme, he brought von Balthasar's argument into sharper focus.

We have seen how Barth has taken up in his doctrine of reconciliation the traditional Protestant notion of "justification" of the human only by faith for Christ's sake (see 19.12). It was just on this point that a sharp controversy broke out in the sixteenth century. This Protestant doctrine was rejected as heresy by the Council of Trent. Justification is, said Trent, more than a declaration. Where the human is justified by God, the human does not remain unchanged but is really renewed. "Good works" then come into view; they are now expected of the human; without such "good works" justification is not complete! Rome and the Reformation parted ways in the sixteenth century as a result of this apparent difference (among others). And Barth put all his cards on the sovereignty of God, and so decisively took the side of the Reformation.

Küng emphatically argued that the conflict that broke out in the sixteenth century had rested on a mutual misunderstanding. It was specifically the doctrine of justification developed by Barth (in line with the sixteenth-century Reformation) that according to Küng was not in conflict with the properly understood Roman Catholic doctrine (as formulated by the Council of Trent). An important point in Küng's argument was his consideration that dogmas, statements of doctrine, are always issued in a concrete situation at the occasion of a current question. They often have a polemic tenor. Over and against what is experienced as error, a particular aspect of the truth of faith is especially illuminated by which, of course, other aspects remain underexposed. Just so, Rome and the Reformation stood opposed to each other in the sixteenth century. Now, some centuries later, it can be seen that the real division was not so great. That Trent had put the emphasis on the individual, on one's involvement in the event of justification, did not mean that one was blind to what the Reformation was centrally about and what Barth, too, is about: that justification was and is the sovereign action of the graceful God himself in Jesus Christ.

Küng's dissertation had appeared in 1957 as a trade edition. That edition included an accompanying text written by Barth, addressed to the author. In it, Barth expressly declared that he fully recognized himself in Küng's reflection of his theology, and therewith stated his surprise with Küng's conclusion. If Küng's interpretation of Roman Catholic doctrine is correct, yes, then "I must certainly admit that my view of justification agrees with the Roman Catholic view," for "the Roman Catholic teaching would then be most strikingly in accord with mine."[6] But is that so? Barth was not completely at ease with that and he wrote that he was waiting with anticipation to see how Küng's book would be received in Roman Catholic circles.

25.6 Encounters in Rome

And now the Second Vatican Council had taken place from 1962 to 1965. It really appeared that studies like those of von Balthasar and Küng had not been mayflies but indeed symptoms of a changing ecumenical situation. Not only a few individual theologians, but the Roman Catholic Church itself had entered the ecumenical movement! Hence, Barth gladly sought the occasion in September 1966 to go to Rome to personally discuss the results of the council. The opportunity was courteously offered to him by Rome, by the Roman Secretariat for Unity (then the office that maintained contact with other Christians and churches).

Barth had prepared himself well that preceding summer. The decisions of the council were recorded in a series of documents. Barth had read them all closely and had formulated already at home a number of questions— partly for information but primarily critical—around them. He brought the questions with him. They became the starting point of discussions that he had with various Roman Catholic dignitaries, most of which lasted about three hours. As he himself wrote, the "dramatic climax" of his stay in Rome was a visit with Pope Paul VI. It was an affable meeting in which gifts were exchanged. Barth had brought with him four of his smaller publications. To which the pope (as Barth told it) responded smilingly with the remark that it would indeed have been cumbersome if Barth had come weighed down with the entire *Church Dogmatics*. Apparently the pope knew the size of the *Church Dogmatics*. Looking back, Barth wrote:

---

6. Küng, *Justification*, lxviii.

If I on my part had opportunity to wish him something, it would be a greater measure of "cheerful confidence" (*parrhesia*) in relation to those inner tensions in his church which in part made the council necessary and in part are the result of the Council.[7]

25.7 Critical Questions

But the questions Barth put to his Roman discussion partners were anything but negligible. He included them all in the booklet that he published shortly after his trip to Rome. The answers to his questions were not included there. He had promised his discussion partners confidentiality. The only thing that he hinted was that some of his questions were not answered. That, in itself, already says a lot. His discussion partners were not all of one mind. The documents of the Second Vatican Council are apparently open to multiple interpretations. The precision of interpretation that Barth was seeking apparently could not always be given.

What Barth himself was about is, in any case, absolutely clear. He wanted to know whether the council had indeed made good on, taken over, empowered the rapprochement with the ecumenical movement as had been manifested by individual theologians like Hans Urs von Balthasar and Hans Küng. Had the council come to a "reformation" or not, a genuine course correction? Opinions on the matter were divided.

The document ("dogmatic constitution") "on divine revelation" was crucial for the evaluation of the meaning of the council for Barth. Does God's revelation really come to us "from the other side," or do we (churchmen) have it in our grasp? The traditional Roman Catholic idea, as formulated by earlier councils, placed Scripture and the Tradition of the church alongside each other as "sources" for our knowledge of revelation, whereby the ecclesiastical teaching office is identified as the body that provides the authoritative interpretation of both. Does that not mean that the church, via its teaching office, makes itself the master of God's revelation? That is precisely against which the Reformers, with their appeal to "Scripture alone," stormed. Here Barth follows in their train. But the question is now, has the Second Vatican Council held to and confirmed or has it corrected the traditional Roman Catholic notion?

Barth had closely studied the council document and had stumbled on a "regrettable unclarity." That struck him specifically in the chapter on "handing on divine revelation." On the one hand, the council says there

---

7. Barth, *Ad Limina Apostolorum*, 16.

that ecclesiastical tradition is the handing on of and testimony to what was received and proclaimed by the apostles as revelation, and what they and their co-workers had also put into writing. Hence, it is said that the Scripture (that is, the "written Word of God") stands and has priority. And concerning the teaching office, it is said that it does "not stand above the Word of God, but serves it."[8] That sounds like an approach to the position of the Reformation.

But on the other hand, it is striking that "Tradition and Scripture" are repeatedly still spoken of in that order. And at the conclusion of the chapter, Tradition, Scripture, and the teaching office (again in this order) are even set next to each other as three. Thereby it is said that they "are so connected and associated that one of them cannot stand without the others. Working together . . . they all contribute effectively to the salvation of souls."[9] Suddenly, there does not appear to be a separate, unique position of authority of the Scripture, here. All the more that in that connection the statement of the sixteenth-century Council of Trent is again cited that "both Scripture and Tradition must be accepted and honored with equal feelings of devotion and reverence."[10]

25.8 God's Mills Grind Slowly

Has the Second Vatican Council achieved here a "reformation" or has it not? Barth put the question with surgical precision. He did not say whether he received an answer and, if so, which answer. In a consideration, added to the report of the visit, he offered his further analysis. There he pointed out that apart from the chapter on "handing on divine revelation," Holy Scripture was a primary topic of discussion in the entire council document. Scripture alone is called "truly the Word of God." It is said that "all the preaching of the church, as indeed the entire Christian religion, should be nourished and ruled by sacred Scripture."[11] The importance of precise biblical translation is underscored. Reading the Bible and Bible study are strongly recommended to all clergy, primarily priests, but also all believers. In fact, Barth maintained, the largest part of the council document is dedicated to the meaning of Holy Scripture.

That is still completely different from what was said earlier in official Roman Catholic documents on divine revelation (and its sources, plural!).

---

8. Vatican Council II, *Dei Verbum*, 756.
9. Vatican Council II, *Dei Verbum*, 756.
10. Vatican Council II, *Dei Verbum*, 755.
11. Vatican Council II, *Dei Verbum*, 762.

Here it points in a new direction; albeit not unambiguously. However that may be, so Barth concluded, the result reached by the Second Vatican Council offers courage for the future. How beautiful it would be if a new council would follow this track in the twenty-first century! His travel report ended equally positively:

> I gained a close acquaintance with a church and a theology which have begun a movement, the results of which are incalculable and slow but clearly genuine and irreversible. In looking at it, we can only wish that we had something comparable, if it could avoid a repetition of at least the worst mistakes we have made since the sixteenth century.[12]

Was this a too optimistic estimate? At best we could say that we, in the over fifty years since the council, experience even more that God's mills grind slowly. But Barth himself had already reckoned with slow grinding mills.

---

12. Barth, *Ad Limina Apostolorum*, 17.

26

A Late Dogmatic Fragment on Baptism

26.1 Plea for the De-Sacramentalization of the Church

BARTH HAD SEEN CONFIRMED in Rome what he already suspected, that a renewal movement was on the way in the Roman Catholic Church, one that he would want "with us" as well, in the Protestant ecclesiastical world. Renewal "also with us" in what sense? He had expressed his thoughts on this already in the early days of the Second Vatican Council, in 1963. That took place specifically in the discussion that he had in November of that year with the youth ministers from Rhineland (see 24.7). To the question of: "What would essentially have to happen spiritually and theologically in our church?"[1] Barth had responded with two core concepts. The church must become *mature*, and it must be *de-sacramentalized*.

The church must become mature in its relation to the state, to society, to science, to philosophy. Since the sixteenth century, Protestant churches have become state churches, *folk* churches. Said differently, they have become too bourgeois. It is time that they be freed from their dependence! The church must not parade as the church of a particular society or a particular class of society. Nor, by the way, as the paladin of the (so-called) "modern man." The church must learn to stand on its own feet in faith.

And besides that, the church must free itself from the idea that it would be "sacramental," the instrument of salvation, as though its real task consists in the distribution of salvation via the "sacraments." It is just the Protestant church that figures in society as the church that regulates baptism and confirmation, marriage and burial as "acts of office." So, as church of the "acts of office," it has its established place in the society. That coheres with the lack of maturity noted above and forms its background. By pretending to be

---

1. Barth, "Conversation with Rhineland Youth Pastors," 205.

"the church of the sacraments," it has given up by definition that maturity. Hence, it should not want to be "sacramental church"!

Already in 1963 Barth had related this second aspect of his plea for church renewal to the church's practice of baptism. He saw that the baptism of children, of infants, in the Protestant churches still existed as an established practice as a symptom par excellence of the ecclesiastical inclination to posit itself as "sacramental" (and thus as indispensable) in society, as though the church would be a sort of divine–human amalgamation! He opposed all ecclesiastical talk of "sacraments."

> Oh, if only we could be rid of this word! . . . [H]ere we would have something to say in a conversation with the Catholic Church, whereas now the Protestant church is actually only a weaker version of the Catholic Church.[2]

Remarkable, Barth sighed, that, also by Protestants in general, the practice of child baptism is considered "holy." It is considered a taboo. Everything, including the most classic Christian truths of faith, can be meddled with at present, but not child baptism. Hence, it can be seen how deep sacramental thought, and in that connection the ecclesiastical inclination to societal immaturity, still exists.

26.2 Sacraments: Indispensable Means of Grace? Early Views

Barth had earlier shown that he could not work with the concept "sacrament" any more. Here he had gone through a complete development. In the preface of the second part of his doctrine of reconciliation, IV/2, he himself pointed that out. Originally, in his early work and so also in the first volumes of his dogmatics, he had, as he said there, still spoken rather carelessly of "sacraments." But now he had become more reserved. He now (he wrote in 1955) almost no longer made use of the concept "sacrament."

In his original use of sacramental terminology, he had adhered to the traditional church language, in particular that of the Reformation (see 12.9). An entire sacramental view had developed in the early and medieval church. The church was increasingly seen as a "sacramental church." The Reformation had broken through that heavy accent on the "sacraments" and the "sacramental." True, it had still used sacramental terminology, but had interpreted it differently. That applies, in particular, of the Reformation insofar as it went back to the work of Calvin and had found its classic expression in the Heidelberg Catechism. Sacraments were described there as

2. Barth, "Conversation with Rhineland Youth Pastors," 209.

"signs and seals, instituted by God so that by our use of them he might make us understand more clearly and seal to us the promise of the gospel" (and as such only baptism and the Lord's Supper were recognized as "instituted by God"). So understood, the sacraments are not about a specific distribution of "salvation" or "grace" beyond that of proclamation. But it is certainly about clarification and confirmation (sealing) of what is proclaimed and already in that proclamation allotted to us. Hence, the sacraments were still retained as having a peculiar function and meaning. Otherwise, would the sacraments not, in fact, be superfluous?

In his earlier work, Barth had in his own way sought a description of what is peculiar to "sacraments." He had done so specifically in the "prolegomena," the introductory considerations of his dogmatics, *CD* I/2, from 1938. Generally speaking, the discussion there was about God's revelation as the basis and starting point of all dogmatic reflection. In that context, he had first talked about revelation as having taken place *objectively*, factually in Jesus Christ. Subsequently he had discussed that and how it actively reaches the human, that is, by the Holy Spirit. Barth called that the *subjectivity* of the same revelation (see 8.2). In that connection, Barth had argued that God's revelation reaches us in particular through *signs* given by God himself. It is via those signs that humans do hear God's Word. God uses them as means in his hand. After Christ, the church is such a sign today, the church, in its visibility, with its apostles, with the apostolic message and with baptism and the Lord's Supper.

It was in that connection that Barth had used the concept of "sacrament" as an indication of how he considered the matter. Not only baptism and the Lord's Supper, but also the (written and spoken) word are at issue here. And still, baptism and the Lord's Supper in particular. And Barth had emphatically pointed out that with these "sacraments" it is about material, palpable "elements": water, bread, and wine. That reminds us that we humans, however spiritual, historical, and moral in nature, are part of the bodily, material reality. Here he could not avoid speaking of something that is peculiar to the sacrament, namely by its externality and visibility

> a sacrament asserts clearly, and with relatively greater eloquence than the word in the narrower sense can ever do, that the *justificatio* or *sanctificatio hominis* which is the meaning of all divine sign-giving, does not rest upon an idea but upon reality, upon an event . . . which has shown itself to be both spiritual and corporeal, the act of a Creator . . . the event of the entry of this Creator into our history, the event of the rolling up of our history . . . [the Word became flesh]([Jn 1:14])—preaching, too,

can and must say this. But in a way which preaching can never do, the sacrament underlines the words [flesh] and [became].[3]

Thus, the sacraments underscore the *reality character* of God's revelation as it reaches us humans. It is precisely that that makes baptism and the Lord's Supper important for us as sacraments. That does not mean, Barth warned, that they would as such be "absolutely necessary for salvation" for us. Still baptism and the Lord's Supper are commanded:

> The authority of the prophets and apostles and through it the grace of the incarnate Word of God is set at the beginning of the Christian Church and therefore at the beginning of our existence as the children of God, just as baptism is put at the beginning of our Christian life as an objective testimony pronounced upon us. And we live by the word of the prophets and apostles ... as we are fed with bread and given wine to drink in the Lord's Supper ... For that reason and in that sense we have to say in all seriousness that sacraments are an indispensable "means of grace."[4]

And extending these considerations, Barth had (as he said, without wanting to fall into "Roman sacramentalism") ventured the statement that the church itself, the church as such, must be seen as sacramental. Living in the church, one finds oneself, he said, by definition "on the way from the baptism already poured out upon him to the Lord's Supper yet to be dispensed to him,"[5] So, the church is the space in which one *begins* to believe, in order exactly in this way to *come* to faith.

26.3 "Jesus Christ, the One and Only Sacrament"

Thus far Barth in 1938. These considerations stand far from the position that Barth would take in the later parts of the dogmatics, specifically in his doctrine of reconciliation. We have heard him remark that there he no longer speaks of "sacraments" or "sacramentality" or does so hardly at all. Baptism and the Lord's Supper are referred to here and there, but always with a warning; they may not be seen as elements, actions, that would make Jesus Christ, his coming and his work present. Does not such a "sacramental making present" after all by definition shortchange the once-for-all nature of what has happened in Jesus Christ and that of the work of the Holy Spirit itself?

3. Barth, *CD*, I/2, 230.
4. Barth, *CD*, I/2, 231–32.
5. Barth, *CD*, I/2, 232.

In this later period of his life and work, Barth no longer appeared to be able to imagine how he ever could have spoken about "sacraments" that have to say, to offer, something to us on behalf of God. He remained convinced that God's revelation is reality, including where it reaches us humans. But in his later work, he distanced himself ever more firmly from the notion that this is underscored because of the fact that a church with sacraments exists. He saw Jesus Christ ever more clearly as the all-determinative center of Christian and ecclesiastical faith and life. God had become human in Christ; he, Christ, now represents us before God and leads our way. It is in that that we humans are reconciled to God, exalted to new life.

We heard how Barth elaborated that in the second part of his doctrine of reconciliation (see 19.3). Now we note that in that same context Barth warned of a misunderstanding. The unity of God and the human in Christ is not comparable with a presupposed unity of divine and human action effecting grace through "sacraments." Of course, one detects that comparison in church history. But Barth deems just that as extremely questionable:

> Was it a wise action on the part of the Church when it ceased to recognise in the incarnation, in the *nativitas Jesu Christi*, in the mystery of Christmas, the one and only sacrament, fulfilled once and for all, by whose actuality it lives . . . ? Has it really not enough to occupy it in the giving and receiving of this one sacrament . . . ?[6]

The only thing the church must do here, said Barth, is to testify to that. But, also in the Reformation, it continued to speak of baptism and the Lord's Supper. Hence, it continued to proceed in such a way that it must (and can) represent, repeat, make present that one sacrament, Jesus Christ himself, as though the church would be a sort of extension of the incarnation! According to the later Barth, that presupposition lacks all legitimacy.

26.4 Baptism: Not a Sacrament but a Human Answer

What meaning still remains for baptism and the Lord's Supper? That had now become clear for Barth: they must be spoken of in ethics where it is about reflection on the Christian life. We heard that Barth had begun his lecture on the ethics of reconciliation that he had given from 1959 to 1961 with the discussion of baptism as (not a sacrament but) human answer to God's salvific actions, that is, as the first step of the Christian life in faithfulness to God (see 23.2). His students at the time were the first to be confronted with

---

6. Barth, *CD*, IV/2, 55.

this view of baptism, one that deviated so widely from the tradition of the church, in the confines of the lecture hall.

They had not yet been published. Barth had already caused quite a stir in earlier publications and statements on baptism. That had happened specifically via his brochure, *Die kirchliche Lehre von der Taufe* [*The Teaching of the Church Regarding Baptism*] of 1943 (see 11.2) In it he still had held to the traditional Reformed (Calvinist) notion of baptism as a sacrament, that is to say, as sign and seal of salvation. But there he had been very critical of the practice of child baptism. In the first place because he had read in the New Testament that in the proper administration of baptism, the baptized does not passively undergo baptism but participates in baptism as "the free partner"[7] and thus consciously accepts and affirms the baptism. In the second place (and primarily) because he saw in the practice of child baptism the effect of the inclination of the church to include all children beforehand, thus, the people as a whole. The church must not desire to be a *folk* church or a state church. It must not be anxious of a position as a minority in society.

Barth had not hidden the fact, when there was the occasion, that, since the publication of his brochure on baptism in 1943, he yet again had developed different thoughts about baptism. In the years following his retirement, he was asked on various occasions about his ideas on baptism. Thus it was in the discussion that he had in June 1962 with the Swiss Protestant booksellers and publishers at their annual gathering. To the question whether he "still" stood behind his brochure on baptism he had answered, yes, but "my views on the matter have become even more radical."[8] Barth had explained: now, more strictly than before, he understood baptism from the baptism that Jesus himself underwent. For Jesus, that baptism was the beginning of the way that he would go as servant in obedience, thus as his conscious acceptance of the task given to him by God. So, Barth had said, it also is the case with our baptism: it is confession, that is, open acceptance of God's call to repent. That means, of course, that baptism must be administered to those who *"know what they are doing"* when they makes this confession. Hence, this baptism cannot be child baptism (in the sense of infant baptism).[9] Barth had stated this last view already in 1943, and he made it clear that now he, nearly twenty years later, had only been confirmed in this notion.

It speaks for itself that this elaboration raised questions. Primarily one question: Is it not that child baptism strikingly expresses that God's goodness already exists for the infant? Certainly, Barth had answered,

7. Barth, *The Teaching of the Church Regarding Baptism*, 54.
8. Barth, "Conversation with Protestant Book Dealers," 234.
9. Barth, "Conversation with Protestant Book Dealers," 235.

Jesus Christ has also come for infants. God's salvation also applies to them. It is the church's task to proclaim that. But that cannot happen by baptizing infants. Baptism comes into view where it is about how humans respond to God's graceful gift. Baptism is a human response, a human answer to God's deed on our behalf.

26.5 Late Dogmatic Fragment on Baptism

Statements like these naturally did not go unnoticed. So, some of what Barth had said on baptism in his lectures about the ethics of reconciliation had leaked out. But only in the winter of 1966 Barth decided to elaborate further on the texts of his lectures on baptism and prepare them for publication. Barth was convinced that the church must be mature and hence a review of baptism and the validity of its baptismal practice was necessary. He was very concerned to show that compared with his brochure of 1943, he had come to new insights about baptism. Moreover, there were growing reports from Germany of ecclesiastical administrations that wanted to suppress any discussion of baptism. There were many within various regional church bodies, including preachers, who questioned the dominant practice of child baptism but had to do with ever more restrictive and disciplinary measures from their church leadership. Barth wanted to support the critical preachers over and against a church leadership that clung to baptismal tradition and, as much as possible, also encourage church leaders to an openness to renewal.

With most of the preceding parts of the *Church Dogmatics* Barth had had the support of Charlotte von Kirschbaum for the editorial work. That could no longer continue. This time it was Eberhard Busch who stood alongside Barth in the technical and substantial completion of the work. The book, Barth's last substantial publication, appeared in the fall of 1967 in the same series as all the preceding parts of the *Church Dogmatics*, as volume IV/4. It was presented as a "fragment" of what Barth had originally had in mind, an entire part dedicated to ethics from the perspective of reconciliation with the title, "The Christian Life." This baptismal "fragment" (still a book of 247 pages!) treated what Barth referred to as the "foundation" of the Christian life. It is in that sense that baptism is discussed.

Barth had given a special dedication to most of the preceding volumes of the *CD*. It was often foreign universities or theological institutes to whom Barth offered thanks in this way because he had received space for the elaboration of his insights. Barth dedicated this last part to his wife Nelly, "in great gratitude." Later, in a circular letter to all who wished him well on the occasion of his eighty-second birthday on May 10, 1968, he would write of the "most harmonious evening of life," that he could experience with her.[10] There had been a great deal of tension between Barth and his wife primarily because of the presence of Charlotte von Kirschbaum in the Barth household (see 4.12). But Barth and his wife had become closer in the final years. Still, even in the last period of Barth's life, the relation between him and his wife continued to be difficult, sometimes tense. It would not become a genuinely harmonious marital relation.

26.6 "Spirit Baptism" and "Water Baptism"

According to what he himself said, Barth owed a great deal to his son Markus for the new view of baptism he had developed. Markus was a New Testament scholar, who, already in 1951, had published a book in which he had argued that baptism must not be seen as a "sacrament." The fundamental point is that Barth now sharply distinguished between two sorts of baptism: (Christian, ecclesiastical) "baptism with water," and (divine) "baptism of the Holy Spirit." It is this distinction that one does not usually make in dealing with baptism; which, according to Barth, has fatal consequences. The New Testament is primarily about "Spirit baptism." John the Baptist declared the coming of one "stronger than I" who "will baptize with the Holy Spirit" (Mark 1:8). It is, also according to Barth, evident that this proclamation anticipates the Pentecostal events narrated in Acts 2, the "outpouring" of the Holy Spirit, and that it is also related to the more particular outpourings of the Spirit narrated later, in which the Pentecostal event apparently continues. So we hear how Peter has spoken to the house of the (Roman) leader Cornelius, witnessing that the "Holy Spirit descended" on all those present, so that they began to "praise God" (Acts 10:44–46; 11:15–16).

What does "Spirit baptism" mean? As Barth described it, it is that action of God in which humans are personally "purified" and receive a new destiny for their life such that they become witnesses of Jesus Christ. Or more generally, it is that divine intervention in a human life where the one involved is "prepared for the Christian life." It is, thus Barth, the unique event, there and then, of the history of Jesus Christ who for concrete humans in this "Spirit baptism" becomes the event of their own renewal. That humans become Christians—and then also see themselves included in the community, the "communion of saints"—is in itself, humanly speaking, impossible. It can only be the consequence of such a "turn from Above, from God," an intervention in their life, a "Spirit baptism." Barth's argument

---

10. Barth, "Circular Letter," May 1968 in *Letters*, 297.

comes down to the claim that everyone who is really Christian must have undergone this sometime in his life. And it is this "Spirit baptism" that Barth characterizes without hesitation as sacrament (as "sacramental" event in the current sense of the word). It is, he said

> effective, causative, even creative action on man and in man. It is, indeed, divinely effective, divinely causative, divinely creative ... It cleanses, renews and changes man truly and totally ... [I]t is ... his being clothed upon with a new garment which is Jesus Christ Himself, his endowment with a new heart controlled by Jesus Christ, his new generation and birth in brotherhood with Jesus Christ, his saving death in the presence of the death which Jesus Christ suffered for him. All this is to be taken realistically, not just significantly and figuratively.[11]

And alongside (after) this "Spirit baptism" there is "water baptism," the baptism that is requested, administered, and received in the Christian community. Of that, it cannot be said, Barth claimed, that it is a "sacrament," a "divinely active action to and in the human." Indeed, "water baptism" is a human action, that responds to "Spirit baptism" as God's deed. Note that that means no depreciation. Its value and glory consist precisely in this human character as response!

26.7 Basis, Goal, and Meaning of Baptism

Barth worked this out by speaking in turn of the basis, goal, and meaning of baptism. From whence, on what basis, did baptism really begin in the Christian community? One obviously refers to the (often so-called) "baptismal command" given, according to Matthew 28:19, by the risen Jesus: "Make disciples of all nations, baptizing them in the name of the Father, and the Son and the Holy Spirit." Earlier, we repeatedly heard Barth claim that Jesus' resurrection and thus the actions and speech of the Resurrected, is revelatory of the scope of all that preceded in his life and death. Barth now related that to the "baptismal command." That cannot simply have fallen from the sky. That the risen Jesus sent his disciples to baptize must certainly mean that this baptism had already been instituted in and with the entirety of Jesus' life and death. And that immediately makes one think of the report in all the gospels of the baptism that Jesus himself had undergone, the baptism of John the Baptist. Jesus' entire further appearance is already programmatically summarized in the report of that baptism. It

---

11. Barth, *CD*, IV/4, 34.

expresses the fact that Jesus submitted to the lordship of God; in that he has taken position on the same foot with all others who are baptized, all who, standing under God's judgment, are in need of the forgiveness of sins, and that he accepted to completely commit himself for their sake. Jesus' own descent into the baptismal water and his emergence from it were already the germ of what would later be fulfilled in the events of cross and resurrection. So it obtains that whoever would become a follower of Jesus must go the way of his Master, follow him through the water of baptism. Barth said that just as Jesus began his appearance by being baptized so it must be for the members of his community: baptism must also be for them the beginning of their new life, in communion with him.

With the fact that, besides speaking of the basis of baptism, he also talks of its goal, he again lets us know as his view: baptism is not a goal, let alone a divine event, in itself. With that, the essential on the meaning of baptism is immediately said. It points away from itself. Christian baptism is fundamentally confession. It is not itself a purification ("washing away") but it is oriented to the purification ("washing away") that *has* happened in God's work of grace and now too *will* happen in the life of the baptized. It comes from the Spirit baptism that is already received. It is the response to it. But as such it anticipates a new Spirit baptism. Here the witness of the Acts of the Apostles is important. On the one hand, in it, people who have already received the Spirit prior to their baptism are portrayed (10:46). On the other hand, people who have received the Spirit following their baptism are portrayed (8:15). In any case, Spirit baptism and water baptism do not coincide. Baptism is not itself guarantee or realization of the gift of the Spirit, or of the forgiveness of sins, but it anticipates them. It is the prayer to receive salvation.

Barth is conscious that with this consideration he comes up squarely against the mainstream of Christian tradition with its retention of baptism as a "sacrament." One had always wanted to find that concept in particular words in the New Testament. It is said of Saul in Damascus that Ananias said to him, "Arise, be baptized, and have your sins washed away" (Acts 22:16). Does this not suggest a direct connection between baptism and the washing away of sins? There are more places in the New Testament that make that suggestion. Barth granted that one could come to a sacramental conception of baptism from such texts. But he strongly contested that such an interpretation must follow from such biblical texts. He deemed it unthinkable that the biblical authors could have had that intention. That God's work and human action may not be intermixed was for him such a fundamental insight that he was not dissuaded from it by the sound of particular biblical texts. In his opinion, essential matters were at issue here.

Meanwhile, it comes down to being careful with baptism. It is indeed, Barth said, about a concrete event, a "washing with water." So it is the image of the purifying, renewing action of God toward us to which it points. Moreover, it takes place in the community. That is represented by the minister and the baptizand together. The baptizand expresses their desire to be adopted into the community; the minister represents the community that recognizes and receives the baptized as a new member. The baptizand and the community together turn to God in repentance to new life. But that repentance must then also bear a binding, obligatory character. It cannot just be something of the inner life. It must take place visibly, in the action of baptism. Naturally, being Christian is not "finished" with baptism; baptism is only the first step on the way of one's Christian life. But precisely as the first step it has a unique, exemplary significance. It is, of course, unrepeatable as the first step. It is that human step at which God, in his engagement with the human, has aimed from eternity:

> This is the step in which the stage of the provisional and the non-obligatory . . . is overhauled and left behind, in which looking at Jesus Christ becomes necessary instead of contingent, fixed instead of vacillating, in which faith becomes solid in spite of unbelief, in which it rings out as man's response, in which his conversion becomes an act which is visible to God and irrevocable, an irreversible event.[12]

26.8 No Place for Child Baptism

There is, of course, no place for child baptism in this view of baptism. According to Barth, the arguments that one has advanced for the practice of child baptism in the Reformation create very much the impression of having been looked for afterwards, in order to be able to justify an already existing custom.

One appeal is to the biblical idea of the covenant of grace that also includes "young children." Or to the biblical story of Jesus blessing the children (Mark 10:13–16). Those are telling data. But it does not say that such young children should now also be baptized. Being a child of Christian parents does not automatically (by inheritance) make you a Christian. To be baptized, to have yourself be baptized, is an act of faith. That faith is expected of the baptizand him- or herself. Others, parents for example, cannot act in faith in his or her place (although the faith of others can certainly support

---

12. Barth, *CD*, IV/4, 151.

the faith of the baptized). True, one used to say that later the baptized can grow in faith; then he can make public confession and thereby still "take responsibility for his baptism." But such an act of "public confession" should have preceded baptism and formed one complete whole with it. Now such "public confession" is often simply a formality, a church (or better, civil) ritual, and just as problematic as child baptism.

An argument often advanced for child baptism is that God's grace precedes all human faith. But if that would obtain as an argument then that would also justify (and eventually require) the baptism of adults without distinction. Moreover, it would imply that the administration of baptism as such is again conceived as the "distribution of grace." As though it would depend on baptism, whether someone stood under God's grace or not!

But when such an emphasis is placed on baptism as an act of confession (by the baptized themselves), is there then not the danger that thereby an arbitrary separation of "sheep" and "goats" takes place? Does it not threaten to result into the formation of a core community of "highly believing baptized" Christians who distance themselves from all that is non-Christian? Is there then not the threat of a chasm that originates between the "church" and the "world"? Such a distance, born of Christian self-sufficiency, would indeed be regrettable. But it is a misunderstanding to claim that it would automatically be the result of the elimination of child baptism. Those who really believe (and thus are baptized) understand and confess their solidarity with those who stand outside (but for whom God's grace also already applies!). Speaking of dangers, is it not much more dangerous that a "Christianity" originates (via the practice of child baptism) to which the members can appeal that they bear no particular responsibility for their "membership"?

Barth ended this reflection with an extraordinarily emotional outburst:

> Enough of this tiresome matter! Theology can and should do no more than advise the Church . . . In this matter of infant baptism, our advice has not been sought, and there is only the faintest hope that it will be heeded. This advice cannot be that in its baptismal practice the Church should continue with a supposedly good conscience . . . This practice is profoundly irregular. It is true that through the centuries and up to our own time the Church has not been destroyed by it (any more than by corrupt preaching or so many other corruptions). But it would be most dangerous . . . to appeal to the fact, or to rely on it, that this practice will not harm it in the future. To all concerned: to theologians, . . . to Christian congregations and their pastors; to Church leaders, presbyterial, synodal or episcopal; to all individual Christians, however simple, let it be said that they should

see to it whether they can and will continue to bear responsibility for what has become the dominant baptismal practice, whether they might not and must not dare to face up to the wound from which the Church suffers at this genuinely vital point with its many-sided implications, whether they could not and should not undertake measures for its healing which do not bear the character of compromise, and which ought not, therefore, to be the last to call for consideration.[13]

26.9 Questions with this New Conception of Baptism

Barth had no illusions that his view of baptism developed here would meet with approval in the church or theology. In the preface of this final part of his *Church Dogmatics* he himself wrote that he anticipated that he would again stand alone in this theological/ecclesiastical area as had always been the case. But he was resigned to it; it simply must be. He was also not lacking in self-assurance. "The day will come when justice will be done to me in this matter too."[14]

Was Barth here too self-assured? Had he overplayed his hand at the end of his life with this newly formulated doctrine of baptism? Had he unnecessarily put up the backs of the defenders of the tradition of the church on this point? One thing is certain. That Barth now represented a radical rejection of the notion that baptism should be a "sacrament" (thus mediating salvation) as well as of the propriety of child baptism was not a bolt from the blue. Whoever had followed the development of Barth's theology, primarily his doctrine of reconciliation, could have seen it coming. It was certainly claimed by critics, including those from the circle of Barth's kindred spirits, that Barth here would have come into conflict with himself. Had Barth himself not always emphasized the priority of God's grace, its character of preceding all human faith decisions? Was not just a principled plea for child baptism to be expected for that reason? But we heard how Barth himself powerfully rejected this argument. All things considered, Barth did that not *despite*, but *because of* the biblical proclamation of the priority of grace. He was convinced that whoever retains child baptism shortchanges this priority, as though it would be bound to ecclesiastical action or administration (of the "sacraments") and does not, also and precisely, precede, transcend that action!

---

13. Barth, *CD*, IV/4, 194–95.
14. Barth, *CD*, IV/4, xii.

It is correctly noted that in his new doctrine of baptism Barth remained faithful to his view of God as the "totally Other," the sovereign (see chapter 2). This "being other" of God implies, after all, that his graceful actions cannot and can never be annexed, taken in hand and manipulated either by humans, or by the church, for example in "sacraments" or "means of grace." So far as Barth had still in his former considerations—under the influence of the tradition of the church—been amenable to the concept of sacrament he had foundationally corrected himself in this last fragment of his dogmatics.

But the question remains whether he did not stand too radically alone. That primarily concerns his sharp distinction of "Spirit baptism" and "water baptism." Do the two not, according to the New Testament, cohere more closely that Barth would have it? In other words, is there not still something of "Spirit baptism" also in water baptism as that is related in the Acts of the Apostles? Not that that would mean that a human, ecclesiastical action could claim to have charge of God's grace. But may it not be said that the ritual of water baptism is performed in the hope and with the prayer that God, by his Spirit, would make use of it in his work?

As Barth speaks of "Spirit baptism" as of a unique event of spiritual renewal of which it may (must) be accepted that it has overcome every truthful, beginning Christian who comes to baptism personally, it sounds a bit artificial. Must one indeed experience that separately, and if so, how? Moreover, it raises the question of how such a separate "Spirit baptism" is related to the event of the (general) outpouring of the Spirit that we hear of in the story of Pentecost. If the latter means that the Spirit is given to us, to us all together, in principle there and then, why must then something extra like an individual Pentecost be considered for every Christian?

Barth's new concept of baptism raises questions. But it certainly provokes thought. His plea for the maturity of the church as it is focused here deserves to be heard. Barth had emphatically laid on the table the idea that along with his baptism, the baptizand also in principle (and fundamentally, publicly for the first time) responds to the reception of grace and confesses his (beginning) faith. Where this insight is taken into account, weighty questions arise concerning the practice of child baptism. We become a member of the community not *by virtue of* but certainly *in* our own, mature decision (affirmation).

27

The Close of a Life

27.1 The *Church Dogmatics* as an Unfinished Symphony

THE LATE VOLUME, *CD* IV/4, on baptism as the foundation of the Christian life, was indeed Barth's last substantial publication. The *Church Dogmatics* would remain incomplete. The fourth and final part of the doctrine of reconciliation that Barth had intended could no longer be completed. And what the final part of his dogmatics was to be, eschatology, the doctrine of "the last things," the great future of God, would remain completely unwritten.

With a certain resignation, Barth had ceased working. It was a loss of strength, physically and spiritually; he was eighty-one years old. In the preface of his fragment on baptism he wrote that most summative theological works of the past also had remained incomplete. He ironically recalled that important medieval cathedrals were never completed and still retained their significance just as in music there are incomplete works (think of Schubert's unfinished symphony) that have remained famous. Who knows what will happen with the incomplete *Church Dogmatics*!

Barth pointed out that what the missing part, the consideration of what the Christian future expectation concerns, was written in various places in the volumes that had already appeared. A picture can indeed be sketched of what he would have elaborated in this missing part. For example, one can consider what he wrote in the third part of his doctrine of reconciliation on Jesus' expected return at the end of time wherein what had come to light with Easter will become fully, universally public (see 22.11). As the expected future, Barth saw the definitive disclosure of what had now, already, come to pass in Christ. Barth had already given that to his readers.

27.2 Nonetheless, Back to Academic Work

Although the time for substantial publications was past, Barth still did not allow himself to be consigned to unemployment. In the summer of 1967, he would not be kept from returning to academic work. He again had the energy to initiate a series of seminars, this time on Calvin. Barth viewed him as the ecumenical theologian par excellence among the Reformers. It was just that aspect that he would illuminate. Hence, he concentrated on Calvin's doctrine of the Holy Spirit as elaborated in the *Institutes*. Witnesses report that there was a large interest in these seminars. Both Swiss and foreigners, including Roman Catholics, were among the participants. With Barth there was no trace of the good-natured retiree to whom everything is not so necessary any more. From the outset, he made it clear that he expected the active participation of those present. The text of Calvin's *Institutes* was foundationally studied.

Following a short, intense loss of energy, he recovered surprisingly quickly in the fall. Another theme continued to capture his thinking, developments in Roman Catholicism. His trip to Rome in September 1966 and his discussions with Vatican authorities there had increasingly impressed him on the importance of what had taken place at the Second Vatican Council. He was convinced that the documents accepted and published by the council were worthy of the highest thought. Directly after his return home he had already, in student groups, given attention to the conciliar document "on divine revelation." Now, a year later, he turned his attention to another document, that on the church.

He also saw that as a key text for the evaluation of the meaning of the council. What, according to this document, does the Roman Catholic Church now think that the church "is"? How does this church understand itself in relation to other churches? What does it think of the relation between office bearers ("hierarchy") and the "laity"? Barth had asked critical questions also of this document during his stay in Rome. What is the case with the distance between Christ as Lord, King, and Judge and his church? Is the laity alone his witness in the world? Is the hierarchy more, more important, than the laity? Is the church as such the manifestation and continuation of the incarnation? Can this really be said? Questions that were still in order following the discussions in Rome but at the same time indicate the continuing importance of this document for the encounter between Roman Catholics and Protestants. All reason for further study. Barth repeatedly emphasized that one may not prematurely deny the possibility of renewal in the Roman Catholic Church. In a series of seminars, from October 1967 to February 1968, the text of the conciliar document was foundationally read and studied. In February, Barth's secretary, Eberhard Busch (who together with his wife had kept a record of all these seminars) had to take his place. Barth's health had again gotten worse; a quick trip to the hospital was necessary.

27.3 Again: Schleiermacher ... and Bultmann

At the end of February, Barth was home again having recovered surprisingly quickly. He took up a new project, a series of seminars on Schleiermacher. Over the course of his life, he had been engaged with the theology of Schleiermacher, a prominent representative of nineteenth-century liberal Protestant theology. Barth had not been able to go along with Schleiermacher's efforts to represent the Christian faith in such a way that it is recognizable to the modern man as an indispensable element in the completion of the culture, that is of the mature human nature. Schleiermacher had taken his starting point in the human, pious, consciousness and that meant, according to Barth, that what is peculiar to the Word of God, as a factor over and against the human, remains out of sight. Still, he always had had the feeling that that was not the end of the matter concerning Schleiermacher. Barth was also convinced that gospel and culture do not simply oppose each other; that it is worthwhile to consider the bridge between the two. After all, the Word of God intends to involve the human, including the modern human. As far as that was what Schleiermacher was about, Barth could not simply reject him (see 6.4). Once more he wanted to expressly put Schleiermacher's theology on the agenda. All the more because he saw Schleiermacher's influence active in the affairs of the church and theology of his own days.

This year, 1968, Schleiermacher's 200th birthday was celebrated. To Barth, that was an extra stimulus. He wanted to offer with his series of seminars a modest contribution to this Schleiermacher jubilee. Again, there was a lot of interest. Between the end of April and the end of June there were weekly Saturday morning sessions.

On the occasion of the Schleiermacher anniversary, a collection of Schleiermacher's texts appeared in a popular German publication. At the request of the publisher, Barth added an epilogue in which he gave an overview of his own history with this "church father of the nineteenth (and also the twentieth!?) century."[1] Just so, he could still publish from what he had discussed in his seminars.

By the way, the epilogue grew into a (brief) autobiography. In it, Barth made clear how the entire course of development of his theology had been

---

1. Barth, *The Theology of Schleiermacher*, 261.

determined by his relation to Schleiermacher. Originally taken by Schleiermacher, later distancing himself from him, he still, when he was a professor at Göttingen, had given lectures on him. But yes, "I still had ringing in my ears the venerable Apostles' and Nicene Creeds. Theologically speaking, I could not revert to Schleiermacher." And then, said Barth in his retrospect, something unexpected happened:

> it came to pass that we "old fighters" from the second and third decades of our rather eventful century suddenly saw ourselves overtaken and overwhelmed by a new theological movement. "Demythologization" and "existentialization" of theological language were its catchwords. And the one who had inaugurated it was none other than our erstwhile companion of old, Rudolf Bultmann.[2]

The entire new theological movement with which Barth had to do since the fifties (see 18.2-3, 24.6) had begun with Bultmann. The existential character of "faith" was emphasized. The Object of faith was thoughtlessly passed over, the One in whom one may believe (and who in fact appears to be the subject of our belief). A true tidal wave. But then a tidal wave with a clearly demonstrable starting point. Bultmann? Yes, but also behind him, Schleiermacher!

> Bultmann was and is a continuator of the great tradition of the nineteenth century, and thus in new guise, a genuine pupil of Schleiermacher . . . That Schleiermacher made the christianly pious person into the criterion and content of his theology, while, after the "death of God" and the state-funeral dedicated to him, one now jubilantly wants to make the christianly impious person into its object and theme, these certainly are two different things. In the end and in principle, however, they probably amount to the same thing . . . I can see no way from Schleiermacher, or from his contemporary epigones, to the chroniclers, prophets, and wise ones of Israel, to those who narrate the story of the life, death, and resurrection of Jesus Christ, to the word of the apostles—no way to the God of Abraham, Isaac, and Jacob and the Father of Jesus Christ, no way to the great tradition of the Christian church.[3]

But in this same connection, Barth also testified his respect for the person of Schleiermacher. He was and remained a man of the church, conscious of his ecclesiastical responsibility. He continued to lead church services into

2. Barth, *The Theology of Schleiermacher*, 267.
3. Barth, *The Theology of Schleiermacher*, 270-72.

his old age. That makes one think. That makes it such, Barth said, that I am still not done with him. Up to now I have indeed thought that I had to distance myself from him. But, have I understood him well? Or has Schleiermacher intended something else so that he and I in essence go the same way? Barth made the latter concrete with the formulation of a few dilemmas—just as he had done in the seminars he had just held.

It appears as though what Schleiermacher presented in his work was nothing other than philosophy clothed in a pious, theological garment. Barth said: then I indeed can have nothing to do with it. But conversely it can also be that for Schleiermacher it is still essentially about theology that he dresses in a philosophical jacket for the sake of his contemporaries. Then that should not simply be rejected.

More focused: it appears as though Schleiermacher starts completely from his own consciousness so that there is no talk of an over and against, a real Other. Barth said: then there is no communication possible between him and me. Or did Schleiermacher intend it still otherwise and took account of the presence of an Other to whom worship and prayer are possible and commanded? Then I want to hear more about it in the hope that I can still connect with Schleiermacher.

Barth had always been engaged with these and other questions. And, as he said here, he rejoiced in advance that later, in heaven, he would be able to exchange thoughts extensively with Schleiermacher. "I can imagine that that will be a very serious matter for both sides, but also that we will both laugh very heartily at ourselves."[4]

27.4 A Dream of the Future

Barth concluded his epilogue and retrospect with a dream of the immediate future. He mused of a "theology of the Holy Spirit."[5] By that he meant a theology in which everything, the entire work of God would be illuminated afresh from a consideration of the work of the Holy Spirit. In the *Church Dogmatics* everything, the entire theological reflection, stands in the light of Christ. But should not all of it be able to happen again, now in the light of the Spirit?

Barth could no longer get to working out this idea. Moreover, it would have had to lead to a radical reconstruction of his theology. In the introductory considerations (the "prolegomena") of the *CD*, the Spirit of God is talked about where it is about how God's revelation, happening objectively

---

4. Barth, *The Theology of Schleiermacher*, 277.
5. Barth, *The Theology of Schleiermacher*, 278.

in Christ, comes to the human (Barth called that the "subjective reality," and also possibility, "of revelation"). In the doctrine of reconciliation as well there is that same strict order and division; there Christ, in whom reconciliation is an (objective) reality is treated first, and following that the subjective realization (the application) of reconciliation, the latter being about the Spirit. Barth had noted at the time in this connection that with Schleiermacher (and his followers, like Bultmann) the theme of application was not the last but the first theme. He could not at all join in that prioritization. But now, in the epilogue on his relation to Schleiermacher, this sharp opposition is replaced by a search for agreement. Must his theology not have been set up differently? Would that still not have to happen?

That he had placed the subjective realization (the application) of reconciliation, thus the reality of being church and being Christian "under the sign of the Holy Spirit," was, he said looking back, rightly sensed. But should he have not spoken of the Spirit earlier? Like in the reflection on the way in which God's reconciling grace comes for the human good, in his justification, sanctification, and call (see 19.12, 22.13)? Or already in his doctrine of creation? Moreover, must not the whole of Christology, the reflection on the meaning of Jesus Christ, be illuminated from the Spirit? Is God, the God of revelation and of the covenant, not himself Spirit?

These are essential questions. Barth saw them here, at nearly the end of his life, confronting him. Answer them himself, he could no longer do that. Others would have to do that. In any case, this indicated the direction of what now must happen in theology! Then Schleiermacher and Bultmann could appear to be not so much misunderstood opponents as discussion partners, to be taken seriously.

27.5 "What Jesus Christ Means to Me"

Shortly after the conclusion of the series of seminars on Schleiermacher, Barth had to deal with a new setback. An emergency operation was necessary. He had still had plans to hold a new series of seminars in the fall, but nothing would come of it. He could still read and did a great deal of it.

Now and then he still responded to a request for a contribution. He was asked by a French magazine to write on the question of what Jesus Christ meant to him. In his answer in a November publication, Barth made it clear that it cannot be about something that is "especially for him personally." He would not allow himself to be caught up in such an old-pietistic or modern-existentialist question!

> Jesus Christ is for me precisely—no more, no less, and no other than—what he was, is, and will be, always and everywhere, for the church which he has called together and commissioned in all its forms, and for the whole world according to the message which he has entrusted to the church.
>
> Jesus Christ is the basis of the covenant, the fellowship, the unbreakable relationship between God and man. I, too, am a man. Hence he is the basis of this covenant for me too.
>
> Jesus Christ in the uniqueness of his existence has made himself known to Christians as the free gift of this covenant proffered to all men. I, too, may be a Christian. Hence he is obviously for me, too, the demonstration of God's grace at work in this covenant—the grace which is free in relation to me but which also frees me.
>
> Jesus Christ is the Word of God spoken to all. As I, too, am one of the all . . . I am empowered, commissioned, and liberated to bear witness to him as this Word of the love of God.[6]

It is like an echo of the Barmen Declaration of 1934 (see 1.2).

27.6 "My Theology Always Had a Strong Political Component"

He took part in a broadcast for Swiss radio under the title "Music for a Guest," also in November. The guest to be interviewed could indicate the music he or she wanted to hear. The choice was clear for Barth, his beloved composer was Mozart. In the intervals he spoke of the course of his life. He had never aspired to an academic career, he said. His intention had been to be a preacher.

> My whole theology, you see, is fundamentally a theology for pastors. It grew out of my own situation when I had to teach and preach and counsel a little. And I found that what I had learned at the university was of little help in this. So I had to make a fresh start and I tried to do this.[7]

He had not experienced his professorship as a break with the life of the preacher. It simply meant that he would practice the same business at another level.

---

6. Barth, "Testimony to Jesus Christ," 13–14.
7. Barth, "Music for a Guest," 23.

Barth's involvement in politics also came up in the interview, primarily considering the era of Hitler and the Cold War. Barth made it clear that that political involvement had not fallen from the sky.

> [T]heology . . . was never a private matter for me. Its theme is God for the world, God for man, heaven for earth. This meant that all my theology always had a strong political side, explicit or implicit.[8]

At the conclusion, the topic of what was central for Barth was discussed, where he was really at home. Was that with God's grace? No, it is better to say, with Jesus Christ, grace in person.

> The last word that I have to say as a theologian or politician is not a concept like grace but a name: Jesus Christ. He is grace and he is the ultimate one beyond world and church and even theology. We cannot lay hold of him. But we have to do with him. And my own concern in my long life has been increasingly to emphasize this name and to say: "In him." . . . In him is the spur to work, warfare, and fellowship. In him is all that I have attempted in my life in weakness and folly.[9]

27.7 Orthodox or Liberal?

In the same period Barth was also interviewed by Swiss radio in another way. It was on the question where he was really to be "placed" on the ecclesiastical/theological spectrum. The interviewer's starting point was the presupposition that Barth was in fact an orthodox theologian, or better, "neo-orthodox." Had he not come to terms with Protestant liberalism? Had he not talked about God as the "totally Other" and with his return to tradition and dogma presented orthodoxy in a new way?

Barth had to laugh at this question. He challengingly called himself liberal. He understood by that being open to all sides in freedom and responsibility, including to the voices of the past. Yes, he had written a thick dogmatics. But is that in conflict with freedom and openness? No, much more, it had emerged from that:

> Most theologians, especially today, write only little pamphlets and articles and Festschrift contributions. I was never content

---

8. Barth, "Music for a Guest," 24.
9. Barth, "Music for a Guest," 29–30.

with this. I said to myself: If I am a theologian, I must try to work out broadly what I think I have perceived as God's revelation.[10]

And "revelation" does not mean that "the truth" has fallen like a block of stone from heaven. Indeed:

> Revelation means that one who was hidden has shown himself. One who was silent has spoken. And one who had not so far heard has perceived something of this . . . it is a history between that one and us. I myself do not see what this has to do with lack of freedom . . . God has acted, acts, and will act among men. And when this is perceptible, it is his revelation. To have a relation to this revelation means, then, to enter into this history of God's action, looking to past, present, and future (so far as one can), and asking what one has to think about it and say about it.[11]

This interview, held in November 1968, was broadcast on April 7, 1969, nearly four months after Barth's death. It again concisely reflected how Barth had conceived his theological work.

27.8 Life's End

On December 3, the request reached Barth to participate in the organization of a gathering in Zürich in January in the context of the week of prayer for Christian unity. He was asked whether he would hold a lecture there for a forum of Roman Catholic and Reformed Christians on "the new ecumenical situation." Barth felt called upon and declared that he was prepared to comply and immediately chose a theme for the lecture, "Starting out—Turning Round—Confessing." He hoped, through his contribution, to be able to bring not so much the churches involved as the "progressives" and the "conservatives" in the churches concerned closer together.

Up to the evening of December 9, he worked on the text of his lecture. He broke off in the middle of a sentence, intending to complete the work on the following day, December 10. But that was not to be. That night he died in his sleep.

On Friday, December 13, the burial took place in Basel among a small circle of family. At the request of the family, Eberhard Busch spoke a few words in remembrance in the aula. He had worked with and for Barth intensively for the last two years. The following day there was a large

---

10. Barth, "Liberal Theology," 36.
11. Barth, "Liberal Theology," 35–36.

memorial gathering in the Münster, the central church of Basel. The church was packed. The service was broadcast by radio. Here the word was offered by speakers on behalf of the theological faculty and the church council of the Evangelical-reformed church of Basel, on behalf of the government of the Basel canton, on behalf of the churches in Germany (Helmut Gollwitzer) and Eastern Europe (J. L. Hromádka), and on behalf of the World Council of Churches (W. A. Visser 't Hooft). Hans Küng spoke as a Catholic theologian ("countless Catholics mourn with you today, theologians and laity from all over the world"). Eberhard Jüngel (recently appointed professor in Zürich, who had often visited Barth in the last years) represented the latest academic generation. The addresses were interchanged with music by Mozart. At the beginning of the service Psalm 103 was read by the minister of the Münster church: "Praise the LORD, O my soul, praise his holy name, Praise the LORD, O my soul, and forget not all his benefits." And at the conclusion the song was sung that Barth had often sung himself, "Now thank we all our God with heart and hands and voices . . ."

Appendix 1
Overview of Karl Barth's Life and Career

1886:	Born, May 10, Basel
1889:	Barth family moves to Bern; Karl's father becomes professor of New Testament and Church History
1892–1904:	School years in Bern; elementary school; gymnasium
1904:	September: begin theological studies in Bern
1906:	Continuation of theological studies in Berlin
1907:	Continuation of theological studies in Marburg, later Tübingen
1908–1909;	Editorial secretary of *Die Christliche Welt*. Final theological examination
1909–1911:	Assistant preacher of the German-speaking congregation in Geneva
1911–1921:	Preacher in Safenwil, Aargau Canton
1912:	February 25: Barth's father dies
1913:	Married to Nelly Hoffmann
1914:	Daughter Franziska born
1915:	Joins the Social Democratic Party of Switzerland (Aargau Canton)
	Son Markus born
	Meeting with Christoph Blumhardt

1917:	Son Christoph born. Publishes a collection of sermons with Eduard Thurneysen, *Suchet Gott, so werdet ihr leben* (Seek the Lord and Live)
1919:	September: Participates in a religious-social conference in Tambach, Germany. Speech at Tambach: *Der Christ in der Gesellschaff* (The Christian's Place in Society)
1919:	Publishes *Der Römerbrief* (*The Epistle to the Romans*)
1921:	Son Matthias born
1921–1925:	Particular professor of Reformed Theology at Göttingen, Germany
1922:	Published *Der Römerbrief,* 2nd, completely new ed.
	Honorary doctorate, University of Münster
	Beginning of the journal *Zwischen den Zeiten*, by Barth together with Thurneysen and Friedrich Gogarten
1924–1925:	Lecture cycle in dogmatics: "Unterricht in der christlichen Religion" ("Instruction in the Christian Religion")
1924:	Publication of a collection of lectures: *Das Wort Gottes und die Theologie* (The Word of God and Theology) (texts from 1916–1923)
	Published collection of sermons with Thurneysen, *Komm Schöpfer Geist* (Come Creator Spirit)
1925:	Son Hans Jakob born
	Acquaintance with Charlotte von Kirschbaum, later Barth's closest co-worker (until 1966)
1925–1929:	Professor of dogmatics and New Testament at Münster
1925:	Completion, at Münster, of the first lecture cycle in dogmatics
1926–1928:	Second lecture cycle in dogmatics: "Christliche Dogmatik" (Christian Dogmatics) at Münster
1926	Receives German citizenship (along with Swiss citizenship)
	First visit to the Netherlands.
	Speech at Amsterdam: "Die Kirche und die Kultur" (Church and Culture)

1927:	Publication of *Die Christliche Dogmatik im Entwurf, I: Die Lehre von Worte Gottes* (Christian Dogmatics in Concept, I: The Doctrine of the Word of God)
1928:	Publication of a second collection of lectures, *Die Theologie und die Kirche* (Theology and Church, texts from 1920–1928)
1930–1935:	Professor of Systematic Theology in Bonn
1930:	Honorary doctorate, University of Glasgow
1931:	Publication of *Fides quaerens intellectum: Anselms Beweis der Existenz Gottes* (Anselm's Proof of the Existence of God)
	Beginning third lecture cycle in dogmatics: Kirchliche Dogmatik (Church Dogmatics)
1932:	Publication of *Die Kirchliche Dogmatik I/1: Die Lehre vom Wort Gottes* (Church Dogmatics I: The Doctrine of the Word of God, Part 1)
1933:	June: Publication of the brochure, *Theologische Existenz heute!* (*Theological Existence Today*)
	September: Ends co-editing the journal *Zwischen den Zeiten* (that ceases shortly thereafter)
	Starts a new series, *Theologische Existenz heute!* (published by Barth and Thurneysen
1934:	January 4: Free synod of the evangelical Reformed congregations at Barmen-Gemarke; acceptance of Barth's proposed declaration
	May 29–31: The first synod of the "Confessing Church" at Barmen; acceptance of the theological declaration proposed by Barth ("Barmen Theses")
	October: publication of the brochure *Nein!* (No!)—against Brunner
	End of October: second synod of the "Confessing Church" in Berlin-Dahlem; Barth becomes member of the administration
	End of November: Barth ends his membership in the administration out of protest against the decision in Berlin that weakened the course taken at Barmen.

November 26: suspended as professor in Bonn

December 20: dismissed as professor in Bonn

1935: Publishes a collection of sermons with Thurneysen, *Die grosse Barmherzigkeit* (God's Search for Men, sermons from 1925–1934)

February 10: Barth takes leave of his students (outside the university)

March 1: Barth is forbidden to speak in Germany

February–March: Second visit to the Netherlands: a series of lectures in Utrecht on the Apostles' Creed, published in the same year under the title: *Credo*.

End of June: named professor at Basel; return to Switzerland

October 7: Again in Barmen, His address on "Gospel and Law" read by the local preacher.

1936: Honorary doctorate University of Utrecht

May 10: Barth's fiftieth birthday, honored with a Festschrift (still published in Germany) *Theologische Aufsätze* (Theological Essays)

1937: March–April: Visit to Scotland; series of lectures (Gifford Lectures) at the University of Aberdeen on the Scots Confession

Honorary doctorate University of St. Andrews

1938: March–April: Again a visit to Scotland. Subsequent series of lectures at Aberdeen on the Scots Confession. These were published in a collection *Gotteserkentnis und Gottesdienst nach reformatorischer Lehre*.

Honorary doctorate University of Oxford.

End of the series "Theologische Existenz heute!"

June: Lecture *Rechfertigung und Recht* ("Church and State"), the first brochure in a new series, "Theologische Studien," published (as henceforth nearly all Barth's work) in Switzerland.

September 5: Barth's mother dies

	September 19: Letter to Josef Hromádka, professor at Prague; appeal for (armed) resistance to Hitler-Germany.
	October: Sale of Barth's publications forbidden in Germany.
	December 5: lecture in Wipkingen/Zürich, *Die Kirche und die politische Frage von heute*, on the Jewish question as a question of faith.
	Publication of *Die Kirchliche Dogmatik I/2: Die Lehre vom Wort Gottes*, second part (Church Dogmatics I: The Doctrine of the Word of God, Part 2)
	Honorary doctorate from the University of Münster withdrawn
1939:	March: Third visit to the Netherlands. Lecture held ad various theological faculties, *Die Souveränität des Wortes Gottes und die Entscheiding des Glaubens* ("The Sovereignty of the Word of God and the Decision of Faith"). In discussion critical on child baptism.
	Publication of *Die Kirchliche Dogmatik II/1: Die Lehre von Gott* (Church Dogmatics II: The Doctrine of God, Part 1)
1939–1942:	Letters and messages to the churches and church representatives in Great Britain and occupied territories.
1941:	June: Barth's third son in a fatal accident in the Swiss mountains
1942:	Publication of *Die Kirchliche Dogmatik II/2: Die Lehre von Gott: Gottes Gnadenwahl and Gottes Gebot* (Church Dogmatics II: The Doctrine of God, Part 2).
1943:	May 7: Lecture to Swiss students, *Die Kirchliche Lehre von der Taufe* ("The Teaching of the Church Regarding Baptism"), later published in the series "Theologische Studien." Rejection of the practice of child baptism.
1944–1945:	Various pleas for solidarity with the German people
1945:	June: publication of *Eine Schweizer Stimme* (*The Church and the War*, collected texts from 1938–1945)
	August: First post-war visit to Germany; participation in a meeting on the reconstruction of German church life in Frankfurt/Maim and Treysa (Hessen)

November 2: Public speech held in Stuttgart (later in Tübingen), *Ein Wort an die Deutschen* ("A Word to the Germans").

Publication of *Die Kirchliche Dogmatik III/1: Die Lehre von der Schöpfung* (Church Dogmatics III: The Doctrine of Creation, Part 1).

Honorary doctorate from the University of Münster awarded to Barth anew

1946: Summer Semester: Guest professor at Bonn. Series of lectures on the Apostles' Creed, later published as *Dogmatik im Grundriss* ("Dogmatics in Outline").

Lecture held at various places in Germany, *Christengemeinde und Bürgergemeinde*, on the relation of church and state

1947: Publication of the brochure *Die Kirche – die lebendige Gemeinde des Lebendigen Herrn Jesus Christus,* (The Living Congregation of the Living Lord Jesus Christ), preparatory text for the assembly of the World Council of churches at Amsterdam; appeal for a congregational church structure.

Summer Semester: Again guest professor at Bonn. Series of lectures on the Heidelberg Catechism, published in 1948.

July–August: Involved in the preparation of the "Darmstadt declaration" of the Confessing Church, on the political course of the German people.

Publication of *Die protestantische Theologie im 19 Jahrhundert* ("Protestant Theology in the 19th Century", lectures held in 1932–1933).

1948: March–April: visit to Hungary, to the Hungarian Reformed Church.

Discussion with Emil Brunner on Barth's report of the Hungarian trip

Publication of *Die Kirchliche Dogmatik III/2* (Church Dogmatics III: The Doctrine of Creation, Part 2: on the human as creature).

August 22–September 4: Participant at the assembly of the World Council of Churches in Amsterdam. Introductory lecture on the main theme: "Man's Disorder and God's Design"

1949: February: Lecture on "The Church between East and West", held at various places in Switzlerland.

Publication of the collection of sermons *Fürchte dich micht* ("Do not be afraid", sermons from 1934–1948)

1950: Publication of *Die Kirchliche Dogmatik III/3* (Church Dogmatics III: The Doctrine of Creation, Part 3, on Providence).

1950–1951: Under fire in the Swiss media on Barth's open letter critical of German rearmament

Correspondence with politician Markus Feldmann

1951: Publication of *Die Kirchliche Dogmatik III/4: Das Gebot Gottes des Schöpfers* (Church Dogmatics III: The Doctrine of Creation, Part 4: Ethics)

September: correspondence with Albert Bereczky, Hungarian Reformed bishop, critical of Bereczky's uncritical pro-communism

1951–1953: Participation in the summer meetings in preparation of the second assembly of the World Council of Churches; collaboration in the commission report on Christian hope

1952: Publication of the brochure *Politische Entscheidung in der Einheit des Glaubens* ("Political Decisions in the Unity of the Faith")

Publication of the brochure *Rudolf Bultmann. Ein Versuch, ihn zu verstehen* (An Attempt to Understand him).

1953: Publication of *Die Kirchliche Dogmatik IV/1. Die Lehre von der Versöhnng: Jesus Christus, der Herr als Knecht* (*Church Dogmatics IV: The Doctrine of Reconciliation, Part 1*)

September: Lecture, *Das Geschenk der Freiheit*, ("The Gift of Freedom") held at Bielefeld, Germany

1954; Honorary doctorate University of Budapest

November 14: Public speech held in Wiesbaden, at meeting organized by the German province Hessen in memory of the victims of war

1955: Publication of *Die Kirchliche Dogmatik IV/2. Die Lehre von der Versöhnung: Jesus Christus, der Knecht als Herr* (*Church Dogmatics IV: The Doctrine of Reconciliation, Part 2*)

	Decision by the University of Basel to continue Barth's professorship after his seventieth birthday
1956:	Honorary doctorate University of Edinburgh
	Publication of *Kurze Erklärung des Römerbriefes* (*A Shorter Commentary on Romans*), lectures at a people's school Basel, 1940–1941)
	May 10: Barth's seventieth birthday, honored with a Festschrift *Antwort*
	September: lecture *Die Menschlichkeit Gottes* ("The Humanity of God"), for the Swiss Preacher's Union
1957:	January: lecture "*Evangelische Theologie im 19, Jahrhundert*, (Evangelical Theology in the 19th Century), in Hanover; a reevaluation
	Publication of a third collection of lectures, *Theologische Fragen und Antworten* (Theological Qustions and Answers, texts from 1923–1942)
1958:	August: Letter to a preacher in the German Democratic Republic, published as an open letter
1959:	Publication of *Die Kirchliche Dogmatik IV/3. Die Lehre von der Versöhnung: Jesus Christus, der wahrhaftige Zeuge* (*Church Dogmatics IV: The Doctrine of Reconciliation, Part 3*)
	Publication of a collection of sermons *Den Gefangenen Befreiung* (*Deliverance to the Captives*, sermons from 1954–1959, held in the Basel prison)
	Honorary doctorate University of Strasburg
1959–1961:	Lectures on "Das christliche Leben" (Christian Life, ethics of reconciliation)
1961;	May 10: On Barth's seventy–fifth birthday the publication of the collection *Der Götze wankelt* (The Idol Falters, texts from 1930–1960), published by Karl Kupisch
	Summer: Barth ends his regular lectures; work on the *Church Dogmatics* broken off
1961–1962:	Extra series of lectures, *Einführung in die evangelische Theologie*, (Evangelical Theology: An Introduction), published Spring 1962

APPENDIX 1: OVERVIEW OF KARL BARTH'S LIFE AND CAREER

1962:	March 1: departure as professor at Basel; retirement
	April: Visit to the United States of America; lectures and panel discussions at various places.
	Honorary doctorate University of Chicago
1962–1963:	Participation in various public discussions; confrontation with "God is dead" theology and other new theological developments
1963:	Honorary doctorate Sorbonne University, Paris
1964–1965:	Periods of illness; a number of operations and hospitalizations
1965:	Publication of a collection of sermons *Rufe mich an* (sermons from 1959–1964, held in the Basel prison)
1966:	May 10: Barth's eightieth birthday, honored with a Festschrift *Parrhèsia*
	September 22–29: Visit to the Vatican in Rome; discussions on the documents of the Second Vatican Council.
	Fall: series of seminars on the Council document, *Dei verbum,* "on divine revelation"
1967:	Publication of *Ad Limina Apostolorum*, report on the visit to the Vatican
	Publication of *Die Kirchliche Dogmatis IV/4* (fragment): *Die Lehre van der Taufe:* (Church Dogmatics IV, The Doctrine of Reconciliation, Part 4, Fragment), on baptism (water baptism) as the first step of the Christian life
	October (until the beginning of 1968): series of seminars on the Council document *Lumen gentium*, Second Vatican Council document on the church
1968:	April–May: series of seminars on Schleiermacher
	Publication of *Nachwort* (Epilogue), in a collection of Schleiermacher texts
	November: Various radio interviews with autobiographical reflections
	December 10: Death in Basel

Appendix 2
Literature: Karl Barth's Works

A complete survey of Barth's publications is included in the Festschrifts: *Antwort*, (1956, through 1955) and *Parrhèsia* (1966, through 1965; together 553 titles).

Barth's main works:

Der Römerbrief, 1919; 2nd edition 1922. English: *The Epistle to the Romans*, 1933.

Die christliche Dogmatik im Entwurf, I, 1927; new ed. 1982.

Fides quaerens intellectum. Anselms Beweis der Existenz Gottes, 1931. English: *Anselm: Fides Quaerens Intellectum : Anselm's Proof of the Existence of God in the Context of His Theological Scheme*, 1960.

Die Kirchliche Dogmatik I/1–IV/4, 4 parts in 13 volumes, 1932–1967. English: *Church Dogmatics*, 1956–1975.

Credo: Die Hauptprobleme der Dogmatik dargestellt im Anschluss an das Apostolische Glaubensbekenntnis, 1935. English: *Credo*, 1936.

Gotteserkenntnis und Gottesdienst nach reformatorischer Lehre, 1938 (on the Scots Confession of 1560). English: *The Knowledge of God and the Service of God, according to the Teaching of the Reformation*, 1938.

Dogmatik im Grundriss, 1947. English: *Dogmatics in Outline*, 1949.

Die protestantische Theologie im 19. Jahrhundert. Ihre Vorgeschichte und Geschichte, 1947. English: *Protestant Theology in the Nineteenth Century: Its Background and History*, 1972.

Die christliche Lehre nach dem Heidelberger Katechismus, 1948. English: *Christian Doctrine according to the Heidelberg Catechism*, in his: *The Heidelberg Catechism for Today*, 1964.

Kurze Erklärung des Römerbriefes, 1956. English: *A Shorter Commentary on Romans*, 1959.

Einführung in die evangelische Theologie, 1962. English: *Evangelical Theology: An Introduction*, 1963.

Collected lectures, addresses and essays in these sources

Das Wort Gottes und die Theologie (texts 1916–1923), 1924. English: *The Word of God and the Word of Man*, 1928 (= *Gesammelte Vorträge* I).

Die Theologie und die Kirche (texts 1920–1928), 1928. English: *Theology and Church*, 1962 (=*Gesammelte Vorträge* II).

Eine Schweizer Stimme, 1938–1945, 1945. Partially translated in English.

Theologische Fragen und Antworten (texts 1923–1942), 1957. Partially translated in English (=*Gesammelte Vorträge* III).

"Der Götze wackelt" (texts 1930–1960), 1961. Partially translated in/from English.

A complete edition in German ("Gesamtausgabe") of Barth's texts, including those texts that had not been published by himself, is being undertaken since 1971, by Theologischer Verlag Zürich. More than fifty volumes have already been published. These are divided in five categories: I sermons; II academic works; III addresses and smaller texts; IV records of discussions in which Barth has participated; V letters (arranged per correspondent or per period).

Appendix 3
Literature concerning Karl Barth

Collections of Essays

Theologische Aufsätze: Karl Barth zum 50.Geburtstag, 1936

Antwort: Karl Barth zum siebzigsten Geburtstag am 10. Mai 1956, 1956

Parrhesia: Karl Barth zum achtzigsten Geburtstag am 10. Mai 1966, edited by Eberhard Busch et al., 1966

Karl Barth 1886–1968: Gedenkfeier im Basler Münster. Theologische Studien 100, 1968

Karl Barth and Radical Politics, edited by George Hunsinger, 1976; 2nd ed. 2017

The Cambridge Companion to Karl Barth, edited by John Webster. Cambridge Companions to Religion, 2000

Karl Barth im europäischen Zeitgeschehen (1935–1950): Widerstand–Bewährung–Orientierung, edited by Michael Beintker et al., 2010

Monographs

Balthasar, Hans Urs von, *The Theology of Karl Barth: Exposition and Interpretation*. Communio Books, 1992

Berkouwer, G. C., *The Triumph of Grace in the Theology of Karl Barth*, 1956

Busch, Eberhard, *Karl Barth: His Life from Letters and Autobiographical Fragments*, 1976

Busch, Eberhard, *Barth*. Abingdon Pillars of Theology, 2008

———. *The Great Passion: An Introduction to Karl Barth's Theology*, edited and annotated by Darrell L. Guder and Judith J. Guder, 2004

———. *Meine Zeit mit Karl Barth: Tagebuch 1965–1968*, 2011

Küng, Hans, *Rechtfertigung: Die Lehre Karl Barths und eine katholische Besinnung*, 1957; English translation: *Justification: The Doctrine of Karl Barth and a Catholic Reflection*, 1964

Kupisch, Karl, *Karl Barth in Selbstzeugnissen und Bilddokumenten*. Rowohlts Monographien 174, 1971; new ed., 1977

Reeling Brouwer, Rinse H., *Karl Barth and Post-Reformation Orthodoxy*, 2015

Weber, Otto, *Karl Barth's Church Dogmatics: An Introductory Report on Volumes I,1 to III,4*, 1953

Bibliography

Balthasar, Hans Urs von. *The Theology of Karl Barth*. Translated by Edward T. Oakes. San Francisco: Ignatius, 1992.
"The Barmen Declaration." In *Creeds of the Churches: A Reader in Christian Doctrine from the Bible to the Present*, edited by John H. Leith, 517–22. 3rd ed. Louisville: John Knox, 1982.
Barth, Karl. "Abschied, 1933." In *Der Götze Wackelt*, edited by Karl Kupich, 63–70. Berlin: Vogt, 1961.
———. *Ad Limina Apostolorum: An Appraisal of Vatican II*. Translated by Keith R. Crim. 1968. Reprint, Eugene, OR: Wipf & Stock, 2016.
———. *Against the Stream: Shorter Post-War Writings 1946–52*. Edited by Ronald Gregor Smith. New York: Philosophical Library, 1954.
———. "An die Christen in Norwegen, 1942." In *Eine Schweizer Stimme: 1938–1945*, 242–43. Zollikon–Zurich: Evangelischer, 1945.
———. "An meine Freunde in den Niederlanden, 1942." In *Eine Schweizer Stimme: 1938–1945*, 244–50. Zollikon–Zurich: Evangelischer, 1945.
———. *Anselm: Fides Quaerens Intellectum. Anselm's Proof for the Existence of God in the Context of his Theological Scheme*. Translated by Ian W. Robertson. London: SCM, 1960.
———. *Barth-Thurneysen Briefwechsel 1921–1930*. Edited by Eduard Thurneysen. Karl Barth Gesamtausgabe V/4. Zurich: Theologischer, 1974.
———. *Barth-Visser 't Hooft Briefwechsel 1916–1966*. Edited by Thomas Herwig. Karl Barth Gesamtausgabe V/43. Zurich: Theologischer, 2006.
———. "Biblical Questions, Insights, and Vistas." In *The Word of God and the Word of Man*. Translated by Douglas Horton, 51–96. Grand Rapids: Zondervan, 1935.
———. "Ein Brief nach Frankreich, 1939." In *Eine Schweizer Stimme: 1938–1945*, 108–117. Zollikon–Zurich: Evangelischer, 1945.
———. "Brief an Prof. Hromádka in Prag, 1938." In *Eine Schweizer Stimme: 1938–1945*, 58–59. Zollikon–Zurich: Evangelischer, 1945.
———. "The Christian Community and the Civil Community." In *Community State, and Church: Three Essays*, 149–89. 1960. Reprint, Eugene, OR: Wipf & Stock, 2004.
———. "The Christian Community in the Midst of Political Change: Documents of a Hungarian Journey." In *Against the Stream: Shorter Post-War Writings 1946–52*, edited by Ronald Gregor Smith, 51–124. New York: Philosophical Library, 1954.

———. *The Christian Life: Church Dogmatics, Volume IV, Part 4: Lecture Fragments.* Translated by Geoffrey W. Bromiley. Grand Rapids: Eerdmans, 1981.

———. "The Christian's Place in Society." In *The Word of God and the Word of Man*, 272-327. Translated by Douglas Horton. Grand Rapids: Zondervan, 1935. Speech at Tambach, Sept. 1919.

———. *Die christliche Dogmatik im Entwurf 1927.* Edited by Gerhard Sauter. Karl Barth Gesamtausgabe II/14. Zurich: Theologischer, 1982.

———. "Church and Culture." In *Theology and Church: Shorter Writings 1920-1928*, 334-54. Translated by Louise Pettibone Smith. 1962. Reprint, Eugene, OR: Wipf & Stock, 2015.

———. *The Church and the Political Problem of Our Day.* New York: Scribner, 1939.

———. "Church and State." In *Community State, and Church: Three Essays*, 101-48. 1960. Reprint, Eugene, OR: Wipf & Stock, 2004.

———. *The Church and the War.* Translated by Antonia H. Froendt. 1944. Reprint, Eugene, OR: Wipf & Stock, 2008.

———. "The Church between East and West." In *Against the Stream: Shorter Post-War Writings 1946-52*, edited by Ronald Gregor Smith, 125-46. New York: Philosophical Library, 1954.

———. *Church Dogmatics.* Edited by G. W. Bromiley and T. F. Torrance. 4 vols. in 14 parts. Edinburgh: T. & T. Clark, 1956-1975.

———. "The Church: The Living Congregation of the Living Lord Jesus Christ." In *God Here and Now*, 75-104. Translated by Paul M. van Buren. London: Routledge Classics, 2003.

———. "Conversation with the Church Brotherhood of Württemberg (July 15, 1963)." In *Barth in Conversation: Volume 2, 1963.* Edited by Eberhard Busch, 28-69. Translated by the Translation Fellows of the Center for Barth Studies. Louisville: Westminster John Knox, 2018.

———. "Conversation With the Protestant Book Dealers (6.24.1962)." In *Barth in Conversation: Volume 1, 1959-1962*, edited by Eberhard Busch, 231-60. Translated by the Translation Fellows of the Center for Barth Studies. Louisville: Westminster John Knox, 2017.

———. "Conversation with the Rhineland Youth Pastors (November 4, 1963)." In *Barth in Conversation: Volume 2, 1963*, edited by Eberhard Busch, 151-213. Translated by the Translation Fellows of the Center for Barth Studies. Louisville: Westminster John Knox, 2018.

———. *Credo.* 1962. Reprint, Eugene, OR: Wipf & Stock, 2005.

———. *Dogmatics in Outline.* Translated by G.T. Thomson. New York: Harper & Row, 1959.

———. *Epistle to the Romans.* Translated by Edwyn C. Hoskyns. London: Oxford University Press, 1968. First published in 1933.

———. *Ethics.* Edited by Dietrich Braun. Translated by Geoffrey W. Bromiley. New York: Seabury, 1981.

———. *Evangelical Theology: An Introduction.* Grand Rapids: Eerdmans, 1979.

———. "Evangelical Theology in the 19th Century." In *The Humanity of God.* Translated by John Newton Thomas and Thomas Wieser, 11-33. Louisville: Westminster John Knox, 1960.

———. *Die Evangelische Kirche in Deutschland nach dem Zusammenbruch des dritten Reiches.* Zollikon-Zurich: .Evangelischer, 1945.

---. *Final Testimonies*. Edited by Eberhard Busch. Translated by Geoffrey W. Bromiley. 1977. Reprint, Eugene OR: Wipf & Stock, 2003.

---. "Foreword." In Heinrich Heppe, *Reformed Dogmatics*. Edited by Ernst Bizer. Translated by G. T. Thomson. London: Allen & Unwin, 1950.

---. "Eine Frage und eine Bitte an die Protestanten von Frankreich, 1940." In *Eine Schweizer Stimme: 1938–1945*, 147–56. Zollikon–Zurich: Evangelischer, 1945.

---. "Die geistigen Voraussetzungen für den Neuaufbau in der Nachkriegszeit, 1945." In *Eine Schweizer Stimme: 1938–1945*, 413–32. Zollikon–Zurich: Evangelischer, 1945. Speech Spiez, May 8, 1945 on what is spiritually necessary for the reconstruction after the war.

---. *The German Church Conflict*. Translated by P. T.A. Parker. Cambridge: Lutterworth, 1965.

---. "The Germans and Ourselves." In *The Only Way: How to Change the German Mind*, translated by Marta K. Neufeld and Ronald Gregor Smith, 63–122. New York: Philosophical Library, 1949.

---. "The Gift of Freedom: Foundation of Evangelical Ethics." In *The Humanity of God*. Translated by John Newton Thomas and Thomas Wieser, 69–96. Louisville: Westminster John Knox, 1960.

---. "Gospel and Law." In *Community, State, and Church: Three Essays*, 71–100. 1960. Reprint, Eugene, OR: Wipf & Stock, 2004.

---. *The Göttingen Dogmatics: Instruction in the Christian Religion*. Edited by Hannelotte Reiffen. Translated by Geoffrey W. Bromiley. Grand Rapids: Eerdmans, 1991.

---. *Gottes Wille und unsere Wünsche*. Munich: Kaiser, 1934.

---. *The Heidelberg Catechism for Today*. Translated by Shirley C. Guthrie. Richmond, VA: John Knox, 1964.

---. "How Can the Germans Be Cured?" In *The Only Way: How to Change the German Mind*, translated by Marta K. Neufeld and Ronald Gregor Smith, 3–59. New York: Philosophical Library, 1949.

---. "The Humanity of God." In *The Humanity of God*. Translated by John Newton Thomas and Thomas Wieser, 37–65. Louisville: Westminster John Knox, 1960.

---. "Im Namen Gottes des Allmächtigen! 1291–1941." In *Eine Schweizer Stimme: 1938–1945*, 201–32. Zollikon–Zurich: Evangelischer, 1945.

---. "Jesus Christ and the Movement for Social Justice" with correspondence with a Swiss entrepreneur. In *Karl Barth and Radical Politics*, edited and translated by George Hunsinger, 1–23. 2nd ed. Eugene, OR: Cascade, 2017.

---. "The Jewish Problem and the Christian Answer." In *Against the Stream: Shorter Post-War Writings 1946–52*, edited by Ronald Gregor Smith, 193–201. New York: Philosophical Library, 1954.

---. *Die Kirche Jesu Christi*. Theologische Existenz Heute 5. München: C. Kaiser, 1933.

---. *The Knowledge of God and the Service of God according to the Teaching of the Reformation*. Translated by J. L. M. Haire and Ian Henderson. 1938. Reprint, Eugene, OR: Wipf & Stock, 2005.

---. *Letters 1961–1968*. Edited by Jürgen Fangmeier and Hinrich Stoevesandt. Translated by Geoffrey W. Bromiley. Grand Rapids: Eerdmans, 1981.

---. *A Letter to Great Britain from Switzerland*. London: Sheldon, 1941.

———. "Liberal Theology—An Interview." In *Final Testimonies*, edited by Eberhard Busch, 31–40. Translated by Geoffrey W. Bromiley. 1977. Reprint, Eugene OR: Wipf & Stock, 2003.

———. "Music for a Guest—A Radio Broadcast." In *Final Testimonies*, edited by Eberhard Busch, 17–30. Translated by Geoffrey W. Bromiley. 1977. Reprint, Eugene OR: Wipf & Stock, 2003.

———. "The Need and Promise of Christian Preaching." In *The Word of God and the Word of Man*. Translated by Douglas Horton, 97–135. Grand Rapids: Zondervan, 1935.

———."No Christian Marshall Plan." *Christian Century* 65.49 (1948) 1330–33.

———. "Die Not der evangelischen Kirche, 1931." In *Der Götze wackelt*, edited by Karl Kupich, 33–62. Berlin: Vogt, 1961.

———. *Offene Briefe 1945–1968*. Edited by Diether Koch. Karl Barth Gesamtausgabe V/15. Zurich: Theologischer, 1984.

———. "Past and Future: Friedrich Naumann and Christoph Blumhardt." In *The Beginnings of Dialectical Theology*, edited by James M. Robinson, 35–45. Translated by Keith R. Crim. Richmond, VA: John Knox, 1968.

———. "Podium Discussion in Chicago (4.25/26.1962)." In *Barth in Conversation: Volume 1, 1959–1962*. Edited by Eberhard Busch, 161–91. Translated by the Translation Fellows of the Center for Barth Studies. Louisville: Westminster John Knox, 2017.

———. "Political Decisions in the Unity of Faith." In *Against the Stream: Shorter Post-War Writings 1946–52*, edited by Ronald Gregor Smith, 147–64. New York: Philosophical Library, 1954.

———. *Protestant Theology in the Nineteenth Century*. New ed. Translated by Brian Cozens and John Bowden. Grand Rapids: Eerdmans, 2002.

———. "Quousque tandem?, 1930." In *Der Götze wackelt*, edited by Karl Kupich, 27–32. Berlin: Vogt, 1961.

———. "Recapitulation Number Three." *Christian Century* 77.3 (1960) 72–76.

———. "Rudolf Bultmann—An Attempt to Understand Him." In *Kerygma and Myth: A Theological Debate*, vol. 2, edited by Hans-Werner Bartsch, 83–132. Translated by Reginald H. Fuller. London: SPCK, 1962.

———. "The Sovereignty of God's Word and the Decision of Faith." In *God Here and Now*, 13–33. Translated by Paul M. van Buren. London: Routledge Classics, 2003.

———. "Starting Out, Turning Round, Confessing." In *Final Testimonies*, edited by Eberhard Busch, 51–60. Translated by Geoffrey W. Bromiley. 1977. Reprint, Eugene OR: Wipf & Stock, 2003.

———. *The Teaching of the Church Regarding Baptism*. Translated by Ernest A. Payne. 1948. Reprint, Eugene, OR: Wipf & Stock, 2006.

———. *Theological Existence To-Day!* Translated by R. Birch Hoyle. 1933. Reprint, Eugene, OR: Wipf & Stock, 2011.

———. *Theologische Existenz Heute!* New ed. Munich: Kaiser, 1984.

———. *Theologische Fragen und Antworten*. Zollikon-Zurich: Evangelischer. 1957.

———. *The Theology of Schleiermacher*. Edited by Dietrich Ritschl. Translated by Geoffrey W. Bromiley. Grand Rapids: Eerdmans, 1982.

———. "Testimony to Jesus Christ" In *Final Testimonies*, edited by Eberhard Busch, 11–15. Translated by Geoffrey W. Bromiley. 1977. Reprint, Eugene OR: Wipf & Stock, 2003.

———. "Verheissung und Verantwortung der christlichen Gemeinde im heutigen Zeitgeschehen, 1944." In *Eine Schweizer Stimme: 1938-1945,* 307-33. Zollikon-Zurich: Evangelischer, 1945.

———. "Volkstrauertag, 1954." In *Der Götze wackelt,* edited by Karl Kupich, 165-76. Berlin: Vogt, 1961. Address in Wiesbaden in memory of the war casualties.

———. "Weihnachtsbotschaft an die Christen in Deutschland, 1941." In *Eine Schweizer Stimme: 1938-1945,* 240-41. Zollikon-Zurich: Evangelischer, 1945.

———. "Ein Wort an die Deutschen, 1945." In *Der Götze Wackelt,* edited by Karl Kupich, 87-97. Berlin: Vogt, 1961.

———. "The Word of God and the Task of Ministry." In *The Word of God and the Word of Man.* Translated by Douglas Horton, 183-217. Grand Rapids: Zondervan, 1935.

———. *The Word of God and the Word of Man.* Translated by Douglas Horton. Grand Rapids: Zondervan, 1935.

Barth, Karl, and Eduard Thurneysen. *Die grosse Barmherzigkeit.* Munich: Kaiser, 1935.

Barth, Karl, and Rudolf Bultman. *Karl Barth–Rudolf Bultmann Letters, 1922-1966.* Edited by Bernd Jaspert and Geoffrey W. Bromiley. Translated by Geoffrey W. Bromiley. Grand Rapids: Eerdmans, 1981.

Berkhof, Hendrikus. *How Karl Barth Changed My Mind.* Edited by Donald K. McKim. 1986. Reprint, Eugene, OR: Wipf & Stock, 1998.

Berkouwer, G. C. *The Triumph of Grace in the Theology of Karl Barth.* Translated by Harry R. Boer. Grand Rapids: Eerdmans, 1956.

Bonhoeffer, Dietrich. *Letters & Papers from Prison.* Enlarged ed. Edited by Eberhard Bethge. New York: Touchstone, 1997.

Brunner, Emil, and Karl Barth. *Natural Theology: Comprising "Nature and Grace" by Professor Dr. Emil Brunner and the Reply "No!" by Dr. Karl Barth.* Translated by Peter Fraenkel. 1946. Reprint, Eugene, OR: Wipf & Stock, 2002.

Busch, Eberhard. *Karl Barth: His Life from Letters and Autobiographical Texts.* Translated by John Bowden. Philadelphia: Fortress, 1976.

Busch, E., M. Geiger, and J. Fangmeier, eds. *Parrhesia: Karl Barth zum 80. Geburtstag am 10. Mai 1966.* Zurich: Evangelischer, 1966.

Daniélou, Jean, Reinhold Niebuhr, and Karl Barth. *Gespräche nach Amsterdam.* Zurich: Evangelischer, 1949.

"Darmstädter Wort." https://dfg-vk-darmstadt.de/Lexikon_Auflage_2/Darmstaedter Wort.htm.

Küng, Hans. *Justification: The Doctrine of Karl Barth and a Catholic Reflection.* 40th Anniversary ed. Louisville: Westminster John Knox, 2004.

Miskotte, K. H. *Karl Barth.* Verzameld Werk 2. Kampen: Kok, 1987.

Rumscheidt, Martin. *Revelation and Theology: An Analysis of the Barth-Harnack Correspondence of 1923.* 1972. Reprint, Eugene, OR: Wipf & Stock, 2011.

Smart, James T., trans. *Revolutionary Theology in the Making: Barth-Thurneysen Correspondence 1914-1925.* Richmond, VA: John Knox, 1964.

Sperna Weiland, J. "Er is iets aan het gebeuren." *Wending* 20 (1965) 617-29.

Vatican Council II. *Dei Verbum.* In *Vatican Council II: The Conciliar and Post Conciliar Documents (Study Edition).* Edited by Austin Flannery, OP. Northport, NY: Costello, 1987.

Wolf, Ernst, ed. *Antwort: Karl Barth zum siebzigsten Geburtstag am 10. Mai 1956.* Zollikon: Evangelischer, 1956.

World Council of Churches. "Constitution and Rules of the World Council of Churches." 2018 revision. https://www.oikoumene.org/resources/documents/constitution-and-rules-of-the-world-council-of-churches.

———. *The Evanston Report.* London: SCM, 1954.

———. Advisory Commission. "Report of the Advisory Commission on the Main Theme of the Second Assembly: Christ—the Hope of the World." *Ecumenical Review* 6 (1954) 430–65.

Name Index

Adenauer, Konrad, 198, 284, 285
Anselm of Canterbury, 39–46, 48, 210, 239–40
Asmussen, Hans, 69, 81, 144–45, 288

Balthasar, Hans Urs von, 336–39
Barth, Christoph, 7, 55, 81, 154, 234, 307, 319
Barth, Franziska, 7
Barth, Hans Jakob, 8
Barth, Johann Friedrich, 6, 8
Barth, Markus, 7, 81, 307, 319, 322, 349
Barth, Matthias, 7, 116
Barth(-Hoffmann), Nelly, 7, 37–38, 217, 330, 332, 348–49
Barth, Peter, 10
Bereczky, Albert, 205–7
Berggrav, Eivind, 108
Berkouwer, G.C., 274–76, 279, 297
Bernhard (Prince), 178
Bethge, Eberhard, 273
Bismarck, Otto von, 123–26
Blumhardt, Christoph, 10–11, 34, 218, 297
Blumhardt, Johann Christoph, 11, 34, 218, 297
Bonhoeffer, Dietrich, 107, 129, 221, 272–74, 325
Breukelman, Frans, 331
Brunner, Emil, 24, 64–65, 137, 175–178, 180–82, 198, 274

Bultmann, Rudolf, 24, 152, 164, 231–34, 236, 246, 251, 262–63, 278, 325–26, 328, 330, 358–61
Busch, Eberhard, 276, 330, 348, 358, 364

Calvin, Jean, 7, 26, 98, 113, 118–19, 357
Churchill, Winston, 321
Cicero, Marcus T.. 51
Colijn, Hendrikus, 97

Daniélou, Jean 334–36
Dibelius, Otto, 52, 54, 198
Dulles, John Foster, 178

Ehrenburg, Ilya, 205
Eijkman, J., 32

Feldmann, Markus, 199–205
Feuerbach, Ludwig, 15, 31
Frederick the Great (King), 23, 125, 139, 189, 320–21

Goethe, Johann Wolfgang von, 155, 281
Gogarten, Friedrich, 23, 24, 63–64
Gollwitzer, Helmut, 315, 365
Graham, Billy, 319

Haitjema, Th.L., 32, 33
Harnack, Adolf von, 6, 22, 314
Heering, G.J., 222
Hegel, G.W.F., 154
Heinemann, Gustav, 198–99
Heppe, Heinrich, 27

Herrmann, Wilhelm, 6–7
Heuss, Theodor, 288
Hindenburg, Paul von, 50, 73
Hitler, Adolf, 1–4, 19, 49–50, 57–60, 70–73, 84–85, 87–88, 93, 95–97, 100–8, 117–20, 122–30, 139–41, 174, 176–8, 182, 186, 198, 221, 223, 226, 263, 273, 322, 363
Hromádka, Josef, 87–89, 91, 93–94, 178, 198, 365
Huizinga, Jan, 97

Iwand, Hans-Joachim, 157

Jaspers, Karl, 288
Juliana (Princess), 178
Jüngel, Eberhard, 365

Khrushchev, Nikita, 283
Kierkegaard, Søren, 15, 34
King, Martin Luther, 321
Kirschbaum, Charlotte von, 37–38, 217, 319, 330, 348–49
Kohlbrugge, Hebe, 108
Kohlbrügge, Hermann Friedrich, 34
Küng, Hans, 337–9, 365
Kupisch, Karl, 313
Kuyper, Abraham, 274

Luther, Martin, 21–23, 66, 68, 95, 98, 103

Merz, Georg, 23, 59, 65
Miskotte, K.H., 76, 98–99, 279, 313
Mussolini, Benito, 87, 88, 93, 118
Naumann, Friedrich, 10

Niebuhr, Reinhold, 178, 266–68, 272, 284, 287, 318
Niemöller, Martin, 66, 73, 84–85, 129–30, 132–3, 144–45, 157, 198–99

Nietzsche, Friedrich, 15, 161, 218
Noordmans, Oepke, 32, 34, 151

Ott, Heinrich, 315

Paul VI (Pope), 338
Pius XII (Pope), 248

Rade, Martin, 7
Rembrandt van Rijn, 32
Ritschl, Albrecht, 154
Robinson, John, 325–6, 328
Rousseau, Jean-Jacques, 154

Sartorius, Anna, 6, 87
Schleiermacher, Friedrich D.E., 6, 24, 31, 54–56, 153, 154, 358–61
Schubert, Franz, 356
Schweitzer, Albert, 218, 219, 284
Sperna Weiland, J., 274
Stalin, Joseph, 118, 198, 200
Stoevesandt, H., 59n8–10

Thurneysen, Eduard, 7, 8, 10, 11, 12, 23–24, 30, 32, 65, 82–83, 279, 314
Tillich, Paul, 325
Troeltsch, Ernst, 155
Tromp, D., 32

Visser 't Hooft, W.A., 268–69, 271–72, 279, 319

Weizsäcker, Carl Friedrich von, 284
Wilhelm I (Kaiser), 125
Wilhelm II (Kaiser), 9, 124–25
Wilhelmina (Queen), 109

Zimmermann, Wolf-Dieter, 198
Zinzendorf, Ludwig Count of, 55
Zwingli, Huldrych, 18

www.ingramcontent.com/pod-product-compliance
Lightning Source LLC
Chambersburg PA
CBHW051204300426
44116CB00006B/431